THE LEASE / BUY DECISION

ROBERT E. PRITCHARD and THOMAS J. HINDELANG

The Lease/Buy Decision

amacom

A DIVISION OF
AMERICAN MANAGEMENT ASSOCIATIONS

Appendix A reprinted with permission from BankAmeriLease Group, BankAmerica Companies, 555 California Street, San Francisco, CA 94104.

Appendix B reprinted with permission from First National State Bank of New Jersey, 550 Broad Street, Newark, N.J. 07102.

Appendix C reprinted from *Business and Financial Tables Desk Book* with permission of the publisher, Institute for Business Planning, Inc., IBP Plaza, Englewood Cliffs, N.J. 07632.

Appendix D reprinted from *The Thorndike Encyclopedia of Banking and Finance Tables* with permission of the publisher, Warren, Gorham & Lamont Inc., 201 South Street, Boston, MA 02111.

Appendix E reprinted from David I. Fisher, *The Corporate Economist,* New York: The Conference Board, 1975, with permission.

Library of Congress Cataloging in Publication Data

Pritchard, Robert E   1941–
  The lease/buy decision.

  Bibliography: p.
  Includes index.
  1. Industrial equipment leases. 2. Lease and rental services. 3. Business enterprises—Finance.
  4. Leases. I. Hindelang, Thomas J., joint author.
  II. Title.
  HG4028.C4P74   658.1′5242   79-23000
  ISBN 0-8144-5557-3

© 1980 AMACOM
A division of American Management Associations, New York.
All rights reserved. Printed in the United States of America.

This publication may not be reproduced, stored in a retrieval system, or transmitted in whole or in part, in any form or by any means, electronic, mechanical, photocopying, recording, or otherwise, without the prior written permission of AMACOM, 135 West 50th Street, New York, N.Y. 10020.

First Printing

For Carol Ann and Chris

PREFACE

The Lease/Buy Decision is a comprehensive guide to leasing and the leasing industry. It assumes no prior knowledge of leasing and leads the reader from basic decisions through state-of-the-art criteria for lease evaluation.

The initial chapters provide a detailed description of the leasing industry. The important points to consider when leasing are described in detail, with the goal being to maximize profits and reduce risk and cash outlays. The book is a practical guide for the lessee, with material organized in a concise readable fashion to lead the user through each step in evaluating alternative lease contracts as well as making lease-versus-purchase decisions.

Risk, which is becoming increasingly more important with the continuing high inflation rates and changes in petroleum prices, is discussed at length. Inflation and forecasting are also considered as a part of the leasing decision. The various tax implications of both leasing and purchasing are discussed. The tax treatment is based on materials prepared by Deloitte, Haskins, and Sells especially for this publication.

The procedures used to evaluate leases and lease-versus-purchase decisions are based on the concepts of discounted cash flow. The discounted cash flow methodology has become a cornerstone for evaluation by both financial and line managers throughout the world. A background in this is, however, not assumed. Rather, procedures are developed step by step and then applied to the leasing decision.

Several specialized chapters are provided to offer additional insights to meet the needs of the reader. The areas covered include the effects of leasing on financial statements and financial reporting; sensitivity analysis, which indicates how "sensitive" cash flows and profits are to any errors in cost and revenue estimates; alternative sources of financing; and the structure of the equipment and automobile leasing industries.

Numerous industrial specialists were consulted during the preparation of *The Lease/Buy Decision*. The authors would like to express their special appreciation to them and others who have provided input and support for this publication:

Leo C. Beebe, Dean, Administrative Studies Division, Glassboro State College

Paul E. Dascher, Dean, College of Business and Administration, Drexel University

Joseph L. Naar, Director of Public Relations, The Conference Board
Diane M. Threlheld, Assistant Editor, Machinery and Allied Products Institute
G. Pat Bacon, Senior Vice President, Control Division Aetna Business Credit, Inc.
Kenneth J. Mathews, President, First National State Leasing Co.
Joseph F. Ward, Vice President, Institute for Business Planning, Inc.
Anthony H. Clay, Vice President, Manufacturers Hanover Leasing Corporation
Michelle Frager, Marketing Officer, Citibank, N.A.
John A. Laurino, Senior Marketing Officer, Citibank, N.A.
Cornelia Yelin, Manager, Public Relations, Frost & Sullivan, Inc.
Peter K. Nevitt, President, BankAmeriLease Group
Arthur H. Rosenfield, Executive Vice President, Warren, Gorham, & Lamont, Inc.
Ralph W. Newkirk, Jr., Managing Partner, Deloitte, Haskins, and Sells
Kenneth B. Everett, Tax Manager, Deloitte, Haskins, and Sells
William Hetts, Managing Partner, Deloitte, Haskins, and Sells
Robert J. Corcoran, Vice President and Senior Loan Officer, First National State Bank of New Jersey
Calvin W. Day, Coordinator, Small Business Development Center, Small Business Administration
Edward J. Bogar, Winner Ford
Paul J. Tully, Vice President, The Johnson Companies.
Robert D. Lynch, Executive Director, The Management Institute in Association with Glassboro State College
William C. Strang, Winner Ford

Our students at Drexel University provided valuable feedback in the class testing of parts of the book. To them go our collective thanks. Special thanks go to Robert Luczak, Michael Bayuk, and Charles Schneider for their comments and suggestions.

We would also like to express our thanks to Peter Reimold, for preparing the copy-edited manuscript, to Gertrude F. Kuck, who carefully and cheerfully typed and retyped the several versions of the manuscript, and to Debora L. Pallante, who patiently coordinated the correspondence and reproduction necessary to the preparation of the manuscript.

Comments from readers are welcomed and encouraged.

Robert E. Pritchard
Thomas J. Hindelang

CONTENTS

1. The Dynamics of Leasing   1
2. Types of Leases   11
3. Taxation, Depreciation, and Cash Flow   29
4. Effects of Leasing on Financial Statements   42
5. Evaluating the Lease-versus-Purchase Decision: An Introduction to Discounted Cash Flow Analysis   48
6. Inflation, Risk, and Forecasting   60
7. Quantitative Methods for Risk Analysis   68
8. Lease-versus-Purchase Analysis   89
9. Sensitivity Analysis   120
10. Tax Aspects of Leasing   140
11. Alternative Sources of Financing   153
12. The Equipment Leasing Industry   167
13. Automobile Leasing   184

Appendix A. Glossary of Lease Terms   193
Appendix B. Sample Equipment Leases   203
Appendix C. Comparative Depreciation Tables   211
Appendix D. Compound Interest and Annuity Tables   219
Appendix E. Sources of Economic and Financial Information from The Conference Board   239
Appendix F. Table of Normal Distribution   259
Bibliography   261
Index   269

CHAPTER 1

The Dynamics of Leasing

Leasing is a most fascinating, dynamic, and frequently misunderstood part of finance. Leasing, as a major industry in the United States, grew from infancy after World War II to a multibillion-dollar complex including, literally, thousands of leasing companies and millions of lessees. The rate of growth has varied appreciably with the changing availability and cost of funds within the money and capital markets and can be expected to undergo further transformation as the newly revised procedures for lease accounting become fully implemented. On the basis of past trends and study of projections within the industry, we foresee continued growth at a rate which will exceed that of the economy overall.

Why have hundreds of thousands of firms turned to leasing as a viable method to acquire the use of plant, equipment, vehicles, and almost anything else that can be purchased? How do financial managers decide to lease rather than purchase—what are the key factors to consider, and do they change over time and from company to company? What are the unique elements of leases for different types of assets, such as vehicles, computers, or production equipment? These are but a few of the questions we will examine. Throughout, our goal is to present needed information so that you can make the best decisions for your firm.

How It Came to Be

On the western coast of the Mediterranean Sea, around 1400 B.C., the Phoenician civilization flourished. In addition to developing an advanced alphabet which was the immediate forerunner of the Greek, they were involved in leasing. *Charter ships were leased to merchants who were more interested in conducting their business than in ownership of vessels*—an attitude whose value many businessmen have only recently learned.

In the Mesopotamian Valley leasing was used to foster the development of unused land. A real estate lease carved on stone (as some are today) and dated 551 B.C. in the Kingdom of Babylon forbade subletting and required the lessee to plant trees and keep the house in good repair.

Land was leased throughout most of the Byzantine period, throughout the Dark Ages, and into the early periods of colonization. As an example, Maryland was a totally leased colony of Lord Baltimore; he owned the land and all inhabitants became his tenants.

The leasing of land proved to be a viable means for the development of our industrialized society. Building increased as tenants had cash to use for this purpose rather than for the purchase of land. Concurrently, land owners enjoyed appreciation of property values with the erection of buildings and rental incomes.

American ingenuity found its way into leasing with the development of the percentage lease. The first recorded percentage lease was for a barber shop in the Grand Terminal Building around 1905-1906.[1] The percentage lease found favor in the Depression period, since rent was adjusted to changing economic conditions.[2] Landlords caught with overavailability of vacant property saw percentage leases as a method to find new tenants.[3] The concept spread to mineral leases, wherein rental was tied to a percentage of the yield. This type of lease removed much of the risk in speculation as to mineral resources.

An interesting factor to be noted in the development of leasing is that its primary purpose was to encourage use of assets (usually property) on the part of the owner. It was not until 1936 that the concept of leasing as a financial tool was recognized. Safeway recognized this potential and developed the sale–leaseback arrangement.[4] Many such leases were transacted with nonprofit organizations, which did not have to pay taxes and, hence, could pass part of this saving to the lessee. In 1949 Macy's of New York built a $4.5 million store and sold it to Connecticut Boola, Inc., wholly owned by Yale University.[5] The loss in tax revenue precipitated the start of an ongoing series of tax reform acts and court decisions defining the tax and legal parameters of leases.

In the context of the growth and development of leasing, the emphasis has been on land and buildings, but equipment leasing has been common since before the turn of the century. In fact nearly everyone has leased equipment—a telephone. However, equipment leasing did not really become popular until the 1950s—and primarily after the end of the

Korean conflict, which saw tax-credit and accelerated-depreciation incentives for investment.[6] Prior to this time, the primary lessors were IBM, AT&T, and United Shoe Machinery, which made sophisticated machinery and held near-monopoly market positions.[7] The tax incentives, together with Revenue Ruling 55-540, in which the IRS clarified the substance of an agreement that would be considered to be a lease for tax purposes, created the setting for the leasing industry as we know it today. Concurrently, Joel Dean, who has been called the father of capital budgeting, wrote his classic publication advocating capital budgeting from an economic viewpoint and introduced the evaluative tools necessary for the task.[8] The tools have been found essential, not only to capital budgeting, which encompasses purchase-versus-lease decisions, but also to the evaluation of leases as vehicles for financing. The outcome was the explosive growth of this new industry in the 1960s—a growth into four primary areas: (1) industrial equipment and facilities, (2) automobiles and trucks, (3) office and data processing equipment, and (4) railroad cars.

As the number of leasing transactions increased, so did the value of assets. The largest were facilitated by the development of leveraged leasing, which involves a syndicate of equity and debt holders. This permitted leasing in the multimillion-dollar category. A typical leveraged leasing arrangement is shown in Figure 1-1.

While the change in tax laws and the availability of tools for economic evaluation of leases were basic to the development of the leasing industry, these alone did not turn the tide to leasing. Other economic factors were, and continue to be, paramount. Inflation and business cycles with their inherent risks accompanied by high interest costs have forced many firms to turn to leasing. Smaller firms, in particular, have been removed, in many instances, from the purchase market, because they simply lack sufficient equity capital to support debt financing. Many larger firms that do not suffer from the lack of internally generated equity resources or access to equity markets have also moved to leasing. An underlying motivation is the cost savings resulting from differentials in capital costs to the leasing company versus an operating company.

Why Lease?

The particular combination of reasons that make a firm decide to lease or to purchase has grounding in basic economics. For some, the reason is a dearth of money—there is no other choice; it is either lease or do without. Unfortunately, this is often the situation for the smaller firm, and the decision then is to find the best leasing arrangement, tailored (if possible) to meet the specific needs of the lessee. The larger firm should weigh the

Figure 1-1. Specialized-equipment financing through a leveraged lease arrangement. (Source: Specialized Equipment Finance Department, Citibank, N.A. Used with permission.)

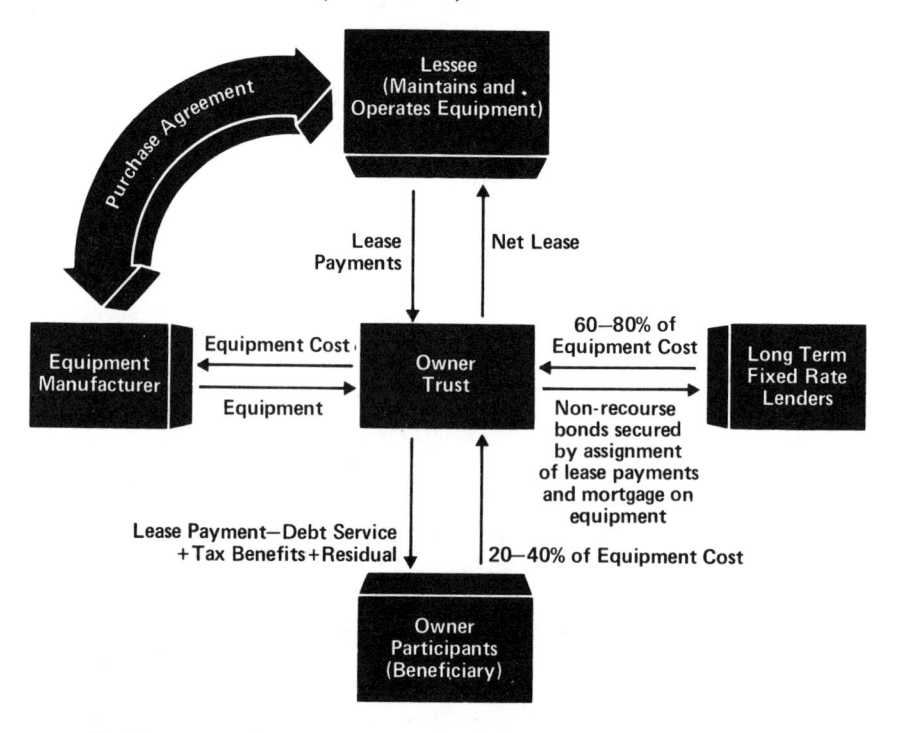

quantifiable economic parameters as well as those which are not so easy to label with a dollar value (possibility of technical or market obsolescence, as examples). Within the area of economic evaluation we will later introduce the discounted cash flow methodology, which is easily applied to the evaluation of lease and lease-versus-purchase decisions.

The primary advantages of leasing are listed below.

1. *Leasing offers potential savings compared to a purchase.* The potential lower cost may come about from two distinct and not mutually exclusive causes. First, a firm may not be able to take full advantage of the tax benefits resulting from accelerated depreciation and investment tax credits. To take advantage of the former, a firm must have sufficient earnings before taxes; to enjoy the latter, the firm must be paying taxes sufficient to equal the allowable tax credit. Many small firms, and also some larger firms, such as airlines and, in particular, bankrupt railroads, cannot take advantage of the tax benefits even when they can raise the funds required for purchase. The lease company can often take full advan-

tage of such benefits and pass them along to the lessee as part of the rental agreement.

Second, due to the lower overall risk posture of a lessor, the cost of funds (both equity and debt) may be significantly less than to an operating firm. This is commonly the situation. Only the most credit-worthy firms have access to the issuing side of the commercial paper markets, for example. Thus, to almost all firms, this relatively low-cost short-term financing is unavailable. Furthermore, many leasing companies are subsidiaries of banks and, as a consequence, have access to funds at lower costs than available to even prime bank customers.

2. *Leasing provides an alternative source of capital.* For firms that have limited funds for capital investment, leasing may provide a viable alternative to increasing the firm's capitalization. At the limit, when the firm's capitalization may no longer be increased, leasing may be the only means for expansion and replacement.

3. *Leasing provides constant cost financing.* Unlike some forms of debt financing that vary in cost as a function of the prime interest rate, lease payments are almost always uniform over the length of the lease (except when specifically tailored otherwise). One common exception is space in shopping malls. Leases for shops usually tie rental to gross sales receipts rather than to the prime interest rate. Later we will briefly examine some of the debt sources of capital and compare them to lease sources.

4. *Leasing extends the length of financing.* In contrast to typical equipment loans, which are generally available only for a period of time significantly less than the economic life of an asset, leases may be obtained for nearly the total length of the asset's life. The result is reduced cash outflow during the initial period of the asset's life, with the cost spread over a longer time period. The benefit is twofold. First, costs tend to be more nearly correlated with revenues over the entire life of the asset. Second, a discounted cash flow analysis will usually indicate a higher return on investment when cash payments are spread out over the entire asset life. This will be demonstrated later in the book.

5. *Leasing allows more flexible cash budgeting.* This is an important corollary to the preceding benefit. Many intermediate-term loans have balloon repayment features, whereby the bulk of the principal is due at the end of the loan and, if the firm maintains its credit rating, forms the basis for a new loan. Such refinancing exposes the firm to additional financial risk if interest rates and/or the availability of capital change. The uncertainty as to availability of refinancing necessitates a more conservative liquidity position. Possible changes (and fluctuations in interest rates, if interest is tied to the prime rate) make cash budgeting more difficult and, again, negatively affect the firm's financial risk posture.

6. *Leasing conserves existing credit.* The use of leasing generally conserves existing sources of credit for other uses and, in most instances, does not restrict a firm's borrowing capacity. Many loan indentures do restrict additional borrowing and may also limit manager/owner compensation and dividend payout.

7. *Leasing provides total financing.* Unlike debt financing, which requires some equity investment, leasing affords 100 percent financing. However, in many instances, a security deposit is required, and the return on this escrow deposit is usually quite low (frequently, current passbook interest rate or lower). Also, lease payments must usually be paid at the start of each period, with the first payment due at the start of the lease. Loan repayments are usually made at the end of each period, with the first payment due at the end of the month (or some other period) after purchase. These factors affect the cash flow budget and the timing of cash flows.

8. *Leasing may provide financing for acquisition plus related costs.* The total acquisition cost, including sales taxes and delivery and installation charges, may be included as a part of the total lease package and spread over the life of the lease. These front-end costs may be substantial and thus result in heavy initial cash outflows if assets are purchased.

9. *Leasing provides a hedge against inflation.* Leasing may provide a hedge against inflation, since the lease payments will be made with "cheaper" dollars. The same line of reasoning may also apply to loan principal and interest repayments, if the latter are constant. If, however, interest rates are tied to the prime rate, then the interest rate will tend to move with the rate of inflation and, hence, the loan will not be as good a hedge against inflation as the fixed lease payment.

While leasing may act as a hedge against inflation, inflation provides the basis for strong arguments supporting ownership. Many firms anticipate purchase or re-leasing of leased assets at the end of the initial lease. With inflation, the actual fair market price may well exceed the price anticipated when the lease was negotiated.

Airlines, in particular, have suffered from this, since airplanes must be maintained with regular overhauls required by the FAA in order to remain in use. In many instances, the fair market value of planes at the lease termination was two to three times the expected amount. Leasing companies benefit greatly from this inflation. In fact, in competitive areas, the primary profit derived by leasing companies results from the sale of the asset at the termination of the lease.

10. *Leasing provides fast, flexible financing.* Leasing tends to be faster and more flexible than borrowing funds. In addition to not containing many of the typical restrictive covenants found in loan agreements, lease

payments may be tailored to the specific need of the lessee. For example, lease payments may be arranged to meet the seasonal cash flows of the lessee. Again, budgeting is facilitated.

11. *Leasing simplifies bookkeeping.* For tax accounting purposes, leasing often avoids the necessity of establishing depreciation schedules and accounting for depreciation and interest.

12. *Leasing provides for tax write-off of land.* Land may not be depreciated. Thus, if land is owned, the only tax benefits realized are through property taxes and interest paid on financing. With leasing, the entire lease payment on land is tax-deductible. While this tax benefit is valuable, it must be considered in the context of generally appreciating land values and the absence of lessee ownership at the end of the lease.

13. *Leasing reduces the risk of obsolescence.* Many lease agreements place the risk of obsolescence on the owner. Computer leasing is a case in point. Introduction of the IBM 370, for example, immediately outdated its predecessor. This is a most important consideration when leasing in areas of rapid technological change.

14. *Leasing provides trial use periods.* In some instances, management, in considering the acquisition of new equipment, may not have sufficient confidence in the estimates of projected cash flows to warrant purchase or long-term leasing. In such instances, it may be possible to lease the equipment for a limited period on a trial basis and then either to extend the lease or purchase.

Each of the areas described above warrants close consideration from the viewpoint of both economic analysis and the practical constraints imposed upon the firm. Those factors that come to bear heavily today may prove to be of lesser consequences in years to come; thus the analysis must be ongoing. Beyond the practical constraints, however, lies the very important factor of ownership: the use of the asset for extended time periods or the enjoyment of residual value. In periods of long-term inflation, it is necessary to estimate as precisely as possible what the fair market value of the asset will be at the end of the lease period. Salvage value should not be thought of in terms of depreciation, since depreciation usually does not even closely approximate asset value change. Depreciation is an accounting tool not appropriate to market value estimation.

The astute reader will have observed the lack of any reference to leases as off-balance-sheet financing. With the implementation of FASB 13, this "advantage" of leasing has been all but lost.[9] Certain types of leases still need not be reported directly on the firm's balance sheet, but for the larger firm these are of little consequence. We will address the question of reporting leases and deal with their impact on accounting statement ratios in detail.

Renting versus Leasing

Along with the growth of business leasing, short-term rentals have also increased dramatically. The American Rental Association indicates that there are at least 10,000 rental stores in the United States. *Renting is generally distinguished from leasing by the duration of time involved;* thus, an automobile is rented for a weekend and leased for a year. The rental and leasing industries are considered to be two separate entities, although some firms that lease also rent (automobiles being the prime example).

From a financial viewpoint, leasing and renting also differ. The underlying financial advantages for leasing are that it *may be* less expensive to lease than to purchase and that leasing may offer the only viable source of funds to acquire needed property.

The profitability in renting, for both owner and renter, comes about from the *rate of utilization* of the rented item. For example, consider a large wheelbarrow costing about $125 and having a useful economic life of 5 years. Such wheelbarrows may be rented for about $4 per day. From the viewpoint of the renter, who may need the wheelbarrow only two or three days a year, purchasing would represent an unwarranted expense. In addition, the wheelbarrow would have to be stored, resulting in the loss of valuable storage space. From the viewpoint of the owner of the wheelbarrow, renting may be very profitable. If, for example, the wheelbarrow were rented only one day in five, the owner would gross $365 \div 5 \times \$4 = \$292$ per year. Over the five-year life, the owner would gross $1,460 on an investment of $125. Of course, the owner would have many expenses, such as the cost of leasing or owning a rental center.

Another example of renting is of hearses and funeral limousines. These vehicles are extremely expensive and their ownership can be justified only if they are used very frequently. Since many small funeral directors have use for such vehicles only once or twice a week, it is much less expensive to rent them as needed. The owner can maintain a fleet of such vehicles and rent them to many funeral directors, frequently with driver included. This ensures both frequent use and economies of scale in maintenance, insurance, storage, and the like.

The American Rental Association[10] indicated in 1975 that gross revenues in the equipment rental industry were over $1 billion in 1974, and projected increases of 10 percent for the next several years. This projection proved to be modest.

Structure of the Leasing Industry

If one were to characterize the leasing industry, it would probably be as nonhomogeneous and fragmented. There are literally thousands of leasing companies, varying in size from thousands of dollars of assets to hundreds of millions. Many automobile dealerships hold captive leasing companies; there are independent lessors; and manufacturer- and distributor-captive leasing is found along with bank-held leasing companies. Insurance companies and financial-service conglomerates are also involved. The industry is complex, with lessors offering widely differing services.

The structure of the industry has changed almost as dramatically as the rate at which the industry has grown. Initially the industry was composed primarily of *third-party leasing companies*. These firms purchase assets and lease them to the ultimate users, raising needed funds through equity and debt financing. The banking community became involved by providing loans and soon realized that it could enjoy the profits of leasing companies, thereby precipitating the rapid growth of bank leasing companies.

Vendor lessors offer greater service than their competitors. They may be able to provide repair service, maintenance, temporary replacement during breakdowns, and so on. Automobile dealers and machinery vendors are examples. In some instances, the lease contract will be with the vendor lessor; in others, the vendor may have a close working relationship with a bank leasing company, which becomes the lessor.

It should be noted that the vendor-related lessor is interested in providing not only financing but customer service as well. Further, being in the business, the vendor may be able to offer a high degree of flexibility in meeting lessee needs—a degree of flexibility that might not be available through a financing lessor. But service has its price, and thus terms must be critically analyzed to obtain the best deal in terms of the lessee's needs.

Third-party lessors, unlike vendor lessors, have no specific interest in the assets leased, but rather act as a financial intermediary. They do not, in general, expect ever to recover the asset, but at lease termination will either re-lease or sell it. The number of independent third-party lessors diminished from 300 in 1972 to 175 in 1975. Many of them were replaced by lessors representing financial institutions, such as commercial banks and investment banks.[11] Thus, a major shift has taken place within the industry, and, as a consequence of the high level of competition, probably only the strongest third-party lessors will survive.

Many larger banks are involved in leasing. While some banks still participate in the leasing industry by lending funds to third-party lessors, their primary, and most profitable, interest is in acting as lessors directly or through subsidiary leasing companies. Frost & Sullivan reports First National Bank of Boston as having two leasing companies.[12] One is within the regular bank structure and deals in leases up to $1 million. The other is a leasing subsidiary for large items. Banks may also put together leveraged leases, which require only a small investment but may result in a large fee. In this area commercial banks are overlapping with investment banks.

Since the primary profit of many insurance companies is derived from their investment portfolio, it is not surprising to note their interest in leasing. Initially insurance companies acted as lenders for large leveraged leases. However, within the limitations of their individual charters, some insurance companies are now moving directly into leasing, and this trend is likely to continue.

The function of investment banks in the leasing industry is primarily, if not exclusively, as financial intermediaries and lease packagers. As in their other investment banking functions, they are very aware of the current availability of capital and the sources thereof. Many have departments to locate sources of capital and structure leases.

In summary, the leasing industry is exhibiting continued growth as a financial, as opposed to service, industry. This trend is likely to continue, and we expect the industry to become dominated by financial institutions—commercial banks for smaller leases and investment banks and insurance companies for larger leases.

NOTES

1. "Percentage Leasing," *Business Week,* January 8, 1938, p. 41.
2. "They Are Beginning to Make a Science of Percentage Leasing," *Business Week,* May 25, 1932, p. 11.
3. "Basing Your Rent on Sales," *Business Week,* June 13, 1936, p. 42.
4. Albert B. Cohen, *Long Term Leases: Problems of Taxation, Finance, and Accounting,* Ann Arbor: University of Michigan Press, 1954.
5. "Moola for Boola," *Time,* November 14, 1949, p. 54.
6. Hugh J. Zick, "Leasing: Its Contribution to the National Economy," *World,* Winter 1977, pp. 3–7.
7. Richard Kartz, "Leasing Is Big Business Today," *The Magazine of Wall Street,* November 14, 1964, p. 214.
8. Joel Dean, *Capital Budgeting: Top Management Policy on Plant Equipment and Product Development.* New York: Columbia University Press, 1951.
9. "Accounting for Leases," Statement of Financial Accounting Standards Board No. 13, Financial Accounting Standards Board, November 1976.
10. *"The Rental Equipment Industry,"* Moline, Illinois: The American Rental Association, 1975.
11. For a detailed description of the leasing industry, and forecasts of future trends, see *The Equipment Leasing Market,* Report No. 382, 1976, Frost & Sullivan, Inc., 106 Fulton Street, New York, N.Y. 10038.
12. Ibid., p. 114.

CHAPTER 2

Types of Leases

In this chapter, we will detail the requirements necessary to a "true" lease as defined by the Internal Revenue Service. In so doing, we will clearly differentiate leases from conditional sales contracts. The primary emphasis of this chapter is, however, on noting and defining various types of leases from two aspects. First, we look to FASB 13 and its definition of lease types and leasing terms for financial reporting purposes. Second, we examine several types of leases from the perspective of the lessee in order to provide him with greater knowledge of and insight into the available packaging of lease financing. Last, we devote a short section to the study of leveraged leases.

A "True" Lease

As noted earlier, one of the primary incentives to leasing lies in the tax benefit: the total cost of leasing is deductible as an expense for computing federal income tax liability. In order to enjoy this benefit, the lease must be a "true" lease rather than a conditional sales contract as defined by the Internal Revenue Service. In general, a conditional sales contract exists if the lessee has acquired or will acquire title or an equity interest in the asset being leased. *In a true lease the lessee does not acquire ownership or title.*

Revenue Ruling 55-540 established the framework for differentiating between a lease and conditional sales agreement. In general, *an agreement will be construed to be a conditional sale if any one or more of the following conditions are present:*

1. Portions of the periodic payment are specifically applicable to equity to be acquired.
2. Title will be acquired upon payment of a stated amount required to be made under the contract.
3. The total payment required for a relatively short period of use constitutes an excessively large portion of the total sum required to be paid to secure transfer of title.
4. The agreed payments materially exceed the current fair lease payment value.
5. The property may be obtained under a purchase option at a price that is nominal in relation to the value of the property at the time the option is exercised.
6. Some portion of the periodic payment is specifically designated as interest or is readily recognizable as the equivalent of interest.
7. Title will be acquired upon payment of an aggregate amount (total of payments plus option price, if any) that approximates the price, plus interest and carrying charges, at which the asset could have been purchased upon entering into the agreement.

On the basis of IRS and tax court rulings, the test of a true lease includes the following elements:[1]

1. The term of the agreement is less than 30 years.
2. The agreement provides a reasonable return to the lessor; usually between 7 percent and 12 percent.
3. If there is a renewal option, then it must be bona fide. This requirement can best be met by providing that the current lessee be given the first option to meet an equal bona fide offer made by a third party.
4. There can be no attempt to transfer ownership at the end of the lease to the lessee at anything other than the fair market value. Further, the lessee may not be granted any significant economic interest in the residual value.
5. At the end of the lease, the expected fair market value of the asset should not be less than 15 percent of the original cost if the lease has a life of 18 years or less. If the lease has a life exceeding 18 years, then the asset should have a value of at least 20 percent at the end of the lease period.
6. The remaining economic life at the end of the lease must be either 20 percent of the life of the lease or 2 years, whichever is less.
7. The lessor must have at least 20 percent interest in the leased asset.

If the agreement is approved as being a true lease, then the lessor will be allowed the tax shelters of ownership and the lessee may deduct the lease payments as expenses for computation of federal income taxes. However, an agreement may be rejected as a lease or classified as a pseudo-lease. In these instances, the agreement could be regarded as either a conditional sales contract or a debt instrument for tax purposes.

Alvin Zises[2] indicates that the following clauses in the agreement could lead to its being classified as a pseudo-lease:

1. A "hell or high water" clause, which makes the lessee's obligation to pay "rent" absolute and unconditional. Under a true lease, the lessee's obligation to pay is conditional upon the future performance of the lessor and the quiet enjoyment of the property.
2. The direct or indirect guarantee by the lessee of the lessor's obligations.
3. The lessor is controlled by the lessee.
4. The lessor has little or no independent economic substance (that is, the lessor is a phantom corporation).
5. The lessee has the right to obtain title to leased assets at less than fair market value.

J. R. Patton, Jr.,[3] has devised the following two-part checklist for distinguishing between a lease and a conditional sales contract:

Factors Indicating a Lease

1. The absence of a provision for the transfer of title to the lessee.
2. The absence of any mention of interest as a factor in rental charges.
3. Rental charges that are competitive with those charged by other lessors of similar equipment.
4. Rental charges that are reasonably related to the loss of value due to the lessee's use of the equipment or that are based on production or use and not necessarily related to purchase price.
5. The assumption of the risk of loss by the lessor.
6. The lessor is required to bear the cost of insurance, maintenance, and taxes.
7. The lessor retains the right to inspect the equipment during the term of the lease.
8. If the lessee has an option to purchase:
   (a) The option price approximates the predicted fair market value of the equipment at the time the option may be exercised.
   (b) Rentals are not applied to the option price.
   (c) Rentals are not so great that the exercise of the purchase option is a virtual certainty.
9. The rentals charged under leasing plans without an option to purchase approximate the rentals charged under plans with such an option.

Factors Indicating a Conditional Sale

1. Portions of the periodic payments are applicable to an equity in the equipment to be acquired by the lessee.
2. The lessee will acquire title upon payment of a fixed amount of rent.
3. The total amount the lessee is required to pay for a relatively short period of use constitutes an inordinately large proportion of the total cost of the equipment, and the lessee has the use of the equipment for the remainder of its useful life at a nominal cost.
4. Some portion of periodic payments is designated as interest.
5. The property may be acquired by exercise of a purchase option which is nominal in relation to the value of the property at the time when the option may be exercised as determined at the time the agreement is entered into.
6. The sum of rental payments and option price approximates the price at which the equipment could have been acquired by purchase plus carrying charges.
7. The lessee assumes the risk of loss of the lessor's investment.
8. The property is leased for substantially its entire useful life.

Most of the lease-with-option cases have been decided in the tax courts. *The criterion generally applied by the courts has been the "economic reality" or "intent to purchase" test.* Essentially, this test says that if the option can be exercised within a period that is clearly less than the useful life of the property, and the lease payments cover what would be the purchase price, then a sale was intended.

The test case for this rule was decided in the Seventh Circuit Court.[4] Beny had an agreement which called for a two-year lease on a farm with payments of $30,000 per year and a $100,000 purchase option. The tax court ruled the transaction to be a purchase and disallowed the lease payments as tax deductions by Beny.

In a later case,[5] the court ruled differently. The parties entered into a lease-and-option-to-purchase agreement that called for a payment of $100,000, payable in 60 annual installments, and an option price of $50,000. The court ruled that there was no equity in the property until the option was exercised and allowed the lease payments as deductions.

A "hell or high water" clause in an agreement may prejudice its status as a lease. Such a clause binds the lessee to pay full value of the leased equipment to the lessor or its assignee (generally a bank) regardless of what happens to the equipment or the lessor. This clause is inserted for the protection of the supplier of the underlying financing in the event of lessor bankruptcy or destruction of the leased equipment. *A "hell or high water" clause puts the owner-borrower's conventional obligations and risk of loss on the lessee. Therefore, the lease agreement may be construed to be a debt obligation or installment purchase contract.*

Another legal question involves the rights of all parties in the event of bankruptcy of one of the parties. A trustee-in-bankruptcy may, under certain conditions, disallow a lease obligation but not a direct debt. Generally, if the lessee becomes bankrupt, it can be held responsible for only one additional year's lease payments. The lessor may reclaim the property, but unless it is readily salable, the lessor may have difficulty with its disposal. In leveraged leases, provisions for lessee bankruptcy are covered in the trust agreement.

Sale-and-leaseback agreements may also result in tax problems. Some assets sold in a sale-and-leaseback agreement qualify as Section 1231 assets—depreciable assets or land used in the taxpayer's trade or business. Section 1231 provides that gains on such sales, to the extent that they exceed recapture of depreciation, be treated as capital gains, while net long-term capital losses may be deducted from ordinary income. This treatment permits a potential lessee great flexibility in timing a sale and leaseback to fit its particular tax needs. For example, in a high-tax year a firm could sell and lease back an asset that had a market value substantially less than its book value and obtain a large ordinary income deduction. The danger here is that the IRS could rule the transaction a sham and disallow the deduction.

In such cases, the IRS has contended that a sale has not really taken place, because the would-be seller has continued to retain control over the asset and merely obtained financing, using the asset as a collateral. The IRS position is strongest when the sale is below market value and the lease is for a long period. The taxpayer's strongest defense is to demonstrate three things: (1) the negotiations were arm's length, (2) the terms of the agreement were based on fair market values for both sale and lease payments, and (3) the basic lease term was under 30 years.[6]

Types of Leases

Within the leasing industry there are various titles or names for leases, and there are several names distinguishing lease arrangements and lease types. Certain lease title designations are based on the duration and monetary value of the lease; others derive from the financial and marketing arrangements. The accounting profession has reinterpreted existing and introduced new lease classifications in order to help resolve the problems in accounting for leases. Further, some leases are known by reference to restrictive covenants contained within the lease agreement. As a consequence, there is a great deal of overlap, and the same type of lease may be known to lessee, lessor, and financial analyst by different names.

In this section, we will provide some of the basic distinctions among types of leases, with two primary goals. First, we want to make the reader aware of the differences in lease types as they pertain to financial reporting and, specifically, to the requirements of FASB 13.[7] Second, through definition and classification, we want to further explore the types of leasing agreements available so as to provide the reader with a sense of the industry and the jargon, thus hopefully placing him in a more favorable bargaining position. We will consider lease designation for financial reporting purposes first.

Before dealing with specifics, it is necessary to recall that there are three types of accounting: managerial, financial reporting, and tax. Unfortunately, the three generally have differing goals and rules. For tax purposes, a lease must meet the various tests described in the previous section; if it does, the IRS shows little interest in the name that is given to the agreement or how it is recorded for financial reporting purposes. *The IRS does not recognize the requirements of FASB 13 for tax reporting purposes.* As a consequence, throughout the following discussions, the reader should be constantly aware that by any other name, an agreement must be a "true" lease by IRS standards if the lessee is to enjoy the tax benefits of leasing.

CAPITAL LEASES

For financial reporting purposes of a lessee, FASB 13 distinguishes two types of leases: capital and operating. For a lease to be considered a *capital lease,* the lease must meet one or more of the following four criteria; otherwise, it is by definition an operating lease. The significance of these two designations will become clear when we discuss lease accounting.[8]

1. The lease transfers ownership of the property to the lessee by the end of the lease term. This term is defined as the fixed noncancelable term of the lease plus any options specified in the contract.

2. The lease contains a bargain option or a provision that allows the lessee at his option to purchase the leased property for a price lower than the expected fair market value of the property.

3. The lease term is equal to 75 percent or more of the estimated economic life of the leased property. If, however, the beginning of the lease falls within the last 25 percent of the total economic useful life of the leased property, including earlier years of use, this criterion is not used for classifying the lease.

4. The present value of the lease at the beginning of the lease term of the minimum lease payments, excluding *executory costs* such as insurance, maintenance, and taxes to be paid by the lessor, including any profit

thereon, equals or exceeds 90 percent of the excess fair market value of the leased property to the lessor at the inception of the lease over any related investment tax credit retained by the lessor and expected to be realized by him. This criterion is not used if the lease term falls within the last 25 percent of the total estimated economic life of the leased property. The lessor computes the present value using the *implicit interest rate*, while the lessee uses his incremental *borrowing rate*, unless he can use the lessor's implicit interest rate. The lessor's implicit interest rate must be used if this rate is less than the incremental borrowing rate.

Several terms from FASB 13 require definition at this juncture to assure understanding of the four criteria.

The *lease term* is the fixed, noncancelable term of the lease plus any other periods under renewal options, if exercise of the option is reasonably assured, plus all periods under renewal or extensions at the lessor's option.

The *fair value of the leased property* is the price at which the property could be sold in an arm's length transaction. In a sales-type lease (wherein a manufacturer-lessor or dealer-lessor both profits on the "sale" of the property and provides lease financing) the fair market value generally is the value at the inception of the lease, less any trade or volume discounts. However, depending on market conditions, it could be a value less than normal selling price or even less than cost. In a financial lease (discussed in detail below), cost and fair market value are ordinarily the same, less any volume or trade discounts. However, in instances where there is a significant lapse of time, fair value is set to reflect existing market conditions.

The *estimated economic life* is the estimated period over which the property will be in the possession of one or more users and used for its intended purpose. The estimated economic life is not limited to the lease term.

The *estimated residual value* is the estimated fair value of the property at the end of the lease term.

The *unguaranteed residual value* is the estimated residual value exclusive of any portion guaranteed by the lessee or a third party.

The *minimum lease payments* over the lease term (excluding the portion applicable to executory costs) are the minimum payments plus any guaranteed residual value, including penalties upon cancelation and bargain purchase options.

The *implicit interest rate* is the discount rate which, when applied to the minimum lease payments and the unguaranteed residual value, cause the present value to equal the fair value of the property, less any investment tax credits retained by the lessor or expected to be retained by him.

The *incremental borrowing rate* is the lessee's rate to borrow funds over a period of the same duration, had the property been purchased.

The *inception of the lease* is the date of the lease agreement or commitment, if earlier, unless the property has yet to be constructed or acquired. If the latter is the case, then the inception is the completed construction date or the date it is acquired by the lessor.

Finally, we need to indicate what a lease is under FASB 13. "A lease is an agreement conveying the right to use property or equipment (land and/or depreciable assets), usually for a stated period of time." Specifically excluded are leases conveying "the rights to explore for or to exploit material resources, such as oil, gas, minerals and timber, [and] licensing agreements for such items as motion picture films, plays, manuscripts, patents and copyrights."

The term capital lease is very broad and includes all lease types other than those defined by FASB 13 as operating leases. Hence, for the lessee's accounting reporting, a capital lease is an umbrella term for many types of leases that may be further distinguished by marketing method, structure, and covenants. The reader should further note that the term capital lease does not in any way distinguish leases as to the type of asset leased.

OPERATING LEASES

The term *operating lease* (or *service* or *maintenance lease*) is used by FASB, the IRS, and the leasing community, but not always in the same context. FASB 13 defines an operating lease in terms of both the lessee and lessor as follows:

- For the lessee it includes all leases that are not capital leases.
- For the lessor it includes all other leases (i.e., those which are not financial, leveraged, etc.).

The leasing community views an operating lease as one having the following characteristics:

- The lease does not involve an extension of credit or a long-term fixed commitment.
- The lessor may provide special services, such as maintenance.
- The lease is of short length compared to the economic life of the asset.
- The lease is cancelable within reasonable restrictions.

McGugan and Caves[9] note that a lease may also be classified as an operating lease if the asset is available only on a lease basis or if the price to purchase is set unrealistically high so as to estop purchase.

In most instances, an operating lease, as defined above, will be construed by the IRS to be a "true" lease. The distinguishing characteristic of an operating lease within this context is the continued ownership of the asset by the lessor, with all the benefits and risks of ownership.

Operating leases offer several special advantages to the lessee who is confronted with the lease-versus-purchase decision.

1. *The lessee may lease a piece of equipment for a short period of time, which provides an opportunity to try it out.* If the equipment performs a needed function economically, then the lessee, armed with the experience gained through its use, may either purchase or opt for a longer-term lease. If the equipment does not perform up to expectations, then the lessee has learned a valuable lesson with only a minimal cost and is not put in the position of having to retain or dispose of marginally useful equipment. In some instances, leasing companies will provide equipment on a trial basis at nominal cost for a short period of time to induce the lessee to take a long-term lease. The lessee should recognize the lessor's experience with the equipment and draw upon the lessor for advice as to the type of equipment that will be most practical and profitable for the lessee.

2. *Operating leases reduce the risk of obsolescence.* Since operating leases are non-full payment and are cancelable upon due notice from the lessee, the risk of obsolescence is borne by the lessor. Naturally, the lessee will be charged a premium over and above the normal rate of return associated with a lease, to compensate the lessor for the risk involved.

C. J. Wilson[10] notes two types of risk that will affect this premium: (1) *military aircraft obsolescence,* where the asset becomes suddenly and totally obsolete and must immediately be replaced; and (2) *improved version obsolescence,* where the equipment need not be replaced immediately, but the lessee is penalized through increasing opportunity costs if it continues to operate a nonoptimal piece of equipment. The lessee would, of course, want to utilize the most profitable equipment available and, therefore, cancel a lease for nonoptimal equipment as soon as practical.

3. *The lessee is not exposed to the risk of ownership under an operating lease.* Obsolescence is a part of the risk of ownership; another part is the burden of selling a second-hand piece of equipment, regardless of the reason underlying the sale. If the lessee had purchased the equipment and later attempted to sell it, he would be at a disadvantage, since his primary form of business is not selling his used equipment. On the other hand, a wise lessor will generally have little difficulty in finding a new lessee for equipment if a lease is not renewed; otherwise he sells the equipment. *Generally, the lessor has direct ties with the manufacturer or is the manufacturer of the equipment and thus enjoys economies of scale with respect to purchasing, leasing, and selling equipment.* Further, the lessor is usually an indus-

try specialist and, by dealing in volume, can frequently obtain equipment at a lower cost than the lessee. However, except for some types of equipment with very low risk of obsolescence, these efficiencies are generally not sufficient to offset the risks of ownership and obsolescence (which are borne by the lessor), and, therefore, operating leases are usually more expensive than ownership or financial leases.

4. *The lessee can take advantage of certain low-cost services provided by the lessor*. Since the lessor is a specialist in dealing with the equipment and operates on large volume, he can provide two important services to the lessee at a cost far less than the cost which the lessee would bear to provide those same services. The first is equipment service and maintenance. The lessor can care for and maintain the equipment efficiently, utilizing trained service technicians, special service equipment, and a full stock of spare parts. Second, the lessor can bring in replacement equipment at short notice if the leased equipment should suffer a major breakdown or require extensive service or maintenance. This reduces production downtime for the lessee and may result in considerable saving in time and expense for the lessee.

5. *The operating lease may provide middle management flexibility*. Normally, major capital expenditures require top management approval, whereas in many firms, operating leasing decisions may be made at middle management levels. This provides flexibility at the branch management level that would otherwise be unavailable.

FINANCIAL LEASES

A *financial lease,* as the word financial connotes, is a method of asset financing whereby the lessor extends credit to the lessee and transfers to the lessee all the responsibilities of ownership, including maintenance, insurance, taxes, and so on, for a period of time close to the economic life of the asset. In most instances, at the termination of the lease, the lessee may either purchase the asset at a price not less than its fair market value, or return the asset to the lessor.[11] The option to purchase generally states the method to be used to determine fair market values (frequently by appraisals by both lessor and lessee). Financial leases are differentiated from conditional sales agreements in that the lease period ends while there is still some economic life remaining.

The lease payments in a financial lease are usually set so that the lessor may recover the purchase price (less investment tax credits and any residual value) and achieve a rate of return approximately equal to the lessee's marginal cost of debt financing over the period of the lease. Most financial leases are *full payout*. In a full-payout lease, the cash returns to the lessor are sufficient to cover the asset cost, the cost of financing, the lessor's overhead, and a rate of return acceptable to the lessor. The full payout is contrasted to the *non-full* payout, in which the lessor must depend upon the salvage value to cover the purchase cost and achieve an acceptable return on investment. Operating leases are usually non-full payout.

Financial leases are similar to mortgage-type loans wherein fixed payments are scheduled for a fixed period of time. The repayment of debt consists of interest and principal repayments. Lease payments similarly may be thought of as having two parts. The first is the amount required by the lessor to recover the investment (essentially the principal repayment). The second is the yield or return the lessor requires on the investment in the asset. The yield is, in essence, an implied interest rate and is a function of several factors:

- The money market conditions, that is, current interest rates, availability of funds, and so on.
- The lessor's required rate of return on investment.
- The conditions of the lease contract.
- The lessor's ability to borrow funds.
- The anticipated sales price of the asset at the end of the lease contract.
- The lessor's expected tax rate during the period of the lease.
- The risks inherent in the ownership of the asset.

Most financial leases are noncancelable and written on a net or net-net basis (as defined below). Furthermore, it is assumed that if the lessee had the capital needed to purchase the asset, he could purchase it at a competitive price.

A special type of financing lease is the leveraged lease, which involves assets having value exceeding approximately $1 million. The leveraged lease requires special attention and is discussed at the end of this chapter.

DIRECT LEASES

The *direct lease* is essentially a hybrid of operating and financial leases. Direct leases are usually full payout and provide for renewal or purchase options, but do not include lessor service such as maintenance.

The FASB includes direct leasing as a type of lease applicable only to lessors. As defined by FASB, a direct lease is one that does not include provision in the lease payment for lessor profit, meets one or more of the criteria used to define a capital lease, and has a reasonably high predictability of collection of lease payments.

Wajnert[12] characterizes direct leases by the following attributes:

1. Duration of three to seven years.
2. The lessor holds title.
3. The lessee may renew or purchase at expiration of lease term.
4. May have mid-stream trade-in option.
5. Usually full payout.

MIDDLE-MARKET LEASES

Middle-market lease is a term applied to a lease that has characteristics of both the direct and leveraged lease:

1. The lease term generally ranges from 5 to 15 years.
2. The assets leased have value ranging from about $500,000 to several million dollars.
3. Financing may be through one or more third parties.

While similar to leveraged leases, the middle-market lease is usually for a shorter duration and involves assets having lower value.

MASTER LEASES

A *master lease* establishes an open-ended contract with rates and terms for both equipment needed at the present time and equipment needed in the future. It is usually written for a term longer than the life of any asset leased, and places responsibility upon the lessor to provide up-to-date equipment throughout the lease period. The quantity of the equipment provided by the lessor may vary seasonally or with the lessee's needs. Master leases are often used for truck and car fleet leasing and computer peripheral equipment leasing.

The master lease is similar to a blanket purchase order and, in effect, also establishes a line of credit between lessee and lessor and eliminates the need to negotiate a new lease contract each time additional equipment is needed.

SALE AND LEASEBACK

Using a *sale-and-leaseback arrangement,* a firm may sell a portion of its assets, such as equipment or buildings, to a lessor and then lease them back. The lessee thus converts fixed assets into cash. The arrangement is beneficial to the lessee in that additional cash is available while the firm still has use of the assets. Furthermore, a profit or recapture of depreciation may be realized in the sale, since market value frequently exceeds book value, especially for buildings and land. If, for example, a firm sold a building that has been fully depreciated and leased it back, it would, in essence, be able to depreciate it twice, since a portion of the lease payments is equivalent to depreciation.

Some lessors tend to be skeptical of sale-and-leaseback transactions, as many firms interested in such transactions have poor liquidity positions. The firms may be, in fact, selling off capital investments to cover the cost of prior financing arrangements.

Another lessee motivation to enter a sale-and-leaseback agreement is to acquire an asset at a fair price. If lease payments arranged by a captive lessor are excessive, a firm may purchase the asset and then sell it to a leasing company for leaseback at a lower cost than through the captive lessor. This complex arrangement may frequently be avoided by arranging directly with a leasing company to purchase the asset and lease it to the firm.

PERCENTAGE LEASES AND MINERAL PROPERTY LEASES

Percentage leases were described briefly in Chapter 1 as the first use of leasing as a financing mechanism. Percentage leases are usually limited to high-powered retail districts, primarily in shopping malls. The lessee pays a flat minimum rental and additional rentals based on a percentage of gross receipts. Lease arrangements may call for lessor improvements to leaseholds to lessee specifications. Percentage leases place a heavy risk burden on the lessor, whose profit is heavily leveraged by the degree of the lessee's success.

Mineral property leases are a special case of percentage leases and are applied when minerals are to be extracted from the ground. The lessee pays a flat rental for the right of use, plus royalties based on the value of the minerals extracted. Mineral property leases do not include improvements, which are usually made by the lessee on the land.

WET AND DRY LEASES

The terms *wet* and *dry* originated in the aircraft industry. A dry lease provided only for financing whereas a wet lease provided for financing as well as fuel and servicing. With respect to lessor service, the provisions of a wet lease are similar to those of an operating lease.

NET AND NET-NET LEASES

The term *net lease* is sometimes applied to a financial lease. The lessee agrees to make lease payments and also bears the costs of maintenance, insurance, taxes, and the like, and assumes the risks of ownership. The net-net lease goes one step further in adding to the lessee's risk burden by requiring the lessee to return to the lessor at lease end an asset having a pre-established value. The lessee is thus responsible for any variation in the actual resale value from the present amount.

There are other characteristics and special terms attached to leases within given segments of the industry. These will be introduced when we examine these areas.

Leveraged Leases

Leveraged leases are similar to financial leases in that they are noncancelable, full-payout, net leases. However, in the case of a leveraged lease there are usually five or six parties involved, while in a financial lease there are only two: the owner (lessor) and the lessee. The difference in the number of parties involved results from the fact that in leveraged leases the owner puts up only a fraction of the investment cost (usually 20 percent to 35 percent) and borrows the rest from other sources. The reason for borrowing on the part of the lessor is the fact that leveraged leases involve significant dollar outlays. Golden and Parrish[13] estimate that leveraged leases run from $5 to $120 million, with $22 million as an average. The products leased through leveraged leasing are large-ticket items and include airplanes, railroad cars, ships, off-shore drilling equipment, nuclear fuel, pipelines, and entire production plants.

The leveraged lease represents a very complex transaction involving several parties and a number of agreements. Manufacturers Hanover Leasing Company[14] has provided the clear explanation of leveraged leasing that follows.

Documentation and Parties to the Typical Leveraged Lease Transaction

The leveraged lease is one of the most complex and legally sophisticated arrangements for financing large capital intensive equipment assets. Numerous entities are parties to the documents. Each major transaction involves negotiation among owners, lenders, lessee, and trustees. A fundamental understanding of the lease's legal structure and the duties and obligations of the various participants is essential to smooth closing of this type of financing transaction. The basic documents found in leveraged lease transactions and the parties to these documents are listed for your information.

The participation agreement

This is the only document executed by all parties to the transaction. It is an agreement in which the commitments and obligations of each participant, including owners, lenders, lessee, trustees, and guarantors, are set forth. It also lists the various conditions precedent for closing the transaction, such as warranties, representations and covenants required, authorities to enter into agreements, opinions of counsel, and specific indemnities of various parties. All important terms are defined and such matters as tax benefits, transfer of Loan and Owner Certificates, citizenship affidavits, liabilities of participants, and other legal matters are included.

The trust agreement

The various equity investors who advance from 20 percent to 50 percent of the cost of the asset are known as OWNER PARTICIPANTS and as such enter into a TRUST AGREEMENT with a corporate trustee (usually a commercial bank's Corporate Trust Department) in which the OWNER PARTICIPANTS agree to advance their prorata share of the equity funds and receive, as evidence of ownership, OWNER CERTIFICATES issued by the OWNER TRUSTEE. The OWNER TRUSTEE agrees to purchase the equipment on behalf of the OWNER PARTICIPANTS and to hold title to the equipment. The TRUST ESTATE includes the equipment subject to a security lien of the lenders, and the assignment of the LEASE and lease rentals. In case of default by the lessee the OWNER TRUSTEE provides written notice to the OWNER PARTICIPANTS, and takes such remedies on their behalf as are provided for under terms of the TRUST AGREEMENT.

Indenture trust

This agreement is entered into by the OWNER TRUSTEE and the INDENTURE TRUSTEE (usually another commercial bank). The agreement provides for issuance by the INDENTURE TRUSTEE of LOAN CERTIFICATES to the various LOAN PARTICIPANTS, representing from 50 percent to 80 percent of the equipment cost. It sets forth the form of the certificates, their term, method of payment, and interest rate. The INDENTURE TRUSTEE receives the periodic rentals from the LESSEE and distributes the rentals first in the form of interest and principal to the LOAN PARTICIPANTS and then any remainder to the OWNER PARTICIPANTS. The INDENTURE TRUSTEE holds for the benefit of the LOAN PARTICIPANTS the security interest or mortgage on the equipment, and in case of LESSEE default can act under remedy provisions of the INDENTURE TRUST to take possession of the equipment for the benefit of the LOAN PARTICIPANTS. If the TRUST ESTATE is liquidated, the INDENTURE TRUSTEE distributes the proceeds first to the LOAN PARTICIPANTS and any remainder to the OWNER PARTICIPANTS.

Lease agreement

The LEASE AGREEMENT is entered into by the user of the equipment, the LESSEE, and the OWNER TRUSTEE. The LESSEE is responsible for specifying the type of equipment and the manufacturer. He also must pay all maintenance costs, insurance, taxes, and fees levied in connection with use of the equipment so that the LEASE is a net lease. The LEASE AGREEMENT sets forth the terms of the transaction, the amount of rental to be paid, the amount and type of insurance required, the obligation of the LESSEE to maintain the equipment, the rights, if any, of

LESSEE to terminate the lease before the expiration of the lease term and the provisions which come into effect in case the equipment is destroyed. The LEASE AGREEMENT also contains a listing of various indemnities that the LESSEE is responsible for.

Purchase agreement and assignment

The LESSEE assigns to the OWNER TRUSTEE his rights, interests, and warranties under the PURCHASE AGREEMENT between the LESSEE and MANUFACTURER of the equipment in the PURCHASE AGREEMENT ASSIGNMENT.

In addition to the documents listed above, there may be various GUARANTEES involved. For example, if a LESSEE is the subsidiary of a larger and more financially substantial parent, a guarantee of the subsidiary's lease obligations may be required.

The chart below can be used as a ready reference to the participants who are parties to these documents.

Leveraged Lease Documentation: Parties to Agreements

Document	Lessee	Participants Owner	Loan	Trustees Owner	Indenture	Manufacturer
Participation agreement	√	√	√	√	√	
Owner trust agreement		√		√		
Indenture trust agreement				√	√	
Lease agreement	√			√		
Purchase agreement	√˙					√
Purchase agreement assignment	√			√		√

In addition to the parties discussed by Manufacturers Hanover Leasing Corporation, a sixth party, called a *packager,* may be included. The packager is usually a major leasing company like Manufacturers Hanover, U.S. Leasing, Itel Leasing, or Citicorp, to name but a few, an investment bank such as Salomon Brothers, Dillon Reed, or Halsey, Stuart & Co., or a commercial bank or bank holding company. The packager gets a fee for bringing the parties together and setting up the lease arrangement. The fee, according to Leatham, may be "up to 3 percent of the deal's total value, depending on the size of the lease." A tombstone announcement of a lease arrangement is usually placed in the leading financial newspapers.

Stiles and Walker[15] note that in a leveraged lease, the lease agreement may require that the "lessee's obligation to pay rent be absolute and unconditional." They also indicate provisions that (1) require the lessee to make a payment of "stipulated loss value" should the equipment be destroyed, lost, or rendered unusable; (2) require payment by the lessee for an optional termination of the lease before the expiration date; (3) require indemnification of participants in the transaction that were injured as a result of changes in the tax laws; (4) contain an "upset clause" should the IRS rule the lease is not a "true" lease; and (5) give the owner the right to perform the lease (that is, meet its terms) on behalf of the lessee in order to forestall a default that could trigger a foreclosure.

The size and complexity of leveraged leases make it absolutely imperative that the lease be a true lease in the eyes of the IRS. To help assure that an agreement is a true lease, the IRS issued Revenue Proceeding 75-21, which sets forth the guidelines the IRS will use for advance ruling purposes in determining whether certain transactions purporting to be leases are in fact leases for federal income tax purposes. Revenue Proceeding 75-28 sets forth a checklist of items to ensure inclusion and order of presentation necessary for initial ruling requests under Proceeding 75-21. Copies of the two Proceedings may be obtained on request from the IRS.

NOTES

1. For a further discussion see Steven J. Weiss and Vincent J. McGugan, "The Equipment Leasing Industry and the Emerging Role of Banking Operations," *The New England Economic Review of the Federal Reserve Banking Position,* November–December 1971.
2. "Pseudo-Lease—A Trap and Time Bomb," *Financial Executive,* August 1973, pp. 21–24. This article also contains a good analysis of the legal aspects of a true lease.
3. "Some Tax Aspects of Equipment Leasing," *Leasing of Industrial Equipment,* Washington, D.C.: Machinery and Allied Products Institute, 1965.
4. Beny, Marvin, 11 TCM 301, December 18, 882 (M).
5. Bruce Veneer and Panel Co., 56-1 USTC, 232 F 2nd 319.
6. For further study of the interpretation of leases, the reader is referred to Thomas F. Cunnane, *Tax Aspects of Buying and Leasing Business Property and Equipment,* Englewood Cliffs, N.J.: Prentice-Hall, 1974.
7. "Accounting for Leases," Statement of Financial Accounting Standards Board No. 13, Financial Accounting Standards Board, November 1976.
8. For further reference on leasing terminology see "Selected Leasing Terminology," *Data Management,* May 1977, p. 34.

9. Vincent J. McGugan and Richard E. Caves, "Integration and Competition in the Equipment Leasing Industry," *Journal of Business,* July 1974, pp. 382–385.
10. "The Operating Lease and the Risk of Obsolescence," *Management Accounting,* December 1973.
11. L. J. Kasper, "Evaluating the Cost of Financial Leases," *Management Accounting,* May 1977, p. 43.
12. T. J. Wajnert, "Purchasing Methods: Leasing Gains Edge for Many Big Buys," *Purchasing,* March 30, 1976.
13. C. L. Golden and K. M. Parrish, "Leasing and Banks," *The Journal of Commercial Bank Lending,* March 1974.
14. "Leveraged Leasing: A Clear Choice for the User of Capital Equipment," New York: Manufacturers Hanover Leasing Corporation. Used with permission.
15. N. B. Stiles and M. A. Walker, "Leveraged Lease Financing of Capital Equipment," *The Journal of Commercial Bank Lending,* July 1973.

CHAPTER 3

Taxation, Depreciation, and Cash Flow

In order to make responsible and meaningful decisions within the context of leasing and capital acquisition, it is necessary to understand the basics of taxation and depreciation, especially as they relate to the acquisition and disposal of assets. The purpose of this chapter is to provide this background and to indicate how it may be integrated to determine after-tax cash flows. These cash flows will be used, after appropriate discounting (described in Chapter 5), to make the lease and lease-versus-purchase decisions.

The reader might inquire as to the importance of calculations involving asset purchase in a book on leasing. The answer is not far to seek: the purchase decision is a part of the leasing decision, whether it be for the principle user or a lessor. Thus, questions involving depreciation, investment tax credits, and the like are applicable to both user-owner and user-lessee. Ultimately, the user will bear the costs and share the benefits inherent in the tax environment.

Depreciation

Depreciation represents a primary consideration in deciding if an asset should be purchased, and it directly impacts the owner's cash flows. Since depreciation is recognized as a tax-deductible expense but requires no outlay of cash, the effect on cash flow is obvious: the greater the depreciation in any given year, the lower the taxes and the higher the after-tax cash flow. Determination of depreciation requires only three pieces of information:

1. *The asset's depreciable value.* This is simply the total asset cost, including shipping, installation, and the like, less any expected salvage value. But the reader should be cautioned at this point to note that although the costs of acquisition, as a general rule, need be capitalized and depreciated, this does not imply that a lender would provide funds to cover these costs. The amount of loan available may cover only asset purchase price, whereas a lease may include total acquisition cost.

2. *The asset's useful life.* This is the period that the asset can be reasonably expected to function in the manner and at the level of efficiency intended. For tax purposes, the useful life of most assets can be established using IRS guidelines. For accounting reporting purposes, the life may be the same, although it is frequently extended as part of the process to stabilize earnings and earnings growth. The length of a lease will frequently equal the economic useful life, and hence, for comparative purposes, it is convenient to select the economic life as the basis for both lease evaluation and book reporting.

3. *The method of depreciation appropriate to the asset.* There are several generally accepted methods of depreciation, with the applicability of each limited by tax law. *Straight-line* is especially important in that it may be used for all new and used property. *Double-declining balance* ranks a close second in application; it may be used for new machinery, vehicles, and equipment and new residential real estate. As such, it is very important to both lessor and prospective lessee. *Sum-of-the-years'-digits* may be used whenever double-declining balance is permitted, but it generally suffers from a lower rate of depreciation during the earlier years of the asset's life and, hence, is not used as frequently. *One and one-half declining balance* may be applied to new real estate, other than residential, and used equipment, machinery, vehicles, and the like. *One and one-quarter declining balance* may be applied to used residential real estate having a life of 20 years or more and is, therefore, generally of little interest to prospective lessees.

Land, of course, may not be depreciated. However, when it is leased, the lessee implicitly depreciates it, since the cost of the land is incorporated into the lease payments. This attractive advantage may, however, be canceled by the loss of any residual value to the owner at lease end.

We assume the reader is familiar with the mechanics of depreciating using the various methods and, hence, will provide only a brief review of the procedures.

The straight-line method requires that salvage value be subtracted from total cost, giving the *depreciable value,* which is divided by the number of years in the asset's life. The result of the division is the annual straight-line depreciation.

The declining-balance method involves depreciating against the total cost (rather than depreciable value), with depreciation ending when the book value equals the salvage value. Commencing with the first year, a factor corresponding to the rate being used (say, double straight-line) is multiplied by the total cost less any accumulated depreciation. The same rate is thus applied to a smaller balance each year so that the annual depreciation decreases as the asset ages.

The sum-of-the-years'-digits method applies a changing rate to the depreciable value. Each year a fraction is multiplied by the depreciable value to obtain that year's depreciation. The numerator of the fraction changes from year to year and represents the number of years of useful life remaining. The denominator is the sum of the digits representing the useful life of the asset.

The reader should note that when a declining-balance method (especially double-declining) is used, two situations may develop. First, if the asset has a salvage value, it is not unusual for the asset to be fully depreciated in a period actually shorter than the depreciable life. Second, if the asset does not have a salvage value, it will be necessary to change depreciation method (generally to straight-line) at some point during the asset's life. If this is not done, the asset will never be fully depreciated. As a guide, if double-declining balance is used, the switch should be made, roughly, two-thirds of the way through the asset life.

EXAMPLE 1

Depreciation

An asset costing $20,000 has a five-year useful life and no expected salvage value. Determine the depreciation using straight-line, sum-of-the-years'-digits, and double-declining balance.

SOLUTION

(a) *Straight-line*

$$\$20,000 \div 5 = \$4,000 \text{ per year}$$

(b) *Sum-of-the-years'-digits*

Year	Basis	Fraction	Depreciation
1	$20,000	$\frac{5}{15}$	$6,667
2	20,000	$\frac{4}{15}$	5,333
3	20,000	$\frac{3}{15}$	4,000
4	20,000	$\frac{2}{15}$	2,667
5	20,000	$\frac{1}{15}$	1,333

(c) *Double-declining balance*

Year	Basis × rate	Yearly Depreciation	Cumulative Depreciation
1	$20,000(.4)	$8,000	$8,000
2	12,000(.4)	4,800	12,800
3	7,200(.4)	2,880	15,680
4	4,320(.5)	2,160	17,840
5	4,320(.5)	2,160	20,000

Note that a switch to straight-line was made in the fourth year. □

Taxation

In this section we briefly review the basic corporate tax laws, with special emphasis on those which have an impact on the acquisition and disposal of capital assets.

ORDINARY INCOME

The corporate taxable income is taxed at a five-tier rate structure[1] as follows:

> First $25,000 taxed at 17%
> Next $25,000 taxed at 20%
> Next $25,000 taxed at 30%
> Next $25,000 taxed at 40%
> Over $100,000 taxed at 46%

If the corporation has a net operating loss, the loss may be carried back three years and forward seven *or* carried forward ten years for pre-1971 carryovers. Thus, if a firm has had profits in the three-year period prior to the loss and if these profits are still available to apply losses against, then the firm may enjoy a tax refund that will at least partially make up for the loss. If the loss is carried forward, then taxes will be reduced in future years.

CAPITAL GAINS AND LOSSES

When a firm purchases and sells assets or securities that are not ordinarily bought and sold as a part of the firm's normal business, capital gains and losses may be incurred. The gain or loss on the sale of a capital asset[2] may be short- or long-term, depending on how long the asset was owned: short-term is less than a year, long-term a year or more. When considering the acquisition and disposal of plant and equipment, we are primarily interested in long-term gains and losses. Long-term capital gains are taxed at the rate applied to ordinary income or 28 percent, *whichever is lower,* while short-term gains are always taxed as a part of ordinary income.

RECAPTURE OF DEPRECIATION

When an asset is sold at a gain or at a price above its book value, recapture of depreciation is involved. When personal property (Section 1245) is sold above book value, the recapture of depreciation is taxed as ordinary income. The tax on real property (Section 1250) depends on method of depreciation used, date of acquisition, and other variables. The reader is referred to a tax service, such as Prentice-Hall or Commerce Clearing House, for specific details.

EXAMPLE 2
Recapture of Depreciation and Capital Gain

Five years ago a corporation acquired machinery for $100,000. The expected life and salvage values were ten years and $20,000. The property is now five years old and has been depreciated using the sum-of-the-years'-digits method. Assuming the machinery can be sold for $120,000 and the corporation has a 46 percent marginal tax rate, determine the additional tax it will have to pay if the machinery is sold.

SOLUTION

The depreciation for the first five years is $58,182, giving a book value of $41,818. The recapture is the difference between purchase price and book value, or $58,182. (In this problem all of the depreciation is recaptured, since the sale price exceeds the purchase price). The capital gain is the sale price less purchase price, or $20,000. The recapture is taxed at 46 percent (the firm's marginal tax rate), whereas the long-term capital gain is taxed at 28 percent.

$$\begin{aligned}
\$58{,}182 \times .46 &= \$26{,}764 \\
20{,}000 \times .28 &= \underline{5{,}600} \\
\text{Total additional tax} &\quad \underline{\underline{\$32{,}364}}
\end{aligned}$$

If the corporation sold the machine, the additional tax would be $32,364. □

CAPITAL LOSSES

For purposes of capital losses, assets are divided into two categories. The first to be considered are Section 1231 assets. Section 1231 assets include two primary types:

1. Real property used in the taxpayer's business and held for more than one year, but not regularly sold to customers as a part of the firm's usual business.
2. Depreciable property used in the taxpayer's business and held for more than one year, but not regularly sold to customers as a part of the firm's usual business.

When dealing with losses incurred on the sale of Section 1231 assets, all long-term capital gains and losses are first netted to determine the net gain or loss. If a net loss has taken place, then the loss may be deducted directly from the firm's ordinary income.

The impact of Section 1231 losses is especially important to the timing of asset acquisition and disposal. Consider a situation where a firm could dispose of two assets. The first will result in a $20,000 Section 1231 loss, the second, in a $20,000 long-term capital gain. If the two are sold in the same year, the gain and loss will just equal, so there will not be any tax effects. If, however, they are sold in different years, assuming no other similar transactions and a 46 percent marginal tax rate, a tax savings will be enjoyed. The loss on the Section 1231 disposal will result in tax savings of $.46 \times \$20,000 = \$9,200$, while the sale of the second asset will result in a tax liability of $.28 \times \$20,000 = \$5,600$. Thus, by timing the sale to two different years, net savings of $3,600 are realized.

For losses other than Section 1231, the process of loss carry-back and carry-forward must be employed. These capital losses may not be deducted from ordinary income but rather must be applied against capital gains enjoyed in prior years or expected in the future. Such capital losses may be carried back three years and forward five years in a manner similar to losses on ordinary income.

INVESTMENT TAX CREDIT

When certain types of assets are acquired, tax law permits up to 10 percent of their cost to be deducted directly from the firm's tax liability. In general, the property must meet the following qualifications to permit the tax credit:

- Be depreciable.
- Have a life of three or more years.
- Be tangible personal property or other tangible property (except buildings and structural components) used in manufacturing, production, or extraction.[3]
- Be placed in use for the production of income during the year in which the credit is taken. Property is considered to be placed in

service in the year depreciation is started or the year the asset is available for service, whichever is earlier.

The types of assets that are of primary interest for purposes of securing investment tax credit include machinery, equipment, vehicles, and property accessories, such as air conditioners, grocery counters, and the like.

The amount of credit that may be taken depends upon the life of the asset selected for tax accounting purposes. Specifically:

- Property having a depreciable life of less than three years does not qualify.
- Property having a depreciable life of three but less than five years qualifies for one-third of the credit.
- Property having a depreciable life of five but less than seven years qualifies for two-thirds of the credit.
- Property having a depreciable life of seven years or over qualifies for the total allowable credit.

If property is disposed of before the end of its depreciable life, then the investment tax credit must be recomputed on the basis of the actual life (rather than the original estimate) and any excess credit recaptured.

To compute investment tax credits, the total price less any allowance for trade-in is used. However, for used property, no more than $100,000 of the cost of the qualifying property may be considered. Furthermore, the amount of investment tax credit taken in any one year is limited to the firm's tax liability or $25,000 plus 60 percent of the firm's tax liability in excess of $25,000, whichever is less.[4] Unused credits may be carried back three years and forward seven years. The two restrictions (trade-in and dollar limit) are especially important to the lease-versus-purchase decision. For an amplification of these limitations see Chapter 10.

Consider the trade-in first. If a firm sells a used asset outright, there is no trade-in and the full credit may be taken on the new asset. The rationale for trade-in is that a vendor may be able and willing to provide a greater trade-in than the owner could get by selling the asset outright.

In leasing, the owner may be able to sell an existing asset to a vendor-lessor for a price equivalent to the trade-in and still enjoy the full benefit of investment tax credit. The lessor will receive the credit and pass it along to the lessee through lower lease payments. The limit in dollar amount of credit frequently imposes a real constraint. Many firms just don't pay sufficient tax to enjoy the full benefit of the tax credit. Leasing provides a way to gain these benefits. When the cost of acquisition may be reduced by 10 percent, this is a most important consideration.

EXAMPLE 3
Investment Tax Credit

A firm is considering the purchase of three assets having the following characteristics:

Asset	Cost	Life
New vehicles	$75,000	5 years
Used equipment	$125,000	10 years
New machine	$50,000	8 years

Determine the total investment tax credit that may be taken this year if the firm's tax, prior to taking investment tax credits, is $18,000.

SOLUTION

First, determine the credit on each asset:

New vehicles	$75,000 × ⅔ × .10 =	$ 5,000
Used equipment	$100,000 × .10 =	10,000
New machine	$50,000 × .10 =	5,000
		$20,000

Since the firm's total tax liability is only $18,000, the investment credit is limited to $18,000 this year. The remaining $2,000 may be first carried back and then forward. □

If, in Example 3, the firm had negligible tax, it could not directly enjoy the benefits of the tax credits. Many smaller and even large going concerns are in this position and look to leasing as the vehicle to take advantage of the credits.

Cash Flows

The primary inputs to the purchase and lease-versus-purchase decisions are the expected after-tax cash flows, both inflows and outflows. These flows are estimated on the basis of sales and marketing forecasts combined with projected costs. We will assume that the appropriate forecasting has been undertaken and that the results are reliable with the same degree of certainty that the firm has enjoyed historically. This assumption does not necessarily mean that the projections are certain, but rather that the decisions based on the current forecasts will not alter the firm's overall risk posture.

In order to determine the cost of asset acquisition, the total funding requirements must be considered:[5]

Land purchased.
Equipment and facilities purchased.
Patents and processes purchased.
All costs relating to purchase (transportation, legal fees, installation, etc.).
Additional working capital required.
Tax liability on sale of replaced assets.
Interest on construction loans and the like.
Property taxes on land and buildings before they are placed in use.

less:

Funds realized from the sale of replaced assets.
Tax benefits arising from the sale of replaced assets.
Investment tax credits.
Tax benefits from payment of construction loan interest and property taxes.

With the exception of additional working capital needed to support the use of a new asset (which is likely to be the same, whether the asset is purchased or leased), all other items may differ in cost to the user depending on whether the asset is leased or purchased. Acquisition costs may be lower to a vendor, for example, than to the lessor, as may tax liabilities and advantages. Thus, when entering a lease–buy decision, it is necessary to find a lessor which can take full advantage of any favorable discounts or strategic market position. It may simply be possible for a lessor to incur fewer costs than another purchaser might, due to the economies which a purchaser might not be able to fully enjoy. Also, interest costs may vary appreciably. Should a firm plan to build facilities, sell them, and lease them back, or should it have them built by another, to specification, and then lease? The answer is not simple and requires detailed analysis of alternative cost data. The items enumerated above are designed to form a checklist that calls attention to the specific points requiring analysis.

In the study of cash flows for asset acquisition, the timing of flows is very important. As the size of the asset increases, this timing becomes especially important. Since inflows and outflows must be coordinated to avoid insolvency and excess cash reserves, it may be necessary to secure financing at times that are not optimal with respect to the firm's position in the money and capital markets.

The after-tax cash outflows must be weighed against the expected after-tax cash inflows expected to result from the asset's use to determine its acceptability as an acquisition candidate. The after-tax cash inflows consist of two components: (1) after-tax profits and (2) depreciation and similar cash throw-offs. Operating cash flows are easily determined, as demonstrated below.

EXAMPLE 4

Cash Flow

An asset costing $20,000 and having a ten-year life with zero expected salvage value is expected to reduce operating costs by $3,000 per year. Assuming it is depreciated using the straight-line method and the owners have a 46 percent marginal tax rate, determine the profitability and after-tax cash flow.

SOLUTION

The profitability may be computed utilizing the normal income statement format.

	Change in Income Statement	Change in Cash Flow
Reduced operating expense	$3,000	$3,000
Less depreciation	−2,000	
Earnings before taxes (EBT)	$1,000	
Less tax	−460	−460
Earnings after taxes (EAT)	$ 540	
Increased Cash Flow		$2,540

Since the depreciation cost does not result in a cash outflow, the owners would have $2,540 cash inflow at year's end for each of the ten years in the asset's life. □

In Example 4 we demonstrated the procedure for computing the cash flow from a project. If the project is depreciated straight-line and all other costs and revenues are held constant, then the yearly earnings after taxes and cash inflows will remain constant over the ten-year life. However, if we elected to utilize an accelerated depreciation method, such as double-declining balance, then the timing of the earnings after taxes and the cash flows will be shifted. The depreciation schedule using double-declining balance (DDB) with a switch to straight-line after the sixth year is shown in Table 3-1.[6]

Using the same income statement format as in Example 4, we can develop the schedule of earnings after taxes and the cash flows. The result is shown in Table 3-2, along with the schedule already developed using straight-line depreciation.

Note that using an accelerated depreciation method only changes the timing; payment of taxes is postponed, earnings after taxes are lower in

TAXATION, DEPRECIATION, AND CASH FLOW

Table 3-1. Depreciation schedule using double-declining balance for an asset costing $20,000, with zero salvage and a ten-year life.

Year	Yearly Depreciation	Cumulative Depreciation
1	$4,000	$ 4,000
2	3,200	7,200
3	2,560	9,760
4	2,048	11,808
5	1,638	13,446
6	1,311	14,757
7	1,311	16,068
8	1,311	17,379
9	1,311	18,690
10	1,310	20,000

the earlier years (and greater later), and cash flows are accelerated to the early years of the project's life. The total earnings after taxes and the cash flows remain constant. Thus, the net result of changing depreciation methods is to change the timing of cash flows and earnings after taxes. This shifting has both positive and negative effects. Accelerating cash

Table 3-2. Comparative earnings and cash flows with straight-line and accelerated depreciation.

Year	Earnings after Taxes Straight-Line	Earnings after Taxes DDB	Cash Inflows Straight-Line	Cash Inflows DDB
1	$540	($540)	$2,540	$3,460
2	540	($108)	2,540	3,092
3	540	238	2,540	2,798
4	540	514	2,540	2,562
5	540	736	2,540	2,373
6	540	912	2,540	2,223
7	540	912	2,540	2,223
8	540	912	2,540	2,223
9	540	912	2,540	2,223
10	540	912	2,540	2,223
Totals	$5,400	$5,400	$25,400	$25,400

flows (and concurrently postponing taxes) is very desirable, while postponing earnings is not.

This leads to the necessity of maintaining two records of depreciation, one for taxes and another for financial reporting purposes. For purposes of tax computation, we generally elect the most rapid form of depreciation and use the shortest depreciable asset life consistent with tax laws. For financial reporting purposes, we generally use straight-line depreciation and may elect a longer depreciable life. This is done to stabilize earnings reported to shareholders.

The goal of tax accounting is to minimize and postpone payment of taxes. Financial reporting accounting seeks to present an accurate picture of the firm's financial position to shareholders—and this includes (if possible) maintaining stability of earnings per share (EPS). Since EPS is a function of earnings after taxes, and since using straight-line depreciation tends to stabilize earnings after taxes, straight-line depreciation is usually chosen for financial reporting purposes.

Summary

In this chapter we have reviewed the methods of depreciation and the tax laws which form crucial parameters for the capital asset acquisition and leasing decisions. Since decisions are based on computations involving after-tax cash flows, it is necessary to be able to perform these calculations. At the conclusion of our discussion, we noted the need to provide for both tax and financial reporting accounting in order to postpone tax payments and stabilize earnings reported to shareholders. In the following chapter, we briefly review the impact of FASB 13 on key financial ratios, and then in Chapter 5 begin the study of discounted cash flow analysis.

NOTES

1. The reader should consult a current tax guide such as those published by Prentice-Hall or Commerce Clearing House for any recent changes in the tax laws. Also see Chapter 10.
2. For purposes of Federal taxation, the IRS has defined capital assets as being any property except the following:
   a. Inventories.
   b. Property held primarily for sale to customers in the ordinary course of business.
   c. Depreciable property used in a trade or business.
   d. Real property used in a trade or business.

    e. Short-term non-interest-bearing government obligations issued at a discount basis.
    f. Copyrights, literary, musical, or artistic composition, letters, or similar property.
    g. Accounts and notes receivable received in the ordinary course of business for services rendered or from the sale of property.

    Land and depreciable property used in a business are not capital assets, but if they are sold or exchanged, in most instances they are treated as capital assets with respect to capital gains and losses and recapture of depreciation.

3. Included in the 1978 Revenue Act is a provision extending the ITC to expenditures incurred to rehabilitate nonresidential structures such as factories, warehouses, hotels, and stores. Additional tax credits are also available for six categories of energy property. Such credits are normally in addition to regular ITC.
4. The 60 percent limitation increases 10 percent annually to 90 percent of the excess after 1981.
5. Source: John J. Clark, Thomas J. Hindelang, and Robert E. Pritchard, *Capital Budgeting: Planning and Control of Capital Expenditures,* Englewood Cliffs, N.J.: Prentice-Hall, 1979. Used with permission.
6. A switch could have been made to sum-of-the-year's digits rather than straight-line. This would have resulted in a further increase in the acceleration of depreciation.

CHAPTER 4

Effects of Leasing on Financial Statements

In Chapter 2 we discussed various types of leases, with emphasis on the definitions of FASB 13. In this chapter we briefly discuss the ramifications of the changes required by FASB 13 for the firm's financial statements. In particular, we re-emphasize the difference in accounting for financial reporting purposes and accounting for federal income taxes. Finally, we examine the impact of FASB 13 reporting on key financial ratios.

Tax and Financial Reporting Accounting

At this juncture, we want to re-emphasize the significant difference between tax accounting and financial reporting accounting. In general, the goal of tax accounting is to reduce the firm's overall tax liability and to postpone tax payments as long as possible. Since a firm's income for tax purposes may differ substantially from that reported to shareholders, financial managers want to minimize income for tax purposes to as great an extent as possible while maximizing (within the parameters that will be examined later) earnings reported to shareholders. These seemingly disparate goals are, of course, obtained by using two methods of bookkeeping.

To demonstrate the process, consider the purchase of a new vehicle costing $10,000, net of any investment tax credits. For tax purposes, the asset may be depreciated using double-declining-balance depreciation over a five-year life. Thus, the initial depreciation (ignoring any added first-year depreciation) would be $4,000. The result is to write off the greatest portion of the cost in the early years of the asset's life. This reduces taxable income and increases cash flow, since cash flow equals the sum of after-tax profits plus depreciation and similar cash throw-offs.

For financial reporting purposes, the asset may be depreciated over a longer life, using straight-line depreciation. With an eight-year life, the depreciation would be only $1,250 per year. Thus, profits reported to shareholders are substantially greater than those subject to federal taxation. Of course, the total profit and cash flow over the entire useful life of the asset will be the same for both tax and financial reporting purposes; the significant difference is the timing of the profits and cash flows.

For both tax and financial reporting purposes, accounting for a purchased asset includes establishing a depreciation schedule, depreciating in accordance with that schedule, and expensing interest on any debt supporting the asset. If an asset is leased, the lease payments are expensed for tax purposes and depreciation need not be considered. This results in an inherent time saving, since record keeping is reduced. The simple accounting procedure just described may not, however, be used in all instances for financial purposes, as we shall soon see.

Financial Reporting for Leases under FASB 13

In Chapter 2, we noted that FASB 13 divides leases into two major categories: operating and capital. For financial reporting purposes, operating leases are handled in the same manner as for tax reporting: the lease is not capitalized on the firm's books, and the lease payment is shown as an expense in the statement. For capital leases the situation is markedly different. FASB 13 requires capitalization of those leases that transfer substantially all benefits and risks of ownership to the lessee (that is, of capital leases). Prior to FASB 13, leases were commonly identified only in the footnotes to the firm's financial statements, and, for financial reporting purposes, the lease expense was shown on the income statement. Under FASB 13, the following items must be disclosed on the firm's balance sheet:

1. The gross amount of assets under capital leases, by major classes. These may be combined with comparable information for owned assets.
2. The minimum lease payments as of the latest financial reporting period and for each of the next five years.

Furthermore, instead of simply expensing the lease cost on the income statement, the income statement must show a statement of depreciation and interest cost, just as if the lessee owned the asset. Under the FASB statement, assets and liabilities under leases meeting the criteria for a capital lease are recorded on the balance sheet at the present value of the future payments.

For reporting earnings, the lessee must establish a depreciation schedule for a capital lease and prepare an amortization table for interest expense. In the early years of the lease, the result is likely to be a larger expense for reporting purposes than the actual lease payment. The reason is not hard to find: *in loan amortization schedules the bulk of the interest is paid in the early periods of the loan.* Thus, while for tax reporting purposes the lease payment remains the single item shown as an expense, for financial reporting purposes we now have two expenses: depreciation and interest.

The impact of FASB 13 has not been fully felt yet, since the statement is to be applied only to leases entered into on or after January 1, 1977. Retroactive reporting is encouraged. Further, in financial statements for periods beginning after December 31, 1981, the statement must be applied retroactively. Starting in 1981, financial statements presented for prior years are to be restated to the extent possible, but at least back to the December 31, 1976, balance sheet. The restatement must include the effects of leases then in force, even if they have since terminated.

The combined effects of capitalizing leases on the balance sheet and reporting expenses as if the asset were owned have direct impact on many of the firm's financial ratios. The requirements of FASB 13 provide for a more accurate picture of the firm's actual position and highlight its total short- and long-term obligations. The impact of FASB 13 on selected financial ratios for the lessee is demonstrated in the next section.

FASB 13 EFFECTS ON FINANCIAL RATIOS*

The lessee reports a capital lease in the property, plant, and equipment sections on the asset side of the balance sheet, with the corresponding liabilities separated according to current and long-term. Accordingly, those ratios that employ fixed assets, current assets and current liabilities, interest charges, operating expenses, and net income will be affected to

---

* For further information on the effects of capitalizing leases on financial ratios, see John J. Kalata, Dennis G. Campbell, and Ian K. Shumaker, "Lease Financing Reporting," *Financial Executive,* March 1977.

the greatest extent by the capitalization of leases. The effect on several key ratios for the lessee is noted below:

Current ratio. The current asset portion will not be changed, but current liabilities increase to reflect the current amount of the lease liability. The result is a *decrease* in the current ratio. The same will, of course, be true for the quick or acid test.

Debt-to-equity ratio. The total outstanding debt, both short- and long-term, increases. Shareholders' equity is affected only negligibly and only as a consequence of the changes in retained earnings that could result from changes in net income. (Net income may increase or decrease as a result of reporting a combination of interest and depreciation expense rather than a lease rental expense.) The result is an *increase* in the debt-to-equity ratio.

Figure 4-1. Balance sheets (Kresge vs. May).

1/29/75 Kresge $(000)			2/1/75 May $(000)	
W/L	Wo/L	Assets	Wo/L	W/L
$1,418,474	$1,418,474	Current Assets	$ 631,226	$ 631,226
59,654	59,654	Investments + Other Assets	53,599	53,599
417,982	417,982	Fixed Assets	520,791	520,791
1,283,210	—	Rights to Use of Leased Property	—	115,000
$3,179,320	$1,896,110	**Total Assets**	$1,205,616	$1,320,616
		Liabilities		
$ 779,302	$ 612,725	Current Liabilities	$ 287,456	$ 298,234
211,683	211,683	Long-Term Debt	355,645	355,645
1,116,633	—	Rental Obligations under lease discounted at the weighted average rate of 7.7% and 5.7%, respectively	—	104,222
49,977	49,977	Deferrals	60,830	60,830
1,021,725	1,021,725	Owner's Equity	501,685	501,685
$3,179,320	$1,896,110	**Total Liabilities + Equity**	$1,205,616	$1,320,616
$1,283,210		Present Value of Leases		$ 115,000
$ 166,577	($179.4 mil. @ 7.7%)	Current Portion due 1975	($11,392 mil. @ 5.7%)	$ 10,778

Reprinted with permission from John J. Kalata, Dennis G. Campbell, and Ian K. Shumaker, "Lease Financing Reporting," *Financial Executive*, March 1977, p. 37.

Figure 4-2. Key financial ratios (Kresge vs. May).

1/29/75 Kresge

2/1/75 May

W/L	Wo/L	Working capital analysis	Wo/L	W/L
1.82x	2.32x	Current Ratio	2.20x	2.12x
.40x	.51x	Acid Test Ratio (Quick Ratio)	1.46x	1.41x
3.9x – 93 days	4.1x – 89 days	Inventory Turnover (Days)	6.7x – 54 days	6.6x – 55 days
42.2x – 8 days	42.2x – 8 days	Receivables Turnover (Days)	4.2x – 87 days	4.2x – 87 days
101 days	97 days	Combined Turnover (Days)	141 days	142 days
8.84x	6.87x	Working Capital Turnover	4.94x	5.10x
		Long-term financial analysis		
32.1%	53.9%	Owner's Equity to Total Assets	41.6%	38.0%
.66x	1.62x	Current Assets to Total Liabilities	.90x	.77x
1.28x/78.1%	1.97x/50.8%	Fixed Assets to Long-Term Liabilities	68.3%/1.46x	72.3%/1.38x
130.0%	20.8%	Long-Term Debt to Owner's Equity	70.9%	91.7%
56.5%	17.2%	Debt to Invested Capital	41.5%	47.8%
43.5%	82.8%	Owner's Equity to Invested Capital	58.5%	52.2%
2.1x	10.7x	Fixed Charges Coverage	6.8x	4.8x
		Profitability analysis		
1.766x	2.962x	Assets Turnover	1.417x	1.293x
3.23%	3.47%	Pre-tax Margin	5.48%	5.48%
5.70%	10.28%	Pre-tax Return on Assets	7.77%	7.09%
3.112x	1.856x	Leverage Factor	2.403x	2.632x
53.7%	53.7%	Tax Retention Rate	49.9%	49.9%
9.53%	10.24%	Net Return on Equity	9.31%	9.31%
72.8%	74.8%	Earnings Retention Rate	47.9%	47.9%
6.94%	7.66%	Net Reinvestment Rate	4.46%	4.46%
9.27%	10.84%	EPS growth/year	10.38%	10.38%
52¢ – 81¢	52¢ – 87¢	(assuming no leasing in 1969)	$1.88 – $3.08	$1.88 – $3.08
29x	29x	Price/Earnings Ratio (3/31/75)	11x	11x
292% – 289%		Relative PER (S & P 425)	81% – 72%	

Reprinted with permission from Kalata, Campbell, and Shumaker, op. cit., p. 39.

Shareholders' equity to property, plant, and equipment. Property, plant, and equipment increase while shareholders' equity is likely to be affected only slightly, as described above. The result is to *decrease* the ratio.

Times interest charges earned. The amount of interest expense increases while net income is likely to be affected only slightly. Usually, the ratio will *decrease*.

Return on assets. Plant, property, and equipment increase while net income will usually be affected only slightly. The return on assets will *decrease*.

Net profit to net working capital. Net working capital decreases while profit remains, for the most part, unaffected. The result is an *increase* in this ratio.

Net sales to net working capital. Sales are unaffected, whereas working capital decreases. The result is a *decrease* in this ratio.

Inventory to net working capital. Inventory remains constant while working capital decreases. The ratio *increases*.

Leased assets to total assets. When leased assets are shown as a portion of total assets (as opposed to recognition through only a footnote), the ratio *increases*.

While capitalization of leases generally has an unfavorable impact on financial ratios, the overall effect is that the ratios become more valid indicators of the firm's true position.

The change to key financial ratios is demonstrated very effectively by Kalata, Campbell, and Shumaker, who compare the balance sheets of Kresge and May stores, providing comparisons with and without leases, as shown in Figure 4-1. Figure 4-2 summarizes financial ratios for both firms, again with and without leasing.

CHAPTER 5

Evaluating the Lease-versus-Purchase Decision: An Introduction to Discounted Cash Flow Analysis

The purpose of this chapter is to introduce the reader to the methodology of discounted cash flow analysis.[1] Once the principles of discounted cash flow are examined, we will apply the procedures to the specific problems found within the leasing arena. Several different methods of lease evaluation have been developed and will be considered in Chapters 7 and 8.

Mathematics of Interest and Discounted Cash Flow

The procedure for computing interest, and its reciprocal, discounting of funds, are basic to the evaluation of capital expenditures, whether they are leasing proposals or capital projects that are purchased outright. In this section, we examine the discounted cash flow calculations and provide examples to illustrate their use. Throughout, we will use the extended interest and present value tables found in Appendix D.

SIMPLE AND COMPOUND INTEREST

Since the computations for simple and compound interest form the basis for discounted cash flow analysis, we examine these first. Simple interest is computed using Equation (1):

$$I = (P)(i)(t) \qquad (1)$$

where I = the dollar amount of simple interest earned
P = principal
i = rate of return (interest rate) per unit of time
t = the time period over which funds are invested

The accumulated fund at the end of the time period in question would simply be the amount of interest earned (I) plus the original principal (P).

When we speak of simple interest, it is assumed that the interest will be withdrawn or paid as soon as it is earned. Compound interest, on the other hand, is earned on the fund consisting of both the principal and previously earned interest; thus, we are earning "interest on interest" to produce the compounding effect. Equation (2) shows how to determine the value of a fund at the end of a period of time over which interest has been left to compound:

$$S_n = P(1 + i)^n \qquad (2)$$

where S_n = compound sum after n years
n = number of years

For computational purposes, we refer to Column 1 in Appendix D, which provides compound interest factors $(1 + i)^n$ for interest rates between 1 percent and 35 percent and time periods up to 50 years. The use of these factors is illustrated in Example 1.

EXAMPLE 1

Simple vs. Compound Interest

An investor places $10,000 in a 6 percent account. How much will he have at the end of six years?

SOLUTION

$$S_6 = \$10,000 \,(1.418519)$$
$$= \$14,185.19$$

The investor will have $14,185.19 in six years. Thus, he has earned $4,185.19 in interest, since he left the interest already earned with the original principal to earn more interest. The amount of simple interest earned each year would be $600, which means that $3,600 of simple interest would have been earned over the six-year period. The extra $585.19 of interest is due to the compounding effect. □

COMPOUND SUM (FUTURE VALUE) OF AN ANNUITY

Sometimes deposits are made regularly on an annual basis into a savings or pension fund. To determine the amount that will accumulate after a number of years, we use Equation (3):

$$F = A \left[\frac{(1 + i)^n - 1}{i} \right] \qquad (3)$$

where F = future value of the annuity payment
A = annual year-end annuity payment
i = rate of return
n = number of years

The factors corresponding to the bracketed portion of Equation (3) are found in Column 2 of Appendix D, again for interest rates from 1 percent to 35 percent and up to 50 years. Their use is demonstrated in Example 2.

EXAMPLE 2

Future Value of an Annuity

An investor places $1,200 per year at the end of each year into an IRA for 20 years. Assuming interest is compounded annually at 7 percent, determine the amount in the account in 20 years.

SOLUTION

F = $1,200 (40.995492)
  = $49,194.59

The investor will have $49,194.59 in 20 years. □

EXAMPLE 3

Future Value of an Annuity

Repeat Example 2 using 5 percent and 9 percent interest rates.

SOLUTION

At 5%, F = $1,200 (33.065954)
      = $39,679.14

At 9%, F = $1,200 (51.160120)
      $61,392.14 □

The large differences in the future annuity values noted in the results to Examples 2 and 3 point to the importance of selecting the correct interest rate for compounding (and also for discounting). The reason for the size of the differences is that the compound interest factors increase exponentially. Interest factors for 5 percent, 7 percent, and 9 percent (from Appendix D, Column 1) are plotted in Figure 5-1 over a 20-year time

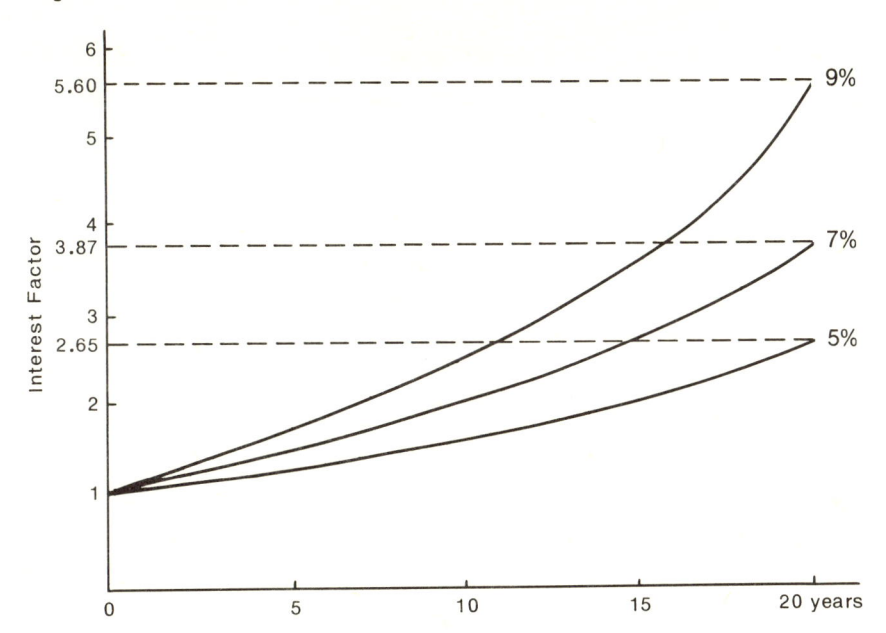

Figure 5-1. Compound interest factors for three interest rates.

horizon to demonstrate the importance of the exponential increase. Note the very large and unequal differences between the values for the three interest rates plotted as the number of years increases.

SINKING FUNDS

A special type of compound annuity is the sinking fund. The creation of a sinking fund involves determining the amount that must be invested each year at a given rate of return in order to pay off a debt or other obligations at the end of the stated time period. Sinking fund factors are provided in Column 3 of Appendix D.

EXAMPLE 4

Sinking Fund

A corporation needs $10 million in 15 years to pay off a bond issue. Assuming it places payments into a 7 percent fund at the end of each year, determine the yearly year-end sinking fund payment necessary to retire the $10 million.

SOLUTION

Payment = $10,000,000 (0.03979462)
= $397,946.20

The annual year-end sinking fund payment is $397,946.20. □

PRESENT VALUE

The goal of present value calculations is to determine the amount of money a firm or investor would accept at present in place of a given amount at some future date. As such, the computation is just the reverse of the compound-interest and compound-sum-of-an-annuity calculations demonstrated earlier. The present value of a sum to be received in the future is found using Equation (4), which is simply a rearrangement of Equation (2).

$$PV = \frac{S}{(1+i)^n} = S \left[\frac{1}{1+i}\right]^n \qquad (4)$$

Appendix D, Column 4, provides the factors corresponding to the bracketed portion $[1/1 + i]^n$ of Equation (4) for n periods, 1 to 50.

EXAMPLE 5

Present Value

A corporation will receive $16,000 in two years as a payment from a customer's note and plans to sell the note to a bank. If the bank discounts the note at 12 percent, how much will it pay the corporation for the note?

SOLUTION

PV = $16,000 (0.797194)
= $12,755.10

The bank would pay $12,755.10 for the note. □

PRESENT VALUE OF AN ANNUITY

Frequently lease payments are made regularly and in constant amounts over the life of the lease. In order to find the present value of a stream of lease payments, we may use the methodology for the present value of an annuity, expressed in Equation (5).

$$PV = A \left[\frac{(1+i)^n - 1}{i(1+i)^n}\right] \qquad (5)$$

The values for the bracketed portion of Equation (5) are found in Column 5 of Appendix D. It should be noted that these factors are for payments made at the *end of each year;* if payments are made at the beginning of each year the approach shown in Example 6 is appropriate.

EXAMPLE 6
Present Value of an Annuity

A lathe may be leased for eight years, with annual payments at the *start of each year* amounting to $2,000. Using an 8 percent discount rate, determine the present value of the lease.

SOLUTION

The lease consists of an initial $2,000 payment plus seven annual year-end payments. The present value is determined as follows:

$$PV = \$2,000 + \$2,000 \ (5.206370)$$
$$= \$2,000 + \$10,412.74$$
$$= \$12,412.74$$

The lease has a present value of $12,412.74 when discounted. Notice that the factor (5.206370) is from the 7-year line for 8 percent in Column 5, Appendix D, since the lease in question will require an initial payment and then at *the end of each of the next seven years.* □

With the introduction to discounted cash flow calculations completed, we will examine the basics of evaluation and the two primary methods useful in evaluating leases: net present value and internal rate of return. Their application to lease decisions will be explored in subsequent chapters.

Basics of Evaluation

While there are at least 35 different evaluative methods in use, those of primary interest fall into the discounted cash flow (DCF) methodology. Specifically, we are concerned with net present value and internal rate of return. However, irrespective of which method is used, as Pflomm[2] points out, it is necessary to keep three factors in mind.

1. The measure used must be applied consistently to all projects (leases).
2. The measure should be used as a guide rather than as the sole basis for approval or disapproval of capital projects and leases.
3. It is necessary for management to completely understand how the computations are made and what the answers really mean.

Net present value involves discounting all expected after-tax cash flows to present value and then taking the difference between the present value of the inflows and the present value of the outflows. The difference is called the net present value (NPV). This method requires the use of a discount rate, which management must determine on the basis of its cost of capital and the degree of risk involved in the project being evaluated vis-à-vis the risk attached to the firm's current composite portfolio of projects. The procedures for determining the most appropriate discount rates to be used in evaluating leases and in making the lease-versus-purchase decision are discussed in Chapters 7 and 8.

The internal rate of return method is similar to net present value. However, rather than determining the net present value using a predetermined discount rate, the goal is to find the discount rate which, when applied to the after-tax cash inflows and outflows, will result in a net present value of zero. This discount rate is called the internal rate of return (IRR) for the project being evaluated.

NET PRESENT VALUE

The net present value method for project evaluation involves algebraically summing the present values of the expected inflows and outflows from the operations of a project. The difference is the net present value, found using Equation (6).

$$\text{NPV} = \sum_{t=0}^{n} \frac{S_t}{(1 + k)^t} - A_0 \qquad (6)$$

where A_0 = present value of the after-tax cost of the project
S_t = cash inflow to be received each period
k = the appropriate discount rate
t = time period

A_0 represents the present value of the cash outflows. If an asset is purchased, the outflow is likely to take place at one point in time, whereas if it is leased, the outflow will be over several periods, as shown in Equation (7).

$$A_0 = \sum_{t=0}^{n} \frac{A_t}{(1 + k)^t} \qquad (7)$$

where A_t = cash outflow in each period

When NPV is used as the criterion for project or lease selection, the goal is to accept those projects (or leases) which have the highest net present value at the appropriate discount rate.

EXAMPLE 7

Present Value

A corporation expects a new asset to result in after-tax cash flows as tabulated below. Using a 10 percent discount rate, determine the net present value of the asset and indicate whether it should be accepted.

Time	Amount
Present	−$10,000
1–8	1,900
8	1,000

SOLUTION

Construct a solution table as shown below and, referring to Appendix D, determine the net present value.

Time	Amount	Discount Factor	Present Value
Present	−$10,000	1	−$10,000
1–8	1,900	5.334926	10,136
8	1,000	.466507	467
		NPV =	$ 603

Since the NPV is positive, the project is a viable candidate for acceptance at a 10 percent discount rate. ☐

EXAMPLE 8

Present Value

Repeat Example 7 using a 12 percent discount rate.

SOLUTION

Time	Amount	Discount Factor	Present Value
Present	−$10,000	1	−$10,000
1–8	1,900	4.967640	9,439
8	1,000	.403883	404
		NPV =	$ −157

Using a 12 percent discount rate, the project is not acceptable. This result points to the importance of selecting the appropriate discount rate. ☐

INTERNAL RATE OF RETURN

As we discussed earlier, the internal rate of return (IRR) is that discount rate which exactly equates the present value of cash inflows and outflows. It may be found using Equation (8).

$$\sum_{t=0}^{n} \frac{S_t}{(1+r)^t} - A_0 = 0 \qquad (8)$$

where r = internal rate of return

EXAMPLE 9
Internal Rate of Return

Determine the internal rate of return for the project in Examples 7 and 8.

SOLUTION

There is no direct method to find the answer. Rather, we select discount rates that are likely to produce NPVs close to zero and then interpolate between these to find the actual IRR. The results of Example 8 indicate a negative NPV of −$157 corresponding to the 12 percent discount rate, while Example 7 indicates a positive NPV of $603 at 10 percent. The NPV at 11 percent should next be determined.

Time	Amount	Discount Factor	Present Value
Present	−$10,000	1	−$10,000
1–8	1,900	5.146123	9,778
8	1,000	0.433926	434
		NPV =	$ 212

The fact that the NPV is positive at 11 percent and negative at 12 percent indicates that the IRR is between 11 percent and 12 percent. It may be found using linear interpolation, as demonstrated below:

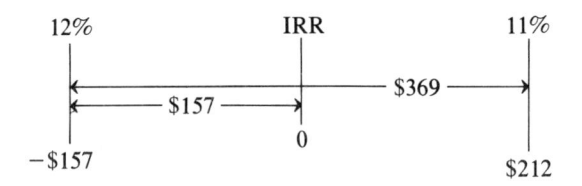

```
     12%              IRR              11%
      |----------------|----------------|
      |<----- $157 ---->|<----- $369 ----->|
                       0
   -$157                                $212
```

The zero point (corresponding to the internal rate of return) is $157/$369 (0.425%) below 12%. Hence, the IRR is 12% − 0.425% = 11.575%. □

The procedures for computing net present value and internal rate of return just described, combined with the materials on depreciation and taxation, provide the analytical basis for the lease-versus-purchase and the leasing decisions. These elements are integrated in Chapters 7 and 8, and the methodology for making the decisions is presented.

Risk Considerations[3]

Within the framework of lease evaluation, it is necessary to consider risk and the effect of leasing on the overall risk position of the firm. As a start, we portray the firm as a portfolio of assets, each having a certain element of risk, and the total of these comprising the business risk portion of the firm's overall risk. *Business risk* is that component of risk arising from the variability in earnings which are a function of the firm's normal operations. Business risk is affected by the changing economic environment and management's decisions with respect to capital intensification, which includes the leasing decision. In general, an increase in capital intensification results in higher fixed costs, and consequently earnings before interest and taxes will vary more with changes in output.

Business risk does not consider variability in earnings as a result of the firm's financing decisions. This brings us to the second primary element of the firm's overall risk posture, financial risk. *Financial risk* results from the variability in earnings which are a function of the firm's financial mix, in particular, the use of debt financing. Increased use of debt results in larger fixed obligation and, thereby, increases the variability of earnings after taxes and earnings per share with output.

The leasing decision may affect both business and financial risk. For example, if capital intensification is achieved through leasing, then the leasing will increase business risk. Concurrently, the firm's fixed obligation will also be increased, and thus, financial risk will also be impacted.

The consequences of leasing on the price of the firm's stock may be positive or negative, depending on how the collective investment community perceives management's ability to effectively employ the new assets. The impact of leasing versus buying on the firm's financial risk as perceived by investors may differ, even if both are recorded on the firm's balance sheet. The underlying reason lies in the difference between the two types of obligations and the restrictive covenants pertaining to each. As an example, if a firm obligates itself to a short-term lease to permit trial use of an asset, the information gained will enhance management's ability to decide if long-term acquisition (whether by lease or purchase) is desirable. This may reduce business risk. Similarly, a constructive sale-and-leaseback arrangement may permit not only further capital acquisition but also the flexibility necessary to establish a more nearly optimum financial structure overall.

The lease decision, then, directly affects the firm's risk posture and, thereby, the price of its stock, the ability to raise additional debt and equity capital, and the cost of both debt and equity capital. The underlying question is how the investor market, viewed collectively, will view the transaction—and this perception will change with market conditions and business trends. Aside from the purely financial analysis, management must be keenly aware of the potential reaction to any acquisition—lease or purchase—by the investment market, and of the importance of timing. The firm desires to retain flexibility for future acquisitions and abandonments. Each decision must be viewed as part of a step-by-step process, leaving the door open to future changes. Management must seek to understand how today's decision will affect the firm's operations in subsequent time periods.

The Firm's Goals

We assume that the primary goal of the firm is to maximize the wealth of the shareholders, in the long run, as reflected by the market price of the common stock. Maximization of net present value generally leads to maximization of shareholders' wealth over the long run. However, the maximization of NPV must be tempered by the evaluation of the impact the investment decision will have on the firm's financial statements. Ranking projects using a discounted cash flow (DCF) technique does not consider ramifications on the firm's accounting statements.

It is possible, in fact, for a DCF analysis to favor projects which, while attractive in the long run, may produce erratic year-to-year earnings. Since management and investors place heavy emphasis on both stability of earnings and regular growth from year to year, we must consider maximization of NPV within the constraints of earnings stability.

Lerner and Rappaport[4] have developed a linear-programming solution to the problem of asset selection within the constraint of maintaining earnings stability. Their approach to the problem is discussed in detail by Clark, Hindelang, and Pritchard.[5] The assumptions underlying the Lerner and Rappaport model are realistic, the solution methodology is straightforward, and the results are consistent with the requirements for regular steady earnings growth. But, as with any other evaluative procedure, there is added cost for the increase in information—which brings us to the next area for managerial consideration.

The Cost of Evaluation

The process of evaluating leases is expensive in manpower, time, and facilities. Generally, the larger the firm, the more sophisticated the process. Also, more expensive projects warrant closer scrutiny. Hence, management may find it desirable to establish cutoff points with respect to project cost and limit the amount of evaluation to be consistent with the decision at hand. Establishing a cost-efficient procedure for lease evaluation is the primary goal. In some instances, the degree of examination is pragmatically limited: the firm may lack sufficient funds to purchase (thus ruling out the lease-versus-purchase question), or the equipment may be available only through a lease (with the same results).

While most of the decision process is centered on asset acquisition, management should follow up with periodic revisits to the asset under lease. Several questions deserve close attention. Are the cash flows consistent with the forecasts, and, if not, why not? Is the project producing the promised profits and internal cash flows? Should the project be abandoned?

The selection process should be updated at regular intervals using current information on actual performance. If mistakes were made, as indicated by large inconsistencies with the forecasts that formed the basis for acquisition, the reasons must be understood and incorporated into the evaluative procedure for future projects.

NOTES

1. This chapter draws heavily upon John J. Clark, Thomas J. Hindelang, and Robert E. Pritchard, *Capital Budgeting: Planning and Control of Capital Expenditures,* Englewood Cliffs, N.J.: Prentice-Hall, 1979, Chapters 4 and 6.
2. N. E. Pflomm, *Managing Capital Expenditures,* New York: The Conference Board, 1963.
3. For a detailed treatment of risk analysis and portfolio theory, see John J. Clark, Thomas J. Hindelang, and Robert E. Pritchard, *Capital Budgeting: Planning and Control of Capital Expenditures,* Englewood Cliffs, N.J.: Prentice-Hall, 1979, Chapters 8 and 9.
4. Eugene M. Lerner and Alfred Rappaport, "Limit DCF Capital Budgeting," *Harvard Business Review,* September–October 1968, pp. 133–138.
5. Op. cit., Chapter 7.

CHAPTER 6

Inflation, Risk, and Forecasting

In our initial discussion of leasing, one of the primary factors emphasized as a necessary input to the lease-versus-purchase decision was the analysis of risk. Risk was seen to arise from several different sources, such as the potential for equipment obsolescence due to changing technology and market demand, volitality in the price of money (interest rate) associated with different types of leases, difficulty in estimating salvage value of equipment at the termination of a lease or at the end of the asset's economic life, and difficulty in estimating an asset's economic life.

The purpose of this chapter is to introduce the concepts of risk, inflation, and forecasting in a qualitative framework. This will provide the groundwork for the mathematical analysis of risk in Chapter 7. Throughout, the reader should bear in mind that the leasing decision is a part of the overall capital expenditure decision. The basic procedures and methodologies described in this and the following chapter have been developed to encompass the broader capital expenditure area.

The Impact of Risk on Capital Investment and Leasing

In order to provide a setting for a discussion of risk, we will briefly describe how risk comes into play at various points in both the capital-investment and the leasing decisions.

The potential for *obsolescence* is heightened in periods of rapid technological change and market volatility. The computer industry is a good example of an area of rapid technological change. Should management consider the purchase or the lease of a computer? The risk of obsolescence is relevant to the decision in two ways. The first has to do with competitive advantage. If the use of a computer is an integral part of a firm's operation and being up to date is essential to continued operation, then the risk of technological obsolescence is great. Management may desire to enter into a short-term lease to avoid this risk rather than purchase a computer even at a low price. If, however, the computer is not an integral element of the firm's mainstream of operations, and change in technology (which generally relates to speed) will not result in a competitive disadvantage beyond slight differentials in labor application, then the wise manager may opt to purchase. Of course, it is necessary to quantify the possible outcomes and attach probabilities to their various likelihoods.

The second relevant aspect of obsolescence risk pertains to residual value. As new computers are introduced, the price of existing units is discounted so as to equate performance capabilities. Introduction of new models may, therefore, result in precipitous price drops of units in use. Leasing reduces or precludes exposure to this risk—but again at a price.

The *volatility of interest rates,* combined with the fact that the interest rate for some types of loans changes in conjunction with market interest rates, may lead to changes in a firm's fixed costs. Leases written under a fixed-lease-charge agreement eliminate this source of risk. But there is a price to pay. In general, lease payments exceed comparable loan terms, since the lessor is assuming the risk. Further, if the general level of interest goes down, the lessee is obligated to pay the fixed lease payment and does not enjoy the decrease in cost.

Estimation of salvage value presents a difficult problem for both lessee and lessor. Some lessors gamble on increasing salvage (fair market) value of residuals and look to this payment for their profit in a leasing arrangement. In the event of either partial or complete obsolescense, the residuals will have limited value. On the other hand, with inflation many assets retained in good working order will depreciate very slowly. Airplanes are a prime example where leasing has proven to be an expensive method of airplane acquisition.

Finally, *estimating an asset's economic life* may be difficult. The economic life of an asset is the period of time during which the asset can be used productively and profitably. Normally, the economic life may be estimated on the basis of experience with similar equipment, in particular, with repair and downtime and relative labor costs. As the cost of labor increases, the cost of downtime increases and the economic life of the asset decreases. If, however, the price of replacements also increases, alternatives for rebuilding or refurbishing may become attractive.

Establishment of the economic life (as opposed to the depreciable life) is the work of industrial engineers in conjunction with cost accountants. However, a persuasive argument can be developed that even with sophisticated talent applied to the problems, errors will result—perhaps due to completely unforeseen events, such as escalating fuel prices. Even so, lessors will generally gamble on longer lives (or higher residuals) than those corresponding to normal depreciation asset life projections. The key question relates to how long the asset will actually be in use, even if only as a backup unit.

We have provided short descriptions of four areas where risk considerations have significant impact. Since almost nothing is known with certainty and there is a cost attached to risk reduction (insurance being one example and fixed-cost lease payments another), management must cope with its preference for risk versus return. All other things being the same, reduction in risk will result in reduction of return. If leasing has less risk associated with it than purchase, expect it to cost more.

Conditions of Certainty, Risk, and Uncertainty

Managers may be faced with conditions that are characterized as "certainty," "risk," or "uncertainty." Conditions of certainty are said to exist if the manager knows precisely what the future holds. Conditions of risk exist if the manager feels that he must use probabilities to describe the likelihood of various events occurring in the future. Uncertain conditions are implied when the manager feels that not all possible outcomes can be specified or that their likelihoods are so difficult to predict that meaningful probabilities cannot be assigned.

We would argue that managers are very seldom faced with conditions of either complete certainty or complete uncertainty. Almost always subjective probabilities can and should be assigned to various outcomes that may occur in the future. Realizing that we face conditions of risk, then, necessitates modification of the approaches to capital expenditure evaluation discussed up to this point. Two additional topics will be treated before we undertake such modification: forecasting and inflation.

The Art and Science of Forecasting

Many volumes have been written on "how to forecast." Our purpose here is not to review or expand upon such dissertations. Rather, our comments will be confined to the importance forecasting plays in the overall capital expenditure evaluation process and to strategies that managers should consider in tackling the forecasting problem.

Clearly, forecasted values play a vital role in the capital budgeting and leasing process, as they do in all managerial decision making. In evaluating the attractiveness of any capital project (on its own merits or as a potential competitor to a lease alternative), forecasts play a role in determining all of the following:

1. The initial outlay required for the project, including purchase price, trade-in values, transportation costs, installation, break-in and training costs, tax effects of the transaction, and working capital requirements of the project.

2. Cash inflows to be generated by the project. These are a function of pricing, demand relationships, reactions of competitors, fixed and variable costs of operation, tax impact, and miscellaneous other effects.

3. The economic life of the asset. This is a function of technological change, obsolescence, wear and tear, feasibility of, and cost involved in, renovating the asset, and the firm's dependence on having the use of this asset in order to maintain a competitive advantage.

4. The market value of the asset at various points throughout its useful life when the firm might consider abandoning it in favor of a replacement, as well as at the end of its useful life. These market values are a function of the inflation rate for this asset, as well as for substitutes, supply and demand factors for both new and used assets of this type, plus other miscellaneous factors.

5. Tax impact on disposition of the asset.

As can be seen from these items, the forecasting activity is very important to obtaining reliable data inputs to evaluate capital investment proposals. Further, it is obvious that all the analysis and evaluation of alternatives will only be as valid as the forecasted values used. The results of the analysis are limited by the quality of the inputs.

Given the importance of forecasted values, the following strategies should prove helpful to managers involved in the forecasting process.

1. We should start by identifying the most important goals to be achieved in forecasting a given item or time series; that is, we should identify the purpose that the forecast will serve, how accurate it needs to be, whether we have a short, intermediate, or long-term horizon of interest, what type of data base is available for determining the forecasted values, what kinds of budgets exist for determining the desired forecast values, what time period is available to arrive at the forecast values, and so on.

2. Given the goals specified above, it is necessary to decide upon the most appropriate forecasting methodology, who should participate in the forecasting group, and how the work should be organized. Obviously, the desired goals will dictate what approach should be used. Given one set of goals, management may decide that a subjective forecast provided by two key individuals at a single meeting would be best. In other circumstances, it may be decided that a sophisticated multiple regression model designed by staff personnel aided by outside consultants, plus the design of a new information system to provide the data for the model (all requiring several man-years of effort), is most desirable.

3. Obtaining additional information and achieving greater forecast accuracy and reliability should be subject to the test: *does the value of such information and/or forecast embellishments exceed the cost of obtaining them (including the cost of delayed action)?*

4. *All forecasts are based on a set of assumptions about the managerial environment.* Such assumptions should be explicitly stated by the responsible forecasting group so as to expose them to the scrutiny and challenges of other knowledgeable individuals within the firm. Further, *every forecasting methodology has inherent limitations*. Thus, managers and users of forecasting models should be aware of such limitations and should have alternative techniques available to supplement or override the primary methodology when the limitations seriously jeopardize the validity of the forecasts.

5. The firm should take steps so that managers and staff specialists learn from the forecasting process. Feedback should be obtained, forecasts should be compared to actual results, significant variations should be investigated and explained, and alternative methodologies should be evaluated. The forecasting group should be held responsible for "controllable" variations.

6. The firm should take steps to encourage the involvement of individuals at all levels within the organization in the forecasting process. Diverse individuals can provide relevant insights and constructive criticism concerning various phases of the forecasting process. Such participation should be encouraged and rewarded.

Inflation

All businessmen and consumers know the meaning and feel the effects of inflation—a condition wherein prices for goods, services, land, labor, capital, and management are generally rising. We will examine how managers can arrive at reasonable anticipations of future inflation rates and the impact that inflation has on the evaluation of the lease-versus-purchase decision.

Future inflation rates are determined by a host of factors, including past price increases, government activities (especially fiscal and monetary policy), consumer behavior patterns in spending and saving, activities of unions in the collective bargaining process, and decisions made by businesses concerning prices for their products and services (which, of course, have a spillover effect on the cost of these products and services to other businesses and consumers).

There is a wealth of information available on the historical trends, as well as the most recent developments, in the above factors. Appendix E contains "Sources of Economic and Financial Information from The Conference Board."[1] Numerous monthly, quarterly, and annual publications are available which provide relevant information for decision makers. The most notable are: *Survey of Current Business, Business Conditions Digest,* and *Statistical Abstract of the United States* (published by the U.S. Department of Commerce); *Federal Reserve Bulletin* (published by the Board of Governors of the Federal Reserve System); *The Economic Report of the President* (published by the Executive Office of the President); *Economic Indicators* (published by the Joint Economic Committee of the U.S. Congress); *The Conference Board Statistical Bulletin, Current Economic Trends, The Conference Board Record, Consumer Attitudes and Buying Plans,* and *The Federal Budget: Its Impact on the Economy* (published by The Conference Board); *Employment and Earnings, The Consumer Price Index,* and *Wholesale Prices and Price Indexes* (published by the Bureau of Labor Statistics of the U.S. Department of Labor).

In addition to these sources, most large banks publish monthly economic letters wherein their chief economists give their views on what the future holds for the economy and on the impact of inflation. Periodicals such as *Business Week, Fortune,* and *U.S. News and World Report* have numerous articles on the economy and inflation, as well as current statistics.

Inflation is but one of the factors which causes difficulties for management in forecasting future costs and benefits of capital investment projects. Further, inflation clouds the picture as company analysts and interested outside parties obtain feedback and evaluate the results of performance. Consider Table 6-1, for example, wherein net sales and earnings per share for a major firm over the ten years 1968–1977 are shown in columns one and two. These reported sales and earnings do not, however, represent real growth over this ten-year period because of the inflation phenomenon. Columns three and four show these same two series in constant 1967 dollars, using the consumers' price index to adjust for infla-

Table 6-1. Net sales and earnings per share 1968–1977, in current and constant dollars, of a major company.

	Current Dollars		Constant Dollars (1967 = 100)	
Year	Net Sales	Earnings per Share	Net Sales	Earnings per Share
1968	$ 652,707	$1.00	$ 626,398	$ .96
1969	666,609	1.02	607,112	.93
1970	792,777	1.40	681,666	1.20
1971	902,453	1.60	743,984	1.32
1972	977,500	1.70	780,128	1.36
1973	1,109,707	1.46	833,739	1.10
1974	1,413,091	1.42	956,731	.96
1975	1,644,979	1.88	1,020,458	1.17
1976	1,441,146	1.23	845,247	.72
1977	1,838,048	2.04	1,012,699	1.12
10th Year Growth Rate	10.91%	7.39%	4.92%	1.55%

tion. Clearly, columns three and four present a different picture from that shown by columns one and two, due to the inflation rate of 5.7 percent compounded annually over the ten-year period.

In addition to the above problems imposed by inflation, another critical one in the lease–purchase decision setting is the fact that conventional accounting financial statements are based on historical costs rather than inflated replacement values. Thus, annual write-offs for depreciation expense, as well as book values for purchased assets, have a very limited relationship, if any, to the fair market value of such assets or to the replacement costs of comparable fixed assets.

Since the 1930s, the accounting profession has debated the merits of modifying conventional accounting statements to reflect the impact of inflation. The Financial Accounting Standard Board proposed general-price-level accounting adjustment of the financial statements as supplemental information, and the Securities and Exchange Commission, through ASR 190, has required certain registrants (estimated to be only 1,000 companies) to provide supplementary replacement cost data on depreciation, fixed assets, inventories, and cost of sales.

At this juncture, we wish to offer a caveat to analysts and managers in the lease–purchase area: inflation has differing impacts on lease and purchase alternatives, which must be estimated and taken into account in evaluating alternatives. Further, relevant costs in decision making are not necessarily those reflected on the financial statements of firms; rather, current replacement costs and market values of existing assets must be incorporated into the analysis. In addition, we would recommend that firms, especially in times of high uncertainty about the future (due to inflation or other factors), consider the possibility of "hedging" by signing a short-term lease, even at a higher annual cost; during the period of the lease a major portion of the uncertainty may be resolved so that probabilities of future outcomes can be more easily assessed. The additional flexibility of being a lessee rather than an owner in such uncertain times could be well rewarded during and at the end of the short-term lease.

This chapter introduced the qualitative aspects of risk analysis and demonstrated the necessity of dealing with risk in the capital-investment and leasing decision. We next dealt with forecasting and inflation. This chapter provides the rationale for the mathematical analysis and methodologies in Chapter 7. The quantitive procedures require close study before they can be fully understood and applied. However, since management will usually call upon staff specialists to carry out such analysis, many readers will want to survey the chapter only to obtain a knowledge of the procedures applicable to dealing with risk and to learn the vocabulary associated with it.

NOTE

1. The Conference Board publications provide an excellent compilation of materials pertaining to economic and business forecasting (as well as other topics) and should be a part of every executive's library.

CHAPTER 7

Quantitative Methods for Risk Analysis

In Chapter 6 we presented the rationale for the study of risk analysis and introduced some examples wherein risk became an important factor in the leasing decision. We also discussed inflation, noting that it adds greatly to the problems of forecasting cash flows, and discussed the underlying concepts of economic and business forecasting.

In this chapter we examine the mathematical procedures for dealing with risk. We introduce measures of return and variability of return and then examine two useful procedures for handling risk: the risk-adjusted discount rate technique and the certainty equivalent technique.

Risk and Return

We have pointed out briefly that when future outcomes must be depicted using a probability distribution, it becomes necessary to identify a measure of both the average or expected value of the distribution and the dispersion or variability within the distribution. These measures are referred to, respectively, as the *expected return* (or just *return*) and the *risk* of the distribution or the decision alternative. Of course, there are several measures of risk and return that may be used to evaluate lease-versus-purchase alternatives. However, the two that have been used traditionally in capital expenditure decisions are the *arithmetic mean*, or *expected value*, and the *standard deviation*.

The expected value of a probability distribution is defined in Equation (1):

$$\bar{R} = \sum_{i=1}^{M} R_i P_i \qquad (1)$$

where $\bar{R}$ = the expected value or expected return
R_i = the return associated with the ith outcome of the probability distribution
P_i = the probability of occurrence of the ith outcome

The standard deviation of a probability distribution is defined in Equation (2).

$$\sigma = \sqrt{\sum_{i=1}^{M} P_i (R_i - \bar{R})^2} \qquad (2)$$

where σ = the standard deviation of the probability distribution

We should point out a number of factors about these two measures. First, the expected value is merely a weighted average of the returns that could occur, where the weights are the likelihood that each of these returns will occur. Thus, if we repeated an experiment a large number of times, the average return that would be earned on each trial of the experiment is shown by the expected value. Second, the standard deviation measures collective differences between the weighted average of each item and the expected value, where the item's "weight" in the calculation is the probability that it will occur. Thus, *the standard deviation measures the average variability of each item around the expected value;* the greater the standard deviation, the greater the risk or variability in the distribution and the less representative is the expected value of the outcomes that could occur. Use of Equations (1) and (2) is illustrated in Example 1.

EXAMPLE 1

Risk vs. Return for Two Investments

A firm is evaluating two investment alternatives, X and Y, which cover the same one-year period. The returns on these two alternatives are dependent upon the state of the economy over the next year. The possible returns for each alternative and the various states of the economy are:

		Possible Investment Returns	
State of the Economy	Probability	X	Y
Great	.2	$2,800	$3,400
Good	.3	2,400	2,600
Fair	.4	2,200	2,000
Poor	.1	1,800	1,600
	1.0		

Compute the expected value, the standard deviation, and the coefficient of variation (which is merely the standard deviation divided by the expected value) for each investment.

SOLUTION

$$\bar{R}_x = (.2)(\$2,800) + (.3)(2,400) + (.4)(2,200) + (.1)(\$1,800)$$
$$= \$2,340$$

$$\bar{R}_y = (.2)(\$3,400) + (.3)(2,600) + (.4)(2,000) + (.1)(\$1,600)$$
$$= \$2,420$$

$$\sigma_x = \sqrt{\begin{array}{l}(.2)(\$2,800 - \$2,340)^2 + (.3)(2,400 - 2,340)^2 \\ + (.4)(2,200 - 2,340)^2 + (.1)(1,800 - 2,340)^2\end{array}}$$
$$= \sqrt{\$42,320 + 1,080 + 7,840 + 29,160}$$
$$= \$283.55$$

$$\sigma_y = \sqrt{\begin{array}{l}(.2)(\$3,400 - 2,420)^2 + (.3)(2,600 - 2,420)^2 \\ + (.4)(2,000 - 2,420)^2 + (.1)(1,600 - 2,420)^2\end{array}}$$
$$= \sqrt{\$192,080 + 9,720 + 70,560 + 67,240}$$
$$= \$582.75$$

$$CV_x = \frac{\sigma_x}{\bar{R}_x} = \frac{\$\ 283.55}{\$2,340.00} = .12$$

$$CV_y = \frac{\sigma_y}{\bar{R}_y} = \frac{\$\ 582.75}{\$2,420.00} = .24$$

These three statistics summarize the differences between the two alternatives. Project Y has a greater expected value, but only by $80. The risk associated with each project is dramatically shown by the standard deviation; project Y's standard deviation is more than twice that of project X. Finally, *the coefficient of variation shows the amount of risk per dollar of expected return:* project X has only 12 cents of risk per dollar of expected return, whereas project Y has 24 cents per dollar.

Which of the two alternatives is preferred by the firm depends upon how management views risk–return trade-offs and how averse it is to taking risk. This is because *neither alternative dominates the other by simultaneously having a greater expected return and a lower degree of risk.* The firm will have to determine whether project Y's additional $80 in expected return plus the opportunity (with probability .2) to earn a very high return of $3,400 (which is $600 greater than the highest return that can be achieved by project X) is worth the additional risk that project Y has—a standard deviation more than twice that of project X, double the amount of risk per dollar of expected return, and a .1 probability of achieving a return of only $1,600, which is $200 below the lowest return for project X. □

We now turn to a discussion of the most widely used method of evaluating capital investment and leasing projects under conditions of risk: *the risk-adjusted discount rate (RADR) technique*. As we will see, this model makes use of the expected value and the standard deviation of the returns on the project throughout its useful life.

Risk-Adjusted Discount Rate Technique[1]

The risk-adjusted discount rate (RADR) technique is a modification of the NPV model discussed in Chapter 5 wherein the discount rate K is adjusted either upward or downward, depending on whether the project under evaluation has greater or less risk than those normally undertaken by the firm. The rationale for adjusting the discount rate is that projects should achieve hurdle rates that reflect their degree of risk; *more risky projects should offer greater expected returns in order to be acceptable to management.*

Advocates of the RADR approach suggest that cash inflows generated by projects should be discounted for both the time value of money (using the risk-free rate[2]) and the degree of risk associated with the project (using a risk premium which is added to the risk-free rate).

Equation (3) shows how the expected net present value is determined using a risk-adjusted discount rate.

$$\overline{RAR} = \sum_{t=0}^{n} \frac{\overline{R_t}}{(1 + r')^t} \qquad (3)$$

where $\overline{RAR}$ = the expected value of the probability distribution of discounted cash flows over the life of the project
$\overline{R_t}$ = the expected value of the distribution of cash flows in period t
r' = the risk-adjusted discount rate based on the perceived riskiness of the project
n = the number of years in the project's life

It should be noticed that since the cash flows for each period are known only by a probability distribution, the discounted cash flows over the project's life will also be a probability distribution which has $\overline{RAR}$ as its expected value. This latter distribution also has a standard deviation σ_{RAR}, which will be discussed momentarily. Furthermore, if the cash flow distributions are all normal, then the discounted cash flow distribution will also be normal.

The way for management to implement the RADR technique is by categorizing projects according to their riskiness and then utilizing the discount rate which is felt appropriate for projects in that risk class. The extent of the risk premium assigned to the various risk classes of projects can differ significantly from firm to firm. Management generally utilizes the following factors to determine the risk premium:

Its perception of the risk associated with the project per se.
Its view of risk–return trade-offs.
The firm's initial wealth position.
The project's impact on the firm's other goals.

Table 7-1 presents one possible approach for classifying projects and the risk premiums that one firm's management felt appropriate after its evaluation of the four factors just enumerated. Example 2 illustrates the use of Equation (3) and Table 7-1.

EXAMPLE 2
Calculation of the Expected RAR Value

A firm is evaluating a project that it has classified as a new investment category II as described in Table 7-1. In addition, management feels that the risk adjustment specified in Table 7-1 for this category of projects (that is, the risk-free rate plus 10 percent) is appropriate for the firm's needs. The probability distributions for the cash flows of this project are:

		Cash Inflows					
Original Cost		Year 1		Year 2		Year 3	
Prob.	Amount	Prob.	Amount	Prob.	Amount	Prob.	Amount
.4	$150,000	.3	$60,000	.2	$ 80,000	.2	$50,000
.6	160,000	.4	75,000	.5	90,000	.4	55,000
		.2	80,000	.2	100,000	.3	60,000
		.1	85,000	.1	105,000	.1	65,000

Management anticipates that the risk-free rate will be 8 percent over the three-year useful life of the project. Determine the expected cash flow for each year and the expected value of the risk-adjusted net present value distribution.

Table 7-1. Return requirements for different investment groups.

Investment Grouping	Required Return
Replacement investments—category I (new machines or equipment, vehicles, etc., which will perform essentially the same function as older equipment which is to be replaced)	Risk-free rate plus 6%
Replacement investments—category II (new machines or equipment which replace older equipment but are more technologically advanced, require different operator skills, require different manufacturing approaches, or the like; examples would include implementation of electronic data processing equipment to replace manual accounting and payroll systems)	Risk-free rate plus 9%
Replacement investments—category III (new facilities such as buildings and warehouses which will replace older facilities; the new plants may be in the same or a different location)	Risk-free rate plus 12%
New investment—category I (new facilities and associated equipment which will produce or sell the same products as already being produced)	Risk-free rate plus 7%
New investment—category II (new facilities or machinery to produce or sell a product line closely related to the existing product line)	Risk-free rate plus 10%
New investment—category III (new facilities or machinery or acquisition of another firm to produce or sell a product line which is unrelated to the company's primary business)	Risk-free rate plus 18%
Research and development—category I (research and development which is directed toward specific goals such as developing new computer circuitry with which the firm's engineers are already very familiar)	Risk-free rate plus 15%
Research and development—category II (research in basic areas where goals have not been precisely defined and the outcome may be unknown)	Risk-free rate plus 25%

Adapted with permission from John J. Clark, Thomas J. Hindelang, and Robert E. Pritchard, *Capital Budgeting: Planning and Control of Capital Expenditures*, Englewood Cliffs, N.J.: Prentice-Hall, 1979.

SOLUTION

First, we compute the expected cash flow in each year.[3]

$$\overline{F}_1 = (.4)(-\$150,000) + (.6)(-\$160,000)$$
$$= -\$156,000$$

$$\overline{R}_1 = (.3)(\$60,000) + (.4)(\$75,000) + (.2)(\$80,000) + (.1)(\$85,000)$$
$$= \$72,500$$

$$\overline{R}_2 = (.2)(\$80,000) + (.5)(\$90,000) + (.2)(\$100,000) + (.1)(\$105,000)$$
$$= \$91,500$$

$$\overline{R}_3 = (.2)(\$50,000) + (.4)(\$55,000) + (.3)(\$60,000) + (.1)(\$65,000)$$
$$= \$56,500$$

Next, we compute $\overline{RAR}$, using Equation (3).

$$\overline{RAR} = -\$156,000 + \left[\frac{\$72,500}{(1.18)} + \frac{\$91,500}{(1.18)^2} + \frac{\$56,500}{(1.18)^3} \right]$$
$$= -\$156,000 + \$161,542 = \underline{\underline{\$5,542}}$$

Since this project has a positive $\overline{RAR}$, it is a candidate for acceptance, but we must also consider the variability in the RAR distribution. □

Variability in the RADR Distribution

In Chapter 5, we saw that the NPV model determined project attractiveness on the basis of whether the computed NPV was positive. Further, projects were ranked according to the magnitude of their NPVs, *since this value shows the increase in shareholders' wealth position due to the project.* Such a criterion is appropriate where the project's cash flows are assumed to be known precisely. However, under conditions of risk, we must consider both the expected value of the risk-adjusted NPV distribution *and* the amount of variability which is present in this distribution. *Under conditions of risk, many firms utilizing the risk-adjusted NPV model have an acceptance criterion which sets a minimum probability that the project will achieve a positive risk-adjusted NPV value over its useful life.* That is, the firm may state that the probability must be at least .80 that the project will achieve a positive NPV value, using a discount rate which is appropriate for the risk class of the project under evaluation.

In order to make such a probability statement, we must determine the standard deviation of the risk-adjusted NPV distribution. Given this standard deviation and the expected value of the distribution, found above, plus the assumption that the cash flow distribution for each year of the project's life is approximately normal, we can determine the probability statement in a straightforward manner. This is accomplished through the use of normal probability tables (see Appendix F) and the widely used Z formula shown in Equation (4).

$$Z = \frac{DV - \overline{RAR}}{\sigma_{RAR}} \qquad (4)$$

where Z = the standardized Z value that will be used to determine probabilities from the normal table
DV = a desired value for the risk-adjusted NPV to exceed for the project under evaluation
$\overline{RAR}$ = the expected value of the risk-adjusted NPV distribution for the project under evaluation
σ_{RAR} = the standard deviation of the risk-adjusted NPV distribution

Note that Equation (4) will determine the standardized Z value associated with any desired risk-adjusted net present value. If the manager were interested in determining the standardized Z value associated with, say, $10,000, this amount would be substituted for DV in Equation (4). Using this standardized Z value, a probability statement could be made about the likelihood that the risk-adjusted NPV for the project under evaluation would exceed $10,000. Of course, *an important value to consider for DV is zero, because the firm is interested in determining how likely it is that the project will increase shareholders' wealth, given the riskiness of the project*. Other positive values, such as $5,000, $10,000, or $50,000, used for DV would show the desired increase in shareholder wealth if the project were accepted and its benefits discounted at a rate consistent with its risk. Example 3 illustrates the use of Equation (4).

EXAMPLE 3
Probability Statements about RAR

For the project shown in Example 2, compute the probability that the risk-adjusted NPV value will equal or exceed:

(a) A value of zero.
(b) A value of $4,000.
(c) A value of $10,000.

For the purposes of this example, assume that σ_{RAR} equals $2,500.

SOLUTION

For the three values shown, we would just substitute each into Equation (4) for DV, using $\overline{RAR}$ from Example 2 and the assumed value of σ_{RAR}.

(A) $$Z = \frac{0 - \$5,542}{\$2,500} = -2.22$$

Looking up the value of 2.22 in Appendix F, we see that it is associated with an area under the normal curve of .4868. The following diagram of the RAR distribution is helpful in arriving at the desired probability statement about the likelihood that the *RAR* value is positive.

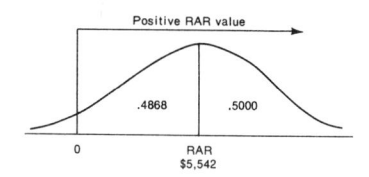

Thus, the probability that the risk-adjusted NPV will be positive is .9868 (.4868 + .5000).

(B) For a desired value of $4,000, we find:

$$Z = \frac{\$4,000 - \$5,542}{\$2,500} = -.62$$

Again, looking up the standardized Z value and using a diagram, we find:

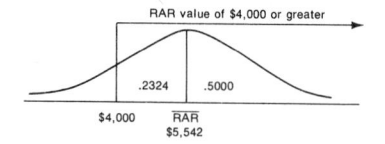

Thus, the probability that the risk-adjusted NPV will equal or exceed $4,000 is .7324.

(C) Finally, for a value of $10,000, we see that the standardized Z value is positive and the desired probability is in just the upper tail of the distribution.

$$Z = \frac{\$10,000 - \$5,542}{\$2,500} = 1.78$$

The area *between* the mean and a Z value of 1.78 is .4625. Thus, the area which lies above a Z value of 1.78 is the difference between .4625 and .5000, or .0375, which is the probability that this project will achieve a risk-adjusted NPV equal to or greater than $10,000. Again, in diagram form:

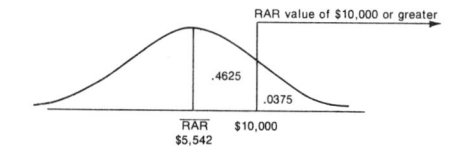

These three probabilities would be compared to the firm's "minimum required probability for acceptance rule," and they would also be used to rank this project with others under evaluation. □

Now that we have seen how the standard deviation for the RAR distribution is used, we should explore the details of its computations. Intuitively, it should make sense that the amount of variability in the risk-adjusted NPV distribution over a project's life (that is, σ_{RAR}) is dependent upon both the risk-free discount rate and the amount of variability that is present in the cash flow distributions in each year of the project's life. A third important factor in determining the magnitude of σ_{RAR} is not as intuitively obvious. This third factor is *the degree of correlation that exists among the cash flow distributions for each year of the life of the project*.

Let us argue to the reasonableness of the above assertion as follows. Consider a project whose yearly cash flow distributions are *independent* of each other; that is, the actual cash flow that occurs in year 1 will have no effect on the cash flow that will occur in any subsequent year (and so on). *The riskiness of this project over its useful life will be relatively low, because cash flows greater than the mean in one year can be offset by cash flows below the respective mean in some later year since there is no systematic relationship in the cash flow distributions from year to year.*

On the other hand, consider a project wherein the cash flow distributions are *perfectly correlated* from year to year with each other. This implies that the number of standard deviations that the actual cash inflow in year 1 is greater (less) than the mean cash inflow for year 1 will provide a perfect prediction of the number of standard deviations that each subsequent year's cash inflow will be greater (less) than its respective mean. *The riskiness of such projects over their useful lives will be quite great, because with each additional year the risk intensifies since there is always variation on the same side of the mean.* Thus, there is no chance for the canceling-out effect that is present in projects where the cash flow distributions are independent.[4] In fact, it can be shown that a project's risk is maximized if *perfect correlation* exists between the cash flow distributions; the risk decreases with the correlation coefficient to a significantly smaller value when the cash flow distributions are independent; finally, with negative correlation between the cash flow distributions, the risk decreases still further.

On the basis of our discussion, we will now present equations for σ_{RAR} for two cases: case I, independent cash flows, and case II, perfectly correlated cash flows over the project's life.[5] Firms participating in highly competitive markets where uncontrollable forces shape the demand for their goods and services are likely to find that cash flow distributions for their usual projects exhibit independence. On the other hand, firms in monopolistically competitive markets are more likely to find that cash flow distributions for their usual projects are highly or perfectly correlated.

Equation (5) shows how σ_{RAR} is computed for independent cash flows:

$$\sigma_{RAR} = \sqrt{\sum_{t=0}^{n} \frac{\sigma_t^2}{(1+i)^{2t}}} \tag{5}$$

where σ_{RAR} = the standard deviation of the risk-adjusted NPV distribution over the project's life
σ_t = the standard deviation of the project's cash flow distribution in year t
i = the risk-free discount rate
n = the useful life of the project

Equation (6) assumes cash flows are perfectly correlated and shows how σ_{RAR} is computed:

$$\sigma_{RAR} = \sum_{t=0}^{n} \frac{\sigma_t}{(1+i)^t} \tag{6}$$

Example 4 illustrates the use of these two expressions.

EXAMPLE 4
Computation of σ_{RAR}

For the project shown in Example 2 determine:
(a) σ_t for each year of the project's life.
(b) σ_{RAR} under the assumption that cash flows are independent over the project's life.
(c) σ_{RAR} under the assumption that cash flows are perfectly correlated over the project's life.
(d) The probability that the project will achieve a positive risk-adjusted NPV under both case I and case II [i.e., using σ_{RAR} found in (b) and (c)].

SOLUTION

(a) $\sigma_0 = \sqrt{.4(\$150{,}000 - \$156{,}000)^2 + .6(\$160{,}000 - \$156{,}000)^2}$
   $= \$4{,}899$

$\sigma_1 = \sqrt{\begin{array}{l}.3(\$60{,}000 - \$72{,}500)^2 + .4(\$75{,}000 - \$72{,}500)^2 \\ + .2(\$80{,}000 - \$72{,}500)^2 + .1(\$85{,}000 - \$72{,}500)^2\end{array}}$
   $= \$8{,}732$

$$\sigma_2 = \sqrt{\begin{array}{l}.2(\$80,000 - \$91,500)^2 + .5(\$90,000 - \$91,500)^2 \\ + .2(\$100,000 - \$91,500)^2 + .1(\$105,000 - \$91,500)^2\end{array}}$$
$$= \$7,762$$
$$\sigma_3 = \sqrt{\begin{array}{l}.2(\$50,000 - \$56,500)^2 + .4(\$55,000 - \$56,500)^2 \\ + .3(\$60,000 - \$56,500)^2 + .1(\$65,000 - \$56,500)^2\end{array}}$$
$$= \$4,500$$

(b) $\sigma_{RAR} = \sqrt{\sum_{t=0}^{n} \dfrac{\sigma_t^2}{(1+i)^{2t}}}$

$$= \sqrt{(\$4,899)^2 + \dfrac{(\$8,732)^2}{(1.08)^2} + \dfrac{(\$7,762)^2}{(1.08)^4} + \dfrac{(\$4,500)^2}{(1.08)^6}}$$

$$= \$12,100$$

(c) $\sigma_{RAR} = \sum_{t=0}^{n} \dfrac{\sigma_t}{(1+i)^t}$

$$= \$4,899 + \dfrac{\$8,732}{(1.08)^1} + \dfrac{\$7,762}{(1.08)^2} + \dfrac{\$4,500}{(1.08)^3}$$

$$= \$23,211$$

(d) The probability that the project will achieve a positive risk-adjusted NPV, assuming cash flows are independent, is found by substituting into Equation (4): zero for DV, $\overline{RAR}$ found in Example 2, and the value found in part (b) for σ_{RAR}:

$$Z = \dfrac{0 - \$5,542}{\$12,100} = -.46$$

This yields an area of .1772, which, added to .5000, yields:

$$Pr\ \{RAR \geq 0\} = .6772$$

To find the comparable probability, assuming that the cash flows are perfectly correlated, we compute:

$$Z = \dfrac{0 - \$5,542}{\$23,211} = -.24$$

This yields an area of .0942 between 0 and $\overline{RAR}$, which, added to .5000, results in:

$$Pr\ \{\overline{RAR} \geq 0\} = .5942 \qquad \square$$

Management would next compare these probabilities to the minimum acceptable probability for achieving a positive risk-adjusted NPV value in order to determine whether the project is a candidate for acceptance. Note that the probability of the project achieving a positive NPV under conditions of perfect correlation of cash flows is .5942, which represents the *worst-case* situation. The probability of achieving a positive NPV under conditions of independent cash flows is .6772 and represents a more desirable risk situation. Risk-adverse managements could use the worst-case value for all projects. However, a more realistic decision rule asks management to judge the relative independence of the cash flows and then estimate a probability value between the two computed probabilities.

Implementation of the Risk-Adjusted NPV Approach

Admittedly, the process of determining the amount of variability in the risk-adjusted NPV distribution is somewhat involved. However, under conditions of uncertainty concerning future cash flows, we must shift our acceptance criterion from a simple "accept if NPV ≥ 0 and reject otherwise" to one which incorporates both the risk and the return of the project. Very often this is accomplished by setting minimum acceptable probabilities that the project will achieve desired levels of risk-adjusted NPV, utilizing a discount rate appropriate for the project under evaluation. Hence, it is necessary for us to determine both $\overline{RAR}$ and σ_{RAR} so that the risky project can be properly evaluated.

Furthermore, it is necessary for firms and divisions to address the difficult questions of how much risk they are willing to take, what impact risky projects will have on their most important goals and objectives, what kinds of trade-offs they are willing to accept between risk and expected return, and how much risk they can afford to take, given their vulnerabilities on several fronts. The answers to these questions are needed in order to arrive at appropriate discount rates for various risk classes of projects, in order to set the minimum acceptable probabilities for desired levels of risk-adjusted NPV over the project's life, and in order to select and implement optimal diversification strategies to reduce variability in returns.

In determining σ_{RAR}, questions can be raised concerning how the degree of correlation between the cash flow distributions can be accurately estimated. We concede that this is usually a thorny problem. However, we would recommend that the analyst determine σ_{RAR} first under the extreme assumption that the cash flow distributions are perfectly correlated. As mentioned above, this assumption produces the maximum value for σ_{RAR}. Thus, *if the project is attractive given the maximum σ_{RAR}, it will be attractive for any degree of correlation that may exist between the cash flow distributions.*

If the project is only marginally attractive or is not attractive under the assumption of perfect correlation, σ_{RAR} should be computed under the assumption of independent cash flow distributions. If the project is now attractive, the firm must address the question of which correlation assumption more accurately portrays the project under evaluation, taking into account similar projects, the general characteristics of the firm, or further analysis such as a simulation study.

Finally, the firm should let the project stand as a candidate for acceptance if it sufficiently satisfies its preferences concerning risk taking, risk–return trade-offs, and its other relevant goals and objectives. That is, the quantitative aspects of any risky project under evaluation (i.e., $\overline{RAR}$, σ_{RAR}, $\overline{R}_t$, σ_t, and the degree of correlation) must be tempered by careful evaluation and judgment and must be balanced against the qualitative aspects of the final decision. These include management's preferences for ranking alternatives on the basis of the degree of risk it is willing to accept, risk–return trade-offs desired, and the impact of the project on all other relevant goals and objectives of the firm.

One final caution to analysts and managers using the risk-adjusted NPV methodology: The use of a constant risk-adjusted discount rate over the life of the project implicitly assumes (due to the compounding process) that the risk of the project is growing exponentially with time. Thus, an increasingly greater penalty for risk is assigned to cash flows that occur progressively later in the project's life. For many projects, this may be appropriate, since there is greater uncertainty later in the project's life and greater forecasting difficulty. However, this is not necessarily the case for all projects. Some projects could very well have less risk associated with later cash flows once the initial uncertainty of the project is resolved. In such cases, and especially if the project has a very long life, the use of a constant risk-adjusted discount rate over its life penalizes the project for its risk. *Recall that the risk-adjusted discount rate approach discounts for the time value of money at the risk-free rate and discounts for the riskiness of the project by adding a risk-premium which is appropriate for the project under evaluation.*

Consider Table 7-2 below, which shows the discount factors and risk penalties for three risk-adjusted discount rates of 10 percent, 15 percent, and 20 percent, assuming a risk-free rate of 6 percent. For a 15 percent risk-adjusted rate, notice that the risk penalty (which is the difference between the risk-free discount factor and the risk-adjusted discount factor) more than doubles from 7.3 percent per dollar of cash inflow in year 1 to 18.2 percent per dollar of cash inflow in year 3, and successively increases to 25 percent, 28.9 percent, and 31.1 percent per dollar of cash inflow in years 5, 7, and 10, respectively (after year 10 the penalty drops off because of the very small values for the risk-adjusted discount factors).

Table 7-2. Discount factors and risk penalties for 10 percent, 15 percent, and 20 percent.

Year	Risk-Free 6%	10% Discount Factor	10% Risk Penalty	15% Discount Factor	15% Risk Penalty	20% Discount Factor	20% Risk Penalty
1	.943	.909	.034	.870	.073	.833	.11
3	.840	.751	.089	.658	.182	.579	.261
5	.747	.621	.126	.497	.250	.402	.345
7	.665	.513	.152	.376	.289	.279	.386
10	.558	.386	.172	.247	.311	.162	.396
15	.417	.239	.178	.123	.294	.065	.352

Thus, a constant risk-adjusted discount rate is appropriate only for projects that are perceived to have risk growing at an increasing rate. If this is not the case for a project under evaluation, then an alternative method is required in order to appropriately adjust for risk. We suggest one of the following:

1. A straightforward, operationally efficient approach would be to estimate an appropriate percentage risk penalty for each year of the project's life and *subtract the decimal equivalent from the discount factor for the risk-free rate in the corresponding year.* For example, suppose that the risk-free rate is 6 percent and a project under evaluation is estimated to require a 10 percent risk penalty in year 1, an 8 percent penalty in year 3, and a 6 percent penalty in year 5; then, the discount factors to be used (see Table 7-2) are .943 − .10, or .843, for year 1; .840 − .08, or .76, for year 3; and .747 − .06, or .687, for year 5.

2. Determine the discount factor by *changing the risk-adjusted discount rate over the life of the project so as to reflect the actual perceived risk of the project.* For example, if the project is perceived as having increasing risk over its life, then a constant risk-adjusted rate at an appropriate level is acceptable; on the other hand, if the project has constant risk over its life, then a decreasing risk-adjusted rate is appropriate. Note here that the discount factors are found in the usual way. Suppose management feels that a 16 percent risk-adjusted rate is appropriate for the first two years of a project's life and thereafter a 14 percent rate is appropriate. The discount factor in year 1 is $\frac{1}{1.16} = .862$; in year 2, $\frac{1}{(1.16)^2} = .743$; in year 3, $\frac{1}{(1.16)^2(1.14)} = .652$; in year 4, $\frac{1}{(1.16)^2(1.14)^2} = .572$, and so on.

3. A significant departure from the risk-adjusted NPV method presented thus far in this chapter is known as the *certainty equivalent method*. The basic approach of this method is to determine "certainty equivalent factors" for each year of the project's life; these factors are then multiplied by $\bar{R}_t$, yielding a dollar amount that the firm would be willing *to accept for certain* rather than taking the chances reflected in the probability distribution for possible cash flows in year t. The certainty equivalent amount for year t is then discounted at the risk-free rate.

It has been argued that the certainty equivalent method is superior to the risk-adjusted NPV approach for two reasons. It is more flexible in handling risk, since it carries no implicit assumption of how risk changes over the life of the project. Also, it divorces the adjustment for risk from the discounting process, which then handles exclusively the time value of money, since the risk-free rate is used. The certainty equivalent method is treated in depth in the following section.

The Certainty Equivalent Method

As we discussed above, the risk-adjusted discount rate (RADR) approach to incorporating risk into the analysis of capital expenditures carries with it an assumption that risk associated with the project increases exponentially over time. An alternative technique for handling risk in the analysis is the certainty equivalent method. The certainty equivalent method is more flexible than the risk-adjusted discount rate approach, since it separates the treatment of risk from the discounting process that reflects the time value of money. By contrast, the RADR approach attempts to treat both risk and the time value of money by discounting at a rate that is appropriate for the project's risk class. *The use of the risk-adjusted discount rate assumes implicitly (due to the compounding process) that risk increases at an increasing rate over time.*

As with the RADR approach, the certainty equivalent (CE) method utilizes the cash flow probability distributions to evaluate project attractiveness. In particular, the CE method requires $\bar{R}_t$ and σ_t (the expected cash flow and the standard deviation of the cash flow distribution in period t) as computed by Equations (1) and (2) respectively. However, as the name implies, the RADR approach discounts cash flows using a risk-adjusted discount rate, whereas the CE method discounts cash flows using the risk-free rate. Before the CE method discounts cash flows, it converts them into amounts that the firm would be willing to accept for certain, using "certainty equivalent factors." The formal definition of the CE method is shown in Equation (7).

$$\overline{CE} = \sum_{t=0}^{n} \frac{\alpha_t \overline{R}_t}{(1 + i)^t} \tag{7}$$

where $\overline{CE}$ = the expected certainty equivalent value over the life of the project
α_t = the certainty equivalent factor for period t
$\overline{R}_t$ = the expected cash flow in period t
i = the risk-free rate

More should be said at this point concerning the α_t values. The range of possible values that α_t can take on is from zero to one. Verbally, the certainty equivalent factor is defined as the number of cents per dollar of expected cash inflow that management is willing to accept *for sure* in place of the probability distribution of possible cash inflows. The closer to one the α_t factor is, the smaller is the penalty assigned by management to the cash flow in period t; the converse is true as the α_t value decreases toward a value of zero. The α_t values are subjectively determined by management for different risk classes of projects and for each year t of a project's life. Management will assign α_t values based on the following factors:

1. The degree of risk which is perceived to be present in the cash flow distribution for year t as measured by the standard deviation or the coefficient of variation (which is the standard deviation divided by the expected value).

2. The degree of aversion that management has to risk taking. Aggressive firms, such as growth companies, will be willing to accept projects with significant risk, and hence the α_t values will be closer to 1 in their analysis than in that of a more conservative firm on the same project.

3. The impact that risky projects will have on the firm's hierarchy of goals or objectives. The greater the potential contribution that more risky projects could make to the achievement of the firm's various objectives, the smaller will be the penalty management assigns to risky cash flows.

Table 7-3 shows various sets of α_t factors that one firm has developed on the basis of its evaluation of the three factors discussed above. Notice that there are both overall risk classes for projects and risk differentials within each class based on the coefficient of variation for each year's cash flow distribution. The use of Equation (7) plus Table 7-3 is illustrated in the following example.

EXAMPLE 5

The Expected CE Value

The firm which developed the certainty equivalent factors shown in Table 7-3 is evaluating a project that would fall into the new-investment risk

Table 7-3. Certainty equivalent factors based on risk classes
and the coefficient of variation.

	Coefficient of Variation (r)	Year 1	Year 2	Year 3	Year 4
Replacement investments—category I (new machines or equipment, vehicles, etc., which will perform essentially the same function as older equipment which is to be replaced)	r ≤ .10	.95	.92	.89	.85
Replacement investments—category II (new machines or equipment which replace older equipment but are more technologically advanced, require different operator skills, require different manufacturing approaches, or the like; examples would include implementation of electronic data processing equipment to replace manual accounting and payroll systems)	.10 < r ≤ .25	.9	.86	.82	.77
Replacement investments—category III (new facilities such as buildings and warehouses which will replace older facilities; the new plants may be in the same or a different location)	r > .25	.84	.79	.74	.68
New investment—category I (new facilities and associated equipment which will produce or sell the same products as already being produced)	r ≤ .10	.92	.88	.85	.80
New investment—category II (new facilities or machinery to produce or sell a product line closely related to the existing product line)	.10 < r ≤ .25	.86	.82	.78	.73
New investment—category III (new facilities or machinery or acquisition of another firm to produce or sell a product line which is unrelated to the company's primary business)	r > .25	.80	.75	.70	.64
Research and development—category I (research and development which is directed toward specific goals such as developing new computer circuitry with which the firm's engineers are already very familiar)	r ≤ .20	.82	.76	.70	.60
Research and development—category II (research in basic areas where goals have not been precisely defined and the outcome may be unknown)	r > .20	.70	.60	.50	0

Reprinted with permission from John J. Clark, Thomas J. Hindelang, and Robert E. Pritchard, *Capital Budgeting: Planning and Control of Capital Expenditures,* Englewood Cliffs, N.J.: Prentice-Hall, 1979.

class. However, rather than placing it into one of the three categories within the new-investment class, the firm feels that the α_t factor for each year should be selected on the basis of the coefficient of variation for the respective year's cash flow distribution. Based on the values for the cash flow distributions shown and a risk-free rate of 8 percent, select the appropriate α_t values from Table 7-3 and compute $\overline{CE}$.

Time	$\overline{R}_t$	σ_t
Present	−$10,000	
1	4,000	$1,200
2	5,000	1,100
3	6,000	500

SOLUTION

In order to compute $\overline{CE}$, we first must select the correct α_t factors from Table 7-3, which in turn requires the computation of the coefficient of variation for each year.

$$CV_1 = \frac{\sigma_1}{\overline{R}_1} = \frac{\$1,200}{\$4,000} = .30$$

$$CV_2 = \frac{\sigma_2}{\overline{R}_2} = \frac{\$1,100}{\$5,000} = .220$$

$$CV_3 = \frac{\sigma_3}{\overline{R}_3} = \frac{\$500}{\$6,000} = .083$$

The appropriate α_t factors are .80, .82, and .85 for years 1, 2, and 3, respectively. Notice that since the risk decreased significantly over the project's life, the firm feels that each dollar of expected cash inflow in period 3 is worth 85 cents, whereas each dollar of expected cash inflow in year 1 was worth only 80 cents. We now compute $\overline{CE}$.

Time	$\overline{R}_t$	α_t	$\alpha_t \overline{R}_t$	Discount Factors at 8%	Discounted $\alpha_t \overline{R}_t$
Present	−$10,000	1.0	−$10,000	1.000	−$10,000
1	4,000	.80	3,200	.926	2,963
2	5,000	.82	4,100	.857	3,514
3	6,000	.85	5,100	.794	4,049
				$\overline{CE}$ =	$ 526

Since this project has a positive $\overline{CE}$ value, it is a candidate for acceptance. □

Variability in the Certainty Equivalent Distribution

The same comments made earlier in this chapter concerning the RADR distribution carry over to the CE distribution. Namely, since the cash flows for the project are known only by probability distributions, the certainty equivalent method will arrive at a distribution of possible CE values over the project's life. This CE distribution has both an expected value ($\overline{CE}$) and a standard deviation (σ_{CE}). We have illustrated the computation of $\overline{CE}$ in Example 5. The σ_{CE} value is computed in exactly the same way as σ_{RAR}, that is, by Equation (5) if the cash flows over the project's life are independent or by Equation (6) if the cash flows are perfectly correlated.

Again, under conditions of risk, the acceptance criterion shifts to one wherein the firm would specify a minimum probability that CE would take on a positive value. Here, Equation (4) again comes into play and is used in exactly the same way as was illustrated above.

Summary

This chapter provided an overview of the important conditions of risk that are characteristic of the usual decision on capital expenditures, including leases. Conditions of risk are present when the manager feels that he must resort to a probability distribution to reflect possible future outcomes and their likelihood of occurrence. The presence of probability distributions for cash flows necessitates the computation of the mean and the standard deviation of such distributions, which are then used in assessing project attractiveness.

The risk-adjusted NPV approach, wherein both $\overline{RAR}$ and σ_{RAR} are determined, was illustrated, since it is the most widely used technique of project evaluation under conditions of risk. Under such conditions, the focus of the project acceptance criterion shifts from one concentrating only on expected return ("accept projects that have positive NPVs") to one that incorporates returns, variability in those returns, and the firm's preferences. The latter approach says, "Accept projects that have a sufficiently high probability of achieving desired returns." Last, we examined the certainty equivalent approach, which is technically superior to the RADR approach. The next two chapters will draw on the approach illustrated here in evaluating the lease alternative.

NOTES

1. This section draws upon John J. Clark, Thomas J. Hindelang, and Robert E. Pritchard, *Capital Budgeting: Planning and Control of Capital Expenditures*, Englewood Cliffs, N.J.: Prentice-Hall, 1979, Chapter 8.

2. The risk-free rate is the rate normally associated with the return on treasury bills. This rate is, of course, not static but constantly changing with money and capital market conditions.
3. The negative value of $\bar{R}_0$ indicates that the $\bar{R}_0$ is a cash outflow (i.e., cost).
4. Technically, the significant increase in the riskiness of projects whose cash flows are perfectly correlated is due to the *covariance* which exists between all pairs of years over the life of the project. The covariance is the product of the correlation coefficient and each of the standard deviations for the two years under consideration. That is, $Cov_{ij} = r_{ij}(\sigma_i)(\sigma_j)$, where r_{ij} is the correlation coefficient between the two years' cash flow distributions, and σ_i and σ_j are the two standard deviations of the respective year's cash flow distributions. Of course, if $r_{ij} = 0$ (i.e., the cash flows are independent), $Cov_{ij} = 0$; on the other hand, if $r_{ij} = +1$ (i.e., the cash flows are perfectly correlated), $Cov_{ij} = (\sigma_i)(\sigma_j)$, which increases the project's riskiness, since here the covariance is positive rather than zero.
5. The reader should note that it is unusual for a project to have either independent or perfectly correlated cash flows from year to year over its life. Rather, these two values represent helpful indications of the magnitude of σ_{RAR}. It would appear that the lower limit of σ_{RAR} would result from independent cash flows, but this is not the case, since if the cash flows were perfectly negatively correlated, σ_{RAR} would equal zero.

CHAPTER 8

Lease-versus-Purchase Analysis

Up to this point, we have introduced the reader to (or refreshed him on) the important prerequisites of performing a complete analysis of the lease-versus-purchase alternatives. Namely, we have discussed the importance of both qualitative and quantitative factors in the evaluation of feasible alternatives. In our discussion of the important quantitative factors, we illustrated the computation of net cash flows based on differing depreciation techniques and relevant tax aspects; the use of discounting techniques which take the time value of money into account; the firm's required rate of return; and various ways of incorporating risk considerations into the analysis. All these tools will be drawn together in this critical chapter, which evaluates leasing alternatives and lease-versus-purchase decisions.

The chapter is divided into several sections in order to facilitate understanding of some of the more complex and controversial topics in leasing. Initially, we review the current literature on the topic of leasing to afford the reader added perspective. The literature is synthesized, and from it a model procedure for lease evaluation is developed, using a detailed flowchart indicating important decision nexuses. The relevant cash flows and appropriate discount rates are next examined. With this baseline established, the remaining two sections deal with the procedures to evaluate alternative leases and lease versus purchase. In each section, we start with an examination of the decision variables, expressed in equation form, and draw on these to provide detailed tabular examples.

An Overview of the Leasing Literature

Although the literature on the analysis of leasing is very extensive, some of it is highly theoretical and thus of limited use to managers and analysts concerned with leasing decisions.

To illustrate, two articles in the June 1976 *Journal of Finance* argued that the net present value of owning an asset *should* always equal the net present value of leasing the asset, because of the equilibrium in the leasing market as well as the equilibrium in the market composed of the users of such leased assets.[1] However, these articles, as well as numerous others, offer little, if any, assistance to practicing managers and analysts who operate under conditions that are anything but in a "state of equilibrium." There are numerous imperfections, including:

- Differences in the rate at which various firms can obtain lease financing and/or debt and equity funds.
- Various tax considerations between lessor and lessee which make the picture anything but crystal-clear.
- The ability of firms to use equipment more efficiently and with lower maintenance costs than their competitors.
- The existence of transaction costs and fees.
- The uncertainty of future equipment obsolescence possibilities.
- The uncertainty of future market prices for new and used assets.
- The lack of perfect communication among lessors, lessees, and other interested parties.

Thus, our position is that such imperfections make it incumbent upon responsible managers and analysts to carefully evaluate feasible alternatives with a sound approach in order to select the one that is best from the firm's standpoint.

Other authors go to great lengths to stress the disagreements they have with approaches recommended to date. For example, Johnson and Lewellen[2] and Mitchell[3] each discuss their differences of opinion with others rather than trying to synthesize and provide practitioners with useful techniques of analysis. Two noteworthy exceptions to the squabbling among authors are articles by Bower[4] and Kasper,[5] who show the points of agreement among the several analytical techniques. Bower, in particular, goes on to suggest ways of resolving disagreements to arrive at easily used decision formats.

Our goal here is to provide the reader with a logical and powerful approach to the leasing problem area; nonetheless, we will demonstrate how easy it is to use the methodology for practical problem solving by managers and analysts who have a grasp of the techniques and approaches illustrated in the previous chapter.

Finally, a recent survey of the 200 largest U.S. industrial firms indicates that of 48 respondents, all but two of the firms utilize lease-versus-purchase analysis techniques that are *inherently biased in favor of the purchase alternative*.[6] The two major reasons for this bias are (1) the failure to adjust for the differential risk present in the cash flows of the alternatives, and (2) the requirement that the investment must be justified on the basis of a purchase *before* leasing is considered.

The results of this survey, when contrasted to those showing the use of sophisticated approaches in strict capital budgeting decisions,[7] indicate the need for a broader exposure of managers and analysts to more advanced and up-to-date lease–purchase evaluative techniques so that correct decisions are facilitated. Thus, our goal in the present chapter will also be to provide coverage of such techniques from a pragmatic and operationally efficient viewpoint.

The Required Data Inputs

In evaluating the lease–purchase decision, there are three critical issues that must be addressed:

1. Is the firm concerned with a capital investment decision, a financing decision, or both?
2. Based on 1, what are the relevant cash flows that must be considered under each of the feasible alternatives?
3. What is the appropriate discount rate for each of the cash flows and each of the feasible alternatives, given the degree of risk present?

In order to arrive at a correct evaluation of the feasible alternatives, each of these issues must be resolved. Figure 8-1 provides an overview of our recommendation for systematically dealing with these issues. Notice that Figure 8-1 stresses the fact that leasing has investment implications, financing implications, renegotiation opportunities, and the need for sensitivity analysis (that is, considering how much conditions would have to change in order to result in a new preferred alternative, as well as incorporating the impact of nonquantifiable factors on the decision). The relevant cash flows and the appropriate discount rates are treated in the two evaluation modules illustrated in subsequent pages.

The *financing evaluation module* would be called upon if the firm has gone through a prior decision process to evaluate the attractiveness of the project and determined that it is a viable candidate for acquisition, *or* if the project is required for the firm's continued existence (sometimes referred to as sustaining investment projects). Under such conditions, the firm

Figure 8-1. Overview of the lease-purchase decision analysis.

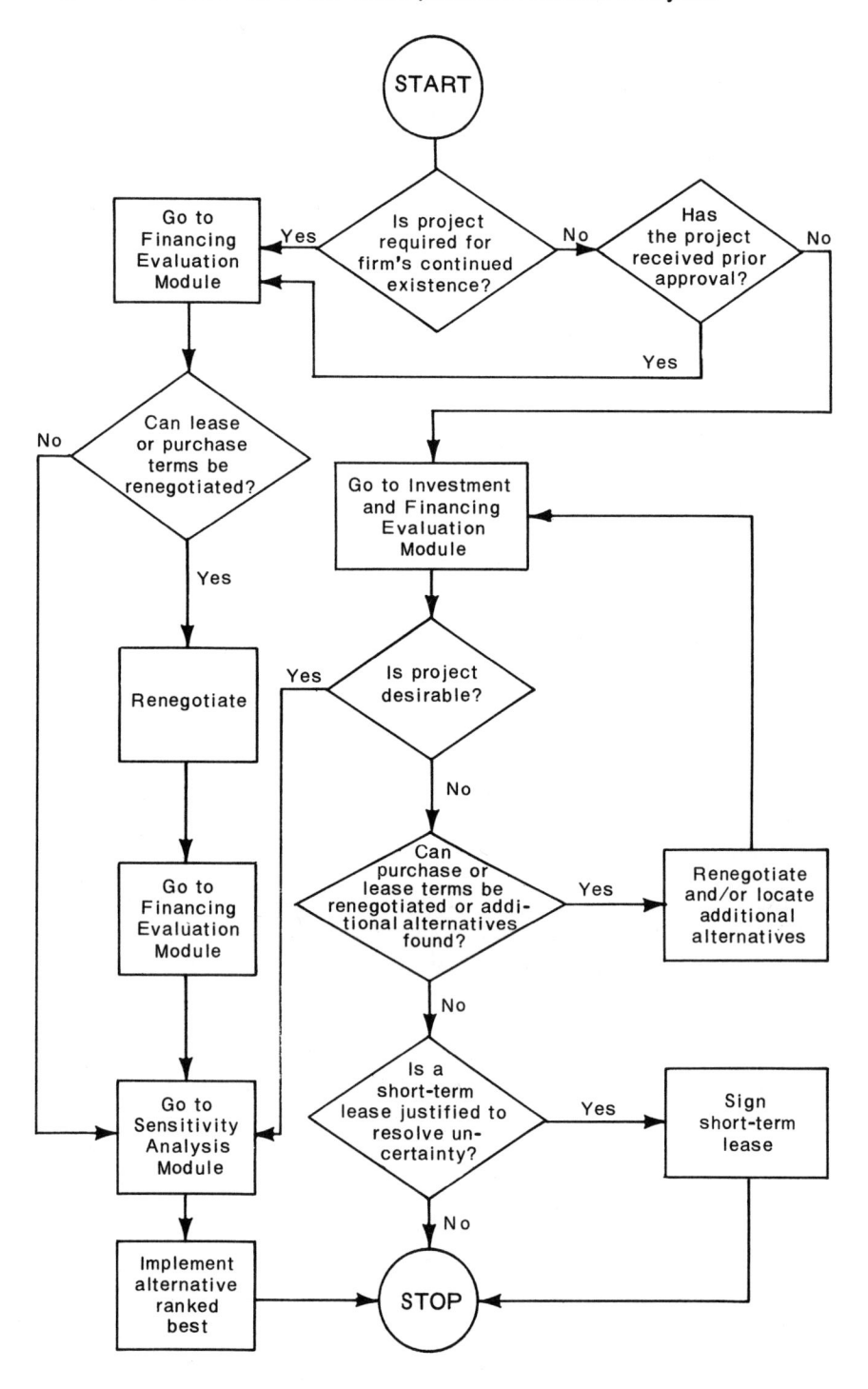

must decide upon the most favorable financing arrangement: purchase for cash, borrow and buy, or enter into one of several leasing contracts. Again, as we shall see, each of these alternatives has its own relevant cash flows and requires the use of appropriate risk-adjusted discount rates.

The *investment and financing evaluation module* simultaneously looks at the attractiveness of the project and the financing of the project. Several authors recommend, to the contrary, that the investment must first be justified on the basis of purchase before the financing decision is considered. We see this as a fallacy and agree with those[8] who argue that such an approach "can never allow a very attractive lease to reverse an original negative purchase decision."[9] Thus, the investment and financing module simultaneously determines whether the expected benefits of the project exceed the operating and financial costs associated with the best financing alternative among those under evaluation, as well as (by necessity) the identity of the best financing alternative.

The major difference between the financing evaluation module and the investment and financing evaluation module is that the latter must consider the benefits that will result from the investment, as well as the operating and financial costs associated with the various financing alternatives, whereas the financing module considers only the relevant operating and financial cash outflows and the related tax effects associated with the various financing alternatives. That is, the revenues or benefits generated by the investment are excluded from consideration in the financing evaluation module, since they will be the same for all the financing alternatives and since the project has already been designated attractive. Thus, *the decision criterion for the investment and financing evaluation module is that the project is attractive if at least one financing alternative has a positive NPV, otherwise it is not attractive.* Further, the best financing alternative is the one with the largest NPV value, considering all relevant cash flows and using appropriate risk-adjusted discount rates. On the other hand, *the decision criterion for the financing evaluation module is that the financing alternative selected has the minimum present value of the operating and financial cash flows.*

We now turn to a discussion of the relevant cash flows associated with the various financing alternatives in the lease-versus-buy decision setting.

Recommended Analysis for the Leasing Alternative

In the lease-versus-purchase decision setting, there are three major classes of financing alternatives: (1) lease the asset under one of several leasing arrangements, (2) buy the asset for cash from the pool of funds available for capital investment, and (3) borrow funds specifically to buy the asset. The third alternative may require a mortgage agreement.

The determination of relevant cash flows, as well as tax impacts and alternative depreciation methods, for the second category has already been discussed in Chapter 3. In addition, Chapter 5 covers the computation of the NPV of such projects. Thus, we will proceed with a discussion of the other two categories and only briefly expand on the prior coverage of category 2.

Under the lease alternative, the obvious cash outflows are the lease payments over the term of the contract. However, these payments can take on a wide variety of patterns: equal monthly payments at the beginning of each month, payments in arrears (at the end of the month), ballooning payments at various times over the lease to meet the needs of the lessor or the lessee, and so on.

In addition, most lease contracts require a security deposit or a prepayment of some number of lease payments, which is an additional cash outflow. A recent survey of 520 financial leases with an average outlay cost to the lessor of $9,863 indicated that the average prepayment requirement was 9.5 percent of the original cost of the asset, with 65 percent of the leases requiring a prepayment between 10 percent and 15 percent of the original cost.[10]

Offsetting the security deposit and the initial lease payments is the possibility that the investment tax credit (ITC) can be passed on to the lessee; the above-mentioned survey indicated that 30 percent of the lease contracts had the ITC passed on to the lessee.[11] It should be noted here that when the ITC is passed on to the lessee, it is computed on the basis of the fair market value of the leased asset.[12]

Other cash outflows related to the lease are those for maintenance, taxes, and insurance (in the case of a net lease), and the amount required to bring the asset up to the pre-established value at the end of the lease (in the case of a net–net lease).

All these cash outflows have the tax shield associated with them. Thus, the net cash outflow will be the after-tax cash outflow—that is:

Before-tax cash outflow × (1 − tax rate on ordinary income)
= after-tax or net cash outflow

The timing of these cash flows is important in that each must be discounted to present value using the appropriate discount rate. Doing so determines the present value of the costs associated with the leasing alternative or the net present value (that is, both benefits and costs) of the project acquired through the lease. The appropriate discount rates are now discussed.

As indicated earlier, there has been considerable debate over the appropriate discount rates to use in evaluating component cash flows in the lease–purchase setting. Further, we indicated that our purpose here would be not to emphasize differences but rather to suggest a correct decision approach and strategies of performing sensitivity analysis before the final decision is made.

The recommended approach in the financing evaluation module will be to find the present value of the after-tax cash outflows related to the lease. As will be illustrated in tabular form below, this requires determining the following items:

1. The present value of the after-tax lease payments over the term of the lease; plus
2. The present value of the after-tax payments for maintenance, property taxes, and insurance required by the lease, if it is a net lease; plus
3. The present value on an after-tax basis of the single payment (if required) at the end of the lease to bring the asset up to a pre-established value; less
4. The present value of the investment tax credit if it is passed on by the lessor to the lessee.

In computing these present values, we recommend using *one risk-adjusted discount rate for all financial cash flows related to the lease* (the first, third, and fourth cash flows enumerated above) and a *second risk-adjusted rate for the cash flows related to the operations of the asset* (the second cash flow described above). Namely, we recommend using the firm's *after-tax borrowing rate* to discount all the financial flows related to the lease, whereas for the operating cash flows we recommend the use of an *after-tax risk-adjusted discount rate* that is appropriate for any asset in the risk class of the project under evaluation.

The firm's after-tax borrowing rate is appropriate for discounting all financial flows of the lease, because it will usually closely approximate the implicit after-tax cost of leasing to the lessee. The second discount rate mentioned is appropriate for the operating cash flows, since, as we argued in the presentation of the risk-adjusted discount rate approach in Chapter 7, *cash flows should be discounted at a rate which is consistent with the uncertainty or variability that exists in their probability distributions of possible outcomes.* The firm is bound to the financial flows by contractual obligations, which necessarily means that very little uncertainty exists about the magnitude of such flows; thus, the low after-tax borrowing rate is appropriate. On the other hand, costs and benefits from the asset's

96   THE LEASE / BUY DECISION

operations are subject to much greater variability, which argues for the higher risk-adjusted discount rate for the appropriate risk class of assets.

Because the tabular approach utilized below is rather comprehensive and the verbal description of our recommended evaluation procedure is quite involved, it is felt that a formal mathematical statement is in order to provide a shorthand summary of how the analysis is carried out. Equation (1) below accomplishes this. We again emphasize that the reader should not be intimidated by the appearance of Equation (1). In fact, like all other equations presented in this chapter, it can be essentially ignored by any reader who is more comfortable with a tabular presentation of the same information. In our example, we will utilize the tabular approach exclusively.

The present value of any lease option can be computed using Equation (1):

$$PV(L) = \sum_{t=0}^{n} \frac{LP_t(1 - t_c)}{(1 + K_d)^t} + \sum_{t=0}^{n} \frac{M_t(1 - t_c)}{(1 + K)^t} + \frac{EP(1 - t_c)}{(1 + K_d)^n} - \frac{(ITC)(FMV)}{(1 + K_d)} \quad (1)$$

where $PV(L)$ = the present value of the after-tax cash outflows associated with leasing the asset

LP_t = the lease payment in period t (note that if a security deposit is required or if one or more payments have to be prepaid, then these amounts are shown as lease payments in period 0.

M_t = the payments for maintenance, tax, and insurance required by the leasing agreement in period t

EP = the estimated payment at the end of the lease to bring the asset up to a pre-established value in a net-net lease

t_c = the firm's marginal tax rate on ordinary income

n = the term of the lease contract

ITC = the relevant investment tax credit rate if passed on by the lessor for the asset under evaluation

FMV = the fair market value at the time of signing the lease of the asset under evaluation

K_d = the firm's after-tax borrowing rate

K = the after-tax discount rate appropriate for the risk class of the asset under evaluation; K will equal the firm's weighted average after-tax cost of capital as long as the asset under evaluation is of similar risk posture to the firm overall

The terms on the right hand side of Equation (1) are arranged to be consistent with the verbal description of our recommended approach provided above. The first term determines the present value of all after-tax lease payments, using the firm's after-tax borrowing rate as the discount rate. The second term finds the present value of the after-tax maintenance, tax, and insurance payments over the term of the lease, using a risk-adjusted discount rate appropriate for the risk class of the asset under evaluation. The third term shows the present value of the single payment (on an after-tax basis) at the end of the lease (if required) to bring the asset up to a pre-established value. Since this is a financial cash flow, it is discounted at the firm's after-tax borrowing rate. Finally, the present value of the ITC (if applicable) passed on by the lessor to the lessee is determined by discounting it back one period at the firm's after-tax borrowing rate, since this financial cash flow is assumed to take place at the end of the first year of the lease.

Equation (1) is contained in the financing evaluation module. For the investment and financing evaluation module, this formula requires a minor modification in order to incorporate the revenue and operating expenses for raw materials, labor, overhead, and so on, as well as the computation of the net present value rather than just the present value of the costs associated with the lease. Equation (2) shows the required computation:

$$NPV(L) = \sum_{t=0}^{n} \frac{[R_t - O_t - M_t][1 - t_c]}{(1 + K)^t} + \frac{(ITC)(FMV)}{(1 + K_d)^1} - \sum_{t=0}^{n} \frac{LP_t(1 - t_c)}{(1 + k_d)^t} - \frac{EP(1 - t_c)}{(1 + k_d)^n} \quad (2)$$

where $NPV(L)$ = the net present value associated with leasing the asset
R_t = the revenue generated by the asset in period t
O_t = the operating expenses for raw materials, direct labor, and overhead of the asset in period t

The first term shows the net after-tax benefits of operating the asset, discounted at the risk-adjusted rate K, to which is added the discounted ITC benefit and from which is subtracted the present value of the after-tax lease payments and the present value of any terminal payment required in a net-net lease.

The following example will illustrate the use of Equation (1). Equation (2) will be illustrated in Example 2.

EXAMPLE 1

Comparison of Two Leasing Options

A firm with a 40 percent marginal tax rate, a before-tax borrowing rate of 10 percent, and a required after-tax rate of return of 14 percent is evaluat-

Table 8-1. Present value of after-tax financing and operating cash flows associated with Lease #1.

	Lease Payments			Final Payment				
End of Year	Before Tax (1)	Tax Shield (40%) × (1) (2)	After-Tax Cash Flow (1) − (2) (3)	Before Tax (4)	Tax Shield (40%) × (4) (5)	After-Tax Cash Flow (4) − (5) (6)	Total After-Tax Financial Cash Flows (3) + (6) (7)	After-Tax Borrowing Rate Discount Factors, 6% (8)
1	$64,700	$25,880	$38,820				$38,820	.943396
2	64,700	25,880	38,820				38,820	.889996
3	64,700	25,880	38,820				38,820	.839619
4	64,700	25,880	38,820				38,820	.792094
5	64,700	25,880	38,820	$3,800	$1,520	$2,280	41,100	.747258

		Maintenance, Insurance, etc.					
End of Year	Present Value of After-Tax Financial Cash Flows (9)	Before Tax (10)	Tax Shield (40%) × (10) (11)	After-Tax Cash Flow (10) − (11) (12)	Discount Factors for After-Tax Risk-Adjusted Rate, 14% (13)	Present Value of After-Tax Operating Cash Flows (12) × (13) (14)	Present Value of All After-Tax Cash Flows (9) + (14) (15)
1	$36,623	$4,600	$1,840	$2,760	.877193	$2,421	$39,044
2	34,550	4,600	1,840	2,760	.759468	2,124	36,674
3	32,594	4,600	1,840	2,760	.674972	1,863	34,457
4	30,749	4,600	1,840	2,760	.592080	1,634	32,383
5	30,712	4,600	1,840	2,760	.519369	1,433	32,145
	$165,228						

Present value of after-tax financial and operating cash outflows: $174,703

ing various financing plans for an asset which is required for one of its major product lines.

The firm feels that its required rate of return is an appropriate risk-adjusted discount rate for this asset. The purchase price of the asset is $250,000, which is the current fair market value of the asset; cost to deliver and install the asset is $16,400; useful life of the asset is five years; and estimated salvage value is $20,000. The firm is considering two leasing plans:

1. A five-year net-net lease wherein annual lease payments paid in arrears amounting to $64,700 would be required. Annual maintenance, tax, and insurance would be $4,600; the ITC would be retained by the lessor; and there would be an estimated payment at the end of the five years of $3,800 to bring the asset up to the value desired by the lessor.

2. A five-year net lease wherein *quarterly* payments in advance of $16,330 would be required, as well as a prepayment of two payments. The ITC would be passed along to the lessee; the annual maintenance, tax, and insurance payment would be $4,600.

Determine the present value of the costs associated with each lease, using the approach outlined above. It can be assumed that the lease is written to cover both the purchase price of the asset and the cost to deliver and install it. The payment for maintenance, tax, and insurance is made at the end of each year, and the benefit for the ITC will be received at the end of the first year.

SOLUTION

The present value calculation for Lease #1 is shown in Table 8-1. As can be seen from the table, the present value of all cash flows associated with Lease #1 is $174,703. It should be pointed out again that the discount factors shown in column 8 are for the firm's after-tax borrowing rate of 6 percent, arrived at by subtracting the tax shield associated with interest from the 10 percent before-tax borrowing rate (that is, 10% − (40%)(10%) = 6%). All financial flows associated with Lease #1 are discounted at 6 percent. Notice also that the discount factors shown in column 13 are for the 14 percent after-tax risk-adjusted discount rate which the firm feels is appropriate for the risk class of the asset under evaluation. All operating cash flows associated with Lease #1 are discounted using this risk-adjusted rate.

We now turn to Lease #2 (see Table 8-2). Notice that this lease requires quarterly payments. This necessitates that we determine discount factors for 1.5 percent per quarter* (the after-tax annual borrowing

---

* The 1.5-percent-per-quarter figure is actually an approximation for the fourth root of the 6 percent annual rate (1.47 percent).

Table 8-2. Present value of after-tax financing and

End of Quarter	Lease Payments Before Tax (1)	Tax Shield (40%) × (1) (2)	After-Tax Cash Flow (1) − (2) (3)	Investment Tax Credit (.0667) ($250K) (4)	Total After-Tax Financial Cash Flows (3) + (4) (5)
Present*	$48,990	$19,595	$29,395		$29,395
1	16,330	6,532	9,798		9,798
2	16,330	6,532	9,798		9,798
3	16,330	6,532	9,798		9,798
4	16,330	6,532	9,798	($16,675)	(6,877)
5	16,330	6,532	9,798		9,798
6	16,330	6,532	9,798		9,798
7	16,330	6,532	9,798		9,798
8	16,330	6,532	9,798		9,798
9	16,330	6,532	9,798		9,798
10	16,330	6,532	9,798		9,798
11	16,330	6,532	9,798		9,798
12	16,330	6,532	9,798		9,798
13	16,330	6,532	9,798		9,798
14	16,330	6,532	9,798		9,798
15	16,330	6,532	9,798		9,798
16	16,330	6,532	9,798		9,798
17	16,330	6,532	9,798		9,798
18	—	—	—		—
19	—	—	—		—
20	—	—	—		—

* The amount shown here represents the first payment in advance, plus the required prepayment of two payments. Notice also that payments only continue until the end of Quarter 17, which completes the 20 payments.

rate of 6 percent divided by four, the number of payments per year, equals 1.5 percent) for 20 periods (five years times four payments per year). These factors can be found by the usual equation (shown in Chapter 3):

$$\text{DF for } 1.5\% \text{ in period } n = \frac{1}{(1.015)^n}$$

These factors are shown in Table 8-2, column 6. Since Lease #2 has the lower present value, it is the *least* costly. The cost savings has a present value equaling the difference between the present values of the two leases, $5,478.

Of equal importance to the comparison of the two lease alternatives is a more complete analysis of why Lease #2 has a lower present value of operating cash flows associated with Lease #2.

End of Quarter	Discount Factors for 6% Annual Rate (6)	PV of After-Tax Financial Cash Flows (5) × (6) (7)	PV of After-Tax Operating Cash Flows† (8)	PV of All After-Tax Cash Flows (7) + (8) (9)
Present*	1.000000	$29,395		$ 29,395
1	.985222	9,653		9,653
2	.970662	9,511		9,511
3	.956317	9,370		9,370
4	.942184	(6,479)	$2,421	(4,058)
5	.928260	9,095		9,095
6	.914542	8,961		8,961
7	.901027	8,828		8,828
8	.887711	8,698	2,124	10,822
9	.874592	8,569		8,569
10	.861667	8,443		8,443
11	.848933	8,318		8,318
12	.836387	8,195	1,863	10,058
13	.824027	8,074		8,074
14	.811849	7,954		7,954
15	.799852	7,837		7,837
16	.788031	7,721	1,634	9,355
17	.776385	7,607		7,607
18	—	—		—
19	—	—		—
20	—	—	1,433	1,433

Present value of after-tax financial and operating cash flows: $169,225

† These values are taken directly from Table 8-1 (column 14) since the present value of the maintenance, tax, and insurance payments are the same under both leases.

cash outflows. Such a summary is provided in the following table:

	PV of Lease Payments	PV of Maintenance, Insurance, Tax Payments	PV of Payment at End of Lease	PV of ITC	Total PV
Lease #1	$163,525	$9,475	$1,703	—	$174,703
Lease #2	175,461	9,475	—	($15,711)	169,225
Difference* (2 − 1)	$ 11,936 U	—	1,703 F	$15,711 F	$ 5,478 F

* F = Favorable difference of Lease #2 over Lease #1.
U = Unfavorable difference of Lease #2 over Lease #1.

Notice that the present value of Lease #2 payments exceeds that of Lease #1 payments by almost $12,000. The maintenance, insurance, and tax payments have equal present values under the two leases. Lease #1 has a disadvantage to the tune of $1,703 due to the final payment required. Finally, *the PV of the ITC which is passed on to the lessee in Lease #2 is $15,711, which is the only reason why Lease #2 has a present value saving of $5,478 compared to Lease #1*. A table such as this should prove helpful in the lessee's attempts to locate other leasing alternatives and in renegotiating the terms of a current lease options.

In addition, firms concerned about possible cash flow problems should find the following summary table of assistance in comparing the impact of the two lease alternatives on their cash budget:

	Before-Tax Security Deposit	Cumulative Before-Tax Cash Outflow over 1st Year	Before-Tax Annual Lease Payments Years 2, 3, 4
Lease #1	—	$64,700	$64,700
Lease #2	$32,660	81,650*	65,320
Difference† (2 − 1)	$32,660 U	$16,950 U	$ 620 U

* Exclusive of security deposit.
† U = Unfavorable difference of Lease #2 over Lease #1.

Notice that during the first year of the lease, Lease #2 requires cash outflows before tax benefits of $49,610 more than Lease #1, due to Lease #2's requirement for a security deposit and payments in advance rather than in arrears as for Lease #1. In fact, before Lease #1's first payment must be made, Lease #2 has required cash outflows of $81,650. The before-tax cash flows are relevant in preparing the cash budget because of the time lag involved in receiving the tax benefits. For example, for Lease #2 (and any lease requiring payments in advance) there could be a time delay of as much as 15 to 18 months in receiving the benefits from the tax shield or the ITC if the lease became effective at the beginning of the firm's fiscal year. The impact of the timing of cash flows and tax benefits could be of significant importance to firms. □

Example 1 illustrated the analysis of two competing leases as it would be carried out in the *financing evaluation module*. Closely related to the above analysis is that which takes place in the *investment and financing evaluation module*. In this module, the net present value of each lease alternative is determined. Two new input variables are required in order to compute the net present value: (1) the revenue generated by the asset in each period of the lease, and (2) the operating expenses of the asset, including raw materials, direct labor, variable overhead, and fixed overhead in each period of the lease. Since both of these cash flows are operating cash flows, the net difference between the two (after-tax) is discounted at the after-tax risk-adjusted discount rate that is appropriate for the risk class of the asset. Thus, in order to determine the net present value of each lease alternative (as will be illustrated in tabular form presently), we must find:

1. The present value of the after-tax net cash flow of the asset. This is determined for each period by subtracting the operating costs (for raw materials, direct labor, and overhead, as well as the operating expenses for maintenance, insurance, and property taxes) from the revenues generated by the asset, subtracting income tax expense, and then discounting at the asset's risk-adjusted discount rate; plus

2. The present value of the investment tax credit, if it is passed on by the lessor to the lessee; minus

3. The present value of the after-tax lease payments over the term of the lease contract; minus

4. The present value on an after-tax basis of the single payment (if required) at the end of the lease to bring the asset up to a pre-established value.

It should be mentioned that each of the last three cash flows (that is, 2, 3, and 4 above) should be discounted at the firm's after-tax borrowing rate, since they represent financial cash flows, as opposed to the operating cash flows described in 1, which are discounted at the appropriate risk-adjusted discount rate for this asset's risk class. Example 2 shows the development of the tabular approach to compute the net present value of the lease.

EXAMPLE 2
Net Present Value Determination for Two Leasing Options

For each of the two leases described in Example 1, find the net present value using the approach just outlined (which is also shown in Equation 2). The asset will generate additional revenue of $190,000, $205,000, $325,000, $350,000, and $480,000 over its five-year life. In addition, direct material, direct labor, and variable overhead are expected to be 55 percent of revenue each year, and fixed expenses are expected to be $40,000 in year 1 and increase by 10 percent each year thereafter. Determine the NPV of each lease.

SOLUTION

In order to determine the NPV of each lease, we use a tabular approach based on the methodology outlined above. The calculation for Lease #1 is shown in Table 8-3. We see that the net present value of Lease #1 is negative. This means that over the term of the lease, the present value of its financial cash outflows exceeds the present value of its net cash inflows from operations by $2,754.

The calculations for Lease #2 are shown in Table 8-4. We see that the net present value of Lease #2 is positive. This means that the present value of its net cash inflows resulting from the operations related to the asset exceeds the present value of the financial flows of Lease #2. *Thus, even though the asset was unattractive if financed through Lease #1 (since it*

Table 8-3. Net present value of Lease #1.

End of Year	*Before-Tax Flows*				
	Revenue (1)	Variable Expenses (2)	Fixed Expenses (3)	Maintenance, Insurance, Tax Expenses (4)	Tax Expense $40\%[(1) - (2) - (3) - (4)]$ (5)
1	$190,000	$104,500	$40,000	$4,600	$16,360
2	205,000	112,750	44,000	4,600	17,460
3	325,000	178,750	48,400	4,600	37,300
4	350,000	192,500	53,240	4,600	39,864
5	480,000	264,000	58,564	4,600	61,134

End of Year	Discount Factors for After-Tax Risk Adjusted Rate, 14% (6)	PV of Operating Net Cash Inflow $[(1) - (2) - (3) - (4) - (5)] \times (6)$ (7)	PV of After-Tax Financial Flows* (8)	Excess of PV of Net Operating Cash Inflows over Financial Cash Outflows (7) − (8) (9)
1	.877193	$ 21,526	$36,623	($15,097)
2	.769468	20,152	34,550	(14,398)
3	.674972	37,765	32,594	5,171
4	.592080	35,404	30,749	4,655
5	.519369	47,627	30,712	16,915

NPV (Lease #1) = ($2,754)

* This column is taken directly from the tabular analysis of Example 1 for Lease #1 (see Table 8-1, column 9).

Table 8-4. Net present value of Lease #2.

End of Quarter	PV of Net Cash Inflows from Operations* (1)	PV of After-Tax Financial Cash Flows† (2)	Excess of PV of Net Operating Cash Inflows over PV of After-Tax Financial Cash Flows (1) − (2) (3)
Present		$29,395	($29,395)
1		9,653	(9,653)
2		9,511	(9,511)
3		9,370	(9,370)
4	$21,526	(6,479)	28,005
5		9,095	(9,095)
6		8,961	(8,961)
7		8,828	(8,828)
8	20,152	8,698	11,454
9		8,569	(8,569)
10		8,443	(8,443)
11		8,318	(8,318)
12	37,765	8,195	29,570
13		8,074	(8,074)
14		7,954	(7,954)
15		7,837	(7,837)
16	35,404	7,721	27,683
17		7,607	(7,607)
18		—	—
19		—	—
20	47,627	—	$47,627

NPV (Lease #2) = $2,724

* This column was taken directly from the preceding tabular analysis for Lease #1 (see Table 8-3, column 7).
† This column was taken directly from the tabular analysis in Example 1 for Lease #2 (see Table 8-2, column 7).

had a negative NPV of $2,754), it is attractive if financed using Lease #2 (since the latter lease has a positive NPV of $2,724). Notice also that Lease #2 is more attractive than Lease #1 by the same margin in present value terms as in Example 1; namely, Lease #1 had a negative NPV here of $2,754 and Lease #2 had a positive NPV of $2,724, making Lease #2 more attractive to the tune of $5,478 ($2,754 + $2,724) in present value terms. This agrees with the difference in favor of Lease #2 shown in Example 1.

Finally, it should be pointed out that in evaluating this asset, we have followed the convention of assuming that the asset's operating cash flows occurred at the end of the year rather than uniformly over the year. The asset becomes much more attractive in NPV terms if we assume that the operating cash flows occur quarterly, consistent with the lease payment, as shown in Table 8-5.

We see from Table 8-5 that the NPV of Lease #2 is now $7,660. This is almost a $5,000 increase over the NPV for Lease #2 under the assumption that operating cash flows did not occur until the end of each year. The

Table 8-5. Net present value of Lease #2, assuming quarterly operating cash flows.

End of Quarter	After-Tax Net Cash Inflow from Operations* (1)	Quarterly Discount Factors for Annual Rate of 6% (2)	PV of After-Tax Net Cash Inflows from Operations (1) × (2) (3)	PV of After-Tax Financial Flows† (4)	Excess of PV of Operating Cash Inflows over PV of After-Tax Financial Flows (3) − (4) (5)
Present	—	1.000000	—	$29,395	($29,395)
1	$ 6,135	.966184	$ 5,928	9,653	(3,725)
2	6,135	.933511	5,727	9,511	(3,784)
3	6,135	.901943	5,533	9,370	(3,837)
4	6,135	.871442	5,346	(6,479)	11,825
5	6,548	.841973	5,513	9,095	(3,582)
6	6,548	.813501	5,327	8,961	(3,634)
7	6,548	.785991	5,147	8,828	(3,681)
8	6,548	.759412	4,973	8,698	(3,725)
9	13,988	.733731	10,263	8,569	1,694
10	13,988	.708919	9,916	8,443	1,473
11	13,988	.684946	9,581	8,318	1,263
12	13,988	.661783	9,257	8,195	1,062
13	14,949	.639404	9,558	8,074	1,484
14	14,949	.617782	9,235	7,954	1,281
15	14,949	.596891	8,923	7,837	1,086
16	14,949	.576706	8,621	7,721	900
17	22,925	.557204	12,774	7,607	5,167
18	22,925	.538361	12,342	—	12,342
19	22,925	.520156	11,925	—	11,925
20	22,925	.502566	11,521	—	11,521

NPV (Lease #2) = $7,660

* The values in this column are computed by taking one-quarter of the annual after-tax net cash inflow computed in Table 8-3 for Lease #1 in Example 2.
† This column is taken directly from the tabular analysis in Example 1 for Lease #2 (see Table 8-2, column 7).

above analysis is more accurate if, in fact, cash flows take place on a quarterly basis rather than at the end of each year. Of course, if we assume quarterly rather than yearly cash flows, Lease #1 will also become more attractive than it was originally. However, Lease #2 will continue to outperform Lease #1 by the present value amount of $5,478 found in our previous analysis in both Examples 1 and 2. □

Recommended Analysis for the Purchase Alternative

As mentioned earlier, we want to discuss both the option of purchasing the asset using the firm's general pool of funds for capital investments and the option of borrowing funds specifically to purchase the asset under evaluation. As was also mentioned, we will only briefly expand on the previous coverage given the first of these two options. Our elaboration will take on the form of the tabular approach similar to that recommended to evaluate the leasing alternative.

As with the lease option, the majority of the relevant "purchase flows" and the corresponding appropriate risk-adjusted discount rates become obvious with a careful examination of the facts. In the *financing evaluation module,* we must determine the present value of (1) all cash flows related to the financing of the asset and (2) the tax shields related to owning the asset. In this module, as was seen in the lease analysis carried out in the preceding section, it is unnecessary to consider the benefits related to the operation of the asset, since the asset's attractiveness or necessity has already been established. Thus, we must find:

1. The present value of the cash outflow required to purchase the asset; less
2. The present value of the investment tax credit associated with the asset; less
3. The present value of the tax shield associated with the depreciation deduction for tax purposes, as well as the interest deduction if the firm entered into a loan agreement specifically to purchase this asset; plus
4. The present value of the after-tax payments for maintenance, property taxes, insurance, and so on, related to ownership of the asset; less
5. The present value of the after-tax cash flow associated with the salvage value of the asset at the end of its useful life.

In computing the present values, in order to be consistent with our analysis of leasing alternatives, the cash flows related to the asset's operations (that is, the depreciation tax shield in 3, as well as the flows described in 4 and 5) should be discounted at the risk-adjusted discount rate that is appropriate for the asset under evaluation*; the ITC (number 2 above) should be discounted at the firm's after-tax borrowing rate; the cash outflows to purchase the asset for cash should be discounted at the firm's weighted average after-tax cost of capital; and the cash outflows less the tax shield associated with interest (when the asset is purchased via a loan) should be discounted at the firm's after-tax cost of borrowing.

These discount rates deserve further comment. The ITC for the purchase alternative should be discounted back one period at the same discount rate as used in evaluating the lease option (hence the recommended use of the firm's after-tax borrowing rate). In a similar way, all cash flows related to the asset's operations require the use of the proper risk-adjusted discount rate to compensate for the risk present in this asset's risk class. Finally, financing cash flows and their related tax shields should be discounted at the rate that corresponds to the after-tax cost of funds utilized. That is, when the asset is purchased for cash from the firm's general pool of funds for capital expenditures, the firm's weighted average after-tax cost of capital is appropriate; on the other hand, when the asset is purchased through a loan, the loan outflows, less tax shields for interest, should be discounted at the firm's after-tax borrowing rate for the loan.

The recommended approach is illustrated in Example 3.

Consistent with our development of the lease analysis, we also want to summarize the recommended approach for the purchase option in equation form. As mentioned earlier, Equation (3) can be skipped by any reader who is more at ease with the tabular approach. Such readers can proceed immediately to Example 3.

Equation (3) again follows the verbal description of the analysis presented above.

$$PV(P) = \sum_{t=0}^{T} \frac{PO_t - t_c I_t}{(1 + K_d)^t} - \frac{(ITC)C}{(1 + K_d)^1}$$
$$+ \sum_{t=0}^{n} \frac{Q_t(1 - t_c)}{(1 + K)^t} - \sum_{t=1}^{n} \frac{t_c(D_t)}{(1 + K)^t} - \frac{SV}{(1 + K)^n} \quad (3)$$

* Some authors argue that the salvage value (that is, cash flow 5) should be discounted at an even higher risk-adjusted discount rate than that specified for the asset's risk class because of the uncertainty involved in estimating residual values. However, we reject this complication because of the already high risk penalty that is attached to the salvage value and because this problem is more efficiently and effectively handled using sensitivity analysis which is discussed in the next chapter.

where $PV(P)$ = the present value of the after-tax cash outflows associated with purchasing the asset
PO_t = the cash outflow associated with the purchase option which is required in period t
I_t = the dollar amount of interest paid in period t
T = the end of the period over which loan repayments must be made
C = the dollar cost of the asset which is relevant for computing the investment tax credit (ITC) at the appropriate rate
Q_t = the cash outflow for insurance, maintenance, taxes, etc., related to operating the asset when it is purchased
D_t = the tax-deductible depreciation expense in period t
SV = the after-tax proceeds from the salvage value of the asset at the end of its useful life, n

Equation (3) states that the present value of the after-tax cash flows associated with the purchase option (whether it is for cash or using a loan) is equal to the five terms on the right-hand side:

The first term includes either the entire cash payment in year 0 or the down payment in year 0 plus the loan repayments in years 1 through T less the tax shield on the interest portion of the loan payment; in the latter case, the after-tax outflow is discounted at the firm's after-tax borrowing rate.

The second term shows the present value of the investment tax credit associated with the asset; this financial flow is discounted at the firm's after-tax borrowing rate.

The next three terms are all operating cash flows, which are discounted at the appropriate risk-adjusted discount rate for this asset's risk class. The third term finds the present value of the after-tax cash outflows related to the asset's operations. The fourth term shows the present value of the tax shield associated with the depreciation on the asset which is deducted for tax purposes. The last term shows the present value of the after-tax proceeds from the asset's salvage value; the variable SV shows the proceeds from the sale of the asset, less any tax liability due to the sale, whether it be recapture of depreciation taxed at ordinary rates or a capital gain taxed at the special rates.

We now turn to the analysis of the purchase options using the tabular approach.

EXAMPLE 3
Evaluation of Purchase Alternatives

For the asset described in Examples 1 and 2, the firm also wants to evaluate the following two purchase alternatives:

1. Purchase for cash.
2. Take out a loan for 75 percent of the *purchase price* of the asset. The firm must pay, in cash, both a 25 percent down payment and the cost to deliver and install the asset. The loan yields the lender 10 percent on the outstanding principal and will be repaid in five equal end-of-the-year payments of $49,462.

The firm uses sum-of-the-years'-digits depreciation for tax purposes and will ignore the salvage value in computing tax depreciation (this will be allowed by the IRS, since it is less than 10 percent of the purchase price of the asset). The firm will incur $5,200 per year for maintenance, insurance, and taxes under either ownership plan.

Determine the present value of the costs associated with each of these alternatives, using a tabular approach.

SOLUTION

1. *Purchase for cash.* The present value calculation for this option is shown in Table 8-6.

2. *Purchase with a loan.* First, under the alternative of purchase with a loan, we must determine what portion of each year's $49,462 payment is interest and what amount is repayment of principal. The amount of the loan is the purchase price of the asset ($250,000) less 25 percent down payment ($62,500), or $187,500. The lender wanted to earn 10 percent on the outstanding principal; thus, the annual payments of $49,462 were determined by multiplying the face value of the loan by the factor from the 10 percent page in Appendix D, column 6 and the five-year line (that is, $187,500 × .26379748 = $49,462). In addition, Table 8-7 will derive the amount of each payment attributable to interest and principal.

Column 3 of Table 8-7 will be relevant in determining the tax shield and the present value for this alternative. Table 8-8 shows the analysis.

We have arrived at an important result. *The present value of the purchase-for-cash alternative equals the present value of the purchase-with-a-loan alternative.* This is because the present value of the tax shields from operating the asset is the same for the two alternatives, as are the present value of the ITC and the after-tax proceeds from salvage value; finally, since we find the present value of the after-tax loan payments by using the after-tax borrowing rate as the discount rate, we arrive at a present value of financial cash flows of $266,400, which is precisely the cash payment made under the purchase-for-cash alternative. The same result will occur for any loan that may be obtained, assuming that we always discount at the correct after-tax borrowing rate.

The results of this example again point to the importance of qualitative factors in evaluating the alternatives. That is, from a quantitative

LEASE-VERSUS-PURCHASE ANALYSIS

Table 8-6. Present value of the purchase-for-cash option.

End of Year	Cash Outflows to Purchase Asset (1)	PV of ITC at Firm's After-Tax Borrowing Rate of 6%* (2)	Operating Expenses Before-Tax Cash Outflow (3)	Tax Shield (.4) × (3) (4)	After-Tax Cash Outflow (3) − (4) (5)	Depreciation: Tax-Deductible Amount (6)
Present	$266,400					
1		$15,731	$5,200	$2,080	$3,120	$88,800
2			5,200	2,080	3,120	71,040
3			5,200	2,080	3,120	53,280
4			5,200	2,080	3,120	35,520
5			5,200	2,080	3,120	17,760
5	Salvage value† $20,000 − $8,000 = $12,000					

End of Year	Depreciation: Tax Shield (.4) × (6) (7)	Discount Factors for After-Tax Risk-Adjusted Rate, 14% (8)	PV of After-Tax Cash Outflow for Operating Expenses (5) × (8) (9)	PV of Depreciation Tax Shields (7) × (8) (10)	PV of After-Tax Operating and Financial Cash Flows (1) − (2) + (9) − (10) (11)
Present		1.000000			$266,400
1	$35,520	.877193	$2,737	$31,158	(44,152)
2	28,416	.769468	2,401	21,865	(19,464)
3	21,312	.674972	2,106	14,385	(12,279)
4	14,208	.592080	1,847	8,412	(6,565)
5	7,104	.519369	1,620	3,690	(2,070)
5		.519369	($6,232)		($6,232)

PV (Purchase for Cash) = $175,638

* The figure shown at the end of year 1 in this column is arrived at by multiplying ($250,000) (.0667)(1/1.06).

† The salvage value of the asset is $20,000. This amount has to be reduced by the tax impact of having a book value for tax purposes of zero (since the firm chose to ignore the salvage value in figuring depreciation for tax purposes), which means that there is a recovery of depreciation of $20,000 which is taxed as ordinary income at 40%, resulting in a tax liability of $8,000. The net cash inflow from disposing of the asset is $20,000 − $8,000 = $12,000 and its present value at 14% is $6,232.

Table 8-7. Computation of interest and principal portion of loan payments.

Year	Principal Amount Owed During Year (1)	Total Payment (2)	Interest Portion of Payment (10%) × (1) (3)	Reduction in Principal (2) − (3) (4)	Principal Amount Owed at End of Year (1) − (4) (5)*
1	$187,500.00	$49,462	$18,750.00	$30,712.00	$156,788.00
2	156,788.00	49,462	15,678.80	33,783.20	123,004.80
3	123,004.80	49,462	12,300.48	37,161.52	85,843.28
4	85,843.28	49,462	8,584.33	40,877.67	44,965.61
5	44,965.61	49,462	4,496.56	44,965.44	.17

* The amount from column 5 is transferred to column 1 for the following year.

standpoint, the two alternatives analyzed here produced equivalent present values; however, this is not to say that all firms should be indifferent in their choice between the two alternatives, because nonquantifiable factors may have an impact on the final decision. Examples would include: the preferences that different firms might have for the cash flow patterns of one alternative vs. the other; preferences that different firms might have for the impact that one alternative has on the firm's balance sheet presentation or future financing requirements; preferences that different firms might have for one alternative because of uncertainties about the future, specifically, about future inflation rates, future investment opportunities, and the like.

Comparing the results here with those obtained in Example 1, we notice that the purchase option has a higher present value of net cash outflows ($175,638) than either Lease #1 ($174,703) or Lease #2 ($169,225). However, these figures, rather than pointing to a clear-cut decision, provide the basis for performing sensitivity analysis and for renegotiating terms on existing financing alternatives or seeking out other financing arrangements before a final decision is made. □

We have now illustrated the recommended approach used in the financing evaluation module for the purchase options. As shown, the analysis is applicable to both purchase-for-cash and purchase-with-a loan options. Furthermore, the present value of the after-tax cash flows will be equivalent under any purchase option. At this point, we can summarize the financing evaluation module, which is done in Figure 8-2.

Next, we will demonstrate the recommended procedure in the investment and financing evaluation module. As with the lease option, the

Table 8-8. Present value of the purchase-with-a-loan option.

End of Year	Cash Outflows to Purchase Asset (1)	Interest Before-Tax Amount (2)	Tax Shield (.4) × (2) (3)	Net Financial Cash Outflows (1) − (3) (4)	Discount Factors for After-Tax Borrowing Rate of 6% (5)
Present	$78,900*			$78,900	1.000000
1	49,462	$18,750.00	$7,500	41,962	.943396
2	49,462	15,678.80	6,272	43,190	.889996
3	49,462	12,300.48	4,920	44,542	.839619
4	49,462	8,584.33	3,434	46,028	.792094
5	49,462	4,496.56	1,799	47,663	.747258
5	Salvage value** $20,000 − $8,000 = $12,000				

End of Year	PV of ITC at 6% (6)†	PV of Net Financial Cash Outflows (4) × (5) − (6) (7)	PV of After-Tax Cash Outflows for Operating Expenses (8)‡	PV of Depreciation Expense Tax Shields (9)§	PV of Operating and Financial Cash Flows (7) + (8) −(9) (10)
Present		$78,900			$78,900
1	$15,731	23,856	$2,737	$31,158	(4,565)
2		38,439	2,401	21,865	18,975
3		37,398	2,106	14,385	25,119
4		36,459	1,847	8,412	29,894
5		35,617	1,620	3,690	33,547
5			($6,232)		($6,232)

PV (Purchase with Loan) = $175,638

* This amount consists of the down payment of $62,500 and the installation expenditure of $16,400. The tax shelter associated with both of these amounts is included in the depreciation expense.
† See footnote for column 2 of Table 8-6.
‡ See column 9 of Table 8-6.
§ See column 10 of Table 8-6.
** See footnote concerning salvage value in Table 8-6.

Figure 8-2. Diagram of financing evaluation module.

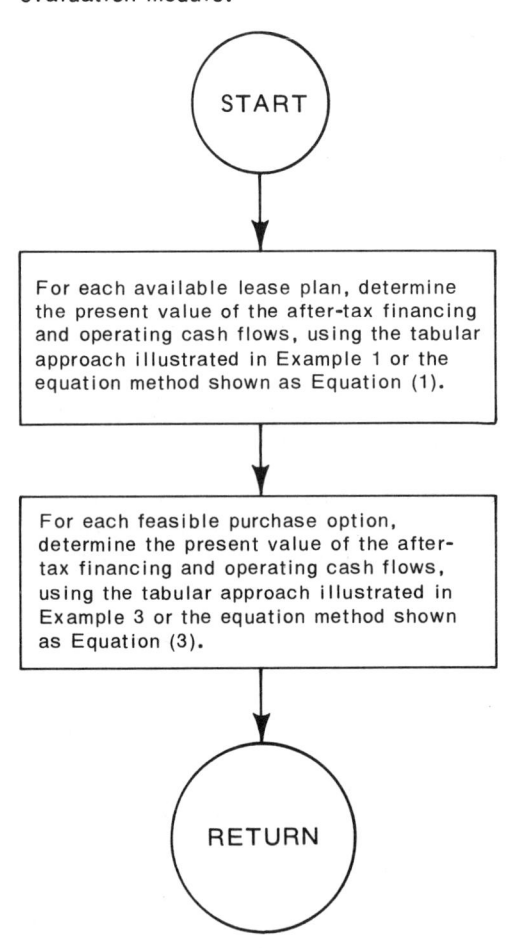

```
                    ┌─────────┐
                    │  START  │
                    └─────────┘
                         │
                         ▼
┌──────────────────────────────────────────────┐
│ For each available lease plan, determine     │
│ the present value of the after-tax financing │
│ and operating cash flows, using the tabular  │
│ approach illustrated in Example 1 or the     │
│ equation method shown as Equation (1).       │
└──────────────────────────────────────────────┘
                         │
                         ▼
┌──────────────────────────────────────────────┐
│ For each feasible purchase option,           │
│ determine the present value of the after-    │
│ tax financing and operating cash flows,      │
│ using the tabular approach illustrated in    │
│ Example 3 or the equation method shown       │
│ as Equation (3).                             │
└──────────────────────────────────────────────┘
                         │
                         ▼
                    ┌─────────┐
                    │ RETURN  │
                    └─────────┘
```

only modification to the analysis is that both the benefits and the costs associated with ownership must be taken into account so that the net present value of the asset can be determined. The parallel approach here will again show that we merely subtract the fixed and variable operating expenses from the revenue generated by the asset in each period, reduce this amount by the tax liability, and then discount to present value using the relevant risk-adjusted discount rate; from this amount is subtracted the present value of the after-tax operating and financial cash flows that were determined in the financing evaluation module. As usual, if the NPV is positive, then the asset is a candidate for purchase.

Example 4 will illustrate the methodology in a tabular framework. However, the equation form of the analysis will be presented first for those desiring this summary.

Equation (4) presents the analysis contained in the investment and financing evaluation module:

$$NPV(P) = \sum_{t=0}^{n} \frac{[R_t - O_t - Q_t][1 - t_c]}{(1 + K)^t} + \frac{(ITC)C}{(1 + K_d)^1}$$
$$- \sum_{t=0}^{T} \frac{PO_t - t_c I_t}{(1 + K_d)^t} + \sum_{t=1}^{n} \frac{t_c D_t}{(1 + K)^t} + \frac{SV}{(1 + K)^n} \quad (4)$$

where $NPV(P)$ = the net present value of the purchase option, and all the other symbols take on their previously defined values.

The first term merely finds the present value of the after-tax net cash benefits of the asset, using the risk-adjusted discount rate. The remaining four terms appeared in Equation (3) with opposite signs, since the present value of the financial operating cash flows are subtracted from the net cash benefits shown in the first term. We now illustrate the analysis for the investment and financing evaluation module.

EXAMPLE 4

NPV Determination for Two Purchase Options

For the same asset described in Examples 1, 2, and 3, determine the NPV for the two purchase options mentioned in Example 3.

SOLUTION

Even though we know in advance that the NPVs for the two purchase options will be equal, we will illustrate the tabular analysis for both so that the reader can prepare the one that may be more relevant for his purposes. Table 8-9 shows the calculation for the first option, purchase for cash; the analysis for the second option, purchase with a loan, is contained in Table 8-10.

As we knew a priori, the NPVs for the two alternatives are equal and are less than either the NPV of Lease #1 of −$2,754 or the NPV of Lease #2 of $2,724. Notice that those who argue that the assessment of an investment's attractiveness must be based on the purchase alternative would have rejected this project, although clearly it has a positive NPV if financed by using Lease #2. Again, we would want to perform a sensitiv-

Table 8-9. Net present value of the purchase-for-cash option.

End of Year	Revenue (1)	Variable Expenses (2)	Fixed Expenses (3)	Insurance, Tax, and Maintenance (4)	After-Tax Cash Flow .6[(1) − (2) − (3) − (4)] (5)	Discount Factors for Risk-Adjusted Rate at 14% (6)
Present						
1	$190,000	$104,500	$40,000	$5,200	$24,180	.877193
2	205,000	112,750	44,000	5,200	25,830	.769468
3	325,000	178,750	48,400	5,200	55,590	.674972
4	350,000	192,500	53,240	5,200	59,436	.592080
5	480,000	264,000	58,564	5,200	91,342	.519369

Operating Benefits and Expenses

End of Year	Present Value of After-Tax Operating Cash Flows (5) × (6) (7)	Present Value of Depreciation Tax Shields (8)*	Cash Outflows to Purchase Asset (9)	PV of ITC at Firm's After-Tax Borrowing Rate of 6% (10)‡	NPV of Financial and Operating Cash Flows (7) + (8) − (9) + (10) (11)
Present			$266,400		($266,400)
1	$21,211	$31,158		$15,731	68,100
2	19,875	21,865			41,740
3	37,522	14,385			51,907
4	35,191	8,412			43,603
5	47,440	3,690			51,130
5	Salvage Value† = ($20,000 − 8,000)(.519369)				6,232

NPV (Purchase for Cash) = ($3,688)

* The figures in this column are taken from column 10 of Table 8-6.
† See the footnote for salvage value in Table 8-6.
‡ See the footnote for column 2 in Table 8-6.

ity analysis and explore renegotiation possibilities before making a final decision. □

This example completes our illustration of the analysis used in the investment and financing evaluation module. Figure 8-3 summarizes the procedure followed in the investment and financing evaluation module.

This rather extensive chapter has given in-depth treatment to lease-versus-purchase analysis. We proceeded through verbal, mathematical, tabular, and flowchart approaches to the recommended evaluation techniques. A powerful, yet flexible approach was illustrated *for analyzing financing alternatives* (lease vs. lease, lease vs. purchase for cash, and lease vs. purchase with a loan) when the project has received prior approval. In addition, the methodology was provided for a *simultaneous consideration of the investment's attractiveness and the best method of financing*. We now are ready for the next vitally important step, sensitivity analysis, which should be performed before the final decision is made. This is the topic of the next chapter.

Table 8-10. Net present value of the purchase-with-a-loan option.

End of Year	Revenue (1)	Variable Expenses (2)	Fixed Expenses (3)	Insurance Tax, and Maintenance (4)	After-Tax Cash Flow .6[(1) − (2) − (3) − (4)] (5)	Discount Factors for Risk-Adjusted Rate at 14% (6)	Present Value of After-Tax Operating Cash Flows (5) × (6) (7)
Present							
1	$190,000	$104,500	$40,000	$5,200	$24,180	.877193	$21,211
2	205,000	112,750	44,000	5,200	25,830	.769468	19,875
3	325,000	178,750	48,400	5,200	55,590	.674972	37,522
4	350,000	192,500	53,240	5,200	59,436	.592080	35,191
5	480,000	264,000	58,564	5,200	91,382	.519369	47,440

End of Year	Present Value of Depreciation Tax Shields (8)*	Net Financial Cash Flows (9)†	Discount Factors for After-Tax Financial Borrowing Rate of 6% (10)	Present Value of Net Financial Cash Flows (9) × (10) (11)	Present Value of ITC at 6% (12)‡	NPV of Financial and Operating Cash Flows (7) + (8) − (11) + (12) (13)
Present		$78,900	1.000000	$78,900		($78,900)
1	$31,158	41,962	.943396	39,587	$15,731	28,513
2	21,865	43,190	.889996	38,439		3,301
3	14,385	44,542	.839619	37,398		14,509
4	8,412	46,028	.792094	36,459		7,144
5	3,690	47,663	.747258	35,617		15,513
5		Salvage Value§ = ($20,000 − 8,000)(.519369)				6,232

NPV (Purchase with Loan) = ($3,688)

* The figures in this column are taken from column 10 of Table 8-6.
† The figures in this column are taken from column 4 of Table 8-8.
‡ See the footnote for column 2 of Table 8-6.
§ See the footnote for salvage value in Table 8-6.

Figure 8-3. Diagram of the investment financing evaluation module.

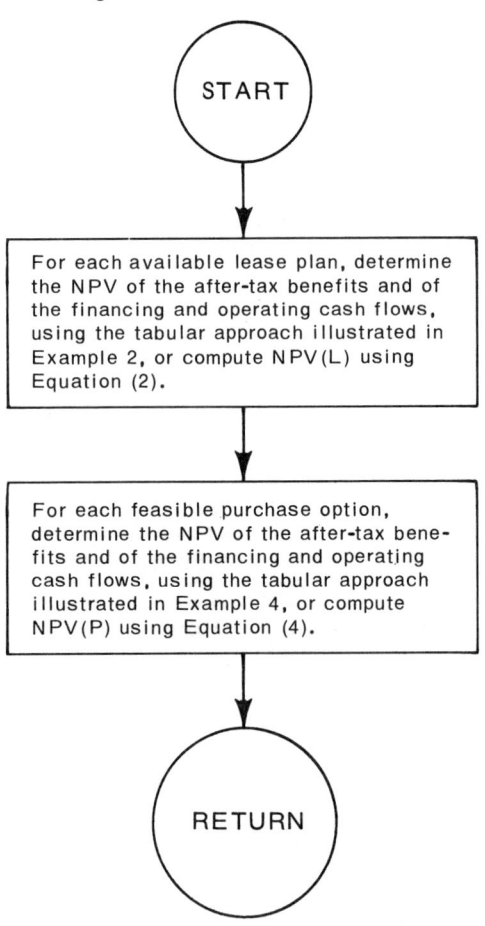

```
                    ┌─────────┐
                    │  START  │
                    └────┬────┘
                         ▼
    ┌──────────────────────────────────────────┐
    │ For each available lease plan, determine │
    │ the NPV of the after-tax benefits and of │
    │ the financing and operating cash flows,  │
    │ using the tabular approach illustrated in│
    │ Example 2, or compute NPV(L) using       │
    │ Equation (2).                            │
    └──────────────────┬───────────────────────┘
                       ▼
    ┌──────────────────────────────────────────┐
    │ For each feasible purchase option,       │
    │ determine the NPV of the after-tax bene- │
    │ fits and of the financing and operating  │
    │ cash flows, using the tabular approach   │
    │ illustrated in Example 4, or compute     │
    │ NPV(P) using Equation (4).               │
    └──────────────────┬───────────────────────┘
                       ▼
                    ┌─────────┐
                    │ RETURN  │
                    └─────────┘
```

NOTES

1. M. H. Miller and C. W. Upton, "Leasing, Buying, and the Cost of Capital Services," *Journal of Finance,* June 1976, pp. 761–786; and W. G. Lewellen, M. S. Long, and J. J. McConnell, "Asset Leasing in Competitive Markets," *Journal of Finance,* June 1976, pp. 787–798.
2. R. W. Johnson and W. G. Lewellen, "Analysis of the Lease or Buy Decision," *Journal of Finance,* September 1972, pp. 815–823.

3. G. B. Mitchell, "After-Tax Cost of Leasing," *The Accounting Review*, April 1970, pp. 308–314.
4. R. S. Bower, "Issues in Lease Financing," *Financial Management*, Winter 1975, pp. 25–34.
5. L. J. Kasper, "Evaluating the Cost of Financial Leases," *Management Accounting*, May 1977, pp. 43–51.
6. P. F. Anderson and J. D. Martin, "Lease vs. Purchase Decisions: A Survey of Current Practice," *Financial Management*, Spring 1977, pp. 41–47.
7. See E. F. Brigham, "Hurdle Rates for Screening Capital Expenditure Proposals," *Financial Management*, Autumn 1975, pp. 17–26; T. Klammer, "Empirical Evidence of the Adoption of Sophisticated Capital Budgeting Techniques," *Journal of Business*, July 1972, pp. 387–397; G. H. Petry, "Effective Use of Capital Budgeting Tools," *Business Horizons*, October 1975, pp. 57–65; J. W. Petty, D. F. Scott, Jr., M. M. Bird, "The Capital Budgeting Decision Making Process of Large Corporations," *The Engineering Economist*, Spring 1975, pp. 159–171.
8. See C. R. Carlson and D. H. Wort, "A New Look at the Lease vs. Purchase Decision," *Journal of Economics and Business*, Spring 1974, pp. 199–202; K. Cooper and R. H. Strawser, "Evaluation of Capital Investment Projects Involving Asset Leases," *Financial Management*, Spring 1975, pp. 44–49; R. W. Johnson and W. G. Lewellen, "Analysis of the Lease-or-Buy Decision," *Journal of Finance*, September 1972, pp. 815–823.
9. R. W. Johnson and W. G. Lewellen, "Reply," *Journal of Finance*, September 1973, p. 1025.
10. I. W. Sorensen and R. E. Johnson, "Equipment Financial Leasing Practices and Costs: An Empirical Study," *Financial Management*, Spring 1977, pp. 33–40.
11. Ibid., p. 34.
12. See R. C. Moyer, "Lease Evaluation and the Investment Tax Credit: A Framework for Analysis," *Financial Management*, Summer 1975, pp. 39–42.

CHAPTER 9

Sensitivity Analysis

In Chapter 8 we provided a detailed exposition of an appropriate analysis of the lease-versus-purchase decision setting. As part of the recommended approach, we identified three modules wherein decision analysis is carried out: the financing evaluation module, the investment and financing evaluation module, and the sensitivity analysis module. The first of these modules commences under the premise that the project under consideration has received prior approval for acceptance or that the project is mandatory if the firm is to continue its operations. The second module, on the other hand, simultaneously ascertains whether the project is an attractive investment for the firm and, if so, what is the preferred method of financing the project's acquisition. The sensitivity analysis module considers:

- Qualitative aspects of the decision setting.
- Quantitative aspects that were too complex to incorporate directly into the former two modules.
- The extent to which conditions would have to change to result in a different preferred alternative.

Chapter 8 examined the first two modules in depth. It remains the task of this chapter to explore the important area of sensitivity analysis.

Qualitative Factors in Lease-versus-Purchase Analysis

Every decision setting is surrounded by both quantifiable and nonquantifiable attributes that require consideration and evaluation in arriving at a final decision. Any model or approach that is called upon to assist in the evaluation of alternatives necessarily must be selective in deciding which aspects of the decision setting can and should be incorporated into the analysis. In general, the strategy is to build in the most critical dimensions which can be accurately estimated or quantified. Hence, many intangible or qualitative factors are not directly incorporated in the analysis. However, such factors can be of significant importance to the firm in either the short or long run. Thus, we recommend that a careful and detailed analysis be performed by the firm concerning the qualitative dimensions of the lease–purchase decision.

The first seven chapters pointed to numerous qualitative considerations that could be relevant to a given firm in a given lease–purchase problem setting and thus should be carefully evaluated. In addition, the following aspects deserve consideration:

1. How will the lease be treated for financial reporting purposes under FASB 13? Does the lease qualify as an *operating lease* and, hence, circumvent "on-balance sheet" treatment? Or does the lease meet one of the four criteria that necessitate classifying it as a *capital lease,* which requires recognition of both an asset and its associated liability on the balance sheet?

There are many complexities involved in answering the above questions, due to the widely varying conditions which can be incorporated into a lease contract and which may also be revised at some later date. Such complexities are evidenced by the fact that the Financial Accounting Standards Board has found it necessary to twice amend FASB 13 within 18 months of its date of issuance with FASB 17 and 22,[1] as well as to issue three interpretations of how to apply FASB 13.[2]

To assist the firm in answering the above questions, Figure 9-1 presents a flowchart designed by Professor William A. Collins,[3] which shows a process to be followed by both lessors and lessees to arrive at an initial classification (Phase 1) and any revisions when modifications are made to existing capital leases, sales-type, or direct financing leases (Phase 2).

2. What are the special tax considerations which must be taken into account in making the lease-purchase decision? The usual tax impacts in capital investment decisions have been discussed in Chapter 3 and were incorporated into the quantitative analysis of the lease and purchase alternatives in Chapter 8. However, the far-reaching nature of tax implications necessitates further discussion and analysis. Thus, we have included an in-depth treatment of tax aspects in Chapter 10.

3. What impact will the financing decision (lease versus borrow-and-buy versus purchase for cash) have on the firm's degree of financial leverage? What impact will the financing decision have on the firm's coverage

THE LEASE / BUY DECISION

Figure 9-1(a). Flowchart for determining initial classifications of leases by lessor.

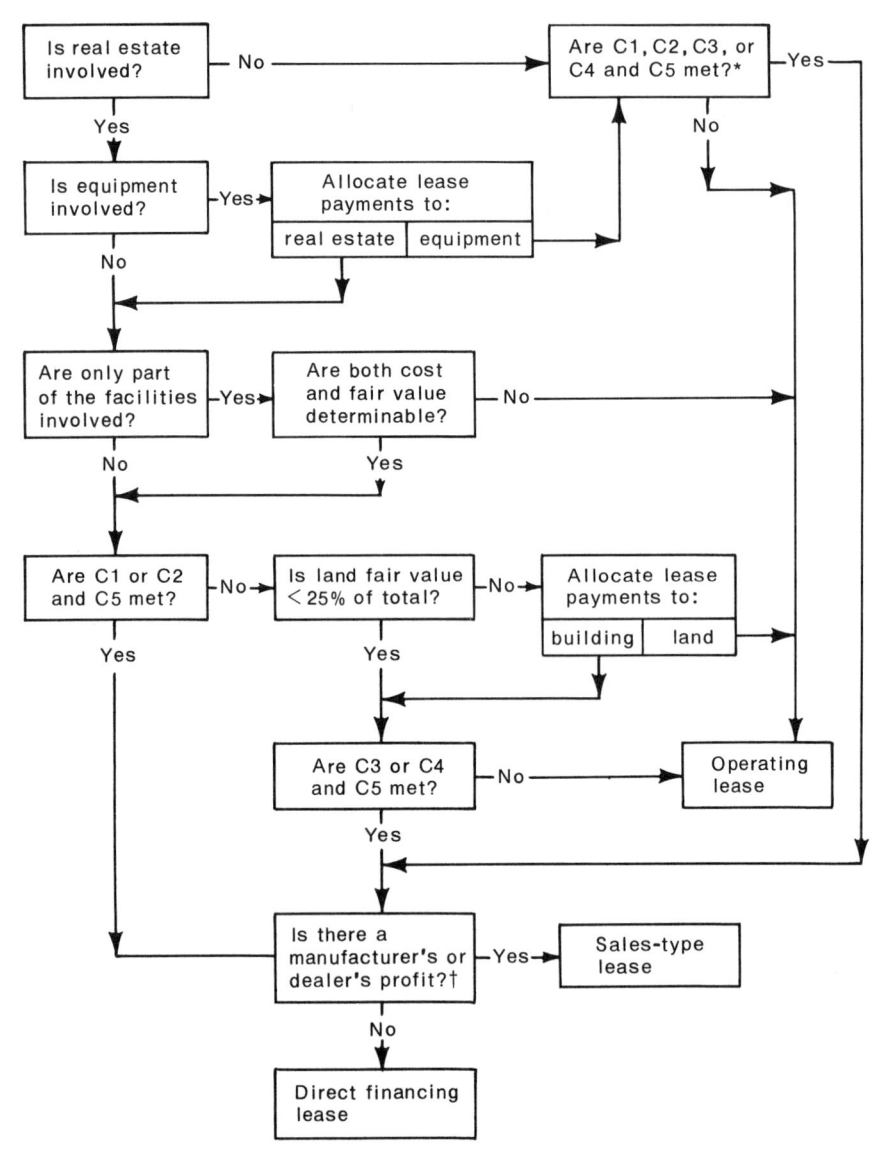

[Flowchart]

*C1: Transfer of ownership
C2: Bargain purchase option
C3: 75% of economic life
C4: 90% of fair value
C5: Collectibility predictable and no important uncertainties

†Sale-leaseback transactions may not be classified as sales-type leases.

SENSITIVITY ANALYSIS

Figure 9-1(b). Flowchart for determining revised classifications of leases by lessor.

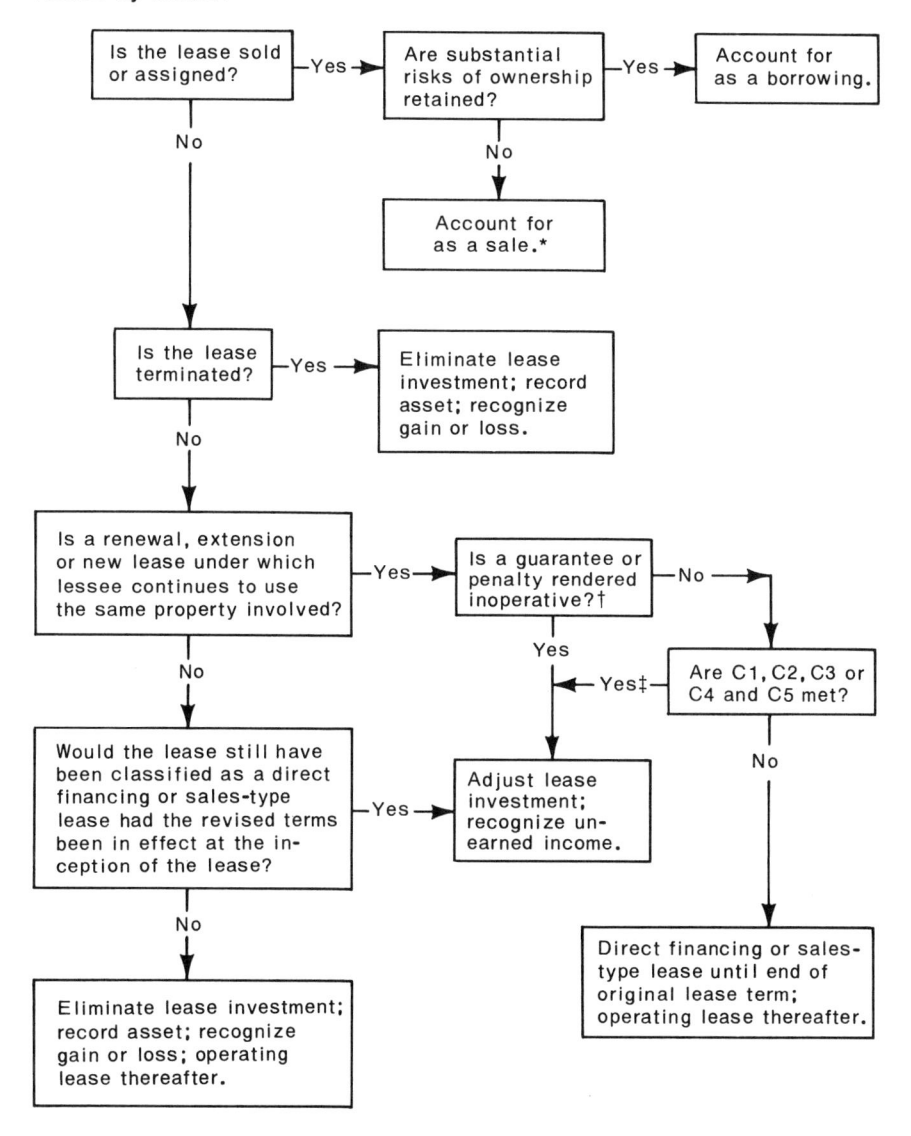

```
[Is the lease sold or assigned?] --Yes--> [Are substantial risks of ownership retained?] --Yes--> [Account for as a borrowing.]
                                                    |
                                                    No
                                                    ↓
                                          [Account for as a sale.*]
     |
     No
     ↓
[Is the lease terminated?] --Yes--> [Eliminate lease investment; record asset; recognize gain or loss.]
     |
     No
     ↓
[Is a renewal, extension or new lease under which lessee continues to use the same property involved?] --Yes--> [Is a guarantee or penalty rendered inoperative?†] --No--> [Are C1, C2, C3 or C4 and C5 met?]
     |                                                          |                                                     |
     No                                                         Yes                              Yes‡ ←---------------|
     ↓                                                           ↓                                                    No
[Would the lease still have been classified as a direct    [Adjust lease investment;                                   ↓
 financing or sales-type lease had the revised terms        recognize unearned income.]                    [Direct financing or sales-
 been in effect at the inception of the lease?] --Yes-->                                                    type lease until end of
     |                                                                                                      original lease term;
     No                                                                                                     operating lease thereafter.]
     ↓
[Eliminate lease investment; record asset; recognize gain or loss; operating lease thereafter.]
```

*The gain or loss is deferred and systematically recognized if the transfer is with recourse.
†These are guarantees and penalties that are included in the minimum lease payments.
‡May only be classified as a direct financing lease.

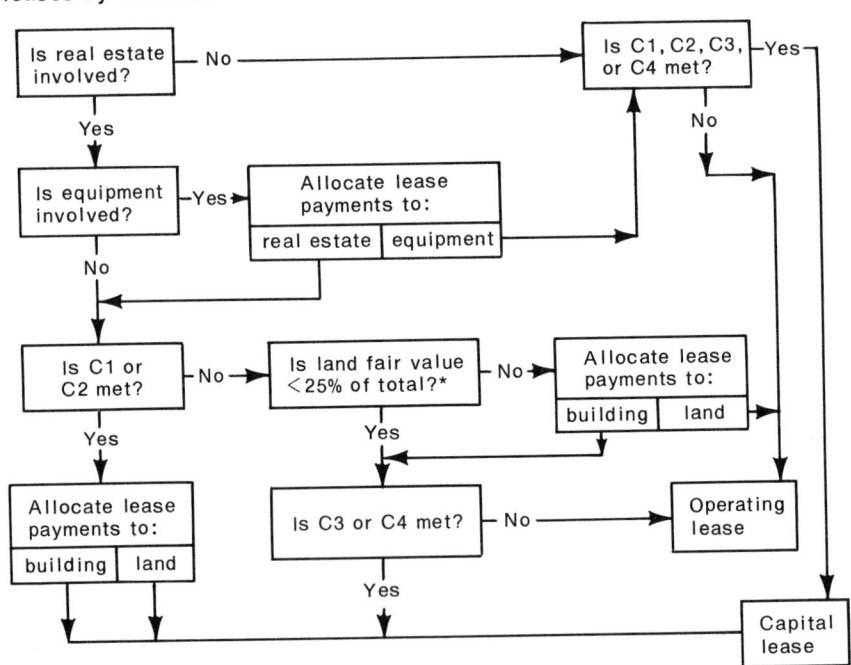

Figure 9-1(c). Flowchart for determining initial classifications of leases by lessees.

*Use the yes path when only part of a building whose fair value is not determinable is leased. Only C3 is then applicable.

of fixed interest and other financial charges? What impact would the financing alternatives have on the firm's existing restrictive covenants in its bond indenture(s)? What impact would there be on future financing decisions? Can the term of the lease be shortened or extended? Could the loan in a borrow-and-buy be renewed or prepaid? Is the loan callable? What impact will the financing decisions have on the combined degree of operating and financial leverage?

4. Among the several lessors that may offer competitive terms to a given lessee, which one should be selected? There are numerous considerations here that must be taken into account. A lessee's checklist for evaluating a lessor, prepared by BankAmeriLease, is included at the end of Chapter 12.

5. What are the alternative sources of financing and their institutional requirements that should be factored into the final decision? Again,

SENSITIVITY ANALYSIS

Figure 9-1(d). Flowchart for determining revised classifications of leases by lessees.

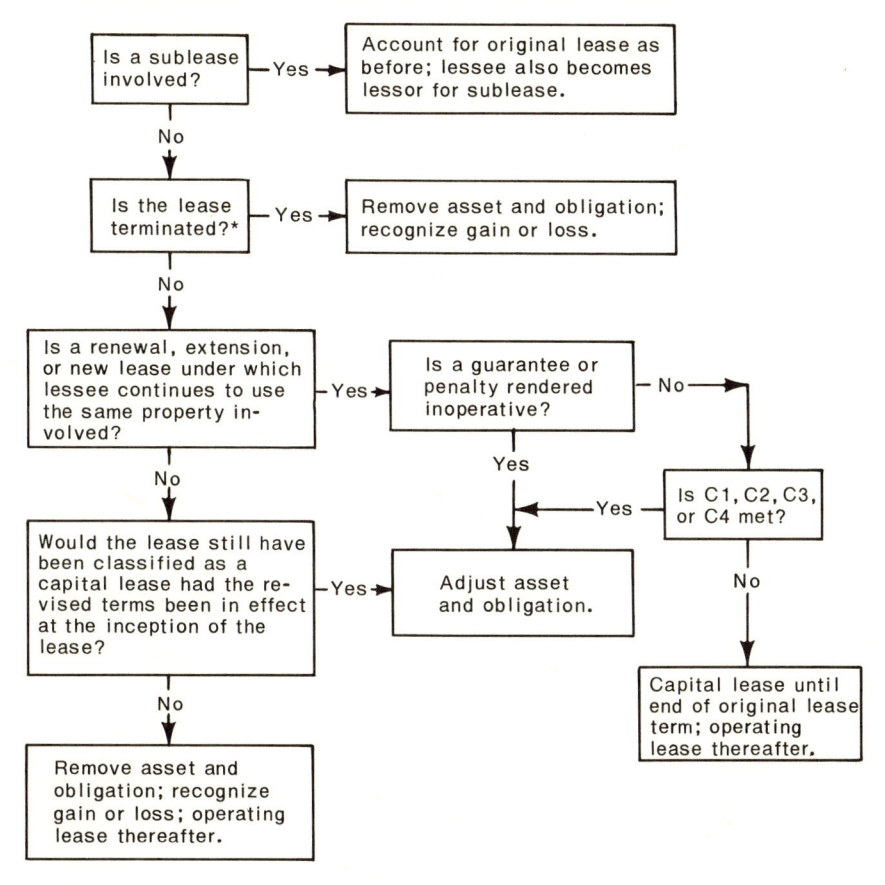

```
┌─────────────┐
│Is a sublease│──Yes──►┌────────────────────────────────┐
│involved?    │        │Account for original lease as   │
└─────────────┘        │before; lessee also becomes     │
      │                │lessor for sublease.            │
      No               └────────────────────────────────┘
      ▼
┌─────────────┐
│Is the lease │──Yes──►┌────────────────────────────────┐
│terminated?* │        │Remove asset and obligation;    │
└─────────────┘        │recognize gain or loss.         │
      │                └────────────────────────────────┘
      No
      ▼
┌──────────────────────┐      ┌──────────────────┐
│Is a renewal, extension│      │Is a guarantee or │
│or new lease under which│─Yes►│penalty rendered  │──No──►
│lessee continues to use │      │inoperative?      │
│the same property in-  │      └──────────────────┘
│volved?                │              │
└──────────────────────┘              Yes
      │                                │
      No                               ▼
      ▼                         ┌──────────────────┐
┌──────────────────────┐  ◄─Yes─│Is C1, C2, C3,    │
│Would the lease still have│    │or C4 met?        │
│been classified as a      │    └──────────────────┘
│capital lease had the re- │─Yes►┌──────────────────┐    │
│vised terms been in effect│    │Adjust asset      │    No
│at the inception of the   │    │and obligation.   │    ▼
│lease?                    │    └──────────────────┘
└──────────────────────┘                        ┌────────────────────┐
      │                                         │Capital lease until │
      No                                        │end of original lease│
      ▼                                         │term; operating     │
┌──────────────────────┐                        │lease thereafter.   │
│Remove asset and      │                        └────────────────────┘
│obligation; recognize │
│gain or loss; operating│
│lease thereafter.     │
└──────────────────────┘
```

*The lease is considered terminated when the lessee is relieved of the primary obligation by a transfer to a third party.

this is a broad topic with several important ramifications. Chapter 11 explores these aspects in detail.

Upon addressing these issues and weighing the advantages and disadvantages they imply for the alternatives under consideration, the evaluation committee should arrive at a summary of the qualitative dimension of the decision. This result will later be merged with that obtained in the next two phases of sensitivity analysis.

Additional Quantitative Factors in the Lease-versus-Purchase Analysis

The recommended approach in Chapter 8, using either the tabular format or the equation formulation, was anything but an obvious or simple analysis of the alternatives under evaluation. Nevertheless, the approach was, in fact, simplified, because a number of additional complexities were not directly incorporated into the analysis. Such additional quantitative complexities include, among others: complete consideration of the conditions of risk surrounding the lease–purchase problem setting; consideration of changes in tax laws; and consideration of the effects of changing the terms of a lease or a loan during the original contract, once it is accepted by the parties.

Our experience indicates that such considerations would render the quantitative analysis of alternatives too complex. Furthermore the marginal benefit in terms of accuracy and additional insight provided is limited. Therefore, we recommend that these complexities be incorporated into the analysis using the approach of the previous section in conjunction with that of the following section. This dual approach should prove more effective and efficient in obtaining greater insight into the decision setting and improved accuracy in specifying the preferred alternative.

We now turn to the third phase in the sensitivity analysis module: analyzing the impact of changes in the data inputs.

Analysis of Changes in the Data Inputs to the Evaluation Modules

The major analytical phase of the sensitivity analysis module is that of determining the impact of changes in the data inputs on the preferred decision alternative. We are interested in determining the extent to which errors made in forecasting future financial and operating cash flows will affect the present value or net present value of the alternatives under evaluation. Of course, various forecasting errors will make the preferred alternative more attractive, while other errors could alter the preferred alternative. In the latter case, the decision maker would want to assess the likelihood of a forecasting error in this direction, and of other errors of this or greater magnitude. If it is felt that the probability is great enough that such forecasting errors could occur, then the new preferred alternative should be considered for implementation. In addition, qualitative factors must be weighed in making the final decision, as was discussed earlier in this chapter.

SENSITIVITY ANALYSIS   127

The basic approach recommended in the sensitivity analysis module will follow that in the financing evaluation module and the investment and financing evaluation module shown in Chapter 8. Thus, in the sensitivity analysis module, values in the various equations or tabular approaches will be modified and their impact on present values or net present values will be determined.

The first change that will be evaluated is the *salvage value* that will accrue to the firm if the asset is purchased. As the salvage value increases, the purchase alternative becomes more attractive relative to the lease alternative; conversely, the lower the salvage value, the more attractive leasing becomes. The analysis is illustrated in Example 1.

EXAMPLE 1
Evaluation of Changes in Salvage Value

For the capital project evaluated in Examples 1 through 4 in Chapter 8, consider the impact on the attractiveness of the alternatives if the salvage value were: $10,000, $25,000, $30,000, $40,000, $40,576, and $50,000, instead of the $20,000 figure used in Chapter 8.

Prepare a table showing the change in the present value (PV) and the net present value (NPV) of the purchase alternative under each of the new salvage values. For each new salvage value compare the present values and net present values of the two leases with the revised values for the purchase alternative. Show the results also using a graphical approach.

SOLUTION

Looking back at Examples 1 through 4 in Chapter 8, we see that:

PV (Lease #1) = $174,703; NPV (Lease #1) = ($2,754)
PV (Lease #2) = $169,225; NPV (Lease #2) = $2,724
PV (Purchase) = $175,638; NPV (Purchase) = ($3,689)

Thus the differences between the purchase alternative and each lease alternative are:

PV (Purchase) − PV (Lease #1) = $935
NPV (Purchase) − NPV (Lease #1) = $935
PV (Purchase) − PV (Lease #2) = $6,413
NPV (Purchase) − NPV (Lease #2) = $6,413

Note that these differences are the same for present values and net present values. An increase in the salvage value will reduce the present value of the purchase and increase the NPV of the purchase by the same dollar amount. Of course, this increase will reduce the difference in present values or NPVs shown above by the same dollar amount. A decrease in the salvage value will have the opposite effect.

Table 9-1 shows the change in present values or NPVs for each of the new salvage values.

Notice that if the salvage value increases by less than $5,000, the purchase alternative becomes more attractive than Lease #1. Furthermore, if the salvage value increases to more than $40,576, the present value of the cost of purchasing is less than the present value of the cost of Lease #2. Figure 9-2 illustrates the impact of changes in the salvage value.

As shown by the horizontal lines for the two leases in Figure 9-2, their present values are invariant under changes in the salvage value. With all salvage values less than $40,576, Lease #2 has a lower present value of cash flows than the purchase alternative (Lease #2 also dominates Lease #1). With a salvage value of exactly $40,576, the firm would be indifferent, from a quantitative standpoint, between Lease #2 and purchasing. Purchasing becomes more advantageous than Lease #2 if the salvage value exceeds $40,576. The firm would then want to address the question: How likely is it that the salvage value in year five will exceed $40,576? The answer points to the firm's preferences for either Lease #2 or the purchase alternative. A graph similar to that in Figure 9-2, but using net

Table 9-1. Changes in present values as salvage value takes on values from $10,000 to $50,000.

	\$10,000	\$25,000	\$30,000	\$40,000	\$40,576	\$50,000
Tax impact*	4,000	10,000	12,000	16,000	16,231	20,000
Net cash inflow	6,000	15,000	18,000	24,000	24,345	30,000
Old net inflow†	12,000	12,000	12,000	12,000	12,000	12,000
Difference	(6,000)	3,000	6,000	12,000	12,345	18,000
Discount factor‡	.519369	.519369	.519369	.519369	.519369	.519369
Change in PV§	$3,116	($1,558)	($3,116)	($6,232)	($6,412)	($9,349)

Salvage Value

* Recall that the book value of this asset was zero for tax purposes so that the salvage value would be recovery of depreciation, which is taxed at 40 percent, the ordinary tax rate.
† The old net cash inflow was the estimated $20,000 salvage value less the tax impact of 40 percent of $20,000 (or $8,000), which equals $12,000.
‡ The discount factor for a 14 percent risk-adjusted discount rate for the end of year 5 is .519369.
§ The increase (decrease) in the present value of the cost of purchasing is the product of the difference in the net cash inflows and the discount factor. If the "difference" is negative, then there will be an increase in the present value of purchasing; otherwise there will be a decrease in this present value. As mentioned before, an increase (decrease) in the present value of the cost of purchasing will lead to a decrease (increase) in the NPV of the purchase alternative.

SENSITIVITY ANALYSIS

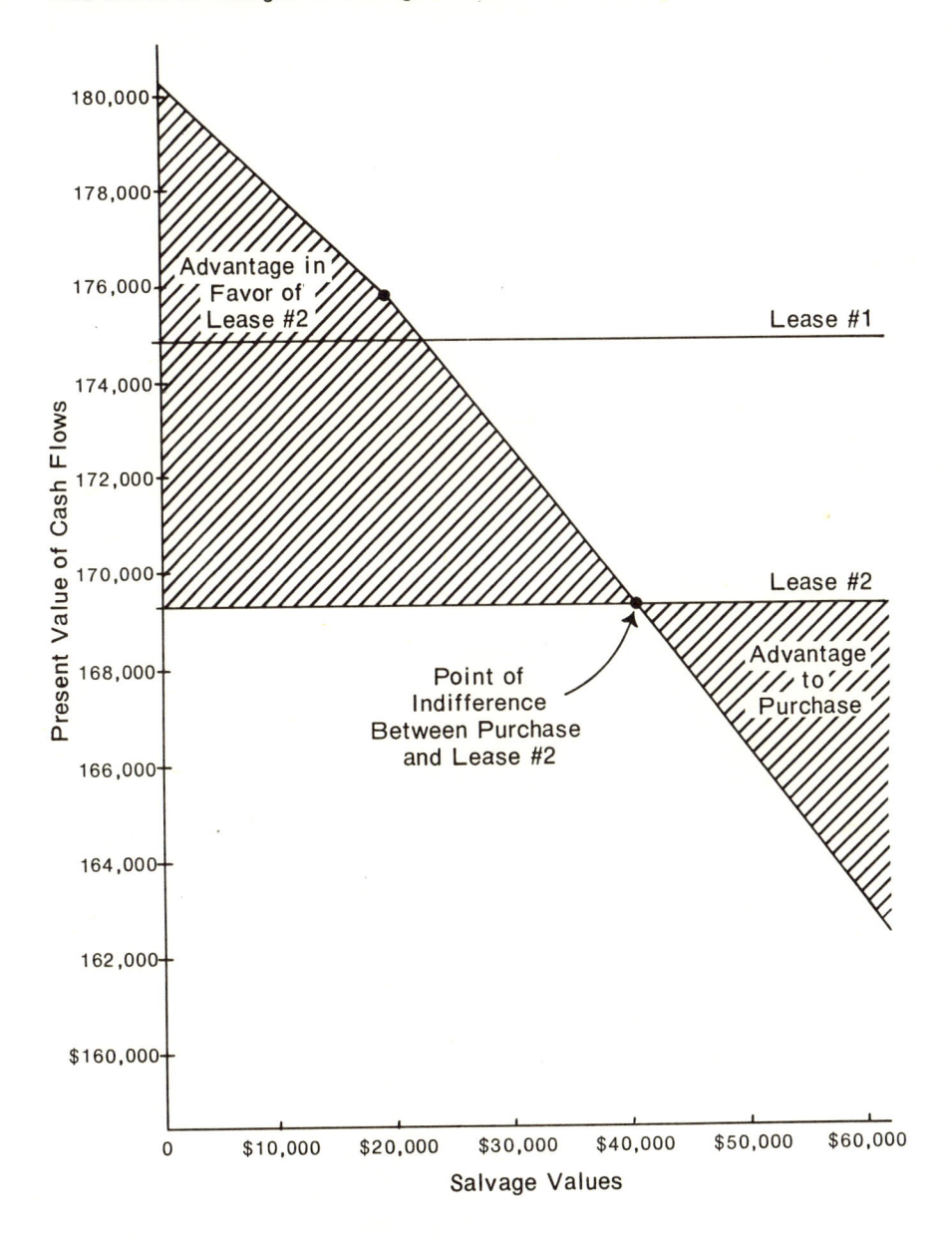

Figure 9-2. Sensitivity of present value of lease #2 and purchase alternative to changes in salvage value.

Figure 9-3. Sensitivity of NPV of lease #2 and purchase alternative to changes in salvage value.

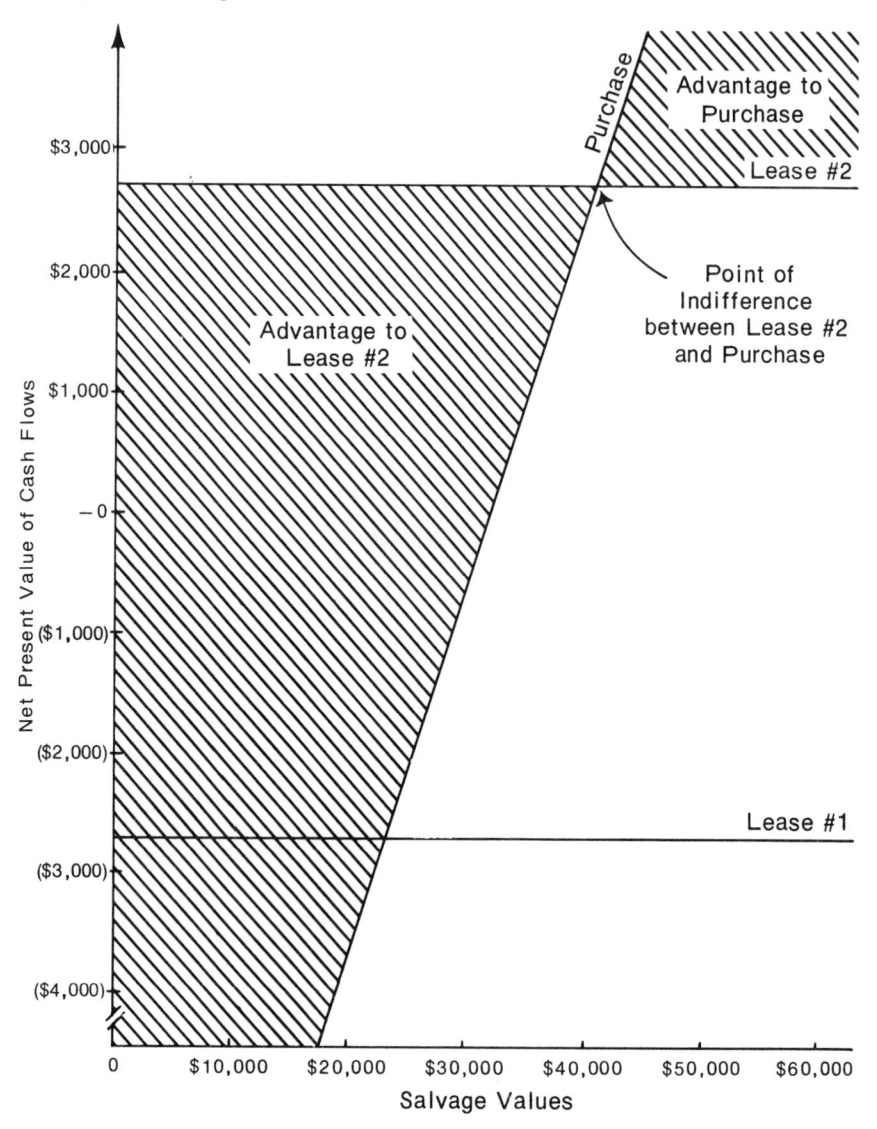

present values instead of present values, is shown in Figure 9-3. The same points of intersection and advantage areas are found.

Notice that the salvage value would have to equal $32,000 before the purchase alternative would have a positive NPV. Of course, since we want to maximize NPV, Lease #2 is advantageous compared to the purchase at all salvage values less than $40,576. □

The second type of evaluation we will take up is *what percent reduction in the net operating cash inflows is required to have the alternative with the greatest NPV equal either zero or the next highest NPV, whichever is larger*. The analysis is illustrated in Example 2.

EXAMPLE 2
Evaluation of the Sensitivity of Net Operating Cash Inflows

For the capital project evaluated in Examples 1 through 4 in Chapter 8, consider the impact of 1 percent, 3 percent, and 5 percent reductions in the net operating cash inflows each year. Determine the NPV of Lease #2 under these modifications. Use both a tabular and graphical approach to demonstrate where the NPV of Lease #2 becomes negative.

SOLUTION

Table 9-2 is helpful in performing this evaluation. As shown in Examples 1 and 2 in Chapter 8, the present value of Lease #2 financial cash flows is $159,750. Thus, Lease #2's NPV will decrease from $2,724 to zero as the present value of the net operating cash inflows decreases from $162,474 to

Table 9.2. NPV of Lease #2 as net cash inflows are reduced 1%, 3%, and 5%.

Year	Current Net Operating Cash Inflow*	1% Reduction Cash Inflow	1% Reduction PV @ 14%	3% Reduction Cash Inflow	3% Reduction PV @ 14%	5% Reduction Cash Inflow	5% Reduction PV @ 14%
1	$24,540	$24,295	$21,311	$23,804	$20,881	$23,313	$20,450
2	26,190	25,928	19,951	25,404	19,548	24,881	19,145
3	55,950	55,391	37,387	54,272	36,632	53,153	35,877
4	59,796	59,198	35,050	58,002	34,342	56,806	33,634
5	91,702	90,785	47,151	88,951	46,198	87,117	45,246
PV of net operating cash inflows			$160,850		$157,601		$154,352
NPV (Lease #2)			$1,100		($2,149)		($5,398)

* See Example 2, Chapter 8.

$159,750; the NPV will be negative whenever the present value of the net operating cash inflows falls below $159,750.

Given Table 9-2, we see that a 1 percent reduction in the net operating cash inflows each year leads to a reduction of $1,624 in Lease #2's NPV (a reduction from $2,724 to $1,100). Furthermore, we see that each 2 percent reduction in the annual net operating cash inflows results in a reduction of $3,249 in Lease #2's NPV. Thus, it would take less than a 2 percent reduction in the annual net operating cash inflows to see Lease #2's NPV become negative.

This clearly indicates that the project's attractiveness, even with the best financing alternative, is highly sensitive to reductions in the net operating cash inflows. In addition, management should be rather hesitant to jump into the project if it has even the remotest feeling that the forecasted net operating cash inflows are at all optimistic. Here, as in Example 1, qualitative factors will enter the picture, as does an informal probability assessment of the likelihood that the annual net cash inflows will drop by 2 percent or more.

Figure 9-4 shows the results pictorially. □

If any other financing alternative had a positive NPV, a similar analysis to that shown in Example 2 could have been performed to determine percent reductions in annual net operating cash inflows to make the NPV of the best alternative just equal to the NPV of the second best financing alternative. In a similar vein, a comparable analysis could consider leaving cash inflows early in the project's life unchanged and reducing only the later cash inflows, where greater forecasting uncertainty exists.

The third modification that will be considered is *variation in the positive direction of the net operating cash inflows.* The purpose of this modification is to determine when another alternative becomes preferred over the current preferred alternative. The analysis again takes the form of either a table or a graphical presentation, as shown in Example 3.

EXAMPLE 3

Evaluation of Upward Changes in Net Operating Cash Flows

For the capital project evaluated in Examples 1 through 4 in Chapter 8, consider that net operating cash inflows will increase by 3 percent, 5 percent, and 10 percent for the leasing alternatives. When the project is purchased, various operating efficiencies can be taken advantage of. Thus, under the purchase alternative, the net operating inflows will increase by 2 percent in excess of the percent increase for the leasing alternatives. Determine the NPV for each of the three alternatives under each of the

Figure 9-4. Sensitivity of NPV of lease #2 to reductions in net cash inflows.

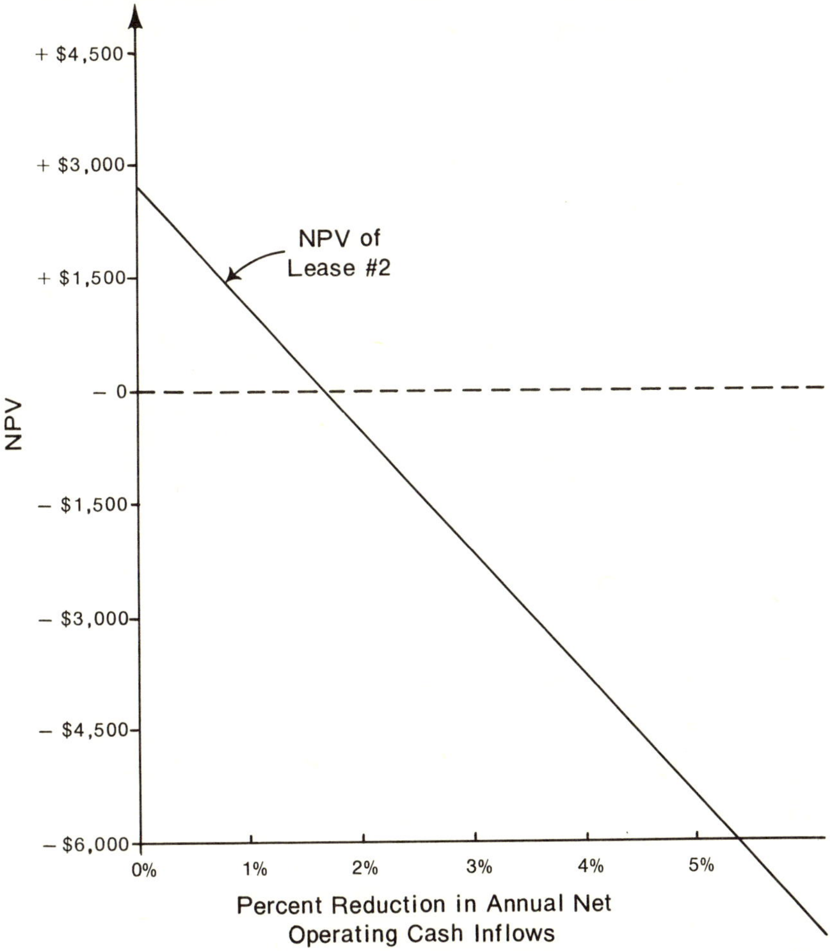

specified increases in net operating cash inflows. Again, use both a tabular and a graphical approach.

SOLUTION

The present value of the *financial cash flows* for each alternative will be unaffected by the changes in the net operating cash inflows specified in this example. These present values were determined in the four examples in Chapter 8: $165,228 for Lease #1, $159,750 for Lease #2, and $250,669 for the purchase alternative. Thus, the NPVs for each of the three alternatives will be obtained by subtracting these present values of financial cash flows from the present value of the revised operating cash inflows. Tables 9-3(a) and (b) show the analysis.

Table 9-3(a). Changes in NPVs of Leases #1 and #2 as cash inflows are increased by 3%, 5%, and 10%.

		3% Increase		5% Increase		10% Increase	
Year	Current Net Operating Cash Inflow	New Cash Inflow	PV @ 14%	New Cash Inflow	PV @ 14%	New Cash Inflow	PV @ 14%
1	$24,540	$25,276	$22,172	$25,767	$22,603	$26,994	$23,679
2	26,190	26,976	20,757	27,500	21,160	28,809	22,168
3	55,950	57,629	38,898	58,748	39,653	61,545	41,541
4	59,796	61,590	36,466	62,786	37,174	65,776	38,944
5	91,702	94,453	49,056	96,287	50,008	100,872	52,390
PV of Net Operating Cash Inflows			$167,349		$170,598		$178,722
NPV (Lease #1)			$2,121		$5,370		$13,494
NPV (Lease #2)			$7,599		$10,848		$18,972

Table 9-3(b). Changes in NPV of purchase alternative as cash inflows are increased 5%, 7%, and 12%.

		5% Increase		7% Increase		12% Increase	
Year	Current Net Operating Cash Inflow*	New Cash Inflow	PV @ 14%	New Cash Inflow	PV @ 14%	New Cash Inflow	PV @ 14%
1	$24,180	$25,389	$22,271	$25,873	$22,696	$27,082	$23,756
2	25,830	27,122	20,870	27,638	21,267	28,930	22,261
3	55,590	58,370	39,398	59,481	40,148	62,261	42,024
4	59,436	62,408	36,951	63,597	37,655	66,568	39,414
5	91,342	95,909	49,812	97,735	50,761	102,303	53,133
PV of Operating Cash Inflows			$169,302		$172,527		$180,588
PV of Financial Cash Flows*			(250,669)		(250,669)		(250,669)
PV of Depreciation Tax Shields*			79,510		79,510		79,510
PV of Salvage Value*			6,232		6,232		6,232
NPV (Purchase)			$4,375		$7,600		$15,661

* These values are taken from Table 8-9. The present value of financial cash flows is the cash outflow of $266,400 less the ITC of $15,731. The present value of depreciation tax shields is the total of column 8 of Table 8-9.

Tables 9-3(a) and (b) provide management with helpful insights into the vulnerability of the current preferred alternative (Lease #2) to increases in net operating income. Recall that the original NPVs of the three alternatives were as follows: NPV (Lease #1) = ($2,754), NPV (Lease #2) = $2,724, and NPV (Purchase) = ($3,688). With a 3 percent increase in the lease alternatives' net operating cash inflows (which yielded a 5 percent increase for the purchase alternative due to operating efficiencies), the purchase alternative ranks second in NPVs, behind Lease #2. With a 5 percent increase, the same rankings exist, but Lease #1 is closing in on the purchase alternative for second place. With a 10 percent increase, the NPV rankings are Lease #2, Lease #1, and Purchase. Lease #2 continued to be the clearly preferred alternative throughout all increases in net operating cash inflows, even with the additional increases in net operating cash inflows for the purchase alternative due to its operating efficiencies. Figure 9-5 also shows the dominance of Lease #2. □

The final change that will be evaluated is that of modifying the *risk-adjusted discount rate or the required rate of return for the project under evaluation*. Here again it was assumed in our analysis in Chapter 8 that the *risk-adjusted discount rate utilized was appropriate for the project under evaluation*. Changes in this discount rate could lead to changes in the preferred alternative. Example 4 illustrates the analysis.

EXAMPLE 4

Evaluation of Changes in the Risk-Adjusted Discount Rate

For the project considered in Examples 1 through 4 in Chapter 8, determine the risk-adjusted NPV, using discount rates of 10 percent and 20 percent so that comparisons can be made with the NPVs using the 14 percent rate.

SOLUTION

As was noted in the solution to Example 3, the present value of the financial cash flows for each alternative will be unaffected by the change in the risk-adjusted discount rate used to discount operating cash flows for the project. These present values of financial cash flows ($165,228 for Lease #1, $159,750 for Lease #2, and $250,669 for the purchase alternative) will be subtracted from the present values of the operating cash inflows in order to determine the NPVs. Tables 9-4(a) and (b) are helpful in analyzing the changes in the risk-adjusted discount rate.

136   THE LEASE / BUY DECISION

Figure 9-5. Sensitivity of NPVs of lease #1, lease #2, and the purchase alternative to increases in net operating cash inflows.

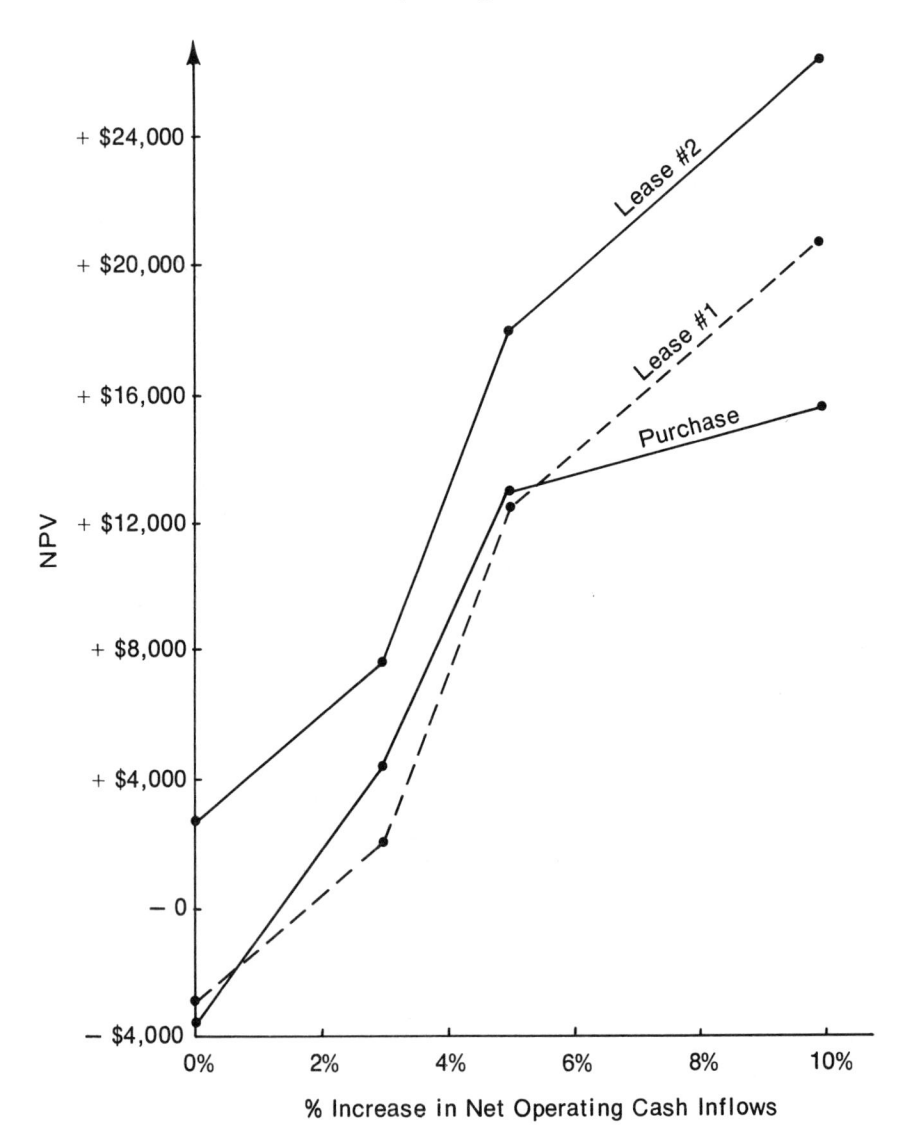

SENSITIVITY ANALYSIS

Table 9-4(a). Changes in NPVs of Lease #1 and Lease #2 as the risk-adjusted discount rate is varied.

		10%		20%	
Year	Operating Cash Inflows	Discount Factors	PV of Cash Inflows	Discount Factors	PV of Cash Inflows
1	$24,540	.909091	$ 22,309	.833333	$ 20,450
2	26,190	.826446	21,645	.694444	18,187
3	55,950	.751315	42,036	.578704	32,378
4	59,796	.683013	40,841	.482253	28,837
5	91,702	.620921	56,940	.401878	36,853
PV of Net Operating Cash Inflows			$183,771		$136,705
NPV (Lease #1)			$18,543		($28,522)
NPV (Lease #2)			$24,021		($23,045)

Table 9-4(b). Changes in NPV of the purchase alternative as the risk-adjusted discount rate is varied.

		10%		20%	
Year	Operating Cash Inflows plus Depreciation Tax Shield	Discount Factors	PV of Cash Flows	Discount Factors	PV of Cash Flows
1	$59,700	.909091	$54,273	.833333	$49,750
2	54,246	.826446	44,831	.694444	37,671
3	76,906	.751315	57,781	.578704	44,506
4	73,644	.683013	50,300	.482253	35,515
5	110,446	.620921	68,578	.401878	44,386
PV of Cash Flows			$275,763		$211,828
NPV (Purchase)			$25,094		($38,841)

To summarize our results:

	Risk-Adjusted Discount Rate		
NPV	10%	14%	20%
Lease #1	$18,543	($2,754)	($28,522)
Lease #2	$24,021	$2,724	($23,045)
Purchase	$25,094	($3,688)	($38,841)

Thus, if the risk-adjusted discount rate were less than 11 percent, the purchase alternative would have the greatest NPV. At all discount rates

Figure 9-6. Sensitivity of NPVs of lease #1, lease #2, and purchase to changes in risk-adjusted discount rates.

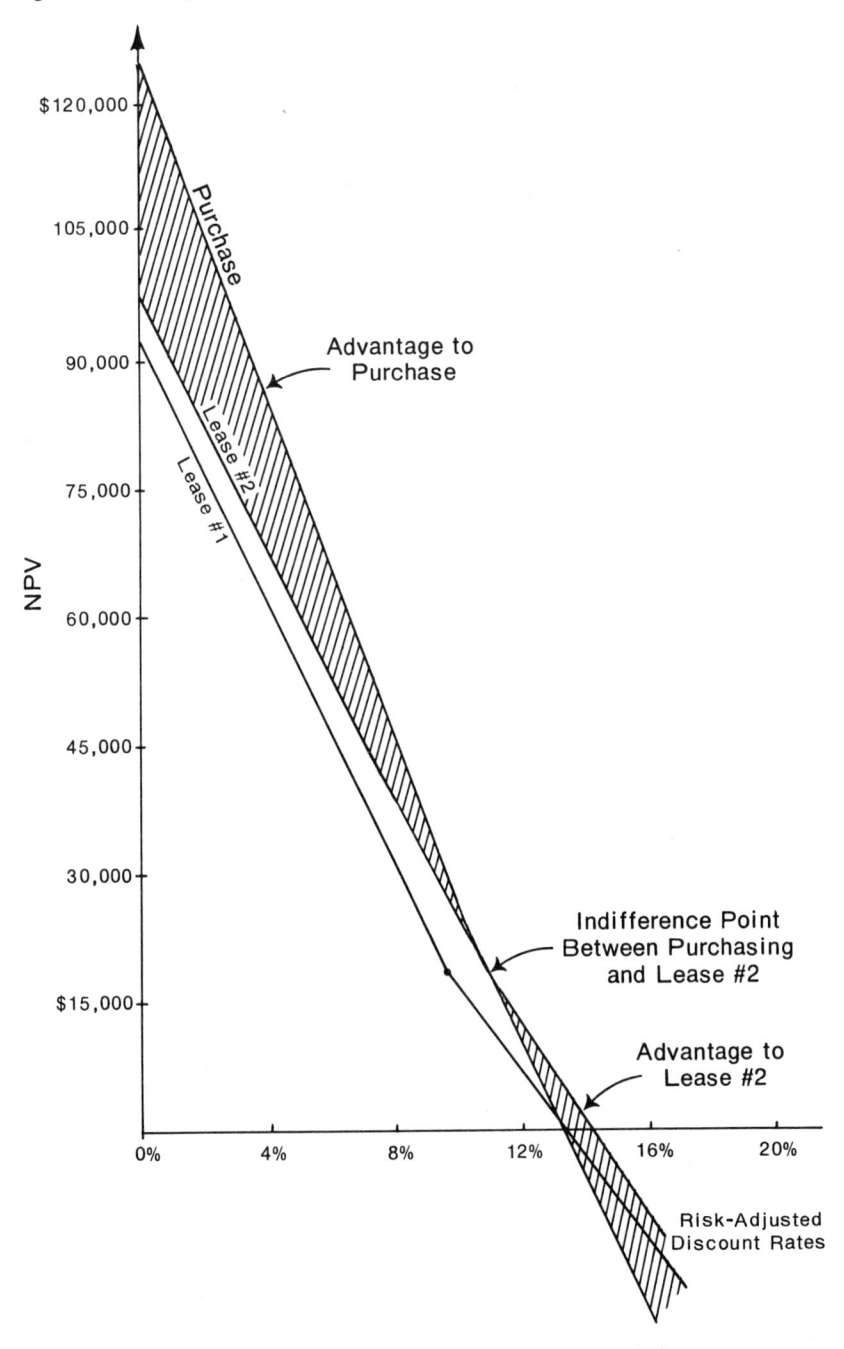

above 11 percent, Lease #2 would have the greatest NPV. Lease #2 would cease to have a positive NPV at all risk-adjusted rates in excess of 15 percent. Once again, management would want to estimate the likelihood that the required rate of return for the project would be less than 11 percent or greater than 15 percent. In the former case, the preferred alternative is no longer Lease #2, but rather the purchase alternative. In the latter case, the project is not attractive from a quantitative standpoint, because no financing alternative generates a positive NPV. Figure 9-6 also shows the results. □

This completes our treatment of the sensitivity analysis area. The impact of various combinations of the changes illustrated in Examples 1 through 4 could be pinpointed by merely integrating such multiple changes in a single table.

This chapter has discussed in depth the importance of incorporating qualitative aspects of the problem setting, as well as the insight gained through sensitivity analysis, into the decision process before selecting the single preferred alternative. Of course, this combined analysis requires management to address complex issues, to call upon subjective estimates or probabilities, and to rank alternatives on the basis of more than just quantitative aspects. However, it is only by a careful analysis and exploration of such dimensions that management improves the decision-making process and increases the likelihood of selecting the optimal alternative.

NOTES

1. Financial Accounting Standards Board, *Statement No. 17: Accounting for Leases—Initial Direct Costs*, Stamford, Conn., November 1977; and *Statement No. 22: Changes in the Provisions of Lease Agreements Resulting from Refundings of Tax Exempt Debt*, Stamford, Conn., June 1978.
2. Financial Accounting Standards Board, *Interpretation No. 19: Lessee Guarantee of the Residual Value of Leased Property*, Stamford, Conn., October 1977; *Interpretation No. 21: Accounting for Leases in a Business Combination*, April 1978; and *Interpretation No. 26: Accounting for Purchase of a Leased Asset During the Term of the Lease*, September 1978.
3. Reprinted with permission from William A. Collins, "Accounting for Leases—Flowcharts," *Journal of Accountancy*, September 1978, pp. 60–63. Copyright © 1978 by the American Institute of Certified Public Accountants, Inc.

CHAPTER 10

Tax Aspects of Leasing

An analysis of the tax consequences of a particular transaction must be based on a determination of the type of transaction involved—in this case, whether the transaction is a true lease or a conditional sale (a transaction that is recognized in law as providing the seller with security interest in the underlying asset until the buyer has satisfied all the items and conditions of the contract)—and knowledge of the applicable rules of the tax law.

Chapter 2 provides guidelines gleaned from Internal Revenue Service pronouncements (Revenue Ruling 55-540 and Revenue Procedure 75-21 are just two of many examples) and from adjudicated cases, which are useful in determining the nature of a particular transaction. But, even though the leasing industry has grown dramatically over the last two decades and a major impetus for this growth has been tax considerations, there still remains uncertainty as to how particular transactions will be treated. Obviously, these transactions are those which do not fall clearly into the definition of either a lease or a conditional sale, but possess some of the characteristics of each.

The authors gratefully acknowledge the preparation of this chapter by Kenneth B. Everett, J. D., Tax Manager, San Francisco office, Deloitte, Haskins, and Sells. Our thanks also go to William Hetts, Managing Partner, San Francisco office, and Ralph W. Newkirk, Jr., Managing Partner, Cherry Hill, N.J., office, Deloitte, Haskins, and Sells, for their sponsorship of the project.

A potential lessee would be ill advised to automatically assume that his "lease" is clearly a lease for tax purposes merely because the value of the leased property is small, or because "everyone is doing it," or because the word "lease" appears on or in the agreement. Because of the conflicting cases and imprecisely worded guidelines published by the Internal Revenue Service decades ago, even common transactions such as automobile leases may fall into the category of questionable transactions and suffer the risk of being treated as conditional sales.

Once a transaction has been analyzed and its character as a lease or a purchase ascertained, reference to Chapter 3 will provide the general tax rules applicable to that transaction—in the case of a true lease, the deduction of the rental payments, or, in the case of an installment purchase, the deduction of interest and recovery of all or part of the cost of the asset through depreciation.

The purpose of this chapter is to integrate the discussions of Chapter 2 and Chapter 3 as they relate to lessees. It should be emphasized that this discussion of taxation is not intended to be the final word on leasing from a lessee's point of view. It is intended to suggest different aspects of the tax law to a lessee and hopefully provide some basic rules for taxation, whether the transaction is a lease or a sale. This chapter will not discuss the general rules used in determining the nature of a transaction, but will concentrate on the Internal Revenue Service's current audit position with respect to leasing.

Current Developments

Although the general guidelines for classifying a transaction as a lease or a sale were stated by the IRS over 20 years ago, there is still controversy over the application of those rules.

During most of this intervening period the IRS has not made a concentrated effort to enforce its own interpretation of the meaning of the published rulings. Recently, however, the level of IRS activity in the leasing area has increased. Previously, leasing companies have been examined superficially. They are now being warned that their next audit will focus on the structure of their transactions, unlike prior examinations, which accepted their leases at face value. In addition to these "promised" reviews, many leasing companies are having the IRS question their leases currently. This increased Internal Revenue Service activity would seem to indicate a toughening of the Service's position with respect to the character of questionable leases.

A prospective lessee must therefore be aware of current IRS activity with respect to lessors, because a holding that a transaction is not a lease but a sale will certainly affect the tax treatment of the transaction by the "lessee." The increased IRS activity and the wide-ranging effect of such increased activity can best be illustrated by the Service's position in a Technical Advice Memorandum (TAM) dated April 26, 1978.

The subject of the TAM was whether certain "leases" written by an automobile leasing company qualified as true leases. Although it is not clear if the lessor was a third-party lessor or a captive leasing company of an automobile dealership, the leases were for terms of three and five years and covered both automobiles and trucks. According to the facts provided, at the end of the years under examination there were more than 2,000 of these suspect agreements, the bulk of which were fleet vehicle leases. As with most vehicle "leases," the agreements provided for a monthly rental, with the lessee bearing all operating expenses, including maintenance and repair, other than warranty expenses.

The particular financing arrangements which the taxpayer had with its banks are not indicated, but it is stated that the "taxpayer borrowed funds (ranging from approximately 93 to 98 percent of the taxpayer's acquisition cost) from 'particular banks.'"

The leasing company calculated the monthly lease payments so that at the end of the lease term, the cost of financing plus a contribution to profit had been recovered, plus an amount equal to (1) the commission paid to the leasing salesman, (2) a markup of 10 to 15 percent to contribute to general overhead and profit, and (3) the cost of the vehicle. These latter three items were referred to as the "original value" of the vehicle, while the first was identified as the "secondary markup." In most transactions, the "original value" was divided by the expected useful life of the vehicle (50 months for cars and 60 months for trucks) to yield a "monthly depreciation reserve"; this amount, when added to the amount of secondary markup divided by the lease term, became the monthly rental.

Upon termination of the lease, the vehicle was to be sold. If the amount received upon sale exceeded the "residual value" ("original value" less cumulative "monthly depreciation reserve"), the lessee would receive the benefit; if, however, the sale proceeds were less than the "residual value," then the lessee was obligated to pay the lessor additional rent to make up the difference between the actual value of the vehicle as determined by sale and the residual value.

As might be expected, the IRS stated that the agreements were not leases but conditional sales agreements, because the benefits and burdens of ownership, and the potential for profit or loss, rested upon the "lessee" and not the "lessor".

The vehicle leasing industry, when faced with this position and the new regulations under the Truth in Lending Rules, revised their leases so that the exposure of the "lessee" for profit or loss was limited to three monthly payments. Thus if the residual value was $1,500, lease payments were $100 per month, and upon sale the proceeds were only $1,000, the lessor would have to bear $200 of loss ($1,500 − $300 − $1,000). Conversely, if the proceeds were $1,900, the lessee would profit by $300, but the lessor would also benefit by $100 ($1,900 − $300 − $100 = $1,500).

Although it is much too early to tell how the IRS will view this new attempt to structure auto leases, it is clear that the Service is taking an increasingly active role in addressing the issue of lease vs. sale and that it is not reluctant to take a position that may affect large numbers of taxpayers. It can only be expected that the IRS will continue to review "leases" critically in light of cases decided by judicial authorities for the taxpayer but not acquiesced to by the Commissioner.

This new critical emphasis can be seen by a case currently being written up by an Internal Revenue agent which would effectively preclude the use of full-payout leases (leases where the total lease payments exceed the lessor's cost for the property) *even* where there is no purchase option contained in the lease agreement. The agent bases his position on language in Rev. Rul. 55-540 at Section 4.05 which states that a presumption exists that a conditional sales contract was intended if the total of the rental payments and any option price payable in addition thereto approximates the price at which the equipment could have been acquired by purchase at the time of entering into the agreement, plus interest and/or carrying charges. The ramifications to the leasing industry and affected lessee if this agent's position is ultimately sustained are obvious when one considers that most lessors and lessees affected by FASB 13 would fall into the category of parties with full-payout leases. Although the ultimate result of this case is not clear, it is representative of the IRS's general attack on the leasing industry on a nationwide basis.

Tax Considerations of the Lessee—True Lease

Because a true lease (one creating a relationship of landlord and tenant) does not grant any continuing right to the lessee for continued use of the leased property beyond the lease term, payments made by a lessee relate to the use of that asset over a specific period of time. Such payments are deductible over that same period as ordinary and necessary business expenses of the lessee doing business.

The term of a lease may simply be for a given period of time, or it may contain renewal options for varying lengths of time. In the latter situation, the rates for such renewal periods may be determined as of the date of renewal, or the lessor and lessee may try to agree in advance what the renewal rental payments will be. The use of renewal periods is so prevalent with respect to many types of leases, especially for office space, that the Internal Revenue Service, in determining the period over which leasehold improvements are amortized, may include the renewal period as part of the fixed lease period. The Internal Revenue Service has recognized this relationship by prohibiting the deduction of prepaid rent, even to a cash basis taxpayer, if the deduction creates a distortion of income in the year paid. Upon the final expiration of the initial lease term plus renewals (if any), the right to possess the asset reverts to the lessor. Not only must the lessee surrender possession to the lessor, he may actually have to bear the cost of returning the asset to the possession of the lessor.

A potential lessee should be aware that a lease subject to renewals for a period which, when combined with the initial lease term, approaches the estimated useful life of the asset, especially when coupled with a reduced renewal rate, may appear to have characteristics of a sale rather than a lease. The IRS has indicated that such terms may be an important factor in determining whether a transaction is actually a sale.

Disposition of leased equipment at the end of a lease term may prove to be a difficult task for a lessor. In an attempt to minimize the burden of locating a purchaser and completing the sale, many lessors grant a purchase option in the lease documents which permits the lessee to acquire the asset at either its then current fair market value or a predetermined price. The existence of a purchase option with a nominal buyout—frequently 1 to 5 percent of the cost of the asset—will probably present difficulties in sustaining the position that a transaction is really a lease. A fair market value buyout appears to be the preferable way to structure a purchase option to avoid the issue of a bargain purchase at the end of the lease term. However, a lessee may wish to place a lid on the potential amount that would have to be paid to exercise an option. If a stated purchase price can be shown to represent the best estimate of the asset's fair market value at the end of the lease term, such an option should not cause the transaction to be considered a sale. Care should be taken, however, that the purchase option is not for such a small amount as to be considered insubstantial with respect to total lease payments or the cost of the equipment.

If the lessee purchases the leased equipment from the lessor, his tax position will no longer be that of a lessee but that of the owner of an asset. Accordingly, attention must be paid to the various tax ramifications of being an owner of used equipment. Clearly, the cost of the purchased asset must be capitalized and not deducted (unless the asset has a remaining useful life of less than one year). The decisions affecting cost recovery through depreciation must be made, such as determining the method of depreciation, the useful life of the asset, and its ultimate salvage value.

In addition, the ex-lessee now has to be aware of the various tax rules relating to the disposition of assets, such as the rules pertaining to depreciation recapture and to holding periods for categorizing potential Section 1231 gains as long- or short-term.

Tax Considerations of the "Lessee"— Conditional Sales Agreement

Because this book focuses on the economic decision in buying or leasing, the tax treatment of a transaction that fails to qualify as a true lease must also be explored.

The initial distinction between a lease and a financing arrangement for a purchase is that the payments made by the "lessee" in a conditional sale are no longer deductible as they are paid. When compared to the true lease situation, where the tenant-landlord relationship exists for a fixed period of time, a proprietary interest in an asset may have no time limitation other than the practicalities of the useful life of the asset. Thus, whereas periodic payments made on account of a lease are deductible over the period to which they relate, the cost of a purchased asset does not relate to a particular period of time and is therefore not deductible under this theory. The cost of purchased assets are, of course, recoverable under a different theory by way of depreciation deductions.

As discussed in Chapter 3, a taxpayer who purchases an asset is entitled to a depreciation deduction which is, under Section 167 of the Internal Revenue Code, a reasonable allowance for the exhaustion and wear and tear (including a reasonable allowance for obsolescence) of the purchased asset. The distinction between the deduction for rental payments and that for depreciation is important. With respect to the former, the deduction relates to the period over which the asset is being used by permission of the owner (lessor), regardless of the asset's useful life, whereas the depreciation deduction theoretically relates to the useful life of the asset.

Frequently the argument is made that if the rental term is shorter than the depreciable life of the asset, cost recovery is accelerated by using a lease arrangement. Although this is frequently true, there are situations where ownership may provide an acceleration of tax benefits.

For instance, the situation may arise where an asset which, when acquired or leased, is expected to last ten years is worthless after five years. The depreciation deduction will permit a write-off of the remaining basis of the asset at the end of the asset's useful life, whereas the rental payments (which under the lease term are to extend over ten years) may be deducted only when paid or accrued.

However, in the normal situation, where the lease term is shorter than or equal to the asset's estimated useful life (if for no other than tax reasons), the rental arrangement should provide a greater total write-off because salvage value, which is considered in determining total depreciation expense, does not have to be considered by the lessee in deducting his rental payments.

Assuming, for purposes of this part, that the transaction is determined to be a conditional sale, what are the tax effects on the "lessee/purchaser"?

An analysis of the total payments to be made by the "lessee/purchaser" indicates that the funds are expended to acquire ownership of the particular asset and, in addition, to compensate the lessor/seller for the privilege of spreading the ownership payments over a period of time. This latter amount—the time price differential—is interest and may be deducted as payments are made or accrued, depending on the purchaser's method of accounting. The cost of the asset, which is the total of the periodic payments, less the interest portion of each payment, plus any purchase option, must be capitalized. Depreciation deductions will then be determined on the basis of the normal criteria provided in the Internal Revenue Code, and judicial or administrative pronouncements.

A "purchaser/lessee," when faced with a purchase transaction, will normally know the components of the total payment obligation. However, the breakdown of any particular payment or number of payments may not be known. For instance, is the interest portion of each installment payment calculated on a straight-line basis over the entire period of the obligation, or is it calculated on a declining-balance method such as the rule of 78's? Because of the rules permitting a current deduction for interest expense, the timing of the interest payment or accrual becomes important. Example 1 clarifies this issue.

EXAMPLE 1
Interest Cost for Lease/Sale

Assume an asset is subject to a transaction deemed to be a purchase and not a lease. The asset cost $12x$, the interest payments are $6x$, and the total payments due are $18x$ over a period of 6 years, or $3x$ per year. Looking only at the interest deduction, on a *straight-line basis,* the annual interest deduction is calculated as follows:

$$\frac{\text{Total interest expense}}{\text{Number of years}} = \text{interest expense per year}$$

In this situation, $\dfrac{\$6x}{6 \text{ years}} = \$1x$ interest per year

The rule of 78's method, the method used by most financial institutions, involves applying a changing fraction to the amount of interest expense. The numerator is the number of years (months) remaining for full payment of interest, and the denominator is the sum of the numbers representing the total years (months) of payment. This method is referred to as the rule of 78's because financial institutions traditionlly use it on a monthly basis, and the denominator, if a loan is for 12 months, is 78 (12 + 11 + 10 + 9 + 8 + 7 + 6 + 5 + 4 + 3 + 2 + 1).

In determining the deduction under the rule of 78's, the following calculation would have to be made.

$$\frac{\text{(Remaining payments)}}{\text{(Sum of numbers representing the total periodic payments)}} \times \text{interest expense} = \text{interest per period}$$

Year 1 $\dfrac{6}{6 + 5 + 4 + 3 + 2 + 1}$ × $6x = $1.7x$
Year 2 $\dfrac{5}{21}$ × $6x = $1.4x$
Year 3 $\dfrac{4}{21}$ × $6x = $1.1x$
Year 4 $\dfrac{3}{21}$ × $6x = $ .9x$
Year 5 $\dfrac{2}{21}$ × $6x = $ .6x$
Year 6 $\dfrac{1}{21}$ × $6x = $ .3x$

A comparison of the two methods (see Table 10-1) shows that under the Rule of 78's a greater part of the early payments is interest. Although the total interest paid and deducted has not increased as a result of using the rule of 78's, the tax deduction has been accelerated. Without any acceleration in payments, the amount of taxes due in the first three years is less

Table 10-1. Comparison of interest deductions calculated by straight-line method and by Rule of 78's.

Year	Straight-Line Method	Rule of 78's	Excess
1	$1.0	$1.7	$ .7
2	1.0	1.4	.4
3	1.0	1.1	.1
4	1.0	.9	(.1)
5	1.0	.6	(.4)
6	1.0	.3	(.7)
	$6.0	$6.0	$0

than the amounts which otherwise would have been due. Clearly, this deferral of taxes, from years 1, 2, and 3 to years 4, 5, and 6, is, in most situations, desirable. □

Because the timing of the interest deduction is important to most taxpayers, care should be taken to ensure that the desired treatment will be obtained if the transaction is ultimately held to be a conditional purchase. The treatment will depend on the terms of the agreement, either explicit language or indirect evidence such as the method of calculating a premature purchase option. Unfortunately, as noted in Chapter 2, the inclusion of an interest factor in the lease agreement is one of the items the Internal Revenue Service will consider in classifying a transaction. Thus the lessee is faced with the dilemma of either defining an interest portion of each payment in the agreement and possibly jeopardizing the lease itself or not indicating the method under which interest is calculated and losing deductions if the transaction is ultimately held to be a conditional sales agreement.

Timing of Deductions

As mentioned previously, the timing of deductions will usually play an important role in the lease–purchase decision. When faced with two alternatives, if all other factors are equal, the least costly in absolute dollars is usually the wisest choice.

However, it is clear from prior discussions of discounted cash flows that merely relying on the cost of an alternative in absolute dollars, without taking into account the time value of money, may result in a more costly decision than previously thought.

The reasons for leasing were discussed in Chapter 1. They included such pragmatic reasons as an inability to purchase the asset (either lease or do without) and the more sophisticated reasons such as 100 percent financing of asset cost and preservation of existing lines of credit. Regardless of the reasons for leasing, which may be quantified, it is almost a truism that leasing an asset will usually be more costly (by 1 or 2 percentage points) than either an outright purchase of the asset or relying on traditional methods of financing, such as bank loans. The reason for this is obvious. The leasing company has its own cost of capital and will incorporate a profit factor in determining the lease rate. The total of these two amounts will usually exceed the lessee's own cost of capital.

Once the additional cost is determined in absolute dollars, the economic cost in terms of the time value of money must be considered. It is at this point that an analysis of the tax affects of each alternative must be made.

Such an analysis would not only point to certain obvious situations, such as the lease of nondepreciable assets (for instance, land), but also compare the benefit of deducting lease payments in total versus the potential interest and depreciation deductions which, due to salvage values, may be less than the cost of the asset.

A popular misconception is that leasing an asset provides an acceleration of deductions over direct ownership. This is not necessarily true. The use of accelerated depreciation methods, short useful lives provided in the Treasury Department rules, first-year bonus depreciation coupled with the privilege of ignoring certain amounts of salvage in determining the total amount of depreciation which may be taken, and the deduction for finance charges can, in fact, provided a greater deduction than the amount of the lease payment at the beginning of the lease term, provided the total cost of acquiring the asset, including financing charges, and the cost of leasing the asset are equal.

Investment Tax Credits

A tax deduction reduces income subject to taxation and, in the absence of other factors, will generally reduce federal corporate income taxes by the amount of the deduction multiplied by the incremental tax rate. Thus, before the Revenue Act of 1978, if a corporation had taxable income in excess of $50,000, an item of income, unless the alternative tax rate applied, would be taxed at 48 percent. If an additional deduction could be generated, the deduction would save 48 percent of the amount of the deduction, provided the new taxable income was in excess of $50,000. As a result of the Revenue Act of 1978, which reduced corporate income tax rates to a maximum of 46 percent, the benefit of each additional dollar of deduction is slightly less than before.

A tax credit, however, provides a dollar-for-dollar reduction in tax liability and is therefore roughly twice as valuable. A deduction of $100,000 may save $46,000 in federal taxes, whereas a credit of $100,000 reduces taxes by $100,000, thus saving an additional $54,000 of taxes.

In an attempt to stimulate the economy, Congress provided that expenditures for certain types of assets will generate credits known as investment tax credits. The rules explaining qualified assets are lengthy and continually being changed, not only by judicial interpretation but also by Congressional or Treasury Department pronouncements. A general definition, however, is that qualified (Section 38) property is tangible personal property or other tangible property (not including a building and its structural components) if the property is used as an integral part of manufacture, production, or extraction or of furnishing transportation, communications, electrical, energy, gas, water, or sewage disposal services. In addition, the property must be depreciable and have a useful life of three years or more.

Assuming that the asset qualifies as Section 38 property and that other requirements are met, the credit is based on a percentage of the basis of the assets placed in service during the taxable year. If the asset has a useful life of three or four years, the applicable percentage is $33\frac{1}{3}$ percent; if the useful life is five or six years, the applicable percentage is $66\frac{2}{3}$ percent; and if the useful life is seven years or more, the applicable percentage is 100 percent. The actual credit is now permanently 10 percent (after enactment of the 1978 tax act) of the total cost of all new Section 38 property after application of the respective applicable percentages. The same applicable percentage rules apply to used Section 38 property; however, there is a limit in that only $100,000 of used property may be considered. If the credit is being claimed with respect to used property, the taxpayer may choose which assets comprise the $100,000.

The resulting credit may then be used to offset the first $25,000 of federal income tax liability and 50 percent (1978 and prior years), 60 percent (1979), 70 percent (1980), 80 percent (1981), or 90 percent (after 1982) of any tax liability in excess of $25,000. If the total amount of the credit is not used in the year generated, it must be carried back three years to reduce past taxes first, and then forward for up to seven years to reduce future taxes.

The investment credit is usually allowable only to a taxpayer having a qualified investment in the property, only for the taxable year during which the property is placed in service by the taxpayer. However, under Code 48(d), a lessor of *new* Section 38 property may elect to treat the lessee as having purchased the property. The Code has six conditions for the pass-through: (1) the property must be Section 38 property in the hands of the lessor, (2) it must be *new* Section 38 property in the hands of the lessor, (3) it would have been new Section 38 property in the hands of the lessee had he actually purchased the equipment, (4) the lessor files the necessary pass-through elections, (5) the lessor is not one of a limited group of lessors such as savings banks and real estate investment trusts, and (6) a condition which relates to transactions where possession of the property was transferred by a lessor prior to February 26, 1964.

Of the conditions mentioned above, two warrant further discussion: first, the requirement that the property be new Section 38 property, and second, the requirement that an election be made to pass the credit through to the lessee.

A lessor may not pass through the credit on used Section 38 property; therefore, the lessee seeking the pass-through must verify that he is the first user of the property. The fact that the lessor has tested the property or attempted to lease it to other parties will not taint the property as being used, but use by the lessor himself will taint it.

In order to pass through the credit to the lessee, a lessor must comply with certain stated rules in the Regulations to the Internal Revenue Code, which regulate the form of the pass-through election. If the election is on a property-by-property basis, the lessor must file a signed statement with the lessee which contains the following: (1) the name, address, and taxpayer identification number of both the lessor and the lessee, (2) the location of the Internal Revenue Service district where both the lessee and the lessor file their income tax returns, (3) a description of each property covered by the election, (4) the date on which possession of the property was transferred to the lessee, (5) the estimated useful life of the property, (6) the basis of the leased property in the hands of the lessor, and (7) if the lessor is itself a lessee, the name, address, and taxpayer identification number of the original lessor as well as the location identification of the district with which the original lessor files his tax return. Instead of making a property-by-property election, a lessor may elect to make a general election for all property leased to a particular lessee during a particular year by filing a signed statement similar to that described above indicating the general election.

Not only must an election be filed with the lessee before the due date of the lessee's tax return for the year during which the property was leased, and copies retained by both the lessor and the lessee, but a summary statement of all property leased on which the investment cash has been passed to lessees must be attached to the lessor's income tax return.

Because of the obvious value of the credit, its pass-through or retention by the lessor will enter into the lease rate. It can be expected that a lessor who retains the investment tax credit will reduce its lease rates to compete with a lessor who chooses to pass through the credit. However, in negotiating a lease, a lessee should keep in mind that many leasing companies have large amounts of unused ITC and that additional ITC is of little value to them. In addition, if the lessor is a noncorporate lessor, sole proprietorship, partnership (unless the partners are corporations), or Subchapter S corporation, the credit may have no value to the lessor because of special rules in Regulation Section 1.46-4(d), which limits its utilization by such a lessor. If the lease was entered into after September 22, 1971, the noncorporate lessor may claim the credit only if (1) the property was manufactured or produced by the lessor in the ordinary course of his business, *or* (2) the term of the lease (including any options to renew) is less than 50 percent of the estimated useful life of the property *and,* during the first 12 months after the property is transferred to the lessee, the lessor's deductions (other than interest, taxes, depreciation, rents, and reimbursed amounts from the lessee) with respect to the property exceed 15 percent of the rental income produced by the property.

Current Business Transactions

As the Internal Revenue Service has become more sophisticated in analyzing "lease" transactions, lessors have become more sophisticated in their marketing. Non-tax considerations frequently control the form of a transaction, and both the lessor and lessee realize that the nominal classification of a transaction as a lease will be disregarded. Hence banks, which are becoming an increasingly important factor in the leasing market, may present different alternatives under which a "lease" may be structured. These alternatives may range from a $1 purchase option to a 10 percent purchase option to a fair market buy-out. The banks offer different interest rates on each alternative, taking into account not only the amount they will receive from the lessee upon termination of the lease, but also whether they qualify to receive tax benefits by being a lessor.

If the size of a transaction warrants the expense, a lessee may wish to obtain the written opinion of legal counsel and accountants and/or obtain a ruling from the Internal Revenue Service on the nature of the transaction. Thus in a transaction structured as a lease which grants a $1 purchase option, the "lessee" might wish to request a ruling from the Internal Revenue Service on ancillary issues that are affected by sale/lease classification or even on the underlying issue of whether the form of the transaction may be disregarded initially by the lessee and the transaction treated as a sale. However, the IRS may become somewhat reluctant to grant a ruling until more definitive rules concerning the requirements for leases are rendered.

From this discussion of the tax aspects of being a lessee, it is clear that once a transaction is determined to be a lease or a sale, the tax options open to the parties in the transaction are limited and fairly well established. However, the determination of the nature of a particular transaction has vexed courts, the Internal Revenue Service, and the leasing industry for years and will apparently continue to do so.

CHAPTER 11

Alternative Sources of Financing

Potential lessees may find lessor dollars elusive or unavailable to them, despite the desirability of using a lease and the fact that the various lease mode criteria may seem to be satisfied. This could be brought about by exogenous factors or for various reasons based on the applicant's own condition. Several reasons are discussed below:

1. The *item* to be acquired *or* the *industry* of the lessee may have had recent reversals; uncertainties may have arisen due to health hazards proclaimed by government agencies, or possible fuel shortages or pollution controls. There is no end to the effect of being "tarred with the same brush."

2. Vagaries of the money markets, particularly in "tight money" periods, can distort interest rates and curtail funds available to financial intermediaries for lease transactions. Since lease arrangements are basically long-term, lessors/lenders generally become wary of extending fixed-rate credit in times when the cost of loanable funds is expected to increase. At best, their quoted rates may be at such a high level that the

---

The authors gratefully acknowledge the help in preparation of this chapter received from Kenneth J. Mathews, President, First National State Bank Leasing Company, and Robert J. Corcoran, Vice President and Senior Commercial Finance Officer, First National State Bank, Newark, New Jersey. Materials from this chapter also draw upon Robert E. Pritchard and Bruce M. Bradway, *Business and Financial Planning and Control for Small Businesses*, 1978, The Management Institute, Glassboro, N.J. Used with permission.

would-be lessee/borrower may well determine that now is not the time to lease.

3. The lessee applicant may also be deemed to be too new in business, having no track record to indicate ability to meet cash flow obligations of a lease transaction; or again, a negative evaluation by the lessor of the lessee's capability to profitably operate the desired equipment may permanently forestall a lease.

The next several sections discuss alternative avenues that the rejected lessee may fruitfully explore.

Commercial Lending Sources

Commercial lending sources offer some short- and intermediate-term solutions to the rejected lessee for acquiring the use of the needed income-producing equipment. More than likely, an asset-based loan arranged through a bank or finance company will offer the needed funding by means of a secured lending plan. The finance company could well be a "captive" of the equipment dealer or may work in close harmony with the manufacturer or its distributors under a "dealer plan," or it may have no particular ties to any manufacturer. (The many commercial banks engaged in this area of funding could also have entered into a dealer plan.)

In the dealer plans there is usually some sharing in the risk or a cooperative remarketing arrangement between dealer and lender. This makes the securing of financing a bit easier for the applicant, but perhaps a trifle more expensive than from a free-standing finance company or with a secured bank loan. In this situation the borrower may trade cost versus availability. There are economic periods, as well as stages of corporate growth, where whittling (or adding to) money costs by "basis points" may be counter-productive to survival or implementing desired expansions. That is, necessity will overcome studied feasibility planning.

Equipment financing generally involves a down payment in cash and/or trade-in, with terms usually up to five years, and in some instances, seven years. Fixed-rate transactions are becoming scarcer, and the interest rate will generally float. That is, the interest rate will be tied to the prime rate and move with it. Thus the interest rate is not fixed but may vary appreciably over the term of the loan. Since, in periods of inflation, the Federal Reserve Board usually tightens money supplies, thereby setting off increases in interest rates, a firm borrowing on a floating rate may be exposed heavily to financial risk. Furthermore, its cost of capital may be increased even to the point that an already accepted project (that is, one acquired and being financed through a loan) may become undesirable as interest rates go up. In the absence of this floating interest, a hefty add-on rate will generally be used. This ensures the lender that no earnings squeeze (due to future rising money costs) will occur during the life of the loan.

Alternatively, a loan may be written for a five-year payout with a three-year term. That is, the loan agreement may call for 35 equal monthly payments based on 1/60th of the loan, with the 36th payment, known as a "balloon" payment, based on the balance. The loan is usually renegotiated prior to the maturing of the "balloon." This procedure limits the risk of rate changes as well as the term risk of the transaction.

An asset-based lender, such as a captive finance company, will insist on a security agreement with the borrower, along with appropriate Uniform Commercial Code (UCC) filings. (UCC exists in all states except Louisiana.) Such a lender may also require additional collateral by the pledge of other equipment assets, which will be "crossed-secured" to reduce the extension of credit to less than prime risks.

While banks have been active in this type of lending for some time, the advent of the UCC in various states (from the 1950s into the early 1960s) has resulted in their becoming more aggressive lenders and has caused the larger banks to acquire finance companies to broaden their expertise and activity in this area. There also remains a full range of non-bank finance companies, such as Aetna Business Credit, The Associates of North America, Commercial Credit Corporation, CIT Corporation, and Walter E. Heller & Co., among the national companies,[1] with many local and regional companies active in equipment funding.

Business Week provides added insight into financing sources available in an article reproduced here.[2]

Financing That Sells Machine Tools

The machine tool industry is enjoying a record $3.3 billion order backlog and claims to foresee no slowdown in its business next year, despite forecasts of a recession. Sales will be countercyclical, bolstered by unusually heavy buying from Detroit as cars are downsized. But tool builders' sales to their bread-and-butter customers—the small job shops—will also be cushioned against a downturn because of expanded financing programs that they have devised to help customers pay for equipment when other sources of credit dry up.

Certainly the financing programs offered by companies such as Warner & Swasey, Cincinnati Milacron, and Ex-Cell-O are no match in size or sophistication for those devised by the manufacturers of heavy equipment and computers. Still, the traditionally conservative industry is now providing a pool of more than $100 million to finance its customers' purchases. Toolmakers are also starting to look at sales financing in a different light: not simply as a marketing tool to boost market share, but as a way "to help support sales activity" in a tight market, notes Frank A. Vitale, vice-president of customer financing at Warner & Swasey Co.

Small customers. Like other tool builders, Warner & Swasey, the industry's No. 2 producer, with $262 million in sales, has been strengthening its program by adding more money and more lenient payment terms. Last December it started a sales plan where the buyer pays nothing for the first six months on a $200,000 piece of equipment. For the next four and a half years, each payment is only about three-quarters of what a bank would require, says Vitale. The big outlay comes with the final payment, which might be $90,000 on the $200,000 machine; but that comes when the buyer is presumably bigger and better able to pay. "We win the small customer who has cash flow considerations," says Vitale. w&s also has nailed down enough money, he says, to finance as much as 20% of this year's sales.

The finance program at w&s, which it runs through a captive finance subsidiary, is probably the most advanced in the industry. But industry leader Cincinnati Milacron Inc. expects its installment sales program to generate more business as interest rates climb. And Ex-Cell-O Corp., which started its own sales financing program two years ago, has been doubling its outlays for the program every year. In addition, the big commercial finance companies, such as CIT Financial Corp. and General Electric Credit Corp., note that they are prepared to buy the toolmakers' receivables—a move that will give producers still more cash to lend. "It's desirable business for us to finance," says Lawrence A. Bossidy, vice-president in charge of General Electric Credit's commercial and industrial division.

Preserving credit lines. Many buyers chose to borrow from toolmakers, even when banks were charging at least 1.5% to 2% less. Inflation has caused prices on many tools almost to triple in 10 years. "If [many of our customers] had to meet the stringent requirements of the banks, they couldn't buy those machines," says Joseph R. Oloffo, Ex-Cell-O's corporate credit manager. And as interest rates climb, "banks will tend to shy away from that kind of financing," admits Charles F. Barnes, president of Detroitbank Corp.'s equipment leasing subsidiary.

Still other buyers say they prefer to preserve their bank credit lines for working capital. Many buyers also feel that manufacturers are more understanding than banks when things go wrong and payments are tough to meet.

Despite such advantages, critics of the machine tool makers' financing programs charge that they are deploying assets that should be invested in toolmaking and taking on credit risks that they are not trained to handle. w&s's Vitale waves away such concerns, noting that in the 1973–74 recession, his company experienced no defaults and had only 20 slow-paying customers. Adds Lawrence R. Cowin Jr., vice-president of finance at Acme-Cleveland Corp.: "We are selling machine tools that would not otherwise be sold."

Commercial Finance Companies

Commercial finance companies, as indicated earlier, may provide alternative financing. The lending functions of commercial finance companies are described in the article[3] by G. Pat Bacon reproduced below.

It is not easy to quantify in a few concise words exactly what services a commercial finance company provides today to a potential borrower. Historically, our function has been to provide operating cash to small and medium sized business firms on a secured loan basis. For many years, members of our industry confined their operations to serving short-term needs of such firms largely through the medium of factoring or accounts receivable financing. To clear up a semantics problem, which exists because these terms are used interchangeably, let me take a moment to review the difference for you.

Factoring is the outright purchase of an account receivable by the factor from a manufacturer or distributor. The factor has preapproved the credit of the client's customer and, following shipment of the merchandise, purchases the receivable from the client. The factor thus assumes the responsibility for collection of the receivable and any possible bad debt risk. Payment for the receivable is generally made by the factor to his client on the due date thereof. The client may borrow funds in advance of the settlement date from the factor should he have the need, and the loan is repaid out of the purchase settlement proceeds.

Receivable financing, however, merely involves the pledge of receivables to a lender to serve as collateral for a loan. The client retains ownership and would continue to be responsible for his own credit and collection function. The lender merely has a lien on the receivables and the proceeds thereof. He advances a stated percentage of the face value of the receivable and is paid back from his client's collections.

Today's commercial finance companies offer a variety of services to their potential clients. Sometimes we are referred to as "department stores of finance" because of the wide spectrum of financing programs available. However, these services have evolved over the years to satisfy the financial needs of many different types of borrowers, who would obviously have varying needs.

Ætna Business Credit, as an example of a modern finance company, is equipped to provide the following programs or variations thereof:

1. *Intermediate Term Commercial Loans.* In this area, we offer term loans ranging from two to ten years, with collateral generally being plant and equipment or receivables with very long maturities. Great consideration is given to the financial strength of the borrower and its demonstrated cash flow ability to retire the loan.
2. *Equipment Financing and Leasing.* Loans secured by existing machinery and equipment or new machinery that is to be purchased are made to industrial firms. Usually, these loans are made on terms up to five years. However, if the customer should prefer, we can provide this type of financing on a lease basis.
3. *Time Sales Financing.* Service is provided to manufacturers, dealers or other sellers of income producing equipment by purchasing either installment notes or lease agreements generated from such sales. The notes and/or leases are secured by the machinery and equipment which has been sold by our client to his customers. Typically, these transactions are payable in monthly installments with maturities ranging from 24 to 60 months.

4. *Factoring Services.* We are also involved in providing credit and collection services in the form of factoring to a wide variety of businesses from whom we purchase current trade accounts receivable on the basis that I outlined for you previously.
5. *Commercial Financing.* These are primarily revolving loans effected on short term basis and are secured by assets primarily consisting of accounts receivable, inventory and machinery and equipment or a combination thereof. Real estate sometimes is included as part of a package loan structure.

Suffice it to say that Ætna's programs reflect the evolution that has taken place within our industry over the years.

At the present time there are approximately 150 companies involved in factoring, commercial financing and related services. Most of these firms are members of the National Commercial Finance Conference, which is our trade association.

There is a wide variance in the characteristics of the finance companies operating today:

1. Some are relatively small and basically operate on a regional or local basis.
2. Others are large public companies operating on a national basis.
3. Approximately half are in some way bank related—either as a direct operating bank department, or are affiliated with a bank holding company.
4. Some are offshoots of consumer finance oriented firms.
5. Some are "captives" of large industrial firms.
6. Ætna Business Credit, at the moment, is the only insurance company owned entity.

The estimated volume of our industry for 1976 was 61 Billion Dollars. We do not consider that to be an insignificant figure, nor a minor contribution to our economy.

Permit me to return to the commercial finance company in its more conventional and historic role as a provider of short-term credit using as a vehicle commercial financing, or revolving secured loans.

As I indicated previously, in this area we are generally serving smaller and medium sized businesses whose financial needs cannot be met on an unsecured basis. Unsecured credit is generally provided by banks, and usually in amounts determined by net worth and measured by working capital and other ratios computed from the borrower's financial statement. Frequently, however, the borrower's needs cannot be met by unsecured credit for any one of many reasons. Examples could be:

1. The firm may be relatively new, and therefore, may not have an operating record sufficient to demonstrate its capacity to adequately repay an unsecured loan.
2. The company could be exhibiting a loss trend which would also cast out on its ability to repay an unsecured loan.

3. There is a possibility that the total cash requirement is beyond the amount acceptable to an unsecured lender.

For similar reasons, the firm may not have access to the equity markets:

1. Again, the operating record of the firm may be too brief to qualify it for consideration in the public market.
2. Its earnings record may have been inadequate to justify an approach to equity financing.
3. The total funding required may not be sufficiently large to interest underwriters from the standpoint of undertaking either a public issue or attempting a private placement.
4. Conceivably the shareholders, in a closely held corporation, might resist the dilution of their positions which would take place if equity financing was consummated.

In such cases, the secured lender may be best equipped to service the borrower through a collateralized loan. Again, the collateral can consist of accounts receivable, inventory, equipment, real estate or combinations thereof.

A profile of the typical commercial finance borrower might resemble the following:

1. A closely held corporation. Closely held by choice, or by the dictates of the market.
2. A growth trend has probably been evident. It may have been accelerated because of new product development, or it may have been less dramatic and developed over time.
3. The firm's outstanding receivables have increased, its inventory is larger, its operating expenses have risen, and its fixed assets may have been expanded—all as a result of the increased volume it is doing.
4. Collection of its receivables is its only source of actual cash inflow supplemented by its ability to borrow on a short-term basis. According to the statistics of your association, the average collection period of receivables—industry wide—approximates 42 days.
5. Cash needs to keep suppliers current, to meet payrolls, to pay taxes and to service term debt requirements continue to mount.
6. Bear in mind that the equity base has remained relatively fixed so we now have what is classically known as "over-trading on equity". The rules governing extension of unsecured credit may well come into play at this time limiting additional amounts available from this source.

How can a secured lender give relief in such a case?

Basically, we attempt to establish a collateral pool sufficiently large to generate the funds necessary to meet the ongoing cash requirements of our clients. Simply, we attempt to recapture cash funds which have been tied up in various asset items and to recycle these funds through the operations so that all current cash requirements are fully satisfied. In essence, we replace debt with debt.

To see how this works, let's use accounts receivable as an example. As soon as one of our clients makes a shipment and prepares an invoice, he has created collateral which can be borrowed against. From a practical standpoint, we are removing the 42 day waiting period involved to collect the receivable before it can generate cash. It could be said that we are creating "instant cash". Normally, we do not advance the full face value of the invoice, but we should more than cover the cost of the item which has been sold.

In a similar manner, we are trying to recapture the cash that may be tied up in inventory and/or machinery and equipment. Again, these recaptured funds flow through the operation to reduce cash pressures.

I believe it's safe to say that you as a credit manager could reasonably expect a customer of yours who has a relationship with a commercial finance company to remain fairly prompt in his payment pattern of purchases from you. If we have done our job correctly, cash availability should come close to meeting total cash needs, and payables should be relatively current.

I think you might be interested in my covering with you some of the areas finance companies review in assessing prospective borrowers:

1. Management
   A. Identification (who they are)
   B. Experience
   C. Operating Record
   D. Use of Management Tools such as formal planning, budgeting, etc.
2. Collateral
   A. Receivables
      Terms of sale
      Historical performance
      Credit ratings of customers
      Concentrations
   B. Inventory
      What it is
      How it is used
      Estimated value
   C. Fixed Assets
      Appraised on liquidation value basis
3. Financial Condition
   A. Current Liabilities
   B. Long Term Liabilities
   C. Capital Structure
   D. Tax Status

With this information base the finance company, in concert with the prospect's management, should then be able to make a determination that the collateral available will support projected loans in amounts sufficient to meet future projected cash needs.

No discussion of commercial financing would be complete without touching on the costs involved. Typically, our industry charges rates ranging from 5 percent to 8 percent over prime rate on its loans. I know that sounds like an astronomical figure, but consideration must be given to the method used in computing the actual interest charge. Finance companies charge for interest on a daily basis for the funds actually used by a client. Our average client usually does not borrow funds every day—many may take a loan advance on a once-a-week basis, or some other similar schedule. Thus, the loan balance will rise when an advance is taken. However, incoming collections serve to reduce the loan balance until another advance is taken. Thus, the interest charge is based on a balance that fluctuates daily. On an effective cost basis—that is interest dollars paid for borrowed dollars actually used—commercial finance company loans costs can be highly competitive with other types of financing.

It is not unusual for a commercial bank to participate in a commercial finance company's loan to a client. As a matter of fact, this joint lending technique is being actively employed in hundreds of outstanding secured loans today. Under these circumstances the customer is charged at the bank's rate of interest on the funds it is providing, and the finance company will charge its rate on its share. The net result is usually a lower overall effective interest cost to the customer.

Our industry does not maintain that we have the ultimate solution to all short-term borrowing requirements for medium and smaller sized firms. However, we do know that thousands of enterprises have been helped on their way to future success by finance companies through their secured lending techniques. These firms were able to obtain short-term assistance, in the amounts needed, to provide for continued growth and prosperity. We hope that we will continue to enjoy the confidence of the business community in the future, and that we will continue to make a strong contribution to the economy.

Borrowing "Short" for Long-Term Purposes

We have cited term borrowings as an alternative to leasing. It should also be pointed out that accounts receivable and inventory are of interest as collateral to asset-based lenders. This is generally known as *commercial finance*. Provided the borrowings against this collateral permit the orderly handling of current liabilities, such as trade payables, taxes, payroll, and general and administrative expenses, there may be room to borrow enough to acquire desired equipment now. Later, this debt can be converted to more conventional long-term funding.

If the receivables and/or inventory are highly seasonal or fluctuate somewhat erratically, this mode of borrowing may not be prudent, despite the exigencies. A cash flow projection that includes collateral values and loan funds available under formula would indicate the feasibility of this mode.

What is suggested here is that commercial finance might be utilized over and above its proven role as a working capital source for growth-oriented or undercapitalized entities. Within bounds, this financing may also allow some fixed-asset acquisition within the accelerated cash flow generated by such borrowings. It is cited in this vein, almost as a last resort, that some lenders may make the fixed-asset loan using the "chattel" as the primary collateral but taking a "blanket" filing and security agreement on the accounts receivable and/or inventory as added collateral protection, without setting up the loan on a full-dress revolving basis.

Funding through Government Agencies

The Small Business Administration has many programs to fund businesses, including equipment acquisition. Its definitions of a "small business" are somewhat liberal. Direct loans are made by the agency, but loans made by a bank sponsor and guaranteed up to 90 percent by the agency are the usual mode. In these cases, the bank loans 100 percent of the money on a loan approved and guaranteed by the agency. Terms are fairly liberal usually, and interest rates generally reflect the guarantee aspect—that is, a shade less than a similar loan negotiated with a bank and without the SBA guarantee.

The SBA will usually require added collateral (similar to the asset-based lenders), personal guarantees of the principals, and even indentures on their homes in some instances where the venture is untried and the business collateral of limited value. The direct SBA loans are often not available in a timely fashion, due to budgetary limitations, and generally have more involved qualifications, including disaster, import competition, job dislocation, or minority status.

The SBA maintains regional offices to assist in processing loan applications. Most commercial banks have officers who specialize in this type of loan and who are also able to render assistance to the borrower. The loan application is a bit tedious, but generally, the information requested can be found in the applicant's financial reports, tax returns, business plan projections, and the like. All these are matters with which the company's controller or CPA is familiar. In addition, personal history of the principals and their personal financial statements are sought. The SBA is quite concerned about any fees paid (other than nominal) to anyone processing the loan application, since it is rightly trying to control influence peddlers that have preyed upon feckless applicants under the guise of "brokers," "consultants," "financial engineers," and similar titles.

SBA PROGRAMS TO CONSIDER[4]

Some broad categories of SBA programs, with brief descriptions of the types of assistance provided, are listed below:

Small Business Loans (Regular Business Loans, or 7(a) Loans). The most frequently used SBA loan. Its purpose is to aid a small business that is unable to obtain financing in the private credit marketplace. It may be direct or guaranteed/insured. Its uses include building and *equipment acquisition.* Manufacturers, wholesalers, and retailers are eligible. Terms, interest rates, and dollar limits keep pace with inflationary trends and money costs, and the 1977 limit of $450,000 has since been raised. A "split" between fixed and varying "prime plus" rate is now in vogue. Current data should be obtained from your local SBA office.

Displaced Business Loans. Applicable where economic injury has been suffered as a result of displacement by, or location in or near, a federally aided project. Loans are available for a 30-year term maximum, with no dollar limit.

Economic Opportunity Loans. Minority, low-income, or disadvantaged applicants may establish, preserve, or strengthen their business loans up to $100,000, with a 15-year term maximum.

State and Local Development Company Loans. The SBA makes direct loans and insured loans to states and to local (for instance, Urban County) development companies that promote economic growth. These are generally called "501" loans and may represent a consortium of, say, J.O.B.S. and an area development group, and an SBA-guaranteed bank participation.

Federal and State EDA (Economic Development Assistance). The federal program will assist in fixed-asset loans for a maximum of 25 years and in loans for working capital up to five years. It will also issue guarantees for the life of the loan or lease. There usually is a 65 percent project limitation on the federal EDA's involvement, 5 percent from state or local development company, 20 percent by a commercial lender; and 10 percent represents the applicant's equity. Applicants must be in a posture of local industrial expansion, creating new permanent jobs, or expanding in certain redevelopment areas, among other qualifying criteria.

State EDA versions vary, but generally do not provide for funds or the liberal federal guarantee. Typically, the state will act as a "pass-through" for enabling the bonds arising out of the project loan to be tax-free, thus offering a tax benefit to a willing buyer of these bonds, at full credit risk to this buyer. Limited state guarantee in some cases is available. Organization expenses for bond counsel, lender's counsel, and the like can make the interest saving uneconomical on relatively small transactions. In New Jersey, for example, a project of less than $200,000 would be uneconomical and less than $500,000 questionable, when comparing tax-free aspects of low interest rate to total closing and underwriting costs.

FARMERS HOME ADMINISTRATION (FmHA) LOANS

These are 90 percent government insured or guaranteed loans and leases to applicants in cities of 50,000 or less, generally to retain or expand production of goods, materials, or commodities, in addition to improving economic and environmental climate in rural areas (including pollution control). Many banks and private financiers have become involved with these loans, which ranged to $10 million per loan in 1977. The maximum term is 30 years for land and building, *up to 15 years for machinery and equipment,* and 7 years for working capital.

Venture Capitalists, SBICs, MESBICs, EQUITY

Venture capitalists may provide the money for new investment. Some have been around for generations, others are fairly recent in their risk money activities. They include basically four types:

1. *Investment Bank Affiliates.* Investment firms have created separate groups to invest in fledgling companies. Once established, these groups will provide customers with corporate financing services.

2. *Insurance Company Affiliates.* A number of insurance companies allocate assets to venture capital subsidiaries.

3. *Small Business Investment Companies (SBICs) and Minority Enterprise Small Business Investment Companies (MESBICs).* Government-backed but privately administered, some SBICs and MESBICs are funded by large banks and insurance companies. It is estimated that 1978 will evidence SBA obligations of $20 million in direct and $100 million in guaranteed loans for equity and venture capital to small businesses and business ventures by the disadvantaged. SBIC debentures having up to a 15-year term with SBA guarantee provide the rediscounting means to make "sound-value" or secured loans that will reasonably assure repayment from successful operations of the small business community.

4. *Independents.* These include family interests, such as the Rockefellers, and those funded by large industrial companies, such as Dow Chemical, Exxon, and Johnson & Johnson. American Research and Development (now part of Textron) was most successful in seeing a $61,000

venture capital investment in Digital Equipment Corporation grow to $382 million when it cashed in DEC stock in 1972!

All venture capitalists seek a "piece of the action," that is, some equity or options on stock ownership, as part of their compensation for risk taking. They will, in varying degrees, supply management guidance and assistance, possibly through joining the company's board of directors. Philosophies and degrees of control or assistance vary among the venture capitalists, and more than one application or contact is indicated in the search for funds. Here, a presentation in the format of a prospectus or 10-K is a good beginning to launch the application.

Other Financing Alternatives

When the business is hard pressed for loan sources, ingenuity (or desperation) may indicate some final alternatives:

1. *Principals/Employees.* Either directly or through friends or relatives, funds may be arranged as a loan, or added equity. Sometimes key employees will choose to make loans to a long-time employer. This also gives rise to the Employee Stock Ownership Plan or Trust (ESOP/ ESOT), which can be a vehicle for fund raising. These are particularly attractive to key employees in high-technology industries.

2. *CSVLI.* Many times the company may be able to borrow significant amounts at nominal rates, based on cash surrender values of insurance policies on key personnel, on which premiums had been paid for a number of years.

3. *Customer or Supplier Loan.* This may be an alternative for specific machinery yielding product improvements or lower costs available to key customers, given a strong working relationship between the firm and its customers or suppliers. Funds may be loaned by the customer to the seller, repayable on a term or "rolling" basis. Conversely, a supplier desirous of increasing sales may consider lending financial assistance toward equipment acquisition that will ensure greater demand for the supplier's product. Settlement can be by royalty or deferred payout terms.

While leasing is an attractive form of financing, it may not always be available, for a variety of reasons described in this chapter. As a consequence, the prospective lessee/borrower is forced to return to the other money and capital market to secure funds. A number of sources are available through private and government agencies. This chapter indicated some of the sources and types of loans available. The intention was to provide not a comprehensive listing but rather a starting point.

NOTES

1. For more information on sources of credit, see National Commerce Finance Conference (NCFC), 1 Penn Plaza, New York, N.Y. 10001.
2. Reprinted from the December 4, 1978, issue of *Business Week* by special permission. Copyright © 1978 by McGraw-Hill, Inc., New York, N.Y. 10020. All rights reserved.
3. "Commercial Finance Companies as Short-Term Lenders," reprint of a speech by G. Pat Bacon, Senior Vice President, Control Division, Aetna Business Credit, Inc., on the occasion of the 81st Annual Credit Congress of the National Association of Credit Management, May 18, 1977.
4. For additional information, see 1977 Catalog of Federal Domestic Assistance (CFDA), Superintendent of Documents, Government Printing Office, Washington, D.C.

CHAPTER 12

The Equipment Leasing Industry

In Chapters 8 and 9 we examined the quantitative methods required to make the lease-versus-purchase and leasing decisions. In this chapter we examine some of the important aspects of the equipment leasing industry, showing trends and additional qualitative rationale for the decisions. The chapter is structured for the lessee, and prospective lessee, to provide added insight into the leasing industry. The authors are especially grateful to the Department of Commerce and to Frost & Sullivan for industrial data contained in this chapter.

Dimensions and Directions of the Equipment Leasing Industry

Statistics as to the size of the equipment leasing industry vary, but reliable estimates are available from at least three major sources: the American Association of Equipment Lessors, Frost & Sullivan, and the Department of Commerce.

Industry estimates indicate a growth from about $20 billion of equipment under lease in 1968 to over $100 billion in 1976. The average annual dollar value of leased equipment has increased at an annual rate of about 15 percent a year, and now approximately 20 percent of all new capital equipment is under lease, with differences existing, of course, from industry to industry. We see this trend as continuing, especially when noting that of the 1,200 largest firms in the United States only about 300 are able to sell public or private debt, sell equity, or borrow from banks in significant amounts.[1]

The Department of Commerce[2] provides an interesting perspective on the growth, versatility, and directions of the leasing industry:

The impressive growth of equipment leasing since the mid-1960s indicates that the industry offers a useful service of the nation's financial marketplace. The dollar value of new leases reached an estimated $15 billion in 1975. The average dollar value of new equipment leased has increased at an estimated 12 percent to 15 percent rate in the past several years.

Industry sources estimate lease-related finance methods account for about one-third of all new industrial and business equipment acquisitions today. General equipment leasing by manufacturers and captives accounts for about half of all lease transactions; third-party lessors—finance companies, independent leasing firms, and bank organizations—for one-third; and the remainder consists of auto and truck leases.

More than half of the respondents to a 1975 industry-sponsored survey of the equipment leasing industry had entered the leasing business since 1970. The survey, conducted by the accounting firm of Deloitte, Haskins, and Sells, indicated that the average cost of equipment leased under direct full-payout leases in fiscal 1974 was $14.4 million.

Production machinery and equipment accounted for 24 percent of all direct, full-payment leases; office machinery and equipment for 18 percent; transportation equipment for 13 percent; and construction machinery for 11 percent. Three-fifths of these leases were not cancelable for three to five years. The noncancelable term for 29 percent of the leases was five to seven years.

Leasing markets have expanded significantly in recent years and almost every type of business is leasing equipment today. All types of transportation equipment are lease financed—jet planes, railroad freight cars, oil tankers, ships, trucks, and automobiles. There is a large demand for leased computers, machine tools, oil refinery processing equipment, and special industrial machinery, including farming, textile, and construction machinery. All kinds of miscellaneous capital goods are leased, including restaurant equipment, complex and costly medical equipment, and pollution abatement equipment. In addition, project lease financing—the leasing of entire manufacturing plants except real estate—is increasing.

Although equipment leasing abroad by U.S. companies only started in the late 1960s, *equipment on lease (at original cost) in Western Europe and Great Britain was estimated at $30 billion by 1975*. One of the reasons for the *growing popularity of leasing as a form of financing new equipment abroad is that European banks generally offer loans for only about three years,* and equipment buyers are therefore required to negotiate two or three loans during the life of a particular piece of equipment. (Italics added)

About 75 *American leasing companies*—independent companies, members of joint ventures, and leasing subsidiaries of American banks—are engaged in leasing activity abroad. In addition, there are about *200 European companies in the leasing business,* many of which belong to Leaseurope Trade Association. *Leasing companies offer three types of financing to European clients*—true leases, conditional sale agreements, and secured loans and chattel mortgages for larger equipment purchases. (Italics added)

As in the United States, all types of equipment are being leased abroad—tankers, railroad cars, computers, machine tools, printing presses, restaurant equipment, mining equipment, and oil-drilling rigs. *In contrast to the equipment leasing industry in this country, leveraged leases are not used internationally and international leases do not offer the benefits of depreciation or the possibility of residual value since foreign laws regarding depreciation and tax credits are different than U.S. laws.* (Italics added)

Different types of lessors handle overseas business differently. One lessor may only operate through affiliates abroad, while another has subsidiaries (mostly joint ventures) in foreign countries. The main object of manufacturer-oriented leasing companies is to assist manufacturing internationally, while bank holding companies essentially provide financing services. *Laws governing lease agreements in European countries vary.* For example, a lessor may not [by law] provide a purchase option in England but must provide a purchase option in France. Depreciation and tax credit rules also differ by country. (Italics added)

While a large portion of overseas equipment leasing serves multinational companies abroad, the bulk of leasing activity for independent companies consists of "cross border financing"—wherein financing is provided in one foreign country and the leased equipment is actually used in another country. These types of lease transactions across international borders are generally not true leases but are conditional sales contracts, since the contracts provide for the purchase of equipment at lease termination.

Most equipment leasing companies are interested in exploring potential leasing markets abroad despite restrictive foreign government regulations regarding percent local ownership requirements, varying tax laws, foreign exchange fluctuations, and funding problems with subsidiaries or affiliates.

From the lessor side of the equipment leasing industry we see, then, at least three types of major firms. The first are the producers of durable goods which have established either captive leasing companies or credit companies to provide outside financing of purchases from the parent firm. Second are the various banks and bank holding companies which provide leases as an alternative to secured loans. The third group are the independent leasing companies which serve as brokers, as well as lessors. Their respective market shares were indicated in the Commerce Department's report above.

Market Nature within the Industry

Studies of the market nature, competitive structure, and trends within the equipment leasing industry indicate important aspects worthy of note by the prospective lessee. Much of the material in this section is drawn from work done by McGugan and Caves[3] in a paper reporting on a survey sponsored by the Federal Reserve Bank of Boston in 1972.

The equipment leasing industry is highly competitive in nature, containing both national and regional structures. Although the number of third-party independent lessors has been on the decline, the growth of the banking industry in the leasing area has maintained a healthy competitive spirit. The leasing market appears to be as highly competitive as the buyer's market, offering both the same variety and sources for typically homogeneous products, as well as generally a variety of sources for highly specialized, and even custom-built, equipment. The leasing industry provides multiple types of financing sources through the use of different types of leases for the same equipment.

Although some of the conclusions from the McGugan and Caves study may be dated since the survey results were taken in 1972, it appears that their analyses of the structural traits are still valid and warrant attention. Their materials, along with other pertinent information, are summarized below:

1. Relevant market size varies with the size of the lessor and lessee. Thus, larger lessors and lessees tend to operate nationally, while smaller ones are regional in nature. The American Association of Equipment Lessors reports that one-third of direct full-payout lease activity was done by firms doing 80 percent or more of their business in one or two states; another third by lessors conducting their business regionally; and the remainder by national lessors.

2. Larger market shares are limited to two types of lessors: (1) those in isolated markets lacking much local competition and (2) large, highly specialized lessors.

3. There do not exist any substantial barriers limiting entrance into the equipment leasing business.

4. Specialization correlates inversely with the size of the lessor; the smaller the lessor, the higher the degree of specialization. A lessor is said to specialize when over 50 percent of its business is limited to a single equipment category.

5. There is little product differentiation within the leasing industry. If a lessor devises a unique lease form, it will be quickly copied.

6. The AAEL sees a growing degree of concentration within the industry. The small independents are tending to go out of business, with

banks picking up market shares. Although there are new independents coming into the industry, the number has been declining.

Frost & Sullivan's Analysis of Industrial Equipment Leasing Market Structure

Frost & Sullivan has undertaken a comprehensive study of the equipment leasing industry.[4] This section relies primarily on its report and provides additional background information to the prospective lessee.

The Frost & Sullivan report provides thorough data using sources including trade journals, U.S. Department of Commerce reports, *Survey of Current Business,* The Conference Board, annual reports of various companies, and data supplied by informed industry personnel. The report segregates the industry into major components: computer equipment; office equipment and retail store fixtures; machine tools; special industrial equipment; materials-handling and "ecology" equipment; instruments for measurement, analysis, and control; medical and dental instruments and equipment; and communications and electronics equipment. Each is discussed briefly below:

1. *Computer equipment.* IBM has been, and continues to be, the dominant force within this sector. While some lessors are involved in total computer lease packages, many are becoming increasingly interested in peripheral equipment that is compatible with IBM systems but is less expensive. The most explosive portion of the computer market is in the minicomputers and microcomputers, data-entry, and telecommunications areas.

A primary difficulty experienced by lessors is that when IBM introduces new higher-speed equipment, the market tends to discount the price of existing equipment to equate price with performance. This, of course, places added high risk on the lessors, which may be to the advantage of lessees. Estimates for 1975 were for about $1 billion of new computer equipment going under lease, and the market is expected to expand.

2. *Office equipment and retail store fixtures.* This market is for small-ticket items, ranging from $2,000 to $17,000. Also, since much of the equipment is electro-mechanical, service and maintenance are very important. The size of leases and the concurrent need for prompt service have led to formation of numerous local leasing companies. Larger lessors usually work this section in conjunction with major product procedures. As examples of the lease market penetration, about 30 percent of calculating and accounting machines and 20 percent of retail store fixtures were leased in 1975, with the percentage being leased on the increase.

Three features of this leasing area warrant attention. First, many firms want to establish sale–leaseback arrangements, that is, sell all their office equipment and desks and lease them back, thus freeing funds to working capital. Second, since many small firms want to lease, credit problems are very common. Third, since office equipment is relatively homogeneous, re-leasing is frequent.

3. *Machine tools.* Machine tools are used by many small and medium-size manufacturers, which frequently do not have the capital required for purchase. Manufacturers of the equipment also generally lack the capital to become lessors. Consequently, this has been a growing area for third-party and bank leasing companies. Frost & Sullivan estimates that leasing accounted for 30 percent of the 1975 market, with continued growth expected. Frequently, machine tool manufacturers establish ongoing relationships with leasing companies as an aid to selling their equipment.

4. *Special industrial equipment.* This is a broad category including farming, construction, oil fields, food production, textiles, and printing trades. Special characteristics of this area include generally low level of obsolescence, high degree of portability, and limited general application of equipment because of high specialization and the cyclical nature of the industries employing the equipment.

Within the farming sector, 35 percent of new shipments were under lease. Leasing appeals to both smaller cash-poor farmers and larger agribusinesses that desire to enhance financial leverage.

Lease and rentals overlap in the construction sector, and in some instances, equipment renters lease the equipment they rent to others. The largest segment of this market is earth-moving equipment. Use of construction equipment varies with GNP, and hence the industry growth pattern is not entirely uniform, but the percentage of leased equipment is steadily growing, from 25 percent in 1972 to 35 percent in 1975.

Leasing has been minimal in the food processing industry, with the percent of new equipment under lease running at about 10 percent. By contrast, the textile industry leases about 30 percent of new shipments. Leasing is firmly established in the printing trade industry. Again, most small printers lack sufficient capital to purchase, and leasing may offer the only viable alternative to asset acquisition.

5. *Materials-handling and "ecology" equipment.* Frost & Sullivan includes conveyors, elevators, cranes, hoists, industrial trucks, and standard emission-control and purifying equipment for industry in this category. Leasing has increased steadily in all these areas, with strongest

activity in the mobile crane and lift-fork truck, easily mobile segments. The fastest-growing portion is the pollution-control equipment. The percentage of new leased materials-handling and ecology-related equipment increased from 15 percent in 1972 to 25 percent in 1975.

6. *Instruments for measurement, analysis, and control.* With both the general complexity of laboratory equipment and the capital intensity increasing, many firms have strained to acquire more sophisticated electronic devices. The capital burden has resulted in a large new market for leasing. While instrumentation is only a very small part of larger firms' total investment, shipments to independent laboratories, for example, represent a large market. Consequently, the major thrust of leasing is to independent laboratories and research firms. The leasing industry has been troubled in this area, since many lessees have been highly specialized and undercapitalized. In the case of business reversals, the leasing companies have been placed in very difficult positions with respect to asset liquidation.

7. *Medical and dental instruments and equipment.* The medical-care industry now ranks third in size, and there has been rapid growth in leasing in this area. From the viewpoint of the public hospitals, the necessity to lease has resulted from low cash resources and the inability to enjoy benefits of investment tax credits. In 1975, 30 percent of new equipment shipments were under lease. Hospitals are increasingly turning to leasing for equipping operating theaters and intensive care units. With the cost of equipping a dental office over $60,000, the need for leasing is obvious.

8. *Communications and electronics equipment.* Until 1968 AT&T dominated the communications industry with an almost perfect monopoly. Although it practiced leasing/renting of equipment to customers, there did not exist the sort of leasing that was prevalent in other industries. After the landmark 1968 decision, other companies were permitted to connect into AT&T equipment. This increase in the freedom of competition has led to leasing. In fact, within the "interconnect" industry, leasing is almost mandated, since customers have been accustomed to leasing equipment.

This summarizes the primary market sectors of leasing and indicates the rapid and continued growth throughout all segments. It appears that the use of leasing will continue to grow and many managers will devote more time to plant operations and the study of leasing alternatives rather than to capital acquisition. One area of leasing of prime importance to many small firms is the leasing of machine tools. We will look at some aspects of this market in the following section.

Leasing in the Machine Tool Industry

In the early 1960s many machine shop owners realized it was time to update their war surplus machine tools in order to retain a competitive market posture. Financing was a critical factor because of rapidly increasing prices and capital insufficiencies. Inflation had an impact in two ways. First, the price of machine tools increased rapidly. Second, the cost of qualified labor necessitated utilization of more productive equipment, further increasing the cost of purchase. While most small owners have typically taken great pride in ownership, for many this option is no longer available.

Typical of machine tool companies that entered the leasing industry is Warner & Swasey Corporation. Warner & Swasey started leasing in 1954. Initial entry was primarily in the textile industry, an industry characterized by intense utilization of machinery, some of which has a relatively short useful life. Recognizing the profitability of leasing, the company quickly extended to machine tools and in 1968 created its own financial subsidiary.

As an example of a popular machine tool that is commonly leased, consider the turret punch press, which punches numerous designs in sheet metal and is commonly used in the machine tool industry. Although these presses are ideally suited for smaller shops, they cost upward of $75,000—an amount frequently well beyond practical purchasing constraints. Thus, leasing has become a popular alternative, and both the number and dollar value of machine tools leased has increased dramatically over the last ten years.

The machine tool leasing industry is dominated by manufacturer-lessors, which lease well over 50 percent of all machine tools. In some instances, it appears that the leasing subsidiary has an exclusive leasing arrangement with the parent company. Other manufacturers have pre-established arrangements with bank leasing companies. The former appear to have a slight competitive edge in some instances in that service may be more easily facilitated and the manufacturer is in a position to deal with the equipment at the end of the lease term. The relative importance of being able to take the equipment back at lease termination may, however, be questioned, since nearly all machine tool leases are written with purchase options—and in most cases the option is exercised. Some industry experts estimate that 90 percent of machine tool leases contain purchase options and that nearly all are exercised. There seem to be two primary reasons underlying this trend. First, with regular maintenance the machines generally have a longer economic life than the lease term, but the fair market value at lease end is usually relatively low, leading to reasonable sale prices. Second, owners of small firms enjoy a pride of ownership and frequently like to purchase at lease end.

The manufacturer-lessors and third-party lessors usually view the market somewhat differently. The manufacturers with regional outlets can afford to write smaller leases than the third-party lessors. The latter frequently are regional in nature with respect to a specific geographic area, but also national in scope. An example is BankAmerica, which has nine lease offices in California and several others located nationally. They establish a lease package minimum of about $25,000 to $50,000 within the California region and a larger minimum for leases written in the rest of the country.

The prospective lessee must bear in mind the fact that manufacturer-lessors are primarily in the manufacturing business (although some may claim to make more profit through lease financing than through manufacturing), whereas third-party lessors are in the money business. The former should offer more product services, and the latter more financial services. Some leases for machine tools require a 10 percent security deposit, which may be increased in instances of poor credit rating. Furthermore, in some cases where the applicant for a lease has marginal credit, personal guarantees may be required. But, within the limits of credit requirements, most lease applications can be approved within a few weeks. Most lease arrangements are for a five- to ten-year period, with renewal available depending upon the economic life of the machine in question. Some leases provide for cancelation, but in this industry, interest seems to be more on early purchase than on cancelation.

Although, as mentioned above, a security deposit may be required, this is generally significantly less than the down payment necessary to purchase. Furthermore, the lease payment schedule usually calls for only one month's payment in advance, with the remaining payments to start when the machine is in operation. This arrangement permits the user to correlate cash inflows from the machine with the outflows necessary to support its existence. Correlation of these cash flows permits stability of working capital—an area of major concern to nearly all small firms.

Depreciation Revisited

Another factor of importance to the lease-versus-purchase decision is depreciation. The underlying rationale for depreciation is that machinery wears out over its useful life and this wasting of assets should be shown as an expense on the firm's income statement.

While the "depreciation expense" is, in fact, only implicit in nature (that is, it does not result in a cash payment), depreciation does affect the firm's total cash flow from operations. The cash flow from operations consists of two parts: the after-tax profits and the depreciation-generated cash throw-offs. The latter result from the fact that depreciation, although shown as an expense, does not require a cash outflow. In theory, depreciation should generate enough cash which, when invested over the life of an asset, will result in funds sufficient to replace the asset. However, with inflation, and interest on invested funds being taxable, this is seldom the case. The process is demonstrated in Example 1.

EXAMPLE 1
Depreciation and Replacement Cost

A firm has purchased a machine for $10,000. The machine has zero salvage and a ten-year life. Management has decided to depreciate the machine straight-line and place the depreciation cash throw-offs in an account bearing 7 percent interest. The funds will be invested at the end of each year. Assuming the price of replacement machinery is expected to increase at an annual rate of 8 percent and the firm has a 20 percent tax rate, determine the projected cost of a replacement in ten years and the amount of money the firm will have set aside to purchase the replacement.

SOLUTION

First, determine the expected cost of the replacement machine, on the basis of an average yearly price increase of 8 percent each year over the next ten years. Refer to Appendix D, column 1.

$$\$10,000 \times 2.158925 = \$21,589.25$$

The price of the machine will more than double in ten years to $21,589.25.

Second, determine the amount the yearly investment of $1,000 will become in ten years. Since the firm has a 20 percent tax rate, the effective after-tax interest rate on savings is 5.5 percent rather than 7 percent (7% − .20 × 7% ≈ 5.5%). We need to find the factor for a ten-year compound of an annuity (column 2 from Appendix D). Since we do not have a table for 5.5 percent, we will take the average of the factors for 5 percent and 6 percent (12.577893 and 13.180795), which is 12.879344. Thus, at the end of ten years the firm would have accumulated $1,000 × 12.879344 = $12,879.34 to purchase the new machine, a shortfall of $8,709.91 or 40 percent of the replacement cost. □

Example 1 points to the almost impossible situation faced by management in periods of high inflation. In order to acquire the needed $21,589.25, management would have to invest $1,676.27 at the end of each year for ten years. In order to make this investment, it would be necessary to invest $676.27 out of after-tax profits each year—an impossibility for nearly all firms. The funds generated through depreciation are not sufficient to cover replacement cost, and hence additional funds are required.

Leasing, of course, negates the whole process of depreciation until the end of the lease term, when the asset may be purchased. Even then, however, the fair market value of the asset is likely to be so low as to render the whole question of investment for replacement mute. The would-be lessee should be cautioned that the same economic process that made the purchase replacement of an asset difficult is also felt in leasing. While the lease cost is fixed for the term of the lease, if the lessee, at the end of the lease, wants to lease a new machine having the same function as the old machine, the cost will likely be twice the current cost. The reason is not hard to find: the cost of the new machine will be twice the cost of the old machine, given the 8 percent inflation postulated above. The fact that the fixed cost of leasing will probably jump in large steps when a lease ends must be weighed as a part of the pricing policy that the lessee establishes. The lessee must not become complacent with a fixed lease cost over a period of years of rising prices. Rather, as a part of his financial planning and managerial accounting, he must plan for increased lease costs as lease terms reach maturity.

Further Considerations

Each lease arrangement should be viewed on a case-by-case basis, utilizing the full scope of managerial expertise ranging from legal to accounting and engineering to operating management. Each of these functional areas may be the source of hidden advantages to leasing or of restrictions that preclude or thwart its possible use.

The initial consideration is the possibility of either loan or existing lease covenants that may restrict further leasing. Restrictive agreements are becoming more common in term loans and revolving credit as the popularity of leasing as a form of debt financing has increased. This factor warrants close attention, and, if possible, the prospective borrower or lessee should attempt to negotiate out of an agreement those terms which may restrict flexibility in the future. Lendors and lessors want maximum protection and design agreements to provide this. However, depending upon the competitive market positions, it may be possible to alter the agreement to the advantage of the lessee.

While a variety of equipment can be leased, equipment categories with the following characteristics[5] present the most viable candidates for leasing:

New. Used equipment does not qualify for the liberal depreciation tax benefits enjoyed by new equipment. Since the full advantages of tax credits and depreciation are at the heart of leasing, new equipment is preferable. Furthermore, a fair market value is more easily ascertainable for new than for used equipment. Lack of information on market value precludes the detailed financial analysis of lease versus purchase.

Durable. Equipment with a short useful life may fail to meet tax law provisions essential to both depreciation and leasing.

Low risk of obsolescence. While much of the risk of obsolescence is borne by the lessor, unless a lease is short-term or readily cancelable (which is unlikely), the lessee may be stuck with outmoded equipment. Selection of equipment with low risk of obsolescence is beneficial to both lessee and lessor.

Low maintenance requirements. Equipment that requires frequent repairs, and especially modifications and alterations, may prove to be disadvantageous to the lessee. The reason is that the principal value underlying the equipment may have been borne by the lessee while accruing to the lessor in terms of residual value.

Portability. To the extent possible, the equipment should be movable from the lessee's premises.

Marketable. Although equipment designed to lessee specification may be leased, equipment that is readily marketable represents the most viable candidate for leasing. Opportunity for resale favors both lessee and lessor by assuring fair lease terms and potential for easily established fair market valuation of residuals.

Distinct. Identification is hampered when equipment lacks specific boundaries. For example, valves, sensors, and related hook-up assemblies of a fire detection system may be identifiable by serial number, but this raises administrative problems when residual value may be less than cost of removal.

Readily identifiable. Some units that may be leased are designed to facilitate rapid interchange and hence may be commingled. Identification through serial number is, again, necessitated.

High unit cost. The higher the cost per unit, the lower the ratio of administrative cost to potential cost savings through leasing. Generally, administrative record-keeping costs increase directly with the number of items under lease. To minimize these costs, it is preferable to lease large-ticket items.

As a further aid in making the lease-versus-purchase decision, we have included sample leases provided by First National State Bank Leasing Company of Newark, New Jersey, in Appendix B. The prospective lessee is encouraged to review them, since they are typical of those currently available in the industry.

Another important consideration to the prospective lessee is the actual selection of a lessor. Two checklists from BankAmeriLease[6] are reproduced on the following pages.

Selection of Lessor

Once a company has decided to finance equipment through leasing, the company must then make a very important decision: choosing a lessor. While the lease rate is certainly a major factor when choosing a lessor, experienced lessees have learned that rate alone is not necessarily the overriding consideration. The ability of the lessor to make a firm commitment and complete the transaction from its own resources as proposed and represented is an essential consideration, since some lessors are merely uncapitalized brokers who will seek to lay off the transaction to a third party for a fee.

There are, of course, many legitimate, established leasing companies and prestigious investment banking firms engaged in brokering leases, and they are thoroughly reliable.

A word of caution, however. There are brokers who, if initially selected, habitually later seek to renegotiate the rate or insist on covenants which add to the cost in order to lay off the transaction. After having "low balled" the transaction to obtain a commitment, they later seek to renegotiate the deal in order to raise the yield to a level which will be satisfactory to investors even after inclusion of the broker's fee. Often the lease ends up at a higher rate than would have been available to the lessee from a legitimate lessor at the outset of the transaction.

The integrity and continuity of the lessor and the lessee's access to the lessor during the lease term are obviously important factors in selecting a lessor.

Lessee's Checklist for Evaluating a Lessor

In evaluating the choice of a lessor, the responsible financial officer should ask the following questions.

Every "no" answer regarding a prospective lessor should raise apprehensions regarding the capability of that lessor to perform as represented and in a satisfactory manner. Furthermore, the degree of risk rises with the number of "no" answers.

It is possible to deal exclusively with a lessor such as a BankAmeriLease company, which rates a "yes" answer on every question.

	Yes	No
1. Will sign a firm commitment subject only to documentation.	___	___
2. Will not broker entire transaction to a third party who may be difficult to deal with.	___	___
3. Is adequately capitalized to back up a firm commitment.	___	___

		Yes	*No*

4. Will furnish an audited statement; will state net worth.
5. Is substantial from a financial and management point of view.
6. Is experienced and has a clear history in the equipment leasing business.
7. Has a good anticipated future in equipment leasing and will be available for consultation throughout term of the lease.
8. Is not a promoter type who will disappear after payment of his fee.
9. Is familiar with the special legal problems related to a lease.
10. Understands and can correctly analyze the income tax considerations.
11. If undercapitalized, will post a deposit to ensure performance.
12. Will disclose the full amount of any fees he will receive in the transaction.
13. The "leasing company" has not purposely submitted a "low ball" bid.
14. If a broker, will not enter into special arrangements for his fee such as "residual sharing" which may jeopardize the "true lease" and result in liability to the lessee under the tax indemnity clause.
15. All material facts will be presented in obtaining the tax ruling since the ruling may be valueless if this is not the case and the lessee's risk of liability under the tax indemnity clause will increase.
16. The transaction may be booked for financial accounting purposes as presented.
17. Has financial resources to do follow-on lease financing of retrofits, improvements, or additions.
18. Will not broker the lease to a number of parties, no one of whom can bind the others and who will be difficult to deal with as a group if changes are later needed.
19. Will not disrupt the lessee's credit standing by contacting financial debt and credit sources all over the country in attempting to broker the transaction.
20. If the commitment is not firm, the broker will disclose in advance how he will go about finding equity participants and whom he will contact.

Yes   No

21. If the broker intends to bring in other brokers to help find equity participants, he will disclose who they are, whom they will contact, the amount of their fees, and who will pay the fees.   ___ ___

22. The broker will make correct representations to the equity participants so they will thoroughly understand their rights and obligations under the lease and not become disgruntled investors with whom it will be difficult to deal should the need arise.   ___ ___

23. The equity participants will be financially able to meet their obligations to the owner trustee.   ___ ___

24. The overall cost of the transaction has not been needlessly raised by a broker's fee.   ___ ___

Equity Investor's Checklist for Evaluating a Packager or Broker

Leverage in a leveraged lease is a double-edged sword. Credit exposure and tax exposure is large in comparison to the equity investment. If an equity investor is not familiar with all facets of leveraged leasing or does not intend to directly negotiate and follow the transaction, the investor is well advised to deal only with a packager which the investor knows he can trust.

The following checklist is intended to be helpful to an investor in determining packagers with whom to deal. Each "no" answer should make an investor apprehensive.

Yes   No

1. The packager has a thorough knowledge of the many facets of leveraged leasing. The packager can be relied upon to correctly describe an investor's rights and liabilities in the transaction.   ___ ___

2. The packager has continuity of interest in the transaction, will have responsible people available for consultation during the term of the lease, and will be concerned with a continuing relationship with the investor.   ___ ___

3. The method of booking the transaction has been explained and the quality of the multiple investment yield has been confirmed by other methods of lease analysis such as standard sinking fund.   ___ ___

4. The packager is not just interested in earning a fee, will not color the facts, and will not attempt to gloss over material facts.   ___ ___

5. The credit analysis of the lessee is correct, and the yield is sufficient to justify a subordinate security interest in the asset.   ___ ___

	Yes	No

6. The packager has explained the significance of the fact that the debt holders' security interest in the asset is superior to the equity investor's and that if the debt obligations are not met, the debt holders can foreclose on the asset. ____ ____

7. If possible, appropriate guarantees by the parent of the lessee have been obtained, are properly drafted, are not mere paper guarantees unenforceable unless and until numerous conditions precedent have been met and other remedies exhausted, and are not subject to numerous suretyship defenses. ____ ____

8. Any residual value assumption in the yield analysis is reasonable and is based upon an in-depth study of the equipment, its use during the lease term, its possible obsolescence, its portability, the cost of transportation and preparation for transportation, and its possible value to a third party. ____ ____

9. The location of the asset has been disclosed and its use at that location will create no special tax problems, licensing problems, or problems with state qualifications in operating a business. ____ ____

10. If the asset is to be used outside of the United States, no foreign-source or other income tax problems will result. ____ ____

11. The transaction may be booked as presented. ____ ____

12. The depreciation election used in the economic analysis presented by the packager is available to the investor. ____ ____

13. All material facts will be presented in obtaining the tax ruling (since the ruling may be valueless if this is not the case). ____ ____

14. The duties and obligations of the owner-trustee are sufficiently passive to prevent adverse discretionary action and to ensure the flow-through of tax benefits. ____ ____

15. If the transaction is supported by a "take-or-pay" contract, the purchaser agrees to pay even though the services or products are not furnished. ____ ____

16. The provisions of the lease as to default, early termination for obsolescence, and casualty loss coincide with the terms of the bonds to permit early prepayment of the bonds. ____ ____

17. Tort liability to third parties with respect to the asset leased (such as in the case of aircraft, nuclear fuel, and oil

	Yes	No
spillage from tankers) has been explained and protected against.	__	__

18. Owning the equipment or entering into the lease will not create additional liability for state income tax or for state franchise tax other than as contemplated.

19. The lease places the burden on the lessee for any sales tax, use tax, stamp tax, excise tax, or license tax.

20. In the event of a default in the lease by the lessee, owner participants have the right to correct or prevent defaults and foreclosures by fulfilling the obligations of the lessee.

21. Owner participants have a right to sell or dispose of their equity participation interests.

22. The lease is designed so the residual is not a negative residual, such as an obsolete piece of equipment which will cost money to remove.

23. Any special approvals required by state or federal regulatory agencies have been disclosed and can be obtained.

24. The extent to which the yield represented is dependent upon reinvestment rate, residual, and present and future income tax rates has been disclosed.

25. Credit exposure and income tax exposure if a default occurs at any time during the lease have been disclosed.

NOTES

1. American Association of Equipment Lessors, "Leasing," *Fortune*, November 1976.
2. U. S. Department of Commerce, *Equipment Leasing and Rental Industries: Trends and Prospects*, Superintendent of Documents, Government Printing Office, Washington, D.C., 1976.
3. Vincent J. McGugan and Richard E. Caves, "Integration and Competition in the Equipment Leasing Industry," *The Journal of Business*, July 1974.
4. *The Equipment Leasing Market*, Report No. 382, 1976, Frost & Sullivan, Inc., 106 Fulton St., New York, N.Y. 10038; used with permission.
5. This section draws on material prepared by Richard G. Turner in an unpublished paper, "Equipment Leasing: The Machine Tool Industry," Drexel University, 1978.
6. *On-the-Spot Leveraged Leasing*, San Francisco, California, BankAmeriLease Group, 1978, pp. 52–55. Used with permission.

CHAPTER 13

Automobile Leasing

In this chapter we examine some of the aspects of automobile leasing and provide a framework for making the lease-versus-purchase decision. The various advantages and disadvantages of leasing automobiles are detailed. The questions of leasing are addressed primarily from the viewpoint of the smaller firm, since most large companies have fleet managers.

The automotive leasing industry is growing rapidly. While only 15 years ago about 7 percent of vehicles were leased, industry experts expect this figure to rise to about 40 percent of the total market by mid-1980.

There are many sources for automotive leasing. Until recently, two independent leasing companies—Peterson, Howell, and Heather, Inc., and Rollins Leasing Inc.—were the largest. Main Line Fleets Inc. specialized in executive and single luxury car leases. Furthermore many automobile dealers leased, but this represented a small part of the market share. Interestingly, dealers frequently have cooperative arrangements so that they will lease various makes of cars.

For the most part, leasing companies purchased cars from a factory-authorized dealer, financed the loan through either a bank or an automotive credit company, and then leased the vehicle. Until recently

The authors gratefully acknowledge the valuable assistance of Paul J. Tully, Vice President, The Johnson Companies, Newtown, Pa., and Edward L. Bogar and William C. Strang, Winner Ford, Cherry Hill, N.J., in the preparation of this chapter.

many automobile dealerships were either unable or unwilling to seriously enter the leasing business. To a large extent, the limitation placed on dealers relates directly to their ability to borrow sufficient funds. Many have found it difficult to obtain adequate financing to meet their normal needs and at the same time provide for the typical 24 or 36 month lease financing costs.

In recent years the market complexion has changed. The automobile manufacturers themselves are pushing leasing through their dealers, using Ford Leasing, Chrysler Leasing, GMAC, and so on. The profitability in leasing is anticipated to grow and become a major factor in the future. Banks also are becoming involved directly with leasing. Thus, we have observed a dramatic increase in the number of leasing companies, to the point that it has now become a buyer's or lessee's market.

A very interesting arrangement involves a franchise plan promoted by some banks, wherein the bank offers a complete financing, billing, and credit service insurance plan to participating dealers. When a bank approves a lease, the participating dealer receives a commission for leasing the automobile. The bank then handles all financing, billing, and resale at lease end.

Types of Leases

There are basically two types of automobile leases: closed-end and open-end. The most common is the closed-end lease, wherein the lessee pays a stated monthly lease payment and returns the vehicle at the end of the lease without further obligation, provided the vehicle has been properly maintained and has not exceeded the stipulated mileage limit.

Most closed-end leases are for 24 or 36 months. An excess mileage fee, generally of five to twenty cents per mile (depending on the vehicle involved), is charged when the lessee exceeds the mileage limit. Lessors attempt to keep mileage below 50,000, since exceeding this amount tends to lower wholesale used-car values. If the lessee is approaching the limit before the end of the lease, it may be advantageous to lease another car. Lessors also favor this.

In establishing the monthly lease payments in a closed-end lease, the lessor estimates the wholesale value at lease end and subtracts this from the price to obtain the depreciation over the lease period. The depreciation is averaged for the number of months and added to the interest, tags, operating expense, profit, and sales tax to get the monthly payment. The key to the lessor's profit or loss comes at the end of the lease. If the wholesale value exceeds the estimate used to figure the lease payments, then the lessor's profit is enhanced. The converse is also true. All risk and profit potential is retained by the lessor.

The open-end lease places the risk burden on the lessee. The vehicle at lease end must yield a predetermined value; if it does not, the lessee must make up the difference. The open-end lease is very similar, in fact, to the old (and now mostly illegal) balloon-repayment auto loans. Lease payments under the open-end method may be substantially lower than under the closed-end method, but the lessee is frequently hit with a large balloon payment at the lease end. As a consequence, some lessors will not participate in open-end agreements.

Many closed-end leases are available with a maintenance program. While some may be expensive, the Ford Maintenance Coupon program costs about $500 over a 36-month lease (not including tires, if necessary). This plan permits dealers to purchase maintenance coupons for the lease period and then charge the maintenance to the company. This shifts the risk of maintenance to the manufacturer.

Four factors deserve further consideration:

1. *Sales tax.* Sales tax is charged on the total monthly lease payment, including interest, tags, and so on. When a car is purchased, the sales tax is added directly to the purchase price, and when the car is traded in, only the additional cost to purchase a new car (price less trade) is subject to sales tax. As a consequence, the total sales tax paid in the lease may exceed the purchase.

2. *Lease term.* When leases are written, the goal is to maximize wholesale value at lease end. Leases are structured to provide for minimum mileage when the cars are turned back to the lessor. This is accomplished by charging an excess mileage rate as described earlier. Most corporate leases are for 18 to 24 months. The lessor will attempt to determine the average yearly mileage the lessee is likely to drive and base the lease term on the expected mileage; the lower the expected yearly mileage, the longer the lease term.

3. *Interest rate.* When cars are purchased and financed on an individual basis through a dealer or bank, the interest is frequently quoted on a discount basis. For example, a 7 percent stated rate converts to a 12.63 percent actual percentage rate on a 36-month basis. (The 7 percent is charged on the entire principal for the loan period, even though a portion of the loan is repaid each month.) If firms purchase large numbers of vehicles, the financing may be through a variety of types of financing discussed earlier in the book, and the interest rates may be more or less than the 12.63 percent figure common to individual purchases. When vehicles are leased, the interest rate applied is generally approximately the rate available to the lessor. As an example, at the time this book was

written, the prime rate was about $9\frac{1}{2}$ percent, and leases were being computed at 10 percent to $10\frac{1}{2}$ percent. For the individual, this provided for about a 2 percent to $2\frac{1}{2}$ percent differential between purchase and lease in favor of leasing.

4. *Investment tax credits.* Investment tax credits may be either retained by the lessor or passed through to the lessee. The lessee should be sure about how this is to be handled, including recapture of investment tax credit at the onset.

Computing Lease Payments

The cost estimate for a 1979 Ford LTD, based on dealer cost, is shown in Table 13-1. On the basis of historical wholesale used-car prices, the dealer assigns a $2,200 value in 36 months, leaving $3,465.15 to be depreciated. The monthly depreciation is $96.25. The interest, based on a $10\frac{1}{4}$ percent rate and averaged over the 36-month period, is $33.05 per month. Operating maintenance, tags, and profit total $33.00. Thus, the total monthly payment is $162.30 plus any sales tax for a closed-end 36-month lease. In New Jersey, sales tax is 5 percent, so the total payment would be $170.42. Normally, a security deposit (which approximates two months' lease payments) and the first lease payment are required, and the lease payments are made at the beginning of each month.

The key factor in determining the lease payment is the estimate of wholesale value at lease end. The primary difference between a closed-

Table 13-1. Cost estimate for a 1979 Ford LTD.

LTD—2-door	$4,653.03
Air conditioner	465.94
Tinted glass	64.66
AM radio	61.58
Automatic transmission	Std.
Power steering	Std.
Power brakes	Std.
WSW	36.94
Freight	268.00
FDAF	40.00
Subtotal (cost to dealer)	$5,590.15
Dealer profit under leasing	75.00
Total	$5,665.15

end and open-end lease is this estimate. An open-end lease might, for example, be written on the basis of a $3,200 terminal value. Obviously, the lease payments will be reduced. If $3,200 turns out to be the actual value, the lessee will benefit. However, the *more likely* situation is that the value will be $2,200 and the lessee will have to pay the lessor an additional $1,000 at lease end.

Insurance costs may be built into the lease. However, it is probably advantageous for the lessee to secure insurance privately rather than to become a part of the lessor's group policy. This results from the fact that there may be "assigned risks" among the group.

Purchase Price and Monthly Payments[1]

Consider the same Ford LTD with a dealer cost of $5,590.15. For this example, we figured an average dealer profit over the sales year of $275, bringing the price to $5,865.15 plus the 5 percent sales tax, or $6,158.41. If the purchase was made in the winter or at the end of the model year, then it might be possible to reduce the $275 figure to a lower amount.

We will assume a down payment of $511.26, which is equal to the two-month security deposit and one-month advance lease payment under the lease option described above. This leaves $5,647.15 plus $39 for tags, for a total of $5,686.15, to be financed. Using a 12.63 percent annual percentage rate, the interest over the three-year period is $1,202.20 and the end-of-month payment $190.26 for *36 months*. This does not include maintenance costs, which were included with the lease option. Thus, to make the two comparable, we must add a monthly average maintenance figure. Over the three-year life, a reasonable figure, excluding tires, would be about $20 per month, for a total of $210.26.

Cash Flow Analyses: Lease versus Purchase

In order to make the quantifiable portion of the decision of lease versus purchase, it is useful to construct a cash flow analysis (see Table 13-2). We use the figures developed in the preceding sections, including the expected $2,200 residual value. All figures are before taxes.

From a financial point of view, the question becomes one of evaluating the differential payment of $1,604.66 (purchase over lease) to obtain an expected $1,859.16 (estimated vehicle value less security deposit refund) at the end of the lease. Of course, the differential payment of $1,604.66 was made in increments over the period of 36 months, so that the return

Table 13-2. Comparative cash flows.

Time	Lease	Purchase	Total Monthly Payments
Present	−$511.26	−$511.26	—
1–35*	−170.42	—	−$5,964.70
1–36	—	−210.26	−7,569.36
36	+340.84†	+2,200.00‡	—
		Difference	$1,604.66

* The initial lease payment of $511.26 includes one month's payment, so only 35 more are due.
† Represents recovery of security deposit.
‡ Represents estimated fair market value of car at end of 3 years.

on all the additional funds needed to obtain the $1,859.16 is about 10 percent. The 10 percent rate is not significant enough to recommend either lease or purchase, so other factors must be considered. These are examined in the following section.

Advantages and Disadvantages of Leasing: A Comparison

Some of the more important advantages and disadvantages are discussed below. After this initial discussion, we look more specifically at open- and closed-end leases.

ADVANTAGES

1. *Leasing may open new credit sources.* Unlike borrowing, leasing does not necessarily restrict further borrowing. The number of restrictive covenants is usually limited.

2. *Leasing has a tax advantage.* This may be the most important advantage, especially to small business. When a vehicle is leased for business purposes, the IRS will seldom question the deduction. However, if the same vehicle is purchased, the deductions for depreciation, interest, and so forth may be questioned, as may be the percentage used for business purposes.

3. *Leasing frees capital.* If vehicles are already owned, the owner may be able to sell them to the lessor, lease new vehicles, and walk away with a substantial amount of cash. Normally, lessors require two months'

security deposit. This may be more than the down payment required to purchase, since banks and finance companies frequently will finance dealer cost plus two or three hundred dollars.

4. *Leasing eliminates used-car sale risk.* The closed-end lease places all the risk of sale on the lessor, so that the lessee is not burdened with this problem.

DISADVANTAGES

1. *With leasing there is no build-up of equity.* When a vehicle is purchased, the owner will enjoy some equity after the vehicle is paid off. The question to be addressed is whether the equity is worth the added monthly payment.

2. *With an open-end lease additional terminal payment may be required.* As discussed earlier, the open-end lease places a high risk burden on the lessee in terms of terminal value payment.

3. *Higher total annualized cost.* When small numbers (less than five) of vehicles are leased, the total annual cost is frequently greater than for a comparable purchase.

4. *Higher sales tax.* Since the total lease payment, including interest and tags, is subject to sales tax, the total annualized tax may be higher than with a purchase.

Corporate Leasing

The initial incentive for many firms to lease is to convert fixed assets into working capital. Corporate fleets now account for about 14 percent of all automobiles on the road. Leasing or purchasing eliminates the prerequisites of an employee owning a car, and it releases employees from the burden of shopping for vehicles—frequently on company time.

The utilization of the maintenance and insurance programs is much more widespread among corporate lessees, since it fixes the maximum rate that a company will spend for repairs and service on their vehicles. This is particularly important when the fleet exceeds 50 vehicles, since the potential costs, not to mention the individual record keeping, could become extremely costly, as well as burdensome.

Open-End and Closed-End Leases

The open-end lease, while exposing the lessee to appreciable risk, is the least costly since the lessor's profit is guaranteed. As with other situations in finance, bearing risk has a cost. By reducing the lessor's risk, the lessee reduces his costs.

During the energy crisis in 1974, large cars, such as Cadillac, Lincoln, and Buick, suffered a substantial decline in value and were often sold for $1,000 to $2,000 below what they normally would have been worth. A lessee in the final months of an open-end or equity lease would have undoubtedly incurred a substantial fee when the leased car was sold at wholesale value. Conversely, many lessees using open-end leases involving foreign models, particularly Mercedes, were pleasantly surprised to find that their three-year-old Mercedes was worth up to $5,000 more than the lease called for. This is due, primarily, to two factors: inflation and the devaluation of the dollar.

In general, open-end leases are most attractive if the lessee drives 12,000 to 15,000 miles a year and selects a car that is likely to have a higher-than-average wholesale value at lease end.

The closed-end lease reduces lessee risk at a cost. The lessee may have the option to purchase the vehicle at fair market value at the termination of the lease. The option price, of course, may not be stipulated if the lease is to be viewed as a "true lease" by the IRS, as opposed to a conditional sales agreement. While an ethical lessor will tailor the lease terms to meet the lessee's driving habits, there is an excess-mileage clause in closed-end leases. The lessor wants to reduce risk of terminal value. This necessitates the excess-mileage premium.

NOTE

1. This example is taken from Robert E. Pritchard and Bruce M. Bradway, *Business and Financial Planning and Control for Small Businesses,* Glassboro, N.J.: The Management Institute, 1978. Used with permission.

APPENDIX A

Glossary of Lease Terms

ADR—Asset Depreciation Range. Refers to regulations under the Internal Revenue Code Section 167 (m) which permits shorter or longer than usual life to be used for tax depreciation. Under certain circumstances, capital equipment may be depreciated over a period which may be up to 20 percent more or less than the applicable class life, rounded to the nearest half-year.

Bargain Purchase Option. A provision allowing the lessee, at his option, to purchase the leased asset for a price which is sufficiently lower than the expected fair market value at the time such option becomes exercisable. The exercise of the option appears, at the inception of the lease, to be reasonably assured.

Bargain Renewal Option. A provision allowing the lessee, at his option, to renew the lease for a rental sufficiently lower than the expected fair rental for the property at the time the option becomes exercisable. The exercise of the option appears, at the inception of the lease, to be reasonably assured.

Bonds. Certificates evidencing indebtedness or loan certificates issued by the owner trustee.

Broker. A company or person who arranges lease transactions between lessees and lessors for a fee.

Burdensome Buyout. A provision in a lease allowing the lessee to purchase the leased equipment at a value to be determined in some fashion when the buyout is exercised, in the event that payments under the tax or general indemnity clauses are deemed by the lessee to be unduly burdensome. Care must be taken if the existence of such a provision is not to invalidate the true lease nature of the transaction and thus, by its existence, make the lessee liable under the tax indemnity clause.

Burn-up Contract. Another name for a nuclear fuel lease.

Call. An option to purchase an asset at a set price at some particular time in the future. Care must be used in negotiating a purchase option or call in a lease agreement. If this is done improperly, many of the advantages of a true lease—such as tax savings—might be disallowed by the Internal Revenue Service.

Capital Lease. A lease is classified and accounted for by a lessee as a *capital lease* if it meets *any* of the following criteria:
a. The lease transfers ownership to the lessee at the end of the lease term;
b. The lease contains an option to purchase property at a bargain price;
c. The lease term is equal to 75 percent or more of the estimated economic life of the property (exceptions for used property leased toward the end of its useful life); or
d. The present value of minimum lease rental payments is equal to 90 percent or more of the fair market value of the leased property less related ITC retained by the lessor.

Casualty Value. See *Insured Value.*

Certificate of Acceptance. A document whereby the lessee acknowledges that the equipment to be leased has been delivered to him, is acceptable to him, and has been manufactured or constructed in accordance with specifications.

Collateral. Collateral under a lease is the equipment which is leased.

Conditional Sale. A transaction for purchase of an asset in which the user, for federal income tax purposes, is treated as the owner of the equipment at the outset of the transaction.

Conditional Sale Lease. A lease which in substance is a conditional sale (sometimes called a hire-purchase agreement).

Contingent Rentals. Rentals in which the amounts are dependent upon some factor other than passage of time.

Debt Service. Payments of principal and interest due lenders.

Direct Financing Lease. A non-leveraged lease by a lessor (not a manufacturer or dealer) in which the lease meets any of the criteria definitions of a *capital* lease, plus two additional criteria as follows:
a. Collectibility of minimum lease payments must be reasonably predictable, and
b. No uncertainties surround the amount of unreimbursable costs to be incurred by the lessor under the lease.

Direct Investor. Refers to the lessor in a direct financing lease.

Direct Lease. Same as a *Direct Financing Lease.*

Economic Life of Leased Property. The estimated period during which the property is expected to be economically usable by one or more users, with normal repairs and maintenance, for the purpose for which it was intended at the inception of the lease.

Equity Participant. The lessor or one of a group of lessors in a leveraged lease. Equity participants hold trust certificates evidencing their beneficial interest as owners under the owner trust. An equity participant is the same as an owner participant, trustor owner, or grantor owner.

Estimated Residual Value of Leased Property. The estimated fair value of the property at the end of the lease term.

Extended Term Agreement. An agreement to renew a lease, commonly used to describe a guaranteed renewal of a lease by a third party.

Fair Rental. The expected rental for equivalent property under similar terms and conditions.

FASB. Financial Accounting Standards Board.

FAS 13. Technically: *Statement of Financial Accounting Standards No. 13, Accounting for Leases;* Financial Accounting Standards Board, Stamford, Connecticut, November 1976. Sets forth financial accounting standards on accounting for leases.

Faz-Bee. Another name for the *FASB,* and sometimes *FAS 13.*

Finance Lease. A financing device whereby a user can acquire use of an asset for most of its useful life. Rentals are net to the lessor, and the user is responsible for maintenance, taxes, and insurance. Rent payments over the life of the lease are sufficient to enable the lessor to recover the cost of the equipment plus a return on its investment. A finance lease may be either a *true lease* or a *conditional sale.*

Financing Agreement. An agreement between the owner trustee, the lenders, the equity participants, the manufacturer, and the lessee, which spells out the obligations of the parties under a leveraged lease. Also called *participation agreement.*

Financing Statement. A notice of a security interest filed under the Uniform Commercial Code.

Floating Rental Rate. Rental which is subject to upward or downward adjustments during the lease term. Floating rents sometimes are adjusted in proportion to prime interest rate or commercial paper rate changes during the term of the lease.

Foreign Source Income. Income earned overseas (net of depreciation and other expenses allocable to such income) as reported for United States federal income tax purposes.

Grantor Trust. A trust used as the owner trust in a leveraged lease transaction, usually with only one equity participant. The Internal Revenue Code refers to such a trust as a grantor trust (see Section 671). With more than one equity participant the grantor trust is usually treated as a partnership.

Heat Supply Contracts. A nuclear fuel lease.

Hell-or-High-Water Clause. A clause in a lease which reiterates the unconditional obligation of the lessee to pay rent for the entire term of the lease, regardless of any event affecting the equipment or any change in the circumstance of the lessee.

Hire-Purchase Agreement. A conditional sale lease.

Inception of a Lease. The date of the lease agreement or commitment, if earlier. (For technical application, consult FAS 13 and subsequent amendments.)

Incremental Borrowing Rate. The interest rate which a person would expect to pay for an additional borrowing at rates prevailing at that time.

Indemnity Agreement. An agreement whereby the owner participants and the lessee indemnify the trustees from liability as a result of ownership of the leased equipment.

Indemnity Clause. Although lease documentation contains various indemnities, the indemnity clause usually refers to the tax indemnity clause whereby the lessee indemnifies the lessor against the loss of tax benefits.

Indenture Trustee. In a leveraged lease, the indenture trustee holds the security interest in the leased equipment for the benefit of the lenders. In the event of default, the indenture trustee exercises the rights of a mortgagee. The indenture trustee also is responsible for receiving rent payments from the lessee and using such funds to pay the amounts due the lenders with the balance being paid to the owner trustee. The indenture trustee verifies that correct filings are made to protect the security interest of the lenders. The bond register is maintained by the indenture trustee, who also acts as transfer agent.

Indenture of Trust. An agreement between the owner trustee and the indenture trustee whereby the owner trustee mortgages the equipment and assigns the lease and rental payments under the lease as security for amounts due to the lenders. The same as a security agreement or mortgage.

Independent Lessor. Any leasing company investing in leases; also, brokers without funds to invest in leases sometimes prefer to call themselves "independent lessors" rather than "brokers."

Initial Direct Costs. Costs incurred by a lessor directly associated with negotiating and completing a transaction. These include commissions, legal fees, costs of credit checkings, documentation costs, allocable sales expenses (including salaries other than commissions), and so forth; but specifically exclude supervisory, administrative, or other indirect or overhead expenses.

Institutional Investors. Investors such as banks, insurance companies, trusts, pension funds, foundations, and educational, charitable, and religious institutions.

Insured Value. A schedule included in a lease which states the agreed value of equipment at various times during the term of the lease, and establishes the liability of the lessee to the lessor in the event the leased equipment is lost or rendered unusable during the lease term, due to a casualty.

Interest Rate Implicit in a Lease (as used in FAS 13). The discount rate which, when applied to *minimum lease payments* (excluding executory costs paid by the lessor) and *unguaranteed residual value,* causes the aggregate present value at the beginning of the lease term to be equal to the fair value of the leased property at the inception of the lease, minus any investment tax credit retained by the lessor and expected to be realized by him.

Interim Rent. Daily rental accruing from delivery, acceptance, and/or funding until a later starting date for a basic lease term. Often used when equipment delivers over a period of time.

ITC. Investment Tax Credit.

Lease Line. A lease line of credit similar to a bank line of credit which allows a lessee to add equipment, as needed, under the same basic terms and conditions without negotiating a new lease.

Lease Rate. The equivalent simple annual interest rate implicit in minimum lease rentals. Not the same as *Interest Rate Implicit in a Lease*.

Lease Term. The fixed, noncancelable term of the lease. Includes, for accounting purposes, all periods covered by fixed-rate renewal options which for economic reasons appear likely to be exercised at the inception of the lease, and for tax purposes, all periods covered by fixed-rate renewal options.

Lease Underwriting. An agreement whereby a packager commits firmly to enter into a lease on certain terms and assumes the risk of arranging any financing.

Lessee. The user of the equipment being leased.

Lessee's Incremental Borrowing Rate. The interest rate which the lessee at the inception of the lease would have incurred to borrow over a similar term the funds necessary to purchase the leased assets. In a leveraged lease the rate on the bonds is normally used.

Lessor. The owner of equipment which is being leased to a lessee or user.

Level Payments. Equal payments over the term of the lease.

Leverage. An amount borrowed. A lease is sometimes referred to as 100% leverage for the lessee. In a leveraged lease, the debt portion of the funds used to purchase the asset represents leverage of the equity holder.

Leveraged Lease. A lease which meets the definition criteria for a *direct financing lease* or a *capital lease,* plus all of the following characteristics:
a. At least three parties are involved: a lessee, a lessor, and a long-term lender.

b. The financing provided by the lender is substantial to the transaction and without recourse to the lessor.

c. The lessor's net investment typically declines during the early years of the lease and rises during the later years of the lease.

Loan Certificates. Debt certificates or bonds issued by the owner trustee to lenders.

Loan Participant. A lender in a leveraged lease; a holder of debt in a leveraged lease evidenced by loan certificates or bonds issued by the owner trustee.

Low Ball Bid. A bid to perform a lease transaction purposely priced below market or with terms not acceptable from a tax or accounting standpoint, with a view to renegotiation of a higher price and/or more expensive terms at a later date once the bid is awarded the low ball bidder and the other interested lessors are no longer available. Typically the low ball bidder raises the price when it is too late for the lessee to seek other leasing sources.

Master Lease. A lease line of credit which allows a lessee to add equipment under the same basic terms and conditions without negotiating a new lease contract.

Minimum Investment. For a leveraged lease to be a *true lease,* the lessor must have a minimum "at risk" investment of at least 20% in a lease when the lease begins, ends, and at all times during the lease term.

Minimum Lease Payments for the Lessee. All payments the lessee is obligated to make or can be required to make in connection with leased property, including residual value guaranteed the lessor and bargain renewal rents or purchase options, but excluding guarantees of lessor's debt (seldom encountered) and executory costs such as insurance, maintenance, and taxes.

Minimum Lease Payments for the Lessor. The payments considered minimum lease payments for the lessee plus any guarantee by a third party of the residual value or rental payments beyond the lease term.

Mortgage. An agreement between the owner trustee and the indenture trustee whereby the owner trustee assigns title to the equipment as security for amounts due the lenders.

Net Lease. In a net lease, the rentals are payable net to the lessor. All costs in connection with the use of the equipment are to be paid by the lessee and are not a part of the rental. For example, taxes, insurance, and maintenance are paid directly by the lessee. Most capital leases and direct financing leases are net leases.

Net-Net Lease. Same as net lease.

Operating Lease. For financial accounting purposes, a lease which does not meet the criteria of a capital lease or direct financing lease. Also, used generally to describe a short-term lease whereby a user can acquire use of an asset for a fraction of the useful life of the asset. The lessor may provide services in connection with the lease such as maintenance, insurance, and payment of personal property taxes.

Owner Participant. The lessor or one of a group of lessors in a leveraged lease holding trust certificates evidencing their beneficial interest as owners under the owner trust. An owner participant is the same as an equity participant, trustor owner, or grantor owner.

Owner Trustee. Also sometimes called grantor trustee. In a leveraged lease, the primary function of the owner trustee is to hold title to the equipment for the benefit of the equity participants. The owner trustee issues trust certificates to the equity participants, maintains the register, and acts as transfer agent for such certificates. The owner trustee issues bonds to the lenders, receives distributions of rent payments from the indenture trustee, pays trustee fees due itself and the indenture trustee, and disburses amounts due the equity participants. The owner trustee makes appropriate filings to perfect and protect the lenders' interest in the collateral. Compliance certificates and other information required from the lessee under the lease are received by the owner trustee and distributed by the owner trustee to the other parties.

Packager. A name used to describe the leasing company, investment banker, or broker who arranges a leveraged lease.

Packer. Another name for packager.

Participation Agreement. An agreement between the owner trustee, the lenders, the equity participants, the manufacturer, and the lessee which spells out the obligations of the parties under the leveraged lease. Also called *financing agreement*.

Present Value. The current equivalent value of cash available immediately for a future payment or a stream of payments to be received at various times in the future. The present value will vary with the discount (interest) factor applied to the future payments.

Purchase Option. An option to purchase leased property at the end of the lease term. In order to protect the tax characteristics of a true lease, an option to purchase property from a lessor by a lessee cannot be at a price less than its fair market value at the time the right is exercised.

Put. An option one person has to sell an asset to another person at a set price at some established point in time in the future. In lease agreements, a lessor sometimes negotiates an option to sell leased equipment to the lessee or to some third party at an established price at the end of the lease term. Care must be used in negotiating a put to a lessee lest the true lease characteristics of the transaction be destroyed and money-saving advantages lost. A lessor may also negotiate a put to a third party as a hedge against future loss on the sale of the asset, although such an arrangement is contrary to IRS advance ruling guidelines.

Related Parties. In leasing transactions: a parent and its subsidiaries; an investor and its investees; provided the parent, owner, or investor has the ability to exercise significant influence over the financial and operating policies of the related party.

Renewal Option. An option to renew the lease at the end of the initial lease term. Here, too, care must be used in granting a renewal option for a fair rental value. If this is not done properly, it may later be ruled that the lease is not a true lease. Tax advantages may be lost and tax indemnity clauses activated.

Residual Insurance. An insurance policy guaranteeing a certain residual value at the end of the lease term.

Residual or Residual Value. The value of equipment at the conclusion of the lease term. To qualify the lease as a "true lease" for tax purposes, the estimated residual value at the end of the lease term must equal at least 20 percent of the original cost of the equipment.

Residual Sharing. An agreement between the lessor and another party providing for a division of the *residual value* between them. Care must be taken in any such agreement, lest the tax benefits be lost and the lessee become liable under the tax *indemnity clause*.

Return on investment. The yield. The interest rate earned by the lessor in a lease which is measured by the rate at which the excess cash flows permit recovery of investment. The rate at which the cash flows not needed for debt service or payment of taxes amortize the investment of the equity participant.

Revenue Procedures. Commonly used in leasing to refer to the IRS Revenue Procedures 75-21, 75-28, and 76-30, which set forth requirements for obtaining a favorable revenue ruling on a leveraged lease.

Revenue Ruling. A written opinion of the Internal Revenue Service requested by parties, which is applicable to assumed facts stated in the opinion. May also refer to published IRS rulings with general applicability.

Sale-Leaseback. A transaction which involves the sale of the property by the owner and a lease of the property back to the seller.

Sale-type Lease. A lease by a lessor who is a manufacturer or dealer, in which the lease meets the criteria definition of a *capital lease* or *direct financing lease*.

Security Agreement. An agreement between the owner trustee and the indenture trustee whereby the owner trustee assigns title to the equipment, the lease, and rental payments under the lease as security for amounts due the lenders. The same as an indenture of trust.

Short-term Lease. Generally refers to an operating lease.

Sinking Fund. A reserve or a sinking fund established or set aside for the purpose of payment of taxes anticipated to become due at a later date. (Generally applicable only in leveraged leases.)

Sinking Fund Rate. The rate of interest allocated to a *sinking fund* set aside for future payment of taxes. (Generally applicable only in leveraged leases.)

Special Purpose Property. Property which is uniquely valuable to the lessee and not valuable to anyone else except as scrap.

Stipulated Loss Value. The same as *insured value*.

Sub-lease. A transaction in which leased property is re-leased by the original lessee to a third party, and the lease agreement between the two original parties remains in effect.

Strip Debt. Debt in connection with a leveraged lease, arranged in tiers with different maturities and amortization to improve the lessor's cash flow and reduce the lessee's costs.

T.A.C.A.R. Pronounced "taker." An unflattering term for a broker of a lease with no investment or continuity in the transaction. The initials stand for: "take a commission and run."

Termination Schedule. Leases sometimes contain provisions permitting a lessee to terminate the lease during the lease term in the event the leased equipment becomes obsolete and surplus to its needs. In such event, the equipment usually must be sold or transferred to some third party unconnected in any way with the lessee. The liability of the lessee in the event of such termination is set forth in a termination schedule which values the equipment at various times during the lease term. If the equipment is sold at a price lower than the amount set forth in the schedule, the lessee pays the difference. In the event the resale is at a price higher than in the termination schedule, such excess amounts belong to the lessor. The termination schedule is not the same as the *casualty value* schedule, *insured value* schedule, or *stipulated loss value* schedule.

True Lease. A true lease is a transaction which qualifies as a lease under the Internal Revenue Code so the lessee can claim rental payments as tax deductions and the lessor can claim tax benefits of ownership such as depreciation and ITC.

Trust Certificate. Document evidencing the beneficial ownership of a trust estate of an equity participant (or owner participant, trustor owner, or grantor owner) in an owner trust.

Trustee. A bank or trust company which holds title to or a security interest in leased property in trust for the benefit of the lessee, lessor, and/or creditors of the lessor. A leveraged lease often has two trustees: owner trustee and indenture trustee.

Trustee Fees. Fees due either the owner trustee or the indenture trustee.

Trustor Owner. The lessor or one of a group of lessors under a leveraged lease holding trust certificates evidencing their beneficial interest as owners under the owner trust. A trustor owner is the same as an equity participant, owner participant, or grantor owner.

Undivided Interest. A property interest held by two or more parties whereby each shares, according to their respective interest, in profits, expenses, and enjoyment; and whereby ownership of the respective interest of each may be transferred but physical partition of the asset is prohibited.

Unguaranteed Residual Value. The portion of residual value "at risk" for a lessor in his yield computation, i.e., for which there is no party obligated to pay.

Useful Life. The period of time during which an asset will have economic value and be usable. Useful life of an asset is sometimes called the economic life of the asset. To qualify as a true lease, the leased property must have a remaining useful life of 20 percent of the original estimated useful life of the leased property at the end of the lease term, and at least a life of one year.

Yield. The interest rate earned by the lessor or equity participant in a lease, which is measured by the rate at which the excess cash flows permit recovery of investment. The rate at which the cash flows not needed for debt service or payment of taxes amortize the investment of the equity participants.

APPENDIX B

Sample Equipment Leases

Agreement for Leasing

First National State Bank
OF NEW JERSEY

550 BROAD STREET, NEWARK, NEW JERSEY 07101

THIS AGREEMENT by and between First National State Bank of New Jersey, a corporation under the laws of the State of New Jersey whose address 550 Broad St., Newark, N.J. (hereinafter referred to as "Lessor"), and the Lessee, whose name and address appear at the end of this agreement (hereinafter referred to as "Lessee").

WITNESSETH:

In order to state the general terms, conditions, covenants and provisions which will be incorporated by reference into future agreements between the parties and in consideration of the mutual covenants contained herein and in such future agreements, the parties agree as follows:

1. **Leasing.** Lessor will use its best efforts to procure items of personal property for leasing to Lessee upon terms and conditions satisfactory to Lessor and Lessee. The parties will from time to time execute leases in substantially the form annexed hereto (sometimes referred to herein as a "short form lease"), describing the property leased, the term of the lease and the commencement thereof, the periodic and total rents, the time for payment thereof, and such other terms and conditions as they shall agree upon. Each such short form lease shall incorporate by reference the terms, conditions, covenants and provisions set forth in Section 2 below.

2. **Lease Provisions.** The following terms, conditions, covenants and provisions shall supplement and become a part of each and every short form lease which shall incorporate this Section 2 by reference (each such short form lease, as supplemented by this section, being hereinafter referred to as a "Lease") and shall apply to all of the leased property described in each Lease (each item of leased property being sometimes referred to as a "Unit"):

   a. **Term** — The letting of, and rent for the leased property, or each Unit thereof, shall commence on the day or days, and shall continue for the period, specified in the Lease.

   b. **Rent** — The rent for the leased property shall be the "total rental" for such property specified in the applicable Lease, payable in successive installments at the times set forth in said Lease. Rent shall be paid to Lessor at the address set forth above, or as otherwise directed by Lessor, free from all claims, demands, or setoffs against Lessor. If Lessor is put to any expense because of any default or breach of the Lease, or other act by Lessee, or because of any compliance with any regulatory law or agency applicable to any Unit or because of any such payment of any amounts provided in the Lease to be paid or repaid by Lessee, then the amount of such expense to, or payment by, Lessor, together with interest at the highest legal contract rate, shall be added to, and become a part of, the installment of rent immediately following such increase, expense, or payment (or, where such increase is payable over a period of months, to the installments of rent payable in such months) and Lessee shall pay the same. Any fee paid by Lessee in connection with the negotiation of this Lease shall be exclusive, and not a part, of the rent hereunder.

   c. **Use, Care and Operation** — Lessee shall, at Lessee's expense:

      (1) **Receipt.** Receive each Unit at, and pay all delivery charges for each Unit to, the "location of original use" specified therefor; and unload, and, if required, assemble and install the same. Lessee shall inspect each Unit within 48 hours after receipt thereof. Unless Lessee within said period of time gives written notice to Lessor, specifying any defect in or other proper objection to any such Unit, Lessee agrees that it shall be conclusively presumed, as between Lessor and Lessee, that Lessee has fully inspected and acknowledged that such Unit is in good operating order, repair, and appearance and that Lessee is satisfied with and has accepted such Unit in such good condition and repair.

      (2) **Fees and Taxes.** Pay all license fees, assessments, and property, sales, use and other tax or taxes, now or hereafter imposed by any State, Federal, or local government or agency upon any Unit leased to Lessee, or upon the leasing, use or operation thereof and all things incidental thereto (excluding only income taxes imposed on Lessor). Lessee shall promptly notify Lessor regarding any tax notices, tax reports, inquiries from taxing authorities concerning taxes, fees, assessments and amounts in lieu thereof.

      (3) **Maintenance.** At all times keep and maintain each Unit in first-class working order, repair, condition, and appearance; install, keep and maintain on each Unit such insignia, identification, and meters or other measuring devices, as Lessor may designate; make all necessary repairs and replacements thereto; and keep the same as specified in the Lease therefor. Lessor will claim the factory warranty for each new Unit to enable Lessee to obtain the customary manufacturer's warranty service therefor; and all repairs, parts, and supplies, while at Lessee's expense, shall be performed and supplied only by such persons as shall be agreeable to Lessor. Lessee shall not, without Lessor's prior written consent, affix or install any accessory, equipment, device, advertising matter or insignia to any Unit if such addition will impair the originally intended function or use of such Unit; and all repairs parts, supplies, accessories, equipment, devices, or other items furnished or affixed to any Unit shall thereupon become Lessor's property (excepting such thereof as may be removed without in anywise affecting or impairing the originally intended function or use of such Unit).

      (4) **Provisioning.** Provide all labor, materials, services, utilities, electric power, lubricants, parts, and other supplies or items consumed or required for, or in connection with the use of, each Unit.

      (5) **Compliance with Law.** Observe and comply with, and perform and execute, all laws, rules, regulations, or orders of all State, Federal, and local governments or agencies which in any way affect or relate to, or are applicable to, any leased Unit, or the use, operation, maintenance or storage thereof; and Lessee shall and does hereby indemnify Lessor and agree to hold Lessor harmless from any and all liability that may arise from any infringement or violation of any such law, rule, regulation, or order, by Lessee, or Lessee's employees, or any other person.

      (6) **Use and Operation.** Not use, operate, maintain, or store any Unit improperly, carelessly, or in violation of the Lease therefor, or any instructions furnished therefor, by the manufacturer or by Lessor; not load any Unit in excess of its specified "rated load capacity"; nor permit anyone to operate the same other than its authorized agents or its employees who must be competent operators.

(7) **Non-Transferability.** Not, without Lessor's prior written consent (or, if any of the rights of Lessor hereunder or in and to any Lease shall have been assigned, without the prior written consent of each assignee or sub-assignee to which such rights have been assigned), except as otherwise herein provided, let, sublet, or use any Unit for hire, nor remove the same from the location for original use specified therefor; nor assign the Lease therefor or any interest therein, or any right or privilege appertaining thereto; or pledge, loan, or part with the possession of, or mortgage or encumber, any Unit, or any part thereof or any interest therein; and, without the prior written consent of Lessor, any such attempted action by Lessee, either by voluntary or involuntary act, or by operation of Law or otherwise, shall, at Lessor's option, terminate the Lease covering such Unit; and any such assignment, transfer, sublease, or other action without such prior written consent of Lessor shall be void; upon obtaining Lessor's prior written consent, the Lessee shall have the right to sublease any Unit to sublessees satisfactory to Lessor, provided that such subleases shall be executed on Lessor's approved form of Lease, and provided, further, that the use by the sublessee of the subleased Unit shall not exceed the normal use of such Unit under conditions similar to those theretofore prevailing in connection with Lessee's operation, and use of such Unit, and provided, further, that notwithstanding such sublease, Lessee shall remain primarily obligated with respect to such subleased Unit. After written demand, all rentals accruing under such subleases shall be paid directly to the Lessor and shall be applied by the Lessor as a payment pro tanto of the Lessee's rental for such Unit, Lessor promptly accounting for and reimbursing to Lessee any excess of the periodic rentals received under such sublease over those due under the Lease covering the subleased Unit, but nothing herein contained shall be construed to release Lessee of its obligations, undertakings, and covenants under the Lease covering such equipment, and such subleases shall be subject and subordinate to the provisions of the Lease covering such subleased equipment, and any breach or default on Lessee's part shall, at Lessor's option, be deemed to constitute a breach and default of such sublease, justifying its immediate termination without further notice to Lessee or its permitted sublessee. No acceptance of rent from a sublessee shall constitute a waiver of the provisions of this sub-paragraph.

(8) **Risk.** Bear, and Lessee hereby assumes, save as hereinafter specifically provided, all risk and liability for each Unit, and for the use, operation, maintenance, and storage thereof, and the loads thereon, and for damages for injury or death to persons and/or property howsoever arising therefrom or because thereof; and Lessee shall save, and does hereby indemnify Lessor and agree to hold, Lessor harmless from any and all claims, liens, demands, or liability arising out of any work done on, or any materials supplied to, or in connection with, the operation, maintenance, or storage of the same, and from all loss of or damage to the same and from all loss, damage, claims, penalties, liability, and expense, including attorneys' fees, howsoever arising or incurred because of any Unit, or the storage maintenance, use, handling, repair, loading, unloading, or operation or alleged use or operation, thereof, or the loads thereon, including (but without being limited to) damages or liability for injuries or death to persons or property and any alleged patent interference or infringement. Lessee will procure, maintain, and pay for workman's compensation insurance upon employee operators of such Units, which may be required in any jurisdiction where such equipment may be used or operated, unless Lessee shall have qualified as a self-insured therefor. If, at any time, such insurance shall not be in effect, Lessee may not, and will not, use or operate any Unit for which such insurance shall not be in effect. Nothing herein shall require Lessor to replace any Unit, or to provide a substitute thereof.

(9) **Inspection.** Upon Lessor's demand, promptly advise Lessor specifically where each such Unit is located and permit Lessor, or its agents or representatives, to enter upon the premises where the same is situate and inspect such Unit, and its manner of use, at any time; and Lessor, or its agents or representatives, shall have the right so to do, or to post notices of non-responsibility for any work done or to be done at the instance of Lessee, or for any other lawful purpose.

(10) **Accidents and Claims.** Without demand, immediately (and in any event within 24 hours thereafter) notify Lessor of each accident involving any Unit, the time, place, and nature of the accident or damage, the names and addresses of parties involved, persons injured, witnesses and owners of property damaged, and such other information as may be known, and promptly advise Lessor of all correspondence, papers, notices, or documents whatsoever received by Lessee in connection with any claim or demand involving or relating to any Unit or its operation, and together with Lessee's employees, aid in the investigation and defense of all such claims and demands, and in the recovery of damages, from third parties liable therefor.

(11) **Notice of Location.** After obtaining Lessor's written consent to change location, without demand, immediately notify Lessor of any change in the location of each Unit from the location of original use.

(12) **Representations.** AND LESSEE DOES HEREBY AGREE THAT EACH UNIT IS OF A SIZE, DESIGN, CAPACITY, AND MATERIAL SELECTED BY LESSEE, AND THAT LESSEE IS SATISFIED THAT EACH SUCH UNIT IS SUITABLE FOR LESSEE'S PURPOSES, AND SUFFICIENTLY DURABLE UNDER THE CONDITIONS OF USAGE THEREOF BY LESSEE, AND THAT LESSOR HAS MADE NO REPRESENTATIONS OR WARRANTIES WITH RESPECT TO THE SUITABILITY OR DURABILITY OF ANY UNIT FOR THE PURPOSES OR USES OF LESSEE, OR WITH RESPECT TO THE PERMISSIBLE LOAD THEREOF, OR ANY OTHER REPRESENTATION OR WARRANTY, EXPRESS OR IMPLIED, WITH RESPECT THERETO.

(13) **Non-Liability of Lessor.** Lessor shall not be liable to Lessee for any loss, damage, or expense of any kind or nature caused, directly, indirectly, or consequentially, by any Unit, or the use, maintenance, operation, handling or storage thereof, or loads thereon, or the repairs, servicing, or adjustment thereto, or because the same is, or has become, unsuitable or unserviceable, or by any delay or failure to provide any unit, or by any interruption of service or loss of use thereof, or for any loss of business or damage whatsoever or howsoever caused; and Lessee expressly waives the benefits and provision of any law to the contrary.

d. **Insurance** — Lessee shall keep the leased property insured against all risks of loss or damage from every cause whatsoever unless otherwise agreed in writing by Lessor, for not less than the full replacement value thereof as determined by manufacturer's current trade-in schedule; and shall carry public liability and property damage insurance covering the leased property. All said insurance shall be in form and amount and with companies approved by Lessor, and shall be in the joint names of Lessor and Lessee. All policies shall provide for a waiver of the Lessee's insurer's rights of subrogation against the Lessor. Lessee shall pay the premiums therefor and deliver said policies, or duplicates thereof, to Lessor. Each insurer shall agree, by endorsement upon the policy or policies issued by it or by independent instrument furnished to Lessor, that it will give Lessor 30 days written notice before the policy in question shall be altered or cancelled. The proceeds of such insurance, at the option of Lessor, shall be applied (a) toward the replacement, restoration or repair of the leased property or (b) toward payment of the obligations of Lessee hereunder. Lessee hereby appoints Lessor as Lessee's attorney-in-fact to make claim for, receive payment of, and execute and endorse all documents, checks or drafts for, loss or damage under any said insurance policy.

e. **Damage.** (1) Should any Unit be damaged by reason of any cause, and be determined by Lessor to be capable of repair, Lessee shall repair the same at Lessee's expense, as quickly as circumstances permit. In such event, should Lessor be indemnified under any insurance policy or policies pursuant to the provisions of the Lease covering such Unit, Lessor shall upon completion of such repair to the satisfaction of Lessor, pay to Lessee the proceeds received by Lessor from such insurance to assist Lessee in defraying the costs and expenses of such repair.

SAMPLE EQUIPMENT LEASES

(2) Should any Unit be determined by Lessor to be lost, stolen, destroyed, or damaged beyond repair by any cause whatsoever, Lessee shall pay Lessor the "Termination Value" for such Unit specified in the Lease covering such Unit, as at the Anniversary Date immediately preceding such loss, theft, destruction or damage (except where such event occurs in the first year of the term of the Lease, the payment shall be the sum of the First Anniversary Termination Value plus the total rental remaining unpaid for such year) less such amount as Lessor shall recover upon adjustment of the loss on such Unit under any policy of insurance provided therefor, after deducting therefrom Lessor's expenses of recovery, including attorneys' fees. Payment of the sums herein provided for shall be made within five (5) days after demand by Lessor and Lessor shall pay to Lessee the net insurance recovery, if any, five (5) days after receipt thereof.

f. **Return of Equipment.** Lessee agrees, by acceptance thereof, that each Unit is in good operating order, repair, and appearance, and that at the expiration or sooner termination of the "term" for the Lease thereof (or any holding over or any extension), Lessee will, at Lessee's cost and expense, return each Unit (or any equal or better Unit which has been substituted with the written consent of the Lessor) to Lessor freight prepaid to such location in the United States as Lessor may designate, free of all advertising or insignia placed thereon by Lessee, and in the same operating condition, order, repair, and appearance, as when received (reasonable wear and tear and damage by any cause for which Lessor has recovered under insurance, excepted). If any such Unit is not so returned within the "term" specified therefor, Lessee shall continue to pay the rental therefor at the rate specified in the Lease therefor, for the last period provided in said Lease, until such Unit is so returned in the aforesaid condition.

g. **Assignment by Lessor.** Lessee acknowledges and understands that Lessor contemplates assigning its interest under this Lease and in and to any Unit leased hereunder to a bank or other lending institution or to others having an interest in the leased property or this transaction, all or some of which will rely upon and be entitled to the benefit of the provisions of this paragraph; and Lessee agrees with Lessor and with such bank or other lending institution and/or such other party (for whose benefit this covenant is expressly made) and in consideration of the provisions hereof, as follows: (1) to recognize any such assignment, (2) to accept the directions or demand of such assignee in place of those of Lessor, (3) to surrender any leased property only to such assignee, (4) to pay all rent payable hereunder to assignee and to do any and all things required of Lessee hereunder and not to terminate this Lease (other than in accordance with paragraph g of this Section 2), notwithstanding any default by Lessor or the existence of any defense, offset, counterclaim, or right of recoupment or abatement as between Lessor and Lessee or the existence of any other liability or obligation of any kind or character on the part of Lessor to Lessee or to any other person or governmental authority whether or not arising hereunder, and (5) not to require any assignee of this Lease to perform any duty, covenant or condition required to be performed by Lessor under the terms of this Lease, all rights of Lessee in any such connection aforesaid being hereby waived as to any and all of such assignees. Lessor's assignee may reassign any or all of such right, title and interest so assigned to it; provided, however, that nothing hereinbefore contained shall relieve Lessor from its obligations to Lessee hereunder.

h. **Default, Enforcement, Remedies.**

(1) **Events of Default.** The occurrence of any one or more of the following events shall constitute an Event of Default hereunder:

(a) If Lessee shall default in the payment of any rent or in making any other payment hereunder when due; or

(b) If Lessee shall default in the payment when due of any indebtedness of Lessee to Lessor under this lease or under any other lease between Lessee and Lessor, or under any other obligation of Lessee to Lessor arising independently of this or any other lease; or

(c) If Lessee shall default in the performance of any other covenant of this lease or of any other lease between Lessee and Lessor, or under any other obligation of Lessee to Lessor arising independently of any lease, and any such default shall continue for ten (10) days after written notice thereof to Lessee by Lessor; or

(d) If Lessee becomes insolvent or makes an assignment for the benefit of creditors; or

(e) If Lessee applies for or consents to the appointment of a receiver, trustee or liquidator of Lessee or of all or a substantial part of the assets of Lessee, or if such receiver, trustee or liquidator is appointed without the application or consent of Lessee; or

(f) If a petition is filed by or against Lessee under the Bankruptcy Act or any amendment thereto (including, without limitation, a petition for reorganization, arrangement or extension) or under any other insolvency law or laws providing for the relief of debtors.

(2) In case an event of default shall occur, Lessor shall have the right to exercise any one or more of the following remedies:

(a) To require Lessee, at Lessee's expense, to return each Unit to Lessor freight prepaid to such location in the United States as Lessor may designate within 15 days from dispatch of such designation, in the same operating condition, order, repair and appearance, as when received (reasonable wear and tear excepted), whereupon, all rights of Lessee in each such Unit shall terminate absolutely;

(b) During or after such 15 day period, without demand or legal process, to enter into any premises where any such Unit may be found and take possession of and remove the same, whereupon all rights of Lessee to each such Unit shall terminate absolutely;

(c) Notwithstanding Lessor's recovery of possession under (a) or (b) above, the Lessee's obligations under the Lease shall not terminate and Lessee, upon demand, shall pay to Lessor upon any such event of default the Termination Value of each and every Unit described in such Lease in default, as at the Anniversary Date next succeeding the date of such event of default (and for the purposes hereof, the Termination Value as at the expiration of the term of the Lease shall be deemed to be zero), plus the unpaid rental from the date of default to such succeeding Anniversary Date; if Lessor incurs any expense because of any default, the amount of the expense shall be deemed paid by Lessor and shall become unpaid rental payable by Lessee prior to such succeeding Anniversary Date. If Lessee shall default in payment, the amount thereof shall bear interest at the highest contract rate permitted by law.

(d) Within 60 days after recovering possession of any Unit, (i) Lessor shall have the option of refunding to Lessee the amount specified in subsection (c) above for each such Unit (or crediting Lessee with the amount thereof if unpaid) and upon such payment or credit by Lessor to Lessee, the Lease shall terminate with respect to such Unit, and neither party thereafter shall have any rights or obligations with respect thereto under such Lease, or (ii) if Lessor shall not have exercised its option to make such refund or credit as aforesaid, then within 30 days after the expiration of the option period, Lessor shall sell such Unit for the highest cash offer then available, if any, Lessor shall be entitled to deduct from the sale proceeds the actual expense incurred in storing, insuring and advertising for sale all such Units and any other expense connected with such sale, including attorney's fees. If such sale is by a public sale on notice to the Lessee, the Lessor shall have the right to purchase such Unit for its own account at such sale. Lessor will refund to Lessee (or credit Lessee with, if unpaid) the net proceeds realized by the Lessor from any such sale, up to but not exceeding the amount specified in subsection (c) above for each such Unit sold.

(e) Lessee shall remain liable to Lessor for the amount specified in subsection (c) for each and every Unit described in such Lease in default, less the amount refunded or credited with respect to such Unit, as in subsection (d) (i) hereof provided, or the net proceeds of the sale of such Unit, as in subsection (d) (ii) hereof provided, up to but not exceeding the amount specified in subsection (c) above for each such Unit sold.

- (f) In no event shall Lessor be required to refund any amounts to Lessee with respect to any Unit, if Lessee shall be indebted or liable to Lessor with respect to any other Unit under the Lease, or any Lease or other agreement between the parties, or otherwise.
- (3) **Remedies not Exclusive.** The remedies herein provided in favor of Lessor or any assignee of Lessor in the case of an Event of Default as hereinabove set forth shall not be deemed to be exclusive, but shall be cumulative and shall be in addition to all other remedies in its favor existing in law, in equity or otherwise, and the exercise or beginning of the exercise by Lessor or any such assignee of any one or more of the remedies provided for in this Lease or otherwise shall not preclude the simultaneous or later exercise by Lessor or such assignee of any or all such other remedies.
- (4) **No Waiver.** No failure by Lessor or Lessee, or any assignee of either of them, to insist upon the strict performance of any term hereof or to exercise any remedy consequent upon a default hereunder, and no acceptance of full or partial rent by Lessor or any assignee of Lessor during the continuance of any default hereunder, shall constitute a waiver of any such term or of any such default. No waiver of any default shall affect or alter this Lease, which shall continue in full force and effect with respect to any other then existing or subsequent default.
- i. **Time of Essence, No Waiver, etc.** Time is of the essence of this agreement and no express or implied waiver by Lessor of any default hereunder, including the acceptance of rent, shall in any way be, or be construed to be, a waiver of any future or subsequent default of Lessee, or a waiver of any rights of Lessor, or a modification of any of the Lease terms, or an extension or enlargement of Lessee's rights under the Lease.
- j. **Notices.** All notices given under the terms and provisions of the Lease shall be in writing and such notices shall become effective when deposited in the United States mail, with proper postage prepaid, addressed to the parties at the respective addresses appearing in the Lease, or at such other address as either party or their permitted assigns may, from time to time, notify the other in writing.
- k. **General.** This is a contract of lease only, and nothing herein shall be construed as conveying to Lessee any right, title, or interest in or to any leased Unit, except as a Lessee only. Title to each leased Unit shall at all times remain in Lessor, and Lessee shall at all times, at Lessee's expenses, protect and defend Lessor's title thereto against all claims, liens and legal processes of Lessee's creditors, or persons claiming through Lessee, and keep all Units free and clear from all liens, claims, and processes. Lessee shall give immediate written notice to Lessor of all such liens, claims and processes. Lessee hereby appoints Lessor as Lessee's attorney-in-fact to execute and file on its behalf any financing statement or other documents that Lessor deems necessary or desirable in order that Lessor's rights hereunder may be made a matter of public notice or record. Lessee will cooperate with Lessor and take whatever action may be necessary to enable Lessor to file, register, or record, and re-file, re-register or re-record, this Lease, financing statements or other documents in such offices as Lessor may determine and whatever required or permitted by law for the proper protection of Lessor's title to such equipment and such Lease, and will pay all costs, charges and expenses incident thereto. Each Unit is, and shall remain, personal property irrespective of its use or manner of attachment to real property, and, on Lessor's demand Lessee shall provide Lessor with an acknowledgment by the owner or mortgagee of the land that such Units are and shall remain personal property. Lessor's obligations shall be suspended to the extent that Lessor is hindered or prevented from complying therewith because of strikes, lockouts, war, acts of God, fires, storms, accidents, governmental regulations or interference or other acts beyond Lessor's control. No obligation of Lessor shall survive the "term" of the Lease, or sooner termination thereof, and should Lessor permit use by Lessee of any Unit beyond the "term" specified therefor, the Lease obligations of Lessee shall continue and such permissive use shall not be construed as a renewal of the term thereof, or as a waiver of any right or continuation of any obligation of Lessor thereunder, and Lessor may take possession of any such Unit at any time upon demand after ten (10) days' notice. This agreement contains the entire understanding between Lessor and Lessee, and any change or modification must be in writing and signed by both parties. This agreement is entered into under, and is to be construed in accordance with the laws of the State of New Jersey.
- l. **Lessor's Performance of Lessee's Obligations.** In the event that Lessee shall fail in the opinion of Lessor to perform any of Lessee's obligations hereunder, then and so often as such events may occur, Lessor notwithstanding any rights and recourses it may have hereunder, shall have the right, but shall not be obligated, to perform such obligation for the account of and at the cost and expense of Lessee.

Entire Agreement. This agreement contains the whole understanding of the parties, except as shall be set forth in "short form" Leases as herein provided; shall be performed in the State of New Jersey and be construed and enforced in accordance with the laws of such state; and shall inure to the benefit of, and be binding upon, the respective legal representatives and heirs of the individual parties, and the successors and assigns of the corporate parties.

IN WITNESS WHEREOF, the parties hereto have executed these presents, the corporate parties by their officers thereunto duly authorized, this _____ day of _____, 19 ___

FIRST NATIONAL STATE BANK   Lessee

By_____   By_____
            Title   Title

                                              _____
                                                        Street

                                              _____
                                              City   State

Lessee No. _____

EQUIPMENT LEASE

No. ....

THIS LEASE made and entered into as of the .... day of .... , 19 .... , by and between

....
(hereinafter sometimes called "Lessor"), and

....
(hereinafter sometimes called "Lessee", whether one or more);

WITNESSETH:

For and in consideration for the mutual covenants and promises hereinafter set forth the parties hereto agree as follows:

1. *Leased Equipment.* Lessor hereby leases and lets unto Lessee, and Lessee hires and takes from Lessor, all of the following described items of equipment and personal property to be located at Lessee's above address unless otherwise specified below:

(all such equipment and personal property so described being hereinafter called "equipment"), together with, and the term "equipment" as herein used shall also include, all personal property used for repair, replacement, additions to parts and substitutions therefor appurtenant to, affixed or a part of said equipment, together with all costs of repairs or installations of same as may be or become necessary in connection with the use and operation of the equipment or property wherever situated. The equipment may either be specific equipment already set aside for Lessee or may be equipment of the same kind and type as described above to be subsequently supplied and furnished by a supplier in which case it shall be specifically identified by invoice from the supplier referring to the above serial number of this instrument.

2. *Term.* The term of this lease shall commence on the Date of Execution of this lease by Lessor as shown below and shall continue in full force and effect for a period of (   ) months from the date of commencement (hereinafter called "initial term") and as long thereafter as renewed in accordance with the renewal provisions hereof, if any, provided Lessee has complied with all of the terms and covenants of this lease.

3. *Rental.* Lessee shall pay to Lessor, or its successors or assigns, at Lessor's office at the address shown above (or as otherwise directed by Lessor in writing), as rent for the use of the equipment during the initial term, (   ) consecutive amounts, each payable in advance, as follows:

SCHEDULE OF RENTALS DURING INITIAL TERM

Number of Rentals	*Frequency of Rental Payments*	*Amount of Each Rental Payment*

The first rental shall be due on the Date of Execution of this Lease by Lessor as shown below, the second rental shall be due on the 10th day of the calendar month or other specified calendar period following date of supplier's shipment of the equipment; however, if such date occurs on or after the 16th day of the month then it shall become due on the 25th day of the following calendar month or other specified calendar period, and the third and each subsequent rental shall be due and payable on the same day of the month in which the second rental is due of each subsequent calendar month or other specified calendar period thereafter until all rentals have been paid.

LD101 (REV. 10-74)

4. *Additional Equipment.* This lease may be amended from time to time to cover additional equipment by the proper execution by Lessor and Lessee of a written instrument of amendment hereof describing the additional equipment to be leased hereunder and specifying the additional rental to be paid therefor and the time or times and place at which same is payable; and upon the execution thereof by Lessor and Lessee such additional equipment shall be and become subject to all of the terms and provisions hereof, as amended, as if same had been described herein initially.

5. *Use.* Lessee shall use the equipment in a careful and proper manner and shall comply with and conform to all national, state, municipal, police and other laws, ordinances and regulations in anywise relating to the possession, use or maintenance of the equipment. If at any time during the term hereof Lessor supplies Lessee with labels, plates, or other markings stating that the equipment is owned by Lessor, Lessee shall affix and keep same in a prominent place on the equipment, and shall permit Lessor to enter into and upon the premises where the equipment is located for the purpose of affixing any such labels, plates or other markings on the equipment.

6. *Lessee's Inspection.* Lessee shall inspect the equipment within two (2) days after receipt thereof. Unless Lessee within said period of time gives written notice to Lessor specifying any defect in or other proper objection to the equipment, Lessee agrees that it shall be conclusively presumed, as between Lessor and Lessee, that Lessee has fully inspected and acknowledged that the equipment is in good condition and repair, and that Lessee is satisfied with and has accepted the equipment in such good condition and repair.

7. *Alterations.* Without the prior written consent of Lessor, Lessee shall not make any alterations, changes, additions or improvements to the equipment except when said changes are initiated and recommended by the manufacturer of the equipment to improve performance or for modernization. All additions and improvements of whatsoever kind or nature made to the equipment shall belong to and become the property of Lessor, and subject to the terms of this lease.

8. *Repairs.* Lessee, at Lessee's own cost and expense and without any obligation or liability whatsoever on the part of Lessor, shall keep the equipment in good repair, condition and working order and shall furnish any and all parts, mechanisms and devices required to keep the equipment in good mechanical and working order, all of which shall become equipment covered by this lease.

9. *Liability of Lessor.* Lessor shall not be liable for any loss or damage which is incurred as a result of delay, strikes, storms, war emergencies, labor troubles, belated receipt of materials, fires, floods, water, Acts of God or other circumstances beyond its control. Lessor shall not be liable for any damages by reason of failure of the equipment to operate or faulty operation of the equipment or system. Lessor shall not be held responsible for any direct or consequential damages or losses resulting from the installation, operation or use of the products or materials furnished by Lessor.

10. *Lessor's Inspection.* Lessor shall at any and all times during business hours have the right to enter into and upon the premises where the equipment may be located for the purpose of inspecting the same or observing its use. Lessee shall give Lessor immediate notice of any attachment or other judicial process affecting any item of equipment and shall, whenever requested by Lessor, advise Lessor of the exact location of the equipment.

11. *Loss and Damage.* Lessee hereby assumes and shall bear the entire risk of loss and damage to the equipment from any and every cause whatsoever, and for the use, operation and storage thereof, and for damage to property or for injuries or death to persons howsoever arising therefrom or because thereof. No loss or damages to the equipment or any part thereof shall impair any obligation of Lessee under this lease which shall continue in full force and effect, including but not limited to the obligation of Lessee to make rental payments, except as follows:

In the event of loss or damage of any kind whatever to any item of equipment, Lessee, at the option of Lessor, shall:

(a) Place the same in good repair, condition and working order; or
(b) Replace the same with like equipment in good repair, condition and working order; or,
(c) If same is determined by Lessor to be lost, stolen, destroyed or damaged beyond repair, Lessee shall pay Lessor therefor in cash the fair market value thereof but in no case less than the remaining rentals during the initial term applicable to such item of equipment. Upon such payment this lease shall terminate with respect to such item of equipment, and Lessee thereupon shall become entitled to such item of equipment as-is and where-is without warranty, express or implied, with respect to any matter whatsoever.

12. *Insurance.* The equipment shall at all times be covered by insurance obtained as follows:

(a) *Risk of Loss or Damage:* Lessee shall keep the equipment insured against all risk of loss or damage from every cause whatever for not less than the full replacement value thereof, except that in the case of oil or gas equipment the insurance, at the election of Lessor, need not include fire and extended coverage on equipment situated beneath the ground; and any such insurance shall be in form and amount with companies approved by Lessor and shall, at the election of Lessor, either be in the joint names of Lessor and Lessee or be for the beneficial interest of Lessor, and Lessee shall pay the premiums therefor and at the request of Lessor deliver said policies or duplicates thereof to Lessor. The proceeds of any such insurance at the option of Lessor, shall be applied (i) toward the replacement, restoration or repair of the equipment including any airplane equipment or (ii) toward payment of the obligations of Lessee hereunder.

(b) Lessee at the election of Lessor shall carry public liability and property damage insurance against any and all damages and liabilities arising out of, connected with, or resulting from the possession, use and operation of such equipment; and any such insurance shall be in form and amount with companies approved by Lessor and shall be in the joint names of Lessor and Lessee, and Lessee shall pay the premiums therefor and at the request of Lessor deliver said policies or duplicates thereof to Lessor.

With respect to all policies of insurance hereinabove required to be obtained by Lessee which are not issued in the joint names of Lessor and Lessee, such policies at the election of Lessor shall effectively provide that the insuror in such policies will give Lessor thirty (30) days' written notice before the policy in question shall be altered or cancelled. If within ten (10) days following notice by Lessor to Lessee the Lessor has not received the policies of insurance herein required to be obtained by Lessee or has not received evidence of the payment by Lessee of the premiums due on any of the policies of insurance required herein, the Lessor shall at Lessor's option have the right to procure such insurance or pay such premiums and any sums so expended by Lessor shall thereafter be reimbursed by Lessee to Lessor and shall become additional rent under this lease and shall be payable in its entirety on the next rental payment date or within sixty (60) days whichever event is sooner.

13. *Surrender.* Upon the expiration or earlier termination of this lease, with respect to any item of equipment, Lessee shall (unless Lessee has paid Lessor in cash the fair market value thereof such item of equipment pursuant to Paragraph 11 hereof) return the same to Lessor in good repair, condition and working order, ordinary wear and tear resulting from proper use thereof alone excepted, in the following manner as may be specified by Lessor:

(a) By delivering such item of equipment at Lessee's cost and expense to such place as Lessor shall specify within the city or county in which the same was delivered to Lessee or to which same was moved with the written consent of Lessor; or
(b) By loading such item of equipment at Lessee's cost and expense on board such carrier as Lessor shall specify and shipping the same, freight collect, to the destination designated by Lessor.

14. *Taxes, Assessments and Licenses.* Lessee shall keep the equipment free and clear of all levies, liens, and encumbrances and shall pay all license fees, registration fees, assessments, charges and taxes, municipal, state and federal which may now or hereafter be imposed upon the ownership, leasing, renting, sale, possession or use of the equipment, excluding, however, all taxes on or measured by Lessor's income. Lessee shall also provide all permits and licenses, if any, necessary for the installation and operation of the equipment or any parts thereof. Lessee shall pay (or reimburse to Lessor forthwith as additional rent hereunder if Lessor is charged for the same) all freight, packing and handling charges (including insurance charges in connection therewith) as billed by manufacturer, vendor or carrier.

15. *Encumbrances.* Lessee shall not lease, sublease, mortgage or otherwise encumber, or part with possession of the equipment or any part thereof, and shall pay to Lessor as additional rent any charges that may be due to cover replacement, broken or missing parts or service at the vendor's regular established price if Lessor shall, at Lessor's sole option, elect to make repairs or replacement.

16. *Warranties.* Lessor makes no warranties, either express or implied, as to any matters whatsoever, including, but without limiting the generality of the foregoing, the condition of the equipment, or its merchantability or its fitness for any purposes; however, Lessor shall extend to Lessee all the vendor's warranties and guarantees but makes no representation or warranty on its own behalf with respect to the equipment.

17. *Indemnity.* Lessee shall indemnify Lessor against, and hold Lessor harmless from, any and all claims, actions, suits, proceedings, costs, expenses, damages and liabilities, including attorneys' fees arising out of, connected with, or resulting from the equipment, including, without limiting the generality of the foregoing, the manufacture, selection, delivery, possession, use operation or return of the equipment.

18. *Default.* If Lessee with regard to any item or items of equipment fails to pay any rent or other amount herein provided when the same shall become due and payable, or if Lessee with regard to any item or items of equipment fails to observe, keep or perform any other provisions of this lease required to be observed, kept or performed by Lessee, or if any execution or other writ of process shall be issued in any action or proceeding against Lessee whereby the said equipment may be taken or distrained, Lessor shall have the right to exercise any one or more of the following remedies:

    (a) To declare the entire amount of rent hereunder immediately due and payable as to any or all items of equipment, without notice or demand to Lessee.
    (b) To sue for and recover all rents and other payments then accrued, or thereafter accruing, with respect to any or all items of equipment.
    (c) To take possession of and remove any or all items of equipment, without demand or notice, wherever the same shall be located, or in lieu of removing any or all items of equipment to make such changes therein so as to prevent the use thereof by Lessee during the continuation of any default by Lessee hereunder, all without any court order or other process of law. Lessee hereby waives any and all damage occasioned by such taking of possession or making of changes. Any said taking of possession or making of changes shall not constitute a termination of this lease as to any or all items of equipment unless Lessor expressly so notifies Lessee in writing.
    (d) To terminate this lease as to any or all items of equipment.
    (e) To pursue any other remedy at law or in equity.

Notwithstanding any said taking of possession, or any other action which Lessor may take, Lessee shall be and remain liable for the full performance of all obligations on its part to be performed under this lease; provided, however, that in the event, but only in the event, all rentals and other amounts hereunder due or to become due are recovered by Lessor in full, Lessor shall allow Lessee a discount at the rate of 6% per annum for any such rentals which are recovered prior to the due date thereof.

All such remedies are cumulative and may be exercised concurrently or separately.

19. *Bankruptcy.* Neither this lease nor any interest therein is assignable or transferable by operation of law. If any proceeding under the Bankruptcy Act, as amended, is commenced by or against Lessee, or if Lessee is adjudged insolvent, or if Lessee makes any assignment for the benefit of his creditors, or if a writ of attachment or execution is levied on any item or items of equipment and may not be released or satisfied within ten (10) days thereafter, or if a receiver is appointed in any proceeding or action to which Lessee is a party with authority to take possession or control of any item or items of the equipment, Lessor shall have the right to exercise any one or more of the remedies set forth in Paragraph 18 hereof; and this lease shall, at the option of Lessor, without notice immediately terminate and shall not be treated as an asset of Lessee after the exercise of said option.

20. *Concurrent Remedies.* No right or remedy herein conferred upon or reserved to Lessor is exclusive of any other right or remedy herein or by law or in equity provided or permitted, but each shall be cumulative of every other right or remedy given hereunder or now or hereafter existing at law or in equity or by statute or otherwise, and may be enforced concurrently therewith or from time to time. The invalidity, or unenforceability in particular circumstances, of any provision of this instrument shall not extend beyond such provision or such circumstances, and no other provision of this instrument shall be affected thereby.

21. *Lessor's Expenses.* Lessee shall pay Lessor all costs and expenses, including attorneys' reasonable fees incurred by Lessor in exercising any of its rights or remedies hereunder or enforcing any of the terms, conditions or provisions hereof.

22. *Lessee's Assignment.* Without the prior written consent of Lessor, the Lessee shall not (a) assign, transfer, pledge or hypothecate this lease, the equipment or any part thereof, or any interest therein, or (b) sublet or lend the equipment or any part thereof, or permit the equipment or any part thereof to be used by anyone other than Lessee or Lessee's employees. Consent to any of the foregoing prohibited acts applies only in the given instance, and is not a consent to any subsequent like act by Lessee or any other person. Subject always to the foregoing, this lease inure to the benefit of, and is binding upon, the heirs, legatees, personal representatives, successors and assigns of the parties hereto.

23. *Lessor's Assignment.* It is understood that Lessor and Lessor's assigns shall have the continuing right to assign this lease and that such assignees shall not be obligated to perform any duty, covenant or condition required to be performed by Lessor under the terms of this lease. All rights of Lessor hereunder may be assigned, transferred, or otherwise disposed of, in whole or in part, without notice to Lessee. If Lessor assigns this lease or the rentals due or to become due hereunder, or any other interest herein, whether as security for any of its indebtedness or otherwise, no breach of default by Lessor hereunder or pursuant to any other agreement between Lessor and Lessee, if any, shall excuse performance by Lessee of any provision hereof, and no such assignee shall be obligated to perform any covenant or condition required to be performed by Lessor under the terms of this lease.

24. *Ownership.* The equipment is, and shall at all times be and remain, the sole and exclusive property of Lessor; and Lessee shall have no right, title or interest therein or thereto except as expressly set forth in this lease.

25. *Personal Property.* The equipment is, and shall at all times be and remain personal property, notwithstanding that the equipment or any part thereof may now be, or hereafter become, in any manner affixed or attached to or imbedded in or permanently resting upon real property or any building thereon, or attached in any manner to what is permanent as by means of cement, plaster, nails, bolts, screws or otherwise.

26. *Independent Contractor.* Lessee in the performance of all of Lessee's obligations hereunder shall at all times be an independent contractor and shall never be deemed an agent or employee of Lessor, and Lessor shall have no control of any nature whatsoever over the operations and activities of Lessee.

27. *Offset.* Lessee hereby waives any and all existing and future claims and offsets against any rent or other payments due hereunder; and agrees to pay the rent and other amounts hereunder regardless of any offset or claims which may be asserted by Lessor or on its behalf.

28. *Non-Waiver.* No covenant or condition of this lease can be waived except by the written consent of Lessor. Forbearance or indulgence by Lessor in any regard whatsoever shall not constitute a waiver of the covenant or condition to be performed by Lessee to which the same may apply, and until complete performance by Lessee of said covenant or condition, Lessor shall be entitled to invoke any remedy available to Lessor under this lease or by law or in equity despite said forbearance or indulgence.

29. *Notices.* All notices to be given under this lease shall be made in writing and mailed to the other party at its address set forth herein, or at such address as such party may provide in writing from time to time. Any such notice mailed to such address shall be effective when deposited in a United States mail depository duly addressed and with postage prepaid.

30. *Gender; Number.* Whenever the context of this lease requires, the masculine gender includes the feminine or neuter, and the singular number includes the plural; and whenever the word "Lessor" is used herein, it shall include all assignees of Lessor. If there is more than one Lessee named in this lease, the liability of each shall be joint and several.

31. *Time.* Time is of the essence in this lease and of each and all of its provisions.

32. *Entire Agreement.* This lease instrument constitutes the entire agreement between the parties hereto, and no representation, agreement, or promise of any officer, employee or agent of the Lessor or of any supplier of equipment not set forth herein shall in any way affect the obligations of the parties hereto as herein set forth; and the terms and provisions of this instrument shall not be modified, amended, altered or changed except by a written agreement signed by Lessee and by a duly authorized officer of Lessor.

33. *Late Charges.* If any rental payment or other invoice hereunder shall be unpaid ten (10) days after the due date thereof, Lessor shall, to the extent permitted by law, have the right to charge interest on the delinquent payment computed from the due date to the date the payment is received.

34. *State Governing.* This contract shall be determined to be made and executed in the State of New Jersey and shall be governed by the laws of the State of New Jersey regardless of where the equipment leased hereunder is or may hereafter be located.

35. *Further Assurances; Financial Statements.* Lessee agrees to provide Lessor with balance sheets and profit and loss statements made available by Lessee to its stockholders in the normal course of its business. Lessee warrants that any such statements and reports are true as of the date made. Lessee warrants that as of the date of this lease there has been no material adverse change in its financial condition since the date of the latest such financial statement.

36. *Additional Provisions.*

IN WITNESS WHEREOF, the parties hereto have executed these presents as of the day and year first above written, in multiple counterparts, any of which may be considered an original, the Date of Execution of this lease by Lessor being the   day of   19

By ....

ATTEST:

....
LESSOR

....
LESSEE

APPENDIX C

Comparative Depreciation Tables

The following tables show the annual and cumulative depreciation for various useful lives under the straight-line, 200%-declining-balance, 150%-declining-balance, 125%-declining-balance, and sum-of-the-years'-digits methods. *All amounts are expressed as percentages of the basis of the property at the time the useful life begins.*

Year	Straight-Line Annual %	Straight-Line Cum. %	200%-Declining-Balance Annual %	200%-Declining-Balance Cum. %	150%-Declining-Balance Annual %	150%-Declining-Balance Cum. %	Sum-of-Digits Annual %	Sum-of-Digits Cum. %
\multicolumn{9}{c}{**3-Year Life**}							
1	33.33	33.33	66.66	66.66	50.00	50.00	50.00	50.00
2	33.33	66.66	22.22	88.88	25.00	75.00	33.33	83.33
3	33.34	100.00	7.41	96.29	12.50	87.50	16.67	100.00
\multicolumn{9}{c}{**4-Year Life**}							
1	25.00	25.00	50.00	50.00	37.50	37.50	40.00	40.00
2	25.00	50.00	25.00	75.00	23.44	60.94	30.00	70.00
3	25.00	75.00	12.50	87.50	14.65	75.59	20.00	90.00
4	25.00	100.00	6.25	93.75	9.15	84.74	10.00	100.00
\multicolumn{9}{c}{**5-Year Life**}							
1	20.00	20.00	40.00	40.00	30.00	30.00	33.33	33.33
2	20.00	40.00	24.00	64.00	21.00	51.00	26.67	60.00
3	20.00	60.00	14.40	78.40	14.70	65.70	20.00	80.00
4	20.00	80.00	8.64	87.04	10.29	75.99	13.33	93.33
5	20.00	100.00	5.18	92.22	7.20	83.19	6.67	100.00
\multicolumn{9}{c}{**6-Year Life**}							
1	16.67	16.67	33.34	33.34	25.00	25.00	28.57	28.57
2	16.67	33.34	22.22	55.56	18.75	43.75	23.81	52.38
3	16.66	50.00	14.81	70.37	14.06	57.81	19.05	71.43
4	16.67	66.67	9.87	80.24	10.55	68.36	14.29	85.72
5	16.67	83.34	6.58	86.82	7.91	76.27	9.52	95.24
6	16.66	100.00	4.39	91.21	5.93	82.20	4.76	100.00
\multicolumn{9}{c}{**7-Year Life**}							
1	14.28	14.28	28.57	28.57	21.43	21.43	25.00	25.00
2	14.28	28.56	20.41	48.98	16.83	38.26	21.43	46.43
3	14.29	42.85	14.58	63.56	13.23	51.49	17.86	64.29
4	14.29	57.14	10.41	73.97	10.40	61.89	14.29	78.58
5	14.29	71.43	7.44	81.41	8.17	70.06	10.71	89.29
6	14.29	85.72	5.31	86.72	6.42	76.48	7.14	96.43
7	14.28	100.00	3.79	90.51	5.04	81.52	3.57	100.00
\multicolumn{9}{c}{**8-Year Life**}							
1	12.50	12.50	25.00	25.00	18.75	18.75	22.22	22.22
2	12.50	25.00	18.75	43.75	15.23	33.98	19.44	41.66
3	12.50	37.50	14.06	57.81	12.38	46.36	16.67	58.33
4	12.50	50.00	10.55	68.36	10.06	56.42	13.89	72.22
5	12.50	62.50	7.91	76.27	8.17	64.59	11.11	83.33
6	12.50	75.00	5.93	82.20	6.64	71.23	8.33	91.66
7	12.50	87.50	4.45	86.65	5.39	76.62	5.56	97.22
8	12.50	100.00	3.34	89.99	4.38	81.00	2.78	100.00

THE LEASE / BUY DECISION

Year	Straight-Line		200%-Declining-Balance		150%-Declining-Balance		125%-Declining-Balance		Sum-of-Digits	
	Annual %	Cum. %	Annual %	Cum. %	Annual %	Cum. %	Annual %	Cum. %	Annual %	Cum. %

9-Year Life

1	11.11	11.11	22.22	22.22	16.67	16.67			20.00	20.00
2	11.11	22.22	17.28	39.50	13.89	30.56			17.78	37.78
3	11.11	33.33	13.44	52.94	11.57	42.13			15.56	53.34
4	11.11	44.44	10.45	63.39	9.65	51.78			13.33	66.67
5	11.11	55.55	8.13	71.52	8.04	59.82			11.11	77.78
6	11.11	66.66	6.32	77.84	6.70	66.52			8.89	86.67
7	11.11	77.77	4.92	82.76	5.58	72.10			6.67	93.34
8	11.11	88.88	3.83	86.59	4.65	76.75			4.44	97.78
9	11.12	100.00	2.98	89.57	3.88	80.63			2.22	100.00

10-Year Life

1	10.00	10.00	20.00	20.00	15.00	15.00			18.18	18.18
2	10.00	20.00	16.00	36.00	12.75	27.75			16.37	34.55
3	10.00	30.00	12.80	48.80	10.84	38.59			14.56	49.09
4	10.00	40.00	10.24	59.04	9.21	47.80			12.73	61.82
5	10.00	50.00	8.19	67.23	7.83	55.63			10.91	72.73
6	10.00	60.00	6.56	73.79	6.66	62.29			9.09	81.82
7	10.00	70.00	5.24	79.03	5.66	67.95			7.27	89.09
8	10.00	80.00	4.19	83.22	4.81	72.76			5.46	94.55
9	10.00	90.00	3.36	86.58	4.09	76.85			3.63	98.18
10	10.00	100.00	2.68	89.26	3.47	80.32			1.82	100.00

15-Year Life

1	6.67	6.67	13.33	13.33	10.00	10.00			12.50	12.50
2	6.66	13.33	11.56	24.89	9.00	19.00			11.67	24.17
3	6.67	20.00	10.01	34.90	8.10	27.10			10.83	35.00
4	6.67	26.67	8.68	43.58	7.29	34.39			10.00	45.00
5	6.66	33.33	7.53	51.11	6.56	40.95			9.17	54.17
6	6.67	40.00	6.51	57.62	5.90	46.85			8.33	62.50
7	6.67	46.67	5.65	63.27	5.32	52.17			7.50	70.00
8	6.66	53.33	4.90	68.17	4.78	56.95			6.67	76.67
9	6.67	60.00	4.25	72.42	4.30	61.25			5.83	82.50
10	6.67	66.67	3.67	76.09	3.88	65.13			5.00	87.50
11	6.66	73.33	3.19	79.28	3.49	68.62			4.17	91.67
12	6.67	80.00	2.76	82.04	3.14	71.76			3.33	95.00
13	6.67	86.67	2.40	84.44	2.82	74.58			2.50	97.50
14	6.66	93.33	2.07	86.51	2.54	77.12			1.67	99.17
15	6.67	100.00	1.80	88.31	2.29	79.41			.83	100.00

20-Year Life

1	5.00	5.00	10.00	10.00	7.50	7.50	6.25	6.25	9.52	9.52
2	5.00	10.00	9.00	19.00	6.94	14.44	5.86	12.11	9.05	18.57
3	5.00	15.00	8.10	27.10	6.42	20.86	5.49	17.60	8.57	27.14
4	5.00	20.00	7.29	34.39	5.94	26.80	5.15	22.75	8.10	35.24
5	5.00	25.00	6.56	40.95	5.49	32.29	4.83	27.58	7.62	42.86
6	5.00	30.00	5.91	46.86	5.08	37.37	4.53	32.11	7.14	50.00
7	5.00	35.00	5.31	52.17	4.70	42.07	4.24	36.35	6.67	56.67
8	5.00	40.00	4.78	56.95	4.35	46.42	3.98	40.33	6.19	62.86
9	5.00	45.00	4.31	61.26	4.02	50.44	3.73	44.06	5.71	68.57
10	5.00	50.00	3.87	65.13	3.71	54.15	3.50	47.55	5.24	73.81
11	5.00	55.00	3.49	68.62	3.44	57.59	3.28	50.83	4.76	78.57
12	5.00	60.00	3.14	71.76	3.18	60.77	3.07	53.90	4.29	82.86
13	5.00	65.00	2.82	74.58	2.94	63.71	2.88	56.79	3.81	86.67
14	5.00	70.00	2.54	77.12	2.72	66.43	2.70	59.49	3.33	90.00
15	5.00	75.00	2.29	79.41	2.52	68.95	2.53	62.02	2.86	92.86

COMPARATIVE DEPRECIATION TABLES

Year	Straight-Line Annual %	Straight-Line Cum. %	200%-Declining-Balance Annual %	200%-Declining-Balance Cum. %	150%-Declining-Balance Annual %	150%-Declining-Balance Cum. %	125%-Declining-Balance Annual %	125%-Declining-Balance Cum. %	Sum-of-Digits Annual %	Sum-of-Digits Cum. %
\multicolumn{11}{c}{**20-Year Life** *(continued)*}
16	5.00	80.00	2.06	81.47	2.33	71.28	2.37	64.39	2.38	95.24
17	5.00	85.00	1.85	83.32	2.15	73.43	2.23	66.62	1.90	97.14
18	5.00	90.00	1.67	84.99	1.99	75.42	2.09	68.70	1.43	98.57
19	5.00	95.00	1.50	86.49	1.84	77.26	1.96	70.66	.95	99.52
20	5.00	100.00	1.35	87.84	1.70	78.96	1.83	72.49	.48	100.00
\multicolumn{11}{c}{**25-Year Life**}
1	4.00	4.00	8.00	8.00	6.00	6.00	5.00	5.00	7.69	7.69
2	4.00	8.00	7.36	15.36	5.64	11.64	4.75	9.75	7.39	15.08
3	4.00	12.00	6.77	22.13	5.30	16.94	4.51	14.26	7.07	22.15
4	4.00	16.00	6.23	28.36	4.98	21.92	4.29	18.55	6.77	28.92
5	4.00	20.00	5.73	34.09	4.68	26.60	4.07	22.62	6.47	35.39
6	4.00	24.00	5.27	39.36	4.40	31.00	3.87	26.49	6.15	41.54
7	4.00	28.00	4.86	44.22	4.14	35.14	3.68	30.17	5.85	47.39
8	4.00	32.00	4.46	48.68	3.89	39.03	3.49	33.66	5.53	52.92
9	4.00	36.00	4.10	52.78	3.66	42.69	3.32	36.98	5.23	58.15
10	4.00	40.00	3.78	56.56	3.43	46.12	3.15	40.13	4.93	63.08
11	4.00	44.00	3.48	60.04	3.23	49.35	2.99	43.12	4.61	67.69
12	4.00	48.00	3.19	63.23	3.03	52.38	2.84	45.96	4.31	72.00
13	4.00	52.00	2.94	66.17	2.86	55.24	2.70	48.67	4.00	76.00
14	4.00	56.00	2.71	68.88	2.68	57.92	2.57	51.23	3.69	79.69
15	4.00	60.00	2.49	71.37	2.52	60.44	2.44	53.67	3.39	83.08
16	4.00	64.00	2.29	73.66	2.37	62.81	2.32	55.99	3.07	86.15
17	4.00	68.00	2.11	75.77	2.23	65.04	2.20	58.19	2.77	88.92
18	4.00	72.00	1.94	77.71	2.10	67.14	2.09	60.28	2.47	91.39
19	4.00	76.00	1.78	79.49	1.97	69.11	1.99	62.26	2.15	93.54
20	4.00	80.00	1.64	81.13	1.85	70.96	1.89	64.15	1.85	95.39
21	4.00	84.00	1.51	82.64	1.74	72.70	1.79	65.94	1.53	96.92
22	4.00	88.00	1.39	84.03	1.64	74.34	1.70	67.65	1.23	98.15
23	4.00	92.00	1.28	85.31	1.54	75.88	1.62	69.26	.93	99.08
24	4.00	96.00	1.17	86.48	1.45	77.33	1.54	70.80	.61	99.69
25	4.00	100.00	1.08	87.56	1.36	78.69	1.46	72.26	.31	100.00
\multicolumn{11}{c}{**30-Year Life**}
1	3.33	3.33	6.67	6.67	5.00	5.00	4.16	4.16	6.45	6.45
2	3.34	6.67	6.22	12.89	4.75	9.75	3.99	8.16	6.24	12.69
3	3.33	10.00	5.81	18.70	4.51	14.26	3.83	11.99	6.02	18.71
4	3.33	13.33	5.42	24.12	4.29	18.55	3.67	15.65	5.81	24.52
5	3.34	16.67	5.06	29.18	4.07	22.62	3.51	19.17	5.59	30.11
6	3.33	20.00	4.72	33.90	3.87	26.49	3.37	22.54	5.37	35.48
7	3.33	23.33	4.40	38.30	3.68	30.17	3.23	25.76	5.17	40.65
8	3.34	26.67	4.12	42.42	3.49	33.66	3.09	28.86	4.94	45.59
9	3.33	30.00	3.84	46.26	3.32	36.98	2.96	31.82	4.73	50.32
10	3.33	33.33	3.58	49.84	3.15	40.13	2.84	34.66	4.52	54.84
11	3.34	36.67	3.34	53.18	2.99	43.12	2.72	37.38	4.30	59.14
12	3.33	40.00	3.12	56.30	2.84	45.96	2.61	39.99	4.09	63.23
13	3.33	43.33	2.92	59.22	2.70	48.66	2.50	42.49	3.87	67.10
14	3.34	46.67	2.72	61.94	2.57	51.23	2.40	44.89	3.65	70.75
15	3.33	50.00	2.53	64.47	2.44	53.67	2.30	47.19	3.44	74.19
16	3.33	53.33	2.37	66.84	2.32	55.99	2.20	49.39	3.23	77.42
17	3.34	56.67	2.21	69.05	2.20	58.19	2.11	51.50	3.01	80.43
18	3.33	60.00	2.07	71.12	2.09	60.28	2.02	53.52	2.80	83.23
19	3.33	63.33	1.92	73.04	1.99	62.27	1.94	55.45	2.58	85.81
20	3.34	66.67	1.80	74.84	1.89	64.16	1.86	57.31	2.36	88.17

213

Year	Straight-Line Annual %	Straight-Line Cum. %	200%-Declining-Balance Annual %	200%-Declining-Balance Cum. %	150%-Declining-Balance Annual %	150%-Declining-Balance Cum. %	125%-Declining-Balance Annual %	125%-Declining-Balance Cum. %	Sum-of-Digits Annual %	Sum-of-Digits Cum. %
					30-Year Life *(continued)*					
21	3.33	70.00	1.68	76.52	1.80	65.96	1.78	59.09	2.15	90.32
22	3.33	73.33	1.56	78.08	1.70	67.66	1.70	60.79	1.94	92.26
23	3.34	76.67	1.46	79.54	1.62	69.28	1.63	62.43	1.72	93.98
24	3.33	80.00	1.37	80.91	1.54	70.82	1.57	63.99	1.61	95.49
25	3.33	83.33	1.27	82.18	1.46	72.28	1.50	65.49	1.29	96.78
26	3.34	86.67	1.19	83.37	1.39	73.67	1.44	66.93	1.07	97.85
27	3.33	90.00	1.11	84.48	1.32	74.99	1.38	68.31	.86	98.71
28	3.33	93.33	1.03	85.51	1.25	76.24	1.32	69.63	.65	99.36
29	3.34	96.67	.97	86.48	1.19	77.43	1.27	70.89	.43	99.79
30	3.33	100.00	.90	87.38	1.13	78.56	1.21	72.11	.21	100.00
					33-1/3-Year Life					
1	3.00	3.00	6.00	6.00	4.50	4.50	3.75	3.75	5.82	5.82
2	3.00	6.00	5.64	11.64	4.30	8.80	3.61	7.36	5.65	11.47
3	3.00	9.00	5.30	16.94	4.10	12.90	3.47	10.83	5.47	16.95
4	3.00	12.00	4.98	21.93	3.92	16.82	3.34	14.18	5.30	22.25
5	3.00	15.00	4.68	26.61	3.74	20.56	3.22	17.40	5.17	27.37
6	3.00	18.00	4.40	31.00	3.57	24.14	3.10	20.49	4.95	32.32
7	3.00	21.00	4.14	35.15	3.41	27.55	2.98	23.47	4.76	37.10
8	3.00	24.00	3.89	39.03	3.16	30.81	2.87	26.34	4.60	41.70
9	3.00	27.00	3.66	42.70	3.11	33.93	2.76	29.11	4.43	46.13
10	3.00	30.00	3.44	46.14	2.97	36.90	2.66	31.77	4.25	50.38
11	3.00	33.00	3.23	49.37	2.84	39.74	2.56	34.32	4.08	54.46
12	3.00	36.00	3.04	52.41	2.71	42.45	2.46	36.79	3.90	58.36
13	3.00	39.00	2.86	55.26	2.59	45.04	2.37	39.16	3.73	62.10
14	3.00	42.00	2.68	57.95	2.47	47.51	2.28	41.44	3.55	65.64
15	3.00	45.00	2.52	60.47	2.36	49.88	2.20	43.63	3.38	69.02
16	3.00	48.00	2.37	62.84	2.26	52.13	2.11	45.75	3.20	72.22
17	3.00	51.00	2.23	65.07	2.15	54.29	2.03	47.78	3.03	75.25
18	3.00	54.00	2.10	67.17	2.06	56.34	1.95	49.74	2.85	78.10
19	3.00	57.00	1.97	69.14	1.96	58.31	1.88	51.63	2.68	80.78
20	3.00	60.00	1.85	71.00	1.88	60.18	1.81	53.44	2.50	83.28
21	3.00	63.00	1.74	72.73	1.79	61.97	1.75	55.19	2.33	85.61
22	3.00	66.00	1.64	74.37	1.71	63.69	1.68	56.87	2.15	87.77
23	3.00	69.00	1.54	75.90	1.63	65.32	1.62	58.48	1.98	89.75
24	3.00	72.00	1.45	77.35	1.56	66.88	1.56	60.04	1.81	91.56
25	3.00	75.00	1.36	78.71	1.49	68.37	1.50	61.54	1.63	93.19
26	3.00	78.00	1.28	79.99	1.42	69.79	1.44	62.98	1.46	94.64
27	3.00	81.00	1.20	81.19	1.36	71.15	1.39	64.37	1.28	95.92
28	3.00	84.00	1.13	82.32	1.30	72.45	1.34	65.71	1.11	97.03
29	3.00	87.00	1.06	83.38	1.24	73.69	1.29	66.99	.93	97.96
30	3.00	90.00	1.00	84.37	1.18	74.88	1.24	68.23	.76	98.72
31	3.00	93.00	.94	85.31	1.13	76.01	1.19	69.42	.58	99.30
32	3.00	96.00	.88	86.19	1.08	77.09	1.15	70.57	.41	99.71
33	3.00	99.00	.93	87.02	1.03	78.12	1.10	71.67	.23	99.94
33⅓	1.00	100.00	.26	87.28	.33	78.45	.35	71.95	.06	100.00
					35-Year Life					
1	2.86	2.86	5.71	5.71	4.29	4.29	3.57	3.57	5.56	5.56
2	2.86	5.72	5.38	11.09	4.10	8.39	3.44	7.02	5.40	10.96
3	2.85	8.57	5.07	16.16	3.93	12.32	3.32	10.34	5.24	16.20
4	2.86	11.43	4.78	20.94	3.76	16.08	3.20	13.54	5.08	21.28
5	2.86	14.29	4.51	25.45	3.60	19.68	3.09	16.63	4.92	26.20

COMPARATIVE DEPRECIATION TABLES

Year	Straight-Line Annual %	Straight-Line Cum. %	200%-Declining-Balance Annual %	200%-Declining-Balance Cum. %	150%-Declining-Balance Annual %	150%-Declining-Balance Cum. %	125%-Declining-Balance Annual %	125%-Declining-Balance Cum. %	Sum-of-Digits Annual %	Sum-of-Digits Cum. %
\multicolumn{11}{c}{**35-Year Life** (continued)}
6	2.85	17.14	4.25	29.70	3.44	23.12	2.98	19.60	4.76	30.96
7	2.86	20.00	4.01	33.71	3.29	26.41	2.87	22.48	4.60	35.56
8	2.86	22.86	3.78	37.49	3.15	29.56	2.77	25.24	4.44	40.00
9	2.85	25.71	3.56	41.05	3.02	32.58	2.67	27.91	4.29	44.29
10	2.86	28.57	3.36	44.41	2.89	35.47	2.57	30.49	4.13	48.42
11	2.86	31.43	3.17	47.58	2.77	38.24	2.48	32.97	3.97	52.39
12	2.85	34.28	2.99	50.57	2.65	40.89	2.39	35.36	3.81	56.20
13	2.86	37.14	2.82	53.39	2.53	43.42	2.31	37.67	3.65	59.85
14	2.86	40.00	2.66	56.05	2.42	45.84	2.23	39.90	3.49	63.34
15	2.85	42.85	2.51	58.56	2.32	48.16	2.15	42.05	3.33	66.67
16	2.86	45.71	2.37	60.93	2.22	50.38	2.07	44.12	3.18	69.85
17	2.86	48.57	2.23	63.16	2.13	52.51	2.00	46.11	3.02	72.87
18	2.85	51.42	2.10	65.26	2.03	54.54	1.92	48.04	2.86	75.73
19	2.86	54.28	1.98	67.24	1.95	56.49	1.86	49.89	2.70	78.43
20	2.86	57.14	1.87	69.11	1.86	58.35	1.79	51.68	2.54	80.97
21	2.86	60.00	1.76	70.87	1.79	60.14	1.73	53.41	2.38	83.35
22	2.86	62.86	1.66	72.53	1.71	61.85	1.66	55.07	2.22	85.57
23	2.86	65.72	1.57	74.10	1.64	63.49	1.60	56.68	2.06	87.63
24	2.85	68.57	1.48	75.58	1.56	65.05	1.55	58.22	1.90	89.53
25	2.86	71.43	1.40	76.98	1.50	66.55	1.49	59.72	1.75	91.28
26	2.86	74.29	1.32	78.30	1.43	67.98	1.44	61.15	1.59	92.87
27	2.85	77.14	1.24	79.54	1.37	69.35	1.39	62.54	1.43	94.30
28	2.86	80.00	1.17	80.71	1.31	70.66	1.34	63.88	1.27	95.57
29	2.86	82.86	1.10	81.81	1.26	71.92	1.29	65.17	1.11	96.68
30	2.85	85.71	1.04	82.85	1.20	73.12	1.24	66.41	.95	97.63
31	2.86	88.57	.98	83.83	1.15	74.27	1.20	67.61	.79	98.42
32	2.86	91.43	.92	84.75	1.10	75.37	1.16	68.77	.63	99.05
33	2.85	94.28	.87	85.62	1.06	76.43	1.12	69.88	.47	99.52
34	2.86	97.14	.82	86.44	1.01	77.44	1.08	70.96	.32	99.84
35	2.86	100.00	.77	87.21	.97	78.41	1.04	72.00	.16	100.00
\multicolumn{11}{c}{**40-Year Life**}
1	2.50	2.50	5.00	5.00	3.75	3.75	3.13	3.13	4.88	4.88
2	2.50	5.00	4.75	9.75	3.61	7.36	3.03	6.15	4.75	9.63
3	2.50	7.50	4.51	14.26	3.47	10.83	2.93	9.09	4.64	14.27
4	2.50	10.00	4.29	18.55	3.34	14.17	2.84	11.93	4.51	18.78
5	2.50	12.50	4.07	22.62	3.22	17.39	2.75	14.68	4.39	23.17
6	2.50	15.00	3.87	26.49	3.10	20.49	2.67	17.34	4.27	27.44
7	2.50	17.50	3.68	30.17	2.98	23.47	2.58	19.93	4.14	31.58
8	2.50	20.00	3.49	33.66	2.87	26.34	2.50	22.43	4.03	35.61
9	2.50	22.50	3.32	36.98	2.76	29.10	2.42	24.85	3.90	39.51
10	2.50	25.00	3.15	40.13	2.66	31.76	2.35	27.20	3.78	43.29
11	2.50	27.50	2.99	43.12	2.56	34.32	2.27	29.48	3.66	46.95
12	2.50	30.00	2.84	45.96	2.46	36.78	2.20	31.68	3.54	50.49
13	2.50	32.50	2.71	48.67	2.37	39.15	2.13	33.82	3.41	53.90
14	2.50	35.00	2.56	51.23	2.28	41.43	2.07	35.88	3.29	57.19
15	2.50	37.50	2.44	53.67	2.20	43.63	2.00	37.89	3.18	60.37
16	2.50	40.00	2.32	55.99	2.11	45.74	1.94	39.83	3.04	63.41
17	2.50	42.50	2.20	58.19	2.03	47.77	1.88	41.71	2.93	66.34
18	2.50	45.00	2.09	60.28	1.96	49.73	1.82	43.53	2.81	69.15
19	2.50	47.50	1.99	62.27	1.88	51.61	1.76	45.30	2.68	71.83
20	2.50	50.00	1.88	64.15	1.81	53.42	1.71	47.01	2.56	74.39

Year	Straight-Line Annual %	Straight-Line Cum. %	200%-Declining-Balance Annual %	200%-Declining-Balance Cum. %	150%-Declining-Balance Annual %	150%-Declining-Balance Cum. %	125%-Declining-Balance Annual %	125%-Declining-Balance Cum. %	Sum-of-Digits Annual %	Sum-of-Digits Cum. %
\multicolumn{11}{c}{**40-Year Life** (continued)}										
21	2.50	52.50	1.79	65.94	1.75	55.17	1.66	48.66	2.44	76.83
22	2.50	55.00	1.71	67.65	1.68	56.85	1.60	50.27	2.32	79.15
23	2.50	57.50	1.62	69.27	1.62	58.47	1.55	51.82	2.19	81.34
24	2.50	60.00	1.53	70.80	1.56	60.03	1.51	53.33	2.07	83.41
25	2.50	62.50	1.46	72.26	1.50	61.53	1.46	54.78	1.94	85.37
26	2.50	65.00	1.39	73.65	1.44	62.97	1.41	56.20	1.82	87.19
27	2.50	67.50	1.32	74.97	1.39	64.36	1.37	57.57	1.71	88.90
28	2.50	70.00	1.25	76.22	1.34	65.70	1.33	58.89	1.59	90.49
29	2.50	72.50	1.19	77.41	1.29	66.99	1.28	60.18	1.46	91.95
30	2.50	75.00	1.13	78.54	1.24	68.23	1.24	61.42	1.34	93.29
31	2.50	77.50	1.07	79.61	1.19	69.42	1.21	62.63	1.22	94.51
32	2.50	80.00	1.02	80.63	1.15	70.57	1.17	63.79	1.10	95.61
33	2.50	82.50	.97	81.60	1.10	71.67	1.13	64.93	.98	96.58
34	2.50	85.00	.92	85.52	1.06	72.73	1.10	66.02	.86	97.44
35	2.50	87.50	.87	83.39	1.02	73.75	1.06	67.08	.73	98.17
36	2.50	90.00	.83	84.22	.98	74.73	1.03	68.11	.61	98.78
37	2.50	92.50	.79	85.01	.95	75.68	1.00	69.11	.49	99.27
38	2.50	95.00	.75	85.76	.91	76.59	.97	70.07	.36	99.63
39	2.50	97.50	.71	86.47	.88	77.47	.94	71.01	.25	99.88
40	2.50	100.00	.68	87.15	.85	78.32	.91	71.92	.12	100.00
\multicolumn{11}{c}{**45-Year Life**}										
1	2.22	2.22	4.44	4.44	3.33	3.33	2.78	2.78	4.35	4.35
2	2.22	4.44	4.24	8.68	3.22	6.55	2.70	5.48	4.25	8.60
3	2.22	6.66	4.05	12.73	3.12	9.67	2.63	8.10	4.15	12.75
4	2.23	8.89	3.87	16.60	3.01	12.68	2.55	10.66	4.06	16.81
5	2.22	11.11	3.70	20.30	2.91	15.59	2.48	13.14	3.96	20.77
6	2.22	13.33	3.54	23.84	2.81	18.40	2.41	15.55	3.86	24.63
7	2.22	15.55	3.38	27.22	2.72	21.12	2.35	17.90	3.77	28.40
8	2.23	17.78	3.23	30.45	2.63	23.75	2.28	20.18	3.67	32.07
9	2.22	20.00	3.09	33.54	2.54	26.29	2.22	22.40	3.57	35.64
10	2.22	22.22	2.95	36.49	2.46	28.75	2.16	24.55	3.48	39.12
11	2.22	24.44	2.82	39.31	2.38	31.13	2.10	26.65	3.38	42.50
12	2.23	26.67	2.69	42.00	2.30	33.43	2.04	28.68	3.28	45.78
13	2.22	28.89	2.57	44.57	2.22	35.65	1.98	30.67	3.19	48.97
14	2.22	31.11	2.46	47.03	2.15	37.80	1.93	32.59	3.09	52.06
15	2.22	33.33	2.35	49.38	2.07	39.87	1.87	34.46	3.00	55.06
16	2.23	35.56	2.25	51.63	2.00	41.87	1.82	36.28	2.90	57.96
17	2.22	37.78	2.15	53.78	1.94	43.81	1.77	38.05	2.80	60.76
18	2.22	40.00	2.05	55.83	1.87	45.68	1.72	39.77	2.70	63.46
19	2.22	42.22	1.96	57.79	1.81	47.49	1.67	41.45	2.61	66.07
20	2.23	44.45	1.87	59.66	1.75	49.24	1.63	43.07	2.51	68.58
21	2.22	46.67	1.79	61.45	1.69	50.93	1.58	44.66	2.42	71.00
22	2.22	48.89	1.71	63.16	1.64	52.57	1.54	46.19	2.32	73.32
23	2.22	51.11	1.63	64.79	1.58	54.15	1.49	47.69	2.22	75.54
24	2.23	53.34	1.56	66.35	1.53	55.68	1.45	49.14	2.13	77.67
25	2.22	55.56	1.49	67.84	1.48	57.16	1.41	50.55	2.03	79.70
26	2.22-	57.78	1.42	69.26	1.43	58.59	1.37	51.93	1.93	81.63
27	2.22	60.00	1.36	70.62	1.38	59.97	1.34	53.26	1.84	83.47
28	2.23	62.23	1.30	71.92	1.33	61.30	1.30	54.56	1.74	85.21
29	2.22	64.45	1.24	73.16	1.29	62.59	1.26	55.82	1.64	86.85
30	2.22	66.67	1.18	74.34	1.25	63.84	1.23	57.05	1.55	88.40

COMPARATIVE DEPRECIATION TABLES

Year	Straight-Line Annual %	Straight-Line Cum. %	200%-Declining-Balance Annual %	200%-Declining-Balance Cum. %	150%-Declining-Balance Annual %	150%-Declining-Balance Cum. %	125%-Declining-Balance Annual %	125%-Declining-Balance Cum. %	Sum-of-Digits Annual %	Sum-of-Digits Cum. %
				45-Year Life *(continued)*						
31	2.22	68.89	1.13	75.47	1.21	65.05	1.19	58.24	1.45	89.85
32	2.23	71.12	1.08	76.55	1.17	66.22	1.16	59.40	1.35	91.20
33	2.22	73.34	1.03	77.58	1.13	67.35	1.13	60.53	1.26	92.46
34	2.22	75.56	.98	78.56	1.09	68.44	1.10	61.63	1.16	93.62
35	2.22	77.78	.94	79.50	1.05	69.49	1.07	62.69	1.06	94.68
36	2.22	80.00	.90	80.40	1.02	70.51	1.04	63.73	.97	95.65
37	2.23	82.23	.86	81.26	.98	71.49	1.01	64.74	.87	96.52
38	2.22	84.45	.82	82.08	.95	72.44	.98	65.72	.77	97.29
39	2.22	86.67	.78	82.86	.92	73.36	.95	66.67	.68	97.97
40	2.22	88.89	.75	83.61	.89	74.25	.93	67.59	.58	98.55
41	2.23	91.12	.72	84.33	.86	75.11	.90	68.49	.48	99.03
42	2.22	93.34	.69	85.02	.83	75.94	.88	69.37	.39	99.42
43	2.22	95.56	.66	85.68	.80	76.74	.85	70.22	.29	99.71
44	2.22	97.78	.63	86.31	.78	77.52	.83	71.05	.19	99.90
45	2.22	100.00	.60	86.91	.75	78.27	.80	71.85	.10	100.00
				50-Year Life						
1	2.00	2.00	4.00	4.00	3.00	3.00	2.50	2.50	3.92	3.92
2	2.00	4.00	3.84	7.84	2.91	5.91	2.44	4.94	3.85	7.77
3	2.00	6.00	3.69	11.53	2.82	8.73	2.38	7.31	3.76	11.53
4	2.00	8.00	3.54	15.07	2.74	11.47	2.32	9.63	3.69	15.22
5	2.00	10.00	3.39	18.46	2.66	14.13	2.26	11.89	3.60	18.82
6	2.00	12.00	3.26	21.72	2.58	16.71	2.20	14.09	3.53	22.35
7	2.00	14.00	3.14	24.86	2.50	19.21	2.15	16.24	3.45	25.80
8	2.00	16.00	3.00	27.86	2.42	21.63	2.09	18.33	3.38	29.18
9	2.00	18.00	2.89	30.75	2.35	23.98	2.04	20.38	3.29	32.47
10	2.00	20.00	2.77	33.52	2.28	26.26	1.99	22.37	3.22	35.69
11	2.00	22.00	2.66	36.18	2.21	28.47	1.94	24.31	3.15	38.82
12	2.00	24.00	2.55	38.73	2.15	30.62	1.89	26.20	3.06	41.88
13	2.00	26.00	2.45	41.18	2.08	32.70	1.84	28.05	2.98	44.86
14	2.00	28.00	2.35	43.53	2.02	34.72	1.80	29.84	2.91	47.77
15	2.00	30.00	2.26	45.79	1.96	36.68	1.75	31.60	2.82	50.59
16	2.00	32.00	2.17	47.96	1.90	38.58	1.71	33.31	2.74	53.33
17	2.00	34.00	2.08	50.04	1.84	40.42	1.67	34.98	2.67	56.00
18	2.00	36.00	2.00	52.04	1.79	42.21	1.63	36.60	2.59	58.59
19	2.00	38.00	1.92	53.96	1.73	43.94	1.58	38.19	2.51	61.10
20	2.00	40.00	1.84	55.80	1.68	45.62	1.55	39.73	2.43	63.53
21	2.00	42.00	1.77	57.57	1.63	47.25	1.51	41.24	2.35	65.88
22	2.00	44.00	1.70	59.27	1.58	48.83	1.47	42.71	2.28	68.16
23	2.00	46.00	1.62	60.89	1.53	50.36	1.43	44.14	2.19	70.35
24	2.00	48.00	1.57	62.46	1.49	51.85	1.40	45.54	2.12	72.47
25	2.00	50.00	1.50	63.96	1.44	53.29	1.36	46.90	2.04	74.51
26	2.00	52.00	1.44	65.40	1.40	54.69	1.33	48.23	1.96	76.47
27	2.00	54.00	1.39	66.79	1.36	56.05	1.29	49.52	1.87	78.35
28	2.00	56.00	1.33	68.12	1.32	57.37	1.26	50.78	1.81	80.16
29	2.00	58.00	1.27	69.39	1.28	58.64	1.23	52.01	1.72	81.88
30	2.00	60.00	1.22	70.61	1.24	59.89	1.20	53.21	1.65	83.53
31	2.00	62.00	1.18	71.79	1.20	61.09	1.17	54.38	1.57	85.10
32	2.00	64.00	1.13	72.92	1.17	62.26	1.14	55.52	1.49	86.59
33	2.00	66.00	1.08	74.00	1.13	63.39	1.11	56.63	1.41	88.00
34	2.00	68.00	1.04	75.04	1.10	64.49	1.08	57.72	1.33	89.33
35	2.00	70.00	1.00	76.04	1.07	65.56	1.06	58.78	1.26	90.59

Year	Straight-Line Annual %	Straight-Line Cum. %	200%-Declining-Balance Annual %	200%-Declining-Balance Cum. %	150%-Declining-Balance Annual %	150%-Declining-Balance Cum. %	125%-Declining-Balance Annual %	125%-Declining-Balance Cum. %	Sum-of-Digits Annual %	Sum-of-Digits Cum. %
					50-Year Life *(continued)*					
36	2.00	72.00	.96	77.00	1.03	66.59	1.03	59.81	1.18	91.77
37	2.00	74.00	.92	77.92	1.00	67.59	1.00	60.81	1.09	92.86
38	2.00	76.00	.88	78.80	.97	68.56	.98	61.79	1.02	93.88
39	2.00	78.00	.85	79.65	.94	69.50	.96	62.75	.94	94.82
40	2.00	80.00	.81	80.46	.92	70.42	.93	63.68	.87	95.69
41	2.00	82.00	.78	81.24	.89	71.31	.91	64.58	.78	96.47
42	2.00	84.00	.75	81.99	.86	72.17	.89	65.47	.71	97.18
43	2.00	86.00	.72	82.71	.84	73.01	.86	66.33	.62	97.80
44	2.00	88.00	.69	83.40	.81	73.82	.84	67.18	.55	98.35
45	2.00	90.00	.67	84.07	.79	74.61	.82	68.00	.47	98.82
46	2.00	92.00	.64	84.71	.76	75.37	.80	68.80	.40	99.22
47	2.00	94.00	.61	85.32	.74	76.11	.78	69.58	.31	99.53
48	2.00	96.00	.59	85.90	.72	76.83	.76	70.34	.24	99.77
49	2.00	98.00	.57	86.47	.70	77.53	.74	71.08	.15	99.92
50	2.00	100.00	.54	87.01	.67	78.20	.72	71.80	.08	100.00

APPENDIX D

Compound Interest and Annuity Tables

3.00 %
ANNUAL

	Amount Of 1	Amount Of 1 Per Period	Sinking Fund Payment	Present Worth Of 1	Present Worth Of 1 Per Period	Periodic Payment To Amortize 1	Constant Annual Percent	Total Interest	Annual Add-on Rate	
	What a single $1 deposit grows to in the future. The deposit is made at the beginning of the first period.	What a series of $1 deposits grow to in the future. A deposit is made at the end of each period.	The amount to be deposited at the end of each period that grows to $1 in the future.	What $1 to be paid in the future is worth today. Value today of a single payment tomorrow.	What $1 to be paid in the future at the end of each period is worth today. Value today of a series of payments tomorrow.	The mortgage payment to amortize a loan of $1. An annuity certain, payable at the end of each period, worth $1 today.	The annual payment, including interest and principal, to amortize completely a loan of $100.	The total interest paid over the term of a loan. The loan is amortized by regular periodic payments.	The average annual interest rate on a loan that is completely amortized by regular periodic payments.	
	$S=(1+i)^n$	$S_{\overline{n}}=\frac{(1+i)^n-1}{i}$	$\frac{1}{S_{\overline{n}}}=\frac{i}{(1+i)^n-1}$	$V^n=\frac{1}{(1+i)^n}$	$A_{\overline{n}}=\frac{1-V^n}{i}$	$\frac{1}{A_{\overline{n}}}=\frac{i}{1-V^n}$				
YR										YR
1	1.030000	1.000000	1.00000000	0.970874	0.970874	1.03000000	103.00	0.030000	3.00	1
2	1.060900	2.030000	0.49261084	0.942596	1.913470	0.52261084	52.27	0.045222	2.26	2
3	1.092727	3.090900	0.32353036	0.915142	2.828611	0.35353036	35.36	0.060591	2.02	3
4	1.125509	4.183627	0.23902705	0.888487	3.717098	0.26902705	26.91	0.076108	1.90	4
5	1.159274	5.309136	0.18835457	0.862609	4.579707	0.21835457	21.84	0.091773	1.84	5
6	1.194052	6.468410	0.15459750	0.837484	5.417191	0.18459750	18.46	0.107585	1.79	6
7	1.229874	7.662462	0.13050635	0.813092	6.230283	0.16050635	16.06	0.123544	1.76	7
8	1.266770	8.892336	0.11245639	0.789409	7.019692	0.14245639	14.25	0.139651	1.75	8
9	1.304773	10.159106	0.09843386	0.766417	7.786109	0.12843386	12.85	0.155905	1.73	9
10	1.343916	11.463879	0.08723051	0.744094	8.530203	0.11723051	11.73	0.172305	1.72	10
11	1.384234	12.807796	0.07807745	0.722421	9.252624	0.10807745	10.81	0.188852	1.72	11
12	1.425761	14.192030	0.07046209	0.701380	9.954004	0.10046209	10.05	0.205545	1.71	12
13	1.468534	15.617790	0.06402954	0.680951	10.634955	0.09402954	9.41	0.222384	1.71	13
14	1.512590	17.086324	0.05852634	0.661118	11.296073	0.08852634	8.86	0.239369	1.71	14
15	1.557967	18.598914	0.05376658	0.641862	11.937935	0.08376658	8.38	0.256499	1.71	15
16	1.604706	20.156881	0.04961085	0.623167	12.561102	0.07961085	7.97	0.273774	1.71	16
17	1.652848	21.761588	0.04595253	0.605016	13.166118	0.07595253	7.60	0.291193	1.71	17
18	1.702433	23.414435	0.04270870	0.587395	13.753513	0.07270870	7.28	0.308757	1.72	18
19	1.753506	25.116868	0.03981388	0.570286	14.323799	0.06981388	6.99	0.326464	1.72	19
20	1.806111	26.870374	0.03721571	0.553676	14.877475	0.06721571	6.73	0.344314	1.72	20
21	1.860295	28.676486	0.03487178	0.537549	15.415024	0.06487178	6.49	0.362307	1.73	21
22	1.916103	30.536780	0.03274729	0.521893	15.936917	0.06274729	6.28	0.380443	1.73	22
23	1.973587	32.452884	0.03081390	0.506692	16.443608	0.06081390	6.09	0.398720	1.73	23
24	2.032794	34.426470	0.02904742	0.491934	16.935542	0.05904742	5.91	0.417138	1.74	24
25	2.093778	36.459264	0.02742787	0.477606	17.413148	0.05742787	5.75	0.435697	1.74	25
26	2.156591	38.553042	0.02593829	0.463695	17.876842	0.05593829	5.60	0.454396	1.75	26
27	2.221289	40.709634	0.02456421	0.450189	18.327031	0.05456421	5.46	0.473234	1.75	27
28	2.287928	42.930923	0.02329323	0.437077	18.764108	0.05329323	5.33	0.492211	1.76	28
29	2.356566	45.218850	0.02211467	0.424346	19.188455	0.05211467	5.22	0.511325	1.76	29
30	2.427262	47.575416	0.02101926	0.411987	19.600441	0.05101926	5.11	0.530578	1.77	30
31	2.500080	50.002678	0.01999893	0.399987	20.000428	0.04999893	5.00	0.549967	1.77	31
32	2.575083	52.502759	0.01904662	0.388337	20.388766	0.04904662	4.91	0.569492	1.78	32
33	2.652335	55.077841	0.01815612	0.377026	20.765792	0.04815612	4.82	0.589152	1.79	33
34	2.731905	57.730177	0.01732196	0.366045	21.131837	0.04732196	4.74	0.608947	1.79	34
35	2.813862	60.462082	0.01653929	0.355383	21.487220	0.04653929	4.66	0.628875	1.80	35
36	2.898278	63.275944	0.01580379	0.345032	21.832252	0.04580379	4.59	0.648937	1.80	36
37	2.985227	66.174223	0.01511162	0.334983	22.167235	0.04511162	4.52	0.669130	1.81	37
38	3.074783	69.159449	0.01445934	0.325226	22.492462	0.04445934	4.45	0.689455	1.81	38
39	3.167027	72.234233	0.01384385	0.315754	22.808215	0.04384385	4.39	0.709910	1.82	39
40	3.262038	75.401260	0.01326238	0.306557	23.114772	0.04326238	4.33	0.730495	1.83	40
41	3.359899	78.663298	0.01271241	0.297628	23.412400	0.04271241	4.28	0.751209	1.83	41
42	3.460696	82.023196	0.01219167	0.288959	23.701359	0.04219167	4.22	0.772050	1.84	42
43	3.564517	85.483892	0.01169811	0.280543	23.981902	0.04169811	4.17	0.793019	1.84	43
44	3.671452	89.048409	0.01122985	0.272372	24.254274	0.04122985	4.13	0.814113	1.85	44
45	3.781596	92.719861	0.01078518	0.264439	24.518713	0.04078518	4.08	0.835333	1.86	45
46	3.895044	96.501457	0.01036254	0.256737	24.775449	0.04036254	4.04	0.856677	1.86	46
47	4.011895	100.396501	0.00996051	0.249259	25.024708	0.03996051	4.00	0.878144	1.87	47
48	4.132252	104.408396	0.00957777	0.241999	25.266707	0.03957777	3.96	0.899733	1.87	48
49	4.256219	108.540648	0.00921314	0.234950	25.501657	0.03921314	3.93	0.921444	1.88	49
50	4.383906	112.796867	0.00886549	0.228107	25.729764	0.03886549	3.89	0.943275	1.89	50

THE LEASE / BUY DECISION

COMPOUND INTEREST AND ANNUITY TABLE

4.00 % ANNUAL

	Amount Of 1	Amount Of 1 Per Period	Sinking Fund Payment	Present Worth Of 1	Present Worth Of 1 Per Period	Periodic Payment To Amortize 1	Constant Annual Percent	Total Interest	Annual Add-on Rate
	What a single $1 deposit grows to in the future. The deposit is made at the beginning of the first period.	What a series of $1 deposits grow to in the future. A deposit is made at the end of each period.	The amount to be deposited at the end of each period that grows to $1 in the future.	What $1 to be paid in the future is worth today. Value today of a single payment tomorrow.	What $1 to be paid at the end of each period is worth today. Value today of a series of payments tomorrow.	The mortgage payment to amortize a loan of $1. An annuity certain, payable at the end of each period, worth $1 today.	The annual payment, including interest and principal, to amortize completely a loan of $100.	The total interest paid over the term of $1. The loan is amortized by regular periodic payments.	The average annual interest rate on a loan that is completely amortized by regular periodic payments.
	$S=(1+i)^n$	$S_n = \frac{(1+i)^n - 1}{i}$	$\frac{1}{S_n} = \frac{i}{(1+i)^n - 1}$	$V^n = \frac{1}{(1+i)^n}$	$A_n = \frac{1-V^n}{i}$	$\frac{1}{A_n} = \frac{i}{1-V^n}$			

YR										YR
1	1.040000	1.000000	1.00000000	0.961538	0.961538	1.04000000	104.00	0.040000	4.00	1
2	1.081600	2.040000	0.49019608	0.924556	1.886095	0.53019608	53.02	0.060392	3.02	2
3	1.124864	3.121600	0.32034854	0.888996	2.775091	0.36034854	36.04	0.081046	2.70	3
4	1.169859	4.246464	0.23549005	0.854804	3.629895	0.27549005	27.55	0.101960	2.55	4
5	1.216653	5.416323	0.18462711	0.821927	4.451822	0.22462711	22.47	0.123136	2.46	5
6	1.265319	6.632975	0.15076190	0.790315	5.242137	0.19076190	19.08	0.144571	2.41	6
7	1.315932	7.898294	0.12660961	0.759918	6.002055	0.16660961	16.67	0.166267	2.38	7
8	1.368569	9.214226	0.10852783	0.730690	6.732745	0.14852783	14.86	0.188223	2.35	8
9	1.423312	10.582795	0.09449299	0.702587	7.435332	0.13449299	13.45	0.210437	2.34	9
10	1.480244	12.006107	0.08329094	0.675564	8.110896	0.12329094	12.33	0.232909	2.33	10
11	1.539454	13.486351	0.07414904	0.649581	8.760477	0.11414904	11.42	0.255639	2.32	11
12	1.601032	15.025805	0.06655217	0.624597	9.385074	0.10655217	10.66	0.278626	2.32	12
13	1.665074	16.626838	0.06014373	0.600574	9.985648	0.10014373	10.02	0.301868	2.32	13
14	1.731676	18.291911	0.05466897	0.577475	10.563123	0.09466897	9.47	0.325366	2.32	14
15	1.800944	20.023588	0.04994110	0.555265	11.118387	0.08994110	9.00	0.349117	2.33	15
16	1.872981	21.824531	0.04582000	0.533908	11.652296	0.08582000	8.59	0.373120	2.33	16
17	1.947900	23.697512	0.04219852	0.513373	12.165669	0.08219852	8.22	0.397375	2.34	17
18	2.025817	25.645413	0.03899333	0.493628	12.659297	0.07899333	7.90	0.421880	2.34	18
19	2.106849	27.671229	0.03613862	0.474642	13.133939	0.07613862	7.62	0.446634	2.35	19
20	2.191123	29.778079	0.03358175	0.456387	13.590326	0.07358175	7.36	0.471635	2.36	20
21	2.278768	31.969202	0.03128011	0.438834	14.029160	0.07128011	7.13	0.496882	2.37	21
22	2.369919	34.247970	0.02919881	0.421955	14.451115	0.06919881	6.92	0.522374	2.37	22
23	2.464716	36.617889	0.02730906	0.405726	14.856842	0.06730906	6.74	0.548108	2.38	23
24	2.563304	39.082604	0.02558683	0.390121	15.246963	0.06558683	6.56	0.574084	2.39	24
25	2.665836	41.645908	0.02401196	0.375117	15.622080	0.06401196	6.41	0.600299	2.40	25
26	2.772470	44.311745	0.02256738	0.360689	15.982769	0.06256738	6.26	0.626752	2.41	26
27	2.883369	47.084214	0.02123854	0.346817	16.329586	0.06123854	6.13	0.653441	2.42	27
28	2.998703	49.967583	0.02001298	0.333477	16.663063	0.06001298	6.01	0.680363	2.43	28
29	3.118651	52.966286	0.01887993	0.320651	16.983715	0.05887993	5.89	0.707518	2.44	29
30	3.243398	56.084938	0.01783010	0.308319	17.292033	0.05783010	5.79	0.734903	2.45	30
31	3.373133	59.328335	0.01685535	0.296460	17.588494	0.05685535	5.69	0.762516	2.46	31
32	3.508059	62.701469	0.01594859	0.285058	17.873551	0.05594859	5.60	0.790355	2.47	32
33	3.648381	66.209527	0.01510357	0.274094	18.147646	0.05510357	5.52	0.818418	2.48	33
34	3.794316	69.857909	0.01431477	0.263552	18.411198	0.05431477	5.44	0.846702	2.49	34
35	3.946089	73.652225	0.01357732	0.253415	18.664613	0.05357732	5.36	0.875206	2.50	35
36	4.103933	77.598314	0.01288688	0.243669	18.908282	0.05288688	5.29	0.903928	2.51	36
37	4.268090	81.702246	0.01223957	0.234297	19.142579	0.05223957	5.23	0.932864	2.52	37
38	4.438813	85.970336	0.01163192	0.225285	19.367864	0.05163192	5.17	0.962013	2.53	38
39	4.616366	90.409150	0.01106083	0.216621	19.584485	0.05106083	5.11	0.991372	2.54	39
40	4.801021	95.025516	0.01052349	0.208289	19.792774	0.05052349	5.06	1.020940	2.55	40
41	4.993061	99.826536	0.01001738	0.200278	19.993052	0.05001738	5.01	1.050712	2.56	41
42	5.192784	104.819598	0.00954020	0.192575	20.185627	0.04954020	4.96	1.080688	2.57	42
43	5.400495	110.012382	0.00908989	0.185168	20.370795	0.04908989	4.91	1.110865	2.58	43
44	5.616515	115.412877	0.00866454	0.178046	20.548841	0.04866454	4.87	1.141240	2.59	44
45	5.841176	121.029340	0.00826246	0.171198	20.720040	0.04826246	4.83	1.171811	2.60	45
46	6.074823	126.870568	0.00788205	0.164614	20.884654	0.04788205	4.79	1.202574	2.61	46
47	6.317816	132.945390	0.00752189	0.158283	21.042936	0.04752189	4.76	1.233529	2.62	47
48	6.570528	139.263206	0.00718065	0.152195	21.195131	0.04718065	4.72	1.264671	2.63	48
49	6.833349	145.833734	0.00685712	0.146341	21.341472	0.04685712	4.69	1.295999	2.64	49
50	7.106683	152.667084	0.00655020	0.140713	21.482185	0.04655020	4.66	1.327510	2.66	50

COMPOUND INTEREST AND ANNUITY TABLE

5.00 % ANNUAL

	Amount Of 1	Amount Of 1 Per Period	Sinking Fund Payment	Present Worth Of 1	Present Worth Of 1 Per Period	Periodic Payment To Amortize 1	Constant Annual Percent	Total Interest	Annual Add-on Rate	
	What a single $1 deposit grows to in the future. The deposit is made at the beginning of the first period. $S=(1+i)^n$	What a series of $1 deposits grow to in the future. A deposit is made at the end of each period. $S_{\overline{n}}=\frac{(1+i)^n-1}{i}$	The amount to be deposited at the end of each period that grows to $1 in the future. $\frac{1}{S_{\overline{n}}}=\frac{i}{(1+i)^n-1}$	What $1 to be paid in the future is worth today. Value today of a single payment tomorrow. $V^n=\frac{1}{(1+i)^n}$	What $1 to be paid at the end of each period is worth today. Value today of a series of payments tomorrow. $A_{\overline{n}}=\frac{1-V^n}{i}$	The mortgage payment to amortize a loan of $1. An annuity certain, payable at the end of each period, worth $1 today. $\frac{1}{A_{\overline{n}}}=\frac{i}{1-V^n}$	The annual payment, including interest and principal, to amortize completely a loan of $100.	The total interest paid over the term on a loan of $1. The loan is amortized by regular periodic payments.	The average annual interest rate on a loan that is completely amortized by regular periodic payments.	
YR										**YR**
1	1.050000	1.000000	1.00000000	0.952381	0.952381	1.05000000	105.00	0.050000	5.00	1
2	1.102500	2.050000	0.48780488	0.907029	1.859410	0.53780488	53.79	0.075610	3.78	2
3	1.157625	3.152500	0.31720856	0.863838	2.723248	0.36720856	36.73	0.101626	3.39	3
4	1.215506	4.310125	0.23201183	0.822702	3.545951	0.28201183	28.21	0.128047	3.20	4
5	1.276282	5.525631	0.18097480	0.783526	4.329477	0.23097480	23.10	0.154874	3.10	5
6	1.340096	6.801913	0.14701747	0.746215	5.075692	0.19701747	19.71	0.182105	3.04	6
7	1.407100	8.142008	0.12281982	0.710681	5.786373	0.17281982	17.29	0.209739	3.00	7
8	1.477455	9.549109	0.10472181	0.676839	6.463213	0.15472181	15.48	0.237775	2.97	8
9	1.551328	11.026564	0.09069008	0.644609	7.107822	0.14069008	14.07	0.266211	2.96	9
10	1.628895	12.577893	0.07950457	0.613913	7.721735	0.12950457	12.96	0.295046	2.95	10
11	1.710339	14.206787	0.07038889	0.584679	8.306414	0.12038889	12.04	0.324278	2.95	11
12	1.795856	15.917127	0.06282541	0.556837	8.863252	0.11282541	11.29	0.353905	2.95	12
13	1.885649	17.712983	0.05645577	0.530321	9.393573	0.10645577	10.65	0.383925	2.95	13
14	1.979932	19.598632	0.05102397	0.505068	9.898641	0.10102397	10.11	0.414336	2.96	14
15	2.078928	21.578564	0.04634229	0.481017	10.379658	0.09634229	9.64	0.445134	2.97	15
16	2.182875	23.657492	0.04226991	0.458112	10.837770	0.09226991	9.23	0.476319	2.98	16
17	2.292018	25.840366	0.03869914	0.436297	11.274066	0.08869914	8.87	0.507885	2.99	17
18	2.406619	28.132385	0.03554622	0.415521	11.689587	0.08554622	8.56	0.539832	3.00	18
19	2.526950	30.539004	0.03274501	0.395734	12.085321	0.08274501	8.28	0.572155	3.01	19
20	2.653298	33.065954	0.03024259	0.376889	12.462210	0.08024259	8.03	0.604852	3.02	20
21	2.785963	35.719252	0.02799611	0.358942	12.821153	0.07799611	7.80	0.637918	3.04	21
22	2.925261	38.505214	0.02597051	0.341850	13.163003	0.07597051	7.60	0.671351	3.05	22
23	3.071524	41.430475	0.02413682	0.325571	13.488574	0.07413682	7.42	0.705147	3.07	23
24	3.225100	44.501999	0.02247090	0.310068	13.798642	0.07247090	7.25	0.739302	3.08	24
25	3.386355	47.727099	0.02095246	0.295303	14.093945	0.07095246	7.10	0.773811	3.10	25
26	3.555673	51.113454	0.01956432	0.281241	14.375185	0.06956432	6.96	0.808672	3.11	26
27	3.733456	54.669126	0.01829186	0.267848	14.643034	0.06829186	6.83	0.843880	3.13	27
28	3.920129	58.402583	0.01712253	0.255094	14.898127	0.06712253	6.72	0.879431	3.14	28
29	4.116136	62.322712	0.01604551	0.242946	15.141074	0.06604551	6.61	0.915320	3.16	29
30	4.321942	66.438848	0.01505144	0.231377	15.372451	0.06505144	6.51	0.951543	3.17	30
31	4.538039	70.760790	0.01413212	0.220359	15.592811	0.06413212	6.42	0.988096	3.19	31
32	4.764941	75.298829	0.01328042	0.209866	15.802677	0.06328042	6.33	1.024973	3.20	32
33	5.003189	80.063771	0.01249004	0.199873	16.002549	0.06249004	6.25	1.062171	3.22	33
34	5.253348	85.066959	0.01175545	0.190355	16.192904	0.06175545	6.18	1.099685	3.23	34
35	5.516015	90.320307	0.01107171	0.181290	16.374194	0.06107171	6.11	1.137510	3.25	35
36	5.791816	95.836323	0.01043446	0.172657	16.546852	0.06043446	6.05	1.175640	3.27	36
37	6.081407	101.628139	0.00983979	0.164436	16.711287	0.05983979	5.99	1.214072	3.28	37
38	6.385477	107.709546	0.00928423	0.156605	16.867893	0.05928423	5.93	1.252801	3.30	38
39	6.704751	114.095023	0.00876462	0.149148	17.017041	0.05876462	5.88	1.291820	3.31	39
40	7.039989	120.799774	0.00827816	0.142046	17.159086	0.05827816	5.83	1.331126	3.33	40
41	7.391988	127.839763	0.00782229	0.135282	17.294368	0.05782229	5.79	1.370714	3.34	41
42	7.761588	135.231751	0.00739471	0.128840	17.423208	0.05739471	5.74	1.410578	3.36	42
43	8.149667	142.993339	0.00699333	0.122704	17.545912	0.05699333	5.70	1.450713	3.37	43
44	8.557150	151.143006	0.00661625	0.116861	17.662773	0.05661625	5.67	1.491115	3.39	44
45	8.985008	159.700156	0.00626173	0.111297	17.774070	0.05626173	5.63	1.531778	3.40	45
46	9.434258	168.685164	0.00592820	0.105997	17.880066	0.05592820	5.60	1.572697	3.42	46
47	9.905971	178.119422	0.00561421	0.100949	17.981016	0.05561421	5.57	1.613868	3.43	47
48	10.401270	188.025393	0.00531843	0.096142	18.077158	0.05531843	5.54	1.655285	3.45	48
49	10.921333	198.426663	0.00503965	0.091564	18.168722	0.05503965	5.51	1.696943	3.46	49
50	11.467400	209.347996	0.00477674	0.087204	18.255925	0.05477674	5.48	1.738837	3.48	50

COMPOUND INTEREST AND ANNUITY TABLE — 6.00 % ANNUAL

	Amount Of 1	Amount Of 1 Per Period	Sinking Fund Payment	Present Worth Of 1	Present Worth Of 1 Per Period	Periodic Payment To Amortize 1	Constant Annual Percent	Total Interest	Annual Add-on Rate	
	What a single $1 deposit grows to in the future. The deposit is made at the beginning of the first period.	What a series of $1 deposits grow to in the future. A deposit is made at the end of each period.	The amount to be deposited at the end of each period that grows to $1 in the future.	What $1 to be paid in the future is worth today.	What $1 to be paid at the end of each period is worth today. Value today of a series of payments tomorrow.	The mortgage payment to amortize a loan of $1. An annuity certain, payable at the end of each period, worth $1 today.	The annual payment, including interest and principal, to amortize completely a loan of $100.	The total interest paid over the term of $1. The loan is amortized by regular periodic payments.	The average annual interest rate on a loan that is completely amortized by regular periodic payments.	
	$S=(1+i)^n$	$S_n = \frac{(1+i)^n - 1}{i}$	$\frac{1}{S_n} = \frac{i}{(1+i)^n - 1}$	$V^n = \frac{1}{(1+i)^n}$	$A_n = \frac{1 - V^n}{i}$	$\frac{1}{A_n} = \frac{i}{1 - V^n}$				
YR										YR
1	1.060000	1.000000	1.00000000	0.943396	0.943396	1.06000000	106.00	0.060000	6.00	1
2	1.123600	2.060000	0.48543689	0.889996	1.833393	0.54543689	54.55	0.090874	4.54	2
3	1.191016	3.183600	0.31410981	0.839619	2.673012	0.37410981	37.42	0.122329	4.08	3
4	1.262477	4.374616	0.22859149	0.792094	3.465106	0.28859149	28.86	0.154366	3.86	4
5	1.338226	5.637093	0.17739640	0.747258	4.212364	0.23739640	23.74	0.186982	3.74	5
6	1.418519	6.975319	0.14336263	0.704961	4.917324	0.20336263	20.34	0.220176	3.67	6
7	1.503630	8.393838	0.11913502	0.665057	5.582381	0.17913502	17.92	0.253945	3.63	7
8	1.593848	9.897468	0.10103594	0.627412	6.209794	0.16103594	16.11	0.288288	3.60	8
9	1.689479	11.491316	0.08702224	0.591898	6.801692	0.14702224	14.71	0.323200	3.59	9
10	1.790848	13.180795	0.07586796	0.558395	7.360087	0.13586796	13.59	0.358680	3.59	10
11	1.898299	14.971643	0.06679294	0.526788	7.886875	0.12679294	12.68	0.394722	3.59	11
12	2.012196	16.869941	0.05927703	0.496969	8.383844	0.11927703	11.93	0.431324	3.59	12
13	2.132928	18.882138	0.05296011	0.468839	8.852683	0.11296011	11.30	0.468481	3.60	13
14	2.260904	21.015066	0.04758491	0.442301	9.294984	0.10758491	10.76	0.506189	3.62	14
15	2.396558	23.275970	0.04296276	0.417265	9.712249	0.10296276	10.30	0.544441	3.63	15
16	2.540352	25.672528	0.03895214	0.393646	10.105895	0.09895214	9.90	0.583234	3.65	16
17	2.692773	28.212880	0.03544480	0.371364	10.477260	0.09544480	9.55	0.622562	3.66	17
18	2.854339	30.905653	0.03235654	0.350344	10.827603	0.09235654	9.24	0.662418	3.68	18
19	3.025600	33.759992	0.02962086	0.330513	11.158116	0.08962086	8.97	0.702796	3.70	19
20	3.207135	36.785591	0.02718456	0.311805	11.469921	0.08718456	8.72	0.743691	3.72	20
21	3.399564	39.992727	0.02500455	0.294155	11.764077	0.08500455	8.51	0.785095	3.74	21
22	3.603537	43.392290	0.02304557	0.277505	12.041582	0.08304557	8.31	0.827003	3.76	22
23	3.819750	46.995828	0.02127848	0.261797	12.303379	0.08127848	8.13	0.869405	3.78	23
24	4.048935	50.815577	0.01967900	0.246979	12.550358	0.07967900	7.97	0.912296	3.80	24
25	4.291871	54.864512	0.01822672	0.232999	12.783356	0.07822672	7.83	0.955668	3.82	25
26	4.549383	59.156383	0.01690435	0.219810	13.003166	0.07690435	7.70	0.999513	3.84	26
27	4.822346	63.705766	0.01569717	0.207368	13.210534	0.07569717	7.57	1.043823	3.87	27
28	5.111687	68.528112	0.01459255	0.195630	13.406164	0.07459255	7.46	1.088591	3.89	28
29	5.418388	73.639798	0.01357961	0.184557	13.590721	0.07357961	7.36	1.133809	3.91	29
30	5.743491	79.058186	0.01264891	0.174110	13.764831	0.07264891	7.27	1.179467	3.93	30
31	6.088101	84.801677	0.01179222	0.164255	13.929086	0.07179222	7.18	1.225559	3.95	31
32	6.453387	90.889778	0.01100234	0.154957	14.084043	0.07100234	7.11	1.272075	3.98	32
33	6.840590	97.343165	0.01027293	0.146186	14.230230	0.07027293	7.03	1.319007	4.00	33
34	7.251025	104.183755	0.00959843	0.137912	14.368141	0.06959843	6.96	1.366346	4.02	34
35	7.686087	111.434780	0.00897386	0.130105	14.498246	0.06897386	6.90	1.414085	4.04	35
36	8.147252	119.120867	0.00839483	0.122741	14.620987	0.06839483	6.84	1.462214	4.06	36
37	8.636087	127.268119	0.00785743	0.115793	14.736780	0.06785743	6.79	1.510725	4.08	37
38	9.154252	135.904206	0.00735812	0.109239	14.846019	0.06735812	6.74	1.559609	4.10	38
39	9.703507	145.058458	0.00689377	0.103056	14.949075	0.06689377	6.69	1.608857	4.13	39
40	10.285718	154.761966	0.00646154	0.097222	15.046297	0.06646154	6.65	1.658461	4.15	40
41	10.902861	165.047684	0.00605886	0.091719	15.138016	0.06605886	6.61	1.708413	4.17	41
42	11.557033	175.950545	0.00568342	0.086527	15.224543	0.06568342	6.57	1.758703	4.19	42
43	12.250455	187.507577	0.00533312	0.081630	15.306173	0.06533312	6.54	1.809324	4.21	43
44	12.985482	199.758032	0.00500606	0.077009	15.383182	0.06500606	6.51	1.860266	4.23	44
45	13.764611	212.743514	0.00470050	0.072650	15.455832	0.06470050	6.48	1.911522	4.25	45
46	14.590487	226.508125	0.00441485	0.068538	15.524370	0.06441485	6.45	1.963083	4.27	46
47	15.465917	241.098612	0.00414768	0.064658	15.589028	0.06414768	6.42	2.014941	4.29	47
48	16.393872	256.564529	0.00389765	0.060998	15.650027	0.06389765	6.39	2.067087	4.31	48
49	17.377504	272.958401	0.00366356	0.057546	15.707572	0.06366356	6.37	2.119515	4.33	49
50	18.420154	290.335905	0.00344429	0.054288	15.761861	0.06344429	6.35	2.172214	4.34	50

COMPOUND INTEREST AND ANNUITY TABLE

7.00 % ANNUAL

	Amount Of 1	Amount Of 1 Per Period	Sinking Fund Payment	Present Worth Of 1	Present Worth Of 1 Per Period	Periodic Payment To Amortize 1	Constant Annual Percent	Total Interest	Annual Add-on Rate	
	What a single $1 deposit grows to in the future. The deposit is made at the beginning of the first period.	What a series of $1 deposits grow to in the future. A deposit is made at the end of each period.	The amount to be deposited at the end of each period that grows to $1 in the future.	What $1 to be paid in the future is worth today. Value today of a single payment tomorrow.	What $1 to be paid at the end of each period is worth today. Value today of a series of payments tomorrow.	The mortgage payment to amortize a loan of $1. An annuity certain, payable at the end of each period, worth $1 today.	The annual payment, including interest and principal, to amortize a loan of $100	The total interest paid over the term on a loan of $1. The loan is amortized completely by regular periodic payments.	The average annual interest rate on a loan that is completely amortized by regular periodic payments.	
	$S=(1+i)^n$	$S_{\overline{n}}=\frac{(1+i)^n-1}{i}$	$\frac{1}{S_{\overline{n}}}=\frac{i}{(1+i)^n-1}$	$V^n=\frac{1}{(1+i)^n}$	$A_{\overline{n}}=\frac{1-V^n}{i}$	$\frac{1}{A_{\overline{n}}}=\frac{i}{1-V^n}$				
YR										YR
1	1.070000	1.000000	1.00000000	0.934579	0.934579	1.07000000	107.00	0.070000	7.00	1
2	1.144900	2.070000	0.48309179	0.873439	1.808018	0.55309179	55.31	0.106184	5.31	2
3	1.225043	3.214900	0.31105167	0.816298	2.624316	0.38105167	38.11	0.143155	4.77	3
4	1.310796	4.439943	0.22522812	0.762895	3.387211	0.29522812	29.53	0.180912	4.52	4
5	1.402552	5.750739	0.17389069	0.712986	4.100197	0.24389069	24.39	0.219453	4.39	5
6	1.500730	7.153291	0.13979580	0.666342	4.766540	0.20979580	20.98	0.258775	4.31	6
7	1.605781	8.654021	0.11555322	0.622750	5.389289	0.18555322	18.56	0.298873	4.27	7
8	1.718186	10.259803	0.09746776	0.582009	5.971299	0.16746776	16.75	0.339742	4.25	8
9	1.838459	11.977989	0.08348647	0.543934	6.515232	0.15348647	15.35	0.381378	4.24	9
10	1.967151	13.816448	0.07237750	0.508349	7.023582	0.14237750	14.24	0.423775	4.24	10
11	2.104852	15.783599	0.06335690	0.475093	7.498674	0.13335690	13.34	0.466926	4.24	11
12	2.252192	17.888451	0.05590199	0.444012	7.942686	0.12590199	12.60	0.510824	4.26	12
13	2.409845	20.140643	0.04965085	0.414964	8.357651	0.11965085	11.97	0.555461	4.27	13
14	2.578534	22.550488	0.04434494	0.387817	8.745468	0.11434494	11.44	0.600829	4.29	14
15	2.759032	25.129022	0.03979462	0.362446	9.107914	0.10979462	10.98	0.646919	4.31	15
16	2.952164	27.888054	0.03585765	0.338735	9.446649	0.10585765	10.59	0.693722	4.34	16
17	3.158815	30.840217	0.03242519	0.316574	9.763223	0.10242519	10.25	0.741228	4.36	17
18	3.379932	33.999033	0.02941260	0.295864	10.059087	0.09941260	9.95	0.789427	4.39	18
19	3.616528	37.378965	0.02675301	0.276508	10.335595	0.09675301	9.68	0.838307	4.41	19
20	3.869684	40.995492	0.02439293	0.258419	10.594014	0.09439293	9.44	0.887859	4.44	20
21	4.140562	44.865177	0.02228900	0.241513	10.835527	0.09228900	9.23	0.938069	4.47	21
22	4.430402	49.005739	0.02040577	0.225713	11.061240	0.09040577	9.05	0.988927	4.50	22
23	4.740530	53.436141	0.01871393	0.210947	11.272187	0.08871393	8.88	1.040420	4.52	23
24	5.072367	58.176671	0.01718902	0.197147	11.469334	0.08718902	8.72	1.092536	4.55	24
25	5.427433	63.249038	0.01581052	0.184249	11.653583	0.08581052	8.59	1.145263	4.58	25
26	5.807353	68.676470	0.01456103	0.172195	11.825779	0.08456103	8.46	1.198587	4.61	26
27	6.213868	74.483823	0.01342573	0.160930	11.986709	0.08342573	8.35	1.252495	4.64	27
28	6.648838	80.697691	0.01239193	0.150402	12.137111	0.08239193	8.24	1.306974	4.67	28
29	7.114257	87.346529	0.01144865	0.140563	12.277674	0.08144865	8.15	1.362011	4.70	29
30	7.612255	94.460786	0.01058640	0.131367	12.409041	0.08058640	8.06	1.417592	4.73	30
31	8.145113	102.073041	0.00979691	0.122773	12.531814	0.07979691	7.98	1.473704	4.75	31
32	8.715271	110.218154	0.00907292	0.114741	12.646555	0.07907292	7.91	1.530333	4.78	32
33	9.325340	118.933425	0.00840807	0.107235	12.753790	0.07840807	7.85	1.587466	4.81	33
34	9.978114	128.258765	0.00779674	0.100219	12.854009	0.07779674	7.78	1.645089	4.84	34
35	10.676581	138.236878	0.00723396	0.093663	12.947672	0.07723396	7.73	1.703189	4.87	35
36	11.423942	148.913460	0.00671531	0.087535	13.035208	0.07671531	7.68	1.761751	4.89	36
37	12.223618	160.337402	0.00623685	0.081809	13.117017	0.07623685	7.63	1.820763	4.92	37
38	13.079271	172.561020	0.00579505	0.076457	13.193473	0.07579505	7.58	1.880212	4.95	38
39	13.994820	185.640292	0.00538676	0.071455	13.264928	0.07538676	7.54	1.940084	4.97	39
40	14.974458	199.635112	0.00500914	0.066780	13.331709	0.07500914	7.51	2.000366	5.00	40
41	16.022670	214.609570	0.00465962	0.062412	13.394120	0.07465962	7.47	2.061045	5.03	41
42	17.144257	230.632240	0.00433591	0.058329	13.452449	0.07433591	7.44	2.122108	5.05	42
43	18.344355	247.776496	0.00403590	0.054513	13.506962	0.07403590	7.41	2.183543	5.08	43
44	19.628460	266.120851	0.00375769	0.050946	13.557908	0.07375769	7.38	2.245338	5.10	44
45	21.002452	285.749311	0.00349957	0.047613	13.605522	0.07349957	7.35	2.307481	5.13	45
46	22.472623	306.751763	0.00325996	0.044499	13.650020	0.07325996	7.33	2.369958	5.15	46
47	24.045707	329.224386	0.00303744	0.041587	13.691608	0.07303744	7.31	2.432760	5.18	47
48	25.728907	353.270093	0.00283070	0.038867	13.730474	0.07283070	7.29	2.495873	5.20	48
49	27.529930	378.999000	0.00263853	0.036324	13.766799	0.07263853	7.27	2.559288	5.22	49
50	29.457025	406.528929	0.00245985	0.033948	13.800746	0.07245985	7.25	2.622992	5.25	50

COMPOUND INTEREST AND ANNUITY TABLE

8.00 % ANNUAL

	Amount Of 1	Amount Of 1 Per Period	Sinking Fund Payment	Present Worth Of 1	Present Worth Of 1 Per Period	Periodic Payment To Amortize 1	Constant Annual Percent	Total Interest	Annual Add-on Rate	
	What a single $1 deposit grows to in the future. The deposit is made at the beginning of the first period.	What a series of $1 deposits grow to in the future. A deposit is made at the end of each period.	The amount to be deposited at the end of each period that grows to $1 in the future.	What $1 to be paid in the future is worth today. Value today of a single payment tomorrow.	What $1 to be paid at the end of each period is worth today. Value today of a series of payments tomorrow.	The mortgage payment to amortize a loan of $1. An annuity certain, payable at the end of each period, worth $1 today.	The annual payment, including interest and principal, to amortize completely a loan of $100.	The total interest paid over the term on a loan of $1. The loan is amortized by regular periodic payments.	The average annual interest rate on a loan that is completely amortized by regular periodic payments.	
	$S=(1+i)^n$	$S_{\overline{n}}=\frac{(1+i)^n-1}{i}$	$\frac{1}{S_{\overline{n}}}=\frac{i}{(1+i)^n-1}$	$V^n=\frac{1}{(1+i)^n}$	$A_{\overline{n}}=\frac{1-V^n}{i}$	$\frac{1}{A_{\overline{n}}}=\frac{i}{1-V^n}$				
YR										YR
1	1.080000	1.000000	1.00000000	0.925926	0.925926	1.08000000	108.00	0.080000	8.00	1
2	1.166400	2.080000	0.48076923	0.857339	1.783265	0.56076923	56.08	0.121538	6.08	2
3	1.259712	3.246400	0.30803351	0.793832	2.577097	0.38803351	38.81	0.164101	5.47	3
4	1.360489	4.506112	0.22192080	0.735030	3.312127	0.30192080	30.20	0.207683	5.19	4
5	1.469328	5.866601	0.17045645	0.680583	3.992710	0.25045645	25.05	0.2522P2	5.05	5
6	1.586874	7.335929	0.13631539	0.630170	4.622880	0.21631539	21.64	0.297892	4.96	6
7	1.713824	8.922803	0.11207240	0.583490	5.206370	0.19207240	19.21	0.344507	4.92	7
8	1.850930	10.636628	0.09401476	0.540269	5.746639	0.17401476	17.41	0.392118	4.90	8
9	1.999005	12.487558	0.08007971	0.500249	6.246888	0.16007971	16.01	0.440717	4.90	9
10	2.158925	14.486562	0.06902949	0.463193	6.710081	0.14902949	14.91	0.490295	4.90	10
11	2.331639	16.645487	0.06007634	0.428883	7.138964	0.14007634	14.01	0.540844	4.92	11
12	2.518170	18.977126	0.05269502	0.397114	7.536078	0.13269502	13.27	0.592340	4.94	12
13	2.719624	21.495297	0.04652181	0.367698	7.903776	0.12652181	12.66	0.644783	4.96	13
14	2.937194	24.214920	0.04129685	0.340461	8.244237	0.12129685	12.13	0.698156	4.99	14
15	3.172169	27.152114	0.03682954	0.315242	8.559479	0.11682954	11.69	0.752443	5.02	15
16	3.425943	30.324283	0.03297687	0.291890	8.851369	0.11297687	11.30	0.807630	5.05	16
17	3.700018	33.750226	0.02962943	0.270269	9.121638	0.10962943	10.97	0.863700	5.08	17
18	3.996019	37.450244	0.02670210	0.250249	9.371887	0.10670210	10.68	0.920638	5.11	18
19	4.315701	41.446263	0.02412763	0.231712	9.603599	0.10412763	10.42	0.978425	5.15	19
20	4.660957	45.761964	0.02185221	0.214548	9.818147	0.10185221	10.19	1.037044	5.19	20
21	5.033834	50.422921	0.01983225	0.198656	10.016803	0.09983225	9.99	1.096477	5.22	21
22	5.436540	55.456755	0.01803207	0.183941	10.200744	0.09803207	9.81	1.156706	5.26	22
23	5.871464	60.893296	0.01642217	0.170315	10.371059	0.09642217	9.65	1.217710	5.29	23
24	6.341181	66.764759	0.01497796	0.157699	10.528758	0.09497796	9.50	1.279471	5.33	24
25	6.848475	73.105940	0.01367878	0.146018	10.674776	0.09367878	9.37	1.341969	5.37	25
26	7.396353	79.954415	0.01250713	0.135202	10.809978	0.09250713	9.26	1.405185	5.40	26
27	7.988061	87.350768	0.01144810	0.125187	10.935165	0.09144810	9.15	1.469099	5.44	27
28	8.627106	95.338830	0.01048891	0.115914	11.051078	0.09048891	9.05	1.533689	5.48	28
29	9.317275	103.965936	0.00961854	0.107328	11.158406	0.08961854	8.97	1.598938	5.51	29
30	10.062657	113.283211	0.00882743	0.099377	11.257783	0.08882743	8.89	1.664823	5.55	30
31	10.867669	123.345868	0.00810728	0.092016	11.349799	0.08810728	8.82	1.731326	5.58	31
32	11.737083	134.213537	0.00745081	0.085200	11.434999	0.08745081	8.75	1.798426	5.62	32
33	12.676050	145.950620	0.00685163	0.078889	11.513888	0.08685163	8.69	1.866104	5.65	33
34	13.690134	158.626670	0.00630411	0.073045	11.586934	0.08630411	8.64	1.934340	5.69	34
35	14.785344	172.316804	0.00580326	0.067635	11.654568	0.08580326	8.59	2.003114	5.72	35
36	15.968172	187.102148	0.00534467	0.062625	11.717193	0.08534467	8.54	2.072408	5.76	36
37	17.245626	203.070320	0.00492440	0.057986	11.775179	0.08492440	8.50	2.142203	5.79	37
38	18.625276	220.315945	0.00453894	0.053690	11.828869	0.08453894	8.46	2.212480	5.82	38
39	20.115298	238.941221	0.00418513	0.049713	11.878582	0.08418513	8.42	2.283220	5.85	39
40	21.724521	259.056519	0.00386016	0.046031	11.924613	0.08386016	8.39	2.354406	5.89	40
41	23.462483	280.781040	0.00356149	0.042621	11.967235	0.08356149	8.36	2.426021	5.92	41
42	25.339482	304.243523	0.00328684	0.039464	12.006699	0.08328684	8.33	2.498047	5.95	42
43	27.366640	329.583005	0.00303414	0.036541	12.043240	0.08303414	8.31	2.570468	5.98	43
44	29.555972	356.949646	0.00280152	0.033834	12.077074	0.08280152	8.29	2.643267	6.01	44
45	31.920449	386.505617	0.00258728	0.031328	12.108402	0.08258728	8.26	2.716428	6.04	45
46	34.474085	418.426067	0.00238991	0.029007	12.137409	0.08238991	8.24	2.789936	6.07	46
47	37.232012	452.900152	0.00220799	0.026859	12.164267	0.08220799	8.23	2.863776	6.09	47
48	40.210573	490.132164	0.00204027	0.024869	12.189136	0.08204027	8.21	2.937933	6.12	48
49	43.427419	530.342737	0.00188557	0.023027	12.212163	0.08188557	8.19	3.012393	6.15	49
50	46.901613	573.770156	0.00174286	0.021321	12.233485	0.08174286	8.18	3.087143	6.17	50

COMPOUND INTEREST AND ANNUITY TABLE

9.00 % ANNUAL

	Amount Of 1	Amount Of 1 Per Period	Sinking Fund Payment	Present Worth Of 1	Present Worth Of 1 Per Period	Periodic Payment To Amortize 1	Constant Annual Percent	Total Interest	Annual Add-on Rate	
	What a single $1 deposit grows to in the future. The deposit is made at the beginning of the first period.	What a series of $1 deposits grow to in the future. A deposit is made at the end of each period.	The amount to be deposited at the end of each period that grows to $1 in the future.	What $1 to be paid in the future is worth today. Value today of a single payment tomorrow.	What $1 to be paid at the end of each period is worth today. Value today of a series of payments tomorrow.	The mortgage payment to amortize a loan of $1. An annuity certain, payable at the end of each period.	The annual payment, including interest and principal, to amortize completely a loan of $100.	The total interest paid over the term on a loan of $1. The loan is amortized by regular periodic payments.	The average annual interest rate on a loan that is completely amortized by regular periodic payments.	
	$S=(1+i)^n$	$S_{\overline{n}}=\frac{(1+i)^n-1}{i}$	$\frac{1}{S_{\overline{n}}}=\frac{i}{(1+i)^n-1}$	$V^n=\frac{1}{(1+i)^n}$	$A_{\overline{n}}=\frac{1-V^n}{i}$	$\frac{1}{A_{\overline{n}}}=\frac{i}{1-V^n}$				

YR										YR
1	1.090000	1.000000	1.00000000	0.917431	0.917431	1.09000000	109.00	0.090000	9.00	1
2	1.188100	2.090000	0.47846890	0.841680	1.759111	0.56846890	56.85	0.136938	6.85	2
3	1.295029	3.278100	0.30505476	0.772183	2.531295	0.39505476	39.51	0.185164	6.17	3
4	1.411582	4.573129	0.21866866	0.708425	3.239720	0.30866866	30.87	0.234675	5.87	4
5	1.538624	5.984711	0.16709246	0.649931	3.889651	0.25709246	25.71	0.285462	5.71	5
6	1.677100	7.523335	0.13291978	0.596267	4.485919	0.22291978	22.30	0.337519	5.63	6
7	1.828039	9.200435	0.10869052	0.547034	5.032953	0.19869052	19.87	0.390834	5.58	7
8	1.992563	11.028474	0.09067438	0.501866	5.534819	0.18067438	18.07	0.445395	5.57	8
9	2.171893	13.021036	0.07679880	0.460428	5.995247	0.16679880	16.68	0.501189	5.57	9
10	2.367364	15.192930	0.06582009	0.422411	6.417658	0.15582009	15.59	0.558201	5.58	10
11	2.580426	17.560293	0.05694666	0.387533	6.805191	0.14694666	14.70	0.616413	5.60	11
12	2.812665	20.140720	0.04965066	0.355535	7.160725	0.13965066	13.97	0.675808	5.63	12
13	3.065805	22.953385	0.04356656	0.326179	7.486904	0.13356656	13.36	0.736365	5.66	13
14	3.341727	26.019189	0.03843317	0.299246	7.786150	0.12843317	12.85	0.798064	5.70	14
15	3.642482	29.360916	0.03405888	0.274538	8.060688	0.12405888	12.41	0.860883	5.74	15
16	3.970306	33.003399	0.03029991	0.251870	8.312558	0.12029991	12.03	0.924799	5.78	16
17	4.327633	36.973705	0.02704625	0.231073	8.543631	0.11704625	11.71	0.989786	5.82	17
18	4.717120	41.301338	0.02421229	0.211994	8.755625	0.11421229	11.43	1.055821	5.87	18
19	5.141661	46.018458	0.02173041	0.194490	8.950115	0.11173041	11.18	1.122878	5.91	19
20	5.604411	51.160120	0.01954648	0.178431	9.128546	0.10954648	10.96	1.190930	5.95	20
21	6.108808	56.764530	0.01761663	0.163698	9.292244	0.10761663	10.77	1.259949	6.00	21
22	6.658600	62.873338	0.01590499	0.150182	9.442425	0.10590499	10.60	1.329910	6.05	22
23	7.257874	69.531939	0.01438188	0.137781	9.580207	0.10438188	10.44	1.400783	6.09	23
24	7.911083	76.789813	0.01302256	0.126405	9.706612	0.10302256	10.31	1.472541	6.14	24
25	8.623081	84.700896	0.01180625	0.115968	9.822580	0.10180625	10.19	1.545156	6.18	25
26	9.399158	93.323977	0.01071536	0.106393	9.928972	0.10071536	10.08	1.618599	6.23	26
27	10.245082	102.723135	0.00973491	0.097608	10.026580	0.09973491	9.98	1.692842	6.27	27
28	11.167140	112.968217	0.00885205	0.089548	10.116128	0.09885205	9.89	1.767857	6.31	28
29	12.172182	124.135356	0.00805572	0.082155	10.198283	0.09805572	9.81	1.843616	6.36	29
30	13.267678	136.307539	0.00733635	0.075371	10.273654	0.09733635	9.74	1.920091	6.40	30
31	14.461770	149.575217	0.00668560	0.069148	10.342802	0.09668560	9.67	1.997254	6.44	31
32	15.763329	164.036987	0.00609619	0.063438	10.406240	0.09609619	9.61	2.075078	6.48	32
33	17.182028	179.800315	0.00556173	0.058200	10.464441	0.09556173	9.56	2.153537	6.53	33
34	18.728411	196.982344	0.00507660	0.053395	10.517835	0.09507660	9.51	2.232604	6.57	34
35	20.413968	215.710755	0.00463584	0.048986	10.566821	0.09463584	9.47	2.312254	6.61	35
36	22.251225	236.124723	0.00423505	0.044941	10.611763	0.09423505	9.43	2.392462	6.65	36
37	24.253835	258.375948	0.00387033	0.041231	10.652993	0.09387033	9.39	2.473202	6.68	37
38	26.436680	282.629783	0.00353820	0.037826	10.690820	0.09353820	9.36	2.554452	6.72	38
39	28.815982	309.066463	0.00323555	0.034703	10.725523	0.09323555	9.33	2.636186	6.76	39
40	31.409420	337.882445	0.00295961	0.031838	10.757360	0.09295961	9.30	2.718384	6.80	40
41	34.236268	369.291865	0.00270789	0.029209	10.786569	0.09270789	9.28	2.801023	6.83	41
42	37.317532	403.528133	0.00247814	0.026797	10.813366	0.09247814	9.25	2.884082	6.87	42
43	40.676110	440.845665	0.00226837	0.024584	10.837950	0.09226837	9.23	2.967540	6.90	43
44	44.336960	481.521775	0.00207675	0.022555	10.860505	0.09207675	9.21	3.051377	6.93	44
45	48.327286	525.858734	0.00190165	0.020692	10.881197	0.09190165	9.20	3.135574	6.97	45
46	52.676742	574.186021	0.00174160	0.018984	10.900181	0.09174160	9.18	3.220113	7.00	46
47	57.417649	626.862762	0.00159525	0.017416	10.917597	0.09159525	9.16	3.304977	7.03	47
48	62.585237	684.280411	0.00146139	0.015978	10.933575	0.09146139	9.15	3.390147	7.06	48
49	68.217908	746.865648	0.00133893	0.014659	10.948234	0.09133893	9.14	3.475608	7.09	49
50	74.357520	815.083556	0.00122687	0.013449	10.961683	0.09122687	9.13	3.561343	7.12	50

COMPOUND INTEREST AND ANNUITY TABLE

10.00 % ANNUAL

	Amount Of 1	Amount Of 1 Per Period	Sinking Fund Payment	Present Worth Of 1	Present Worth Of 1 Per Period	Periodic Payment To Amortize 1	Constant Annual Percent	Total Interest	Annual Add-on Rate	
	What a single $1 deposit grows to in the future. The deposit is made at the beginning of the first period.	What a series of $1 deposits grow to in the future. A deposit is made at the end of each period.	The amount to be deposited at the end of each period that grows to $1 in the future.	What $1 to be paid in the future is worth today. Value today of a single payment tomorrow.	What $1 to be paid at the end of each period is worth today. Value today of a series of payments tomorrow.	The mortgage payment to amortize a loan of $1. An annuity certain, payable at the end of each period, worth $1 today.	The annual payment, including interest and principal, to amortize completely a loan of $100.	The total interest paid over the term of $1. The loan is amortized by regular periodic payments.	The average annual interest rate on a loan that is completely amortized by regular periodic payments.	
	$S=(1+i)^n$	$S_{\overline{n}}=\frac{(1+i)^n-1}{i}$	$\frac{1}{S_{\overline{n}}}=\frac{i}{(1+i)^n-1}$	$V^n=\frac{1}{(1+i)^n}$	$A_{\overline{n}}=\frac{1-V^n}{i}$	$\frac{1}{A_{\overline{n}}}=\frac{i}{1-V^n}$				
YR										YR
1	1.100000	1.000000	1.00000000	0.909091	0.909091	1.10000000	110.00	0.100000	10.00	1
2	1.210000	2.100000	0.47619048	0.826446	1.735537	0.57619048	57.62	0.152381	7.62	2
3	1.331000	3.310000	0.30211480	0.751315	2.486852	0.40211480	40.22	0.206344	6.88	3
4	1.464100	4.641000	0.21547080	0.683013	3.169865	0.31547080	31.55	0.261883	6.55	4
5	1.610510	6.105100	0.16379748	0.620921	3.790787	0.26379748	26.38	0.318987	6.38	5
6	1.771561	7.715610	0.12960738	0.564474	4.355261	0.22960738	22.97	0.377644	6.29	6
7	1.948717	9.487171	0.10540550	0.513158	4.868419	0.20540550	20.55	0.437838	6.25	7
8	2.143589	11.435888	0.08744402	0.466507	5.334926	0.18744402	18.75	0.499552	6.24	8
9	2.357948	13.579477	0.07364054	0.424098	5.759024	0.17364054	17.37	0.562765	6.25	9
10	2.593742	15.937425	0.06274539	0.385543	6.144567	0.16274539	16.28	0.627454	6.27	10
11	2.853117	18.531167	0.05396314	0.350494	6.495061	0.15396314	15.40	0.693595	6.31	11
12	3.138428	21.384284	0.04676332	0.318631	6.813692	0.14676332	14.68	0.761160	6.34	12
13	3.452271	24.522712	0.04077852	0.289664	7.103356	0.14077852	14.08	0.830121	6.39	13
14	3.797498	27.974983	0.03574622	0.263331	7.366687	0.13574622	13.58	0.900447	6.43	14
15	4.177248	31.772482	0.03147378	0.239392	7.606080	0.13147378	13.15	0.972107	6.48	15
16	4.594973	35.949730	0.02781662	0.217629	7.823709	0.12781662	12.79	1.045066	6.53	16
17	5.054470	40.544703	0.02466413	0.197845	8.021553	0.12466413	12.47	1.119290	6.58	17
18	5.559917	45.599173	0.02193022	0.179859	8.201412	0.12193022	12.20	1.194744	6.64	18
19	6.115909	51.159090	0.01954687	0.163508	8.364920	0.11954687	11.96	1.271390	6.69	19
20	6.727500	57.274999	0.01745962	0.148644	8.513564	0.11745962	11.75	1.349192	6.75	20
21	7.400250	64.002499	0.01562439	0.135131	8.648694	0.11562439	11.57	1.428112	6.80	21
22	8.140275	71.402749	0.01400506	0.122846	8.771540	0.11400506	11.41	1.508111	6.86	22
23	8.954302	79.543024	0.01257181	0.111678	8.883218	0.11257181	11.26	1.589152	6.91	23
24	9.849733	88.497327	0.01129978	0.101526	8.984744	0.11129978	11.13	1.671195	6.96	24
25	10.834706	98.347059	0.01016807	0.092296	9.077040	0.11016807	11.02	1.754202	7.02	25
26	11.918177	109.181765	0.00915904	0.083905	9.160945	0.10915904	10.92	1.838135	7.07	26
27	13.109994	121.099942	0.00825764	0.076278	9.237223	0.10825764	10.83	1.922956	7.12	27
28	14.420994	134.209936	0.00745101	0.069343	9.306567	0.10745101	10.75	2.008628	7.17	28
29	15.863093	148.630930	0.00672807	0.063039	9.369606	0.10672807	10.68	2.095114	7.22	29
30	17.449402	164.494023	0.00607925	0.057309	9.426914	0.10607925	10.61	2.182377	7.27	30
31	19.194342	181.943425	0.00549621	0.052099	9.479013	0.10549621	10.55	2.270383	7.32	31
32	21.113777	201.137767	0.00497172	0.047362	9.526376	0.10497172	10.50	2.359095	7.37	32
33	23.225154	222.251544	0.00449941	0.043057	9.569432	0.10449941	10.45	2.448480	7.42	33
34	25.547670	245.476699	0.00407371	0.039143	9.608575	0.10407371	10.41	2.538506	7.47	34
35	28.102437	271.024368	0.00368971	0.035584	9.644159	0.10368971	10.37	2.629140	7.51	35
36	30.912681	299.126805	0.00334306	0.032349	9.676508	0.10334306	10.34	2.720350	7.56	36
37	34.003949	330.039486	0.00302994	0.029408	9.705917	0.10302994	10.31	2.812108	7.60	37
38	37.404343	364.043434	0.00274692	0.026735	9.732651	0.10274692	10.28	2.904383	7.64	38
39	41.144778	401.447778	0.00249098	0.024304	9.756956	0.10249098	10.25	2.997148	7.68	39
40	45.259256	442.592556	0.00225941	0.022095	9.779051	0.10225941	10.23	3.090377	7.73	40
41	49.785181	487.851811	0.00204980	0.020086	9.799137	0.10204980	10.21	3.184042	7.77	41
42	54.763699	537.636992	0.00185999	0.018260	9.817397	0.10185999	10.19	3.278120	7.81	42
43	60.240069	592.400692	0.00168805	0.016600	9.833998	0.10168805	10.17	3.372586	7.84	43
44	66.264076	652.640761	0.00153224	0.015091	9.849089	0.10153224	10.16	3.467418	7.88	44
45	72.890484	718.904837	0.00139100	0.013719	9.862808	0.10139100	10.14	3.562595	7.92	45
46	80.179532	791.795321	0.00126295	0.012472	9.875280	0.10126295	10.13	3.658096	7.95	46
47	88.197485	871.974853	0.00114682	0.011338	9.886618	0.10114682	10.12	3.753901	7.99	47
48	97.017234	960.172338	0.00104148	0.010307	9.896926	0.10104148	10.11	3.849991	8.02	48
49	106.718957	1057.189572	0.00094590	0.009370	9.906296	0.10094590	10.10	3.946349	8.05	49
50	117.390853	1163.908529	0.00085917	0.008519	9.914814	0.10085917	10.09	4.042959	8.09	50

COMPOUND INTEREST AND ANNUITY TABLES 227

COMPOUND INTEREST AND ANNUITY TABLE 11.00 % ANNUAL

	Amount Of 1	Amount Of 1 Per Period	Sinking Fund Payment	Present Worth Of 1	Present Worth Of 1 Per Period	Periodic Payment To Amortize 1	Constant Annual Percent	Total Interest	Annual Add-on Rate	
	What a single $1 deposit grows to in the future. The deposit is made at the beginning of the first period.	What a series of $1 deposits grow to in the future. A deposit is made at the end of each period.	The amount to be deposited at the end of each period that grows to $1 in the future.	What $1 to be paid in the future is worth today. Value today of a single payment tomorrow.	What $1 to be paid at the end of each period is worth today. Value today of a series of payments tomorrow.	The mortgage payment to amortize a loan of $1. An annuity certain, payable at the end of each period, worth $1 today.	The annual payment, including interest and principal, to amortize completely a loan of $100.	The total interest paid over the term of $1. The loan is amortized by regular periodic payments.	The average annual interest rate on a loan that is completely amortized by regular periodic payments.	
	$S=(1+i)^n$	$S_n=\frac{(1+i)^n-1}{i}$	$\frac{1}{S_n}=\frac{i}{(1+i)^n-1}$	$V^n=\frac{1}{(1+i)^n}$	$A_n=\frac{1-V^n}{i}$	$\frac{1}{A_n}=\frac{i}{1-V^n}$				
YR										YR
1	1.110000	1.000000	1.00000000	0.900901	0.900901	1.11000000	111.00	0.110000	11.00	1
2	1.232100	2.110000	0.47393365	0.811622	1.712523	0.58393365	58.40	0.167867	8.39	2
3	1.367631	3.342100	0.29921307	0.731191	2.443715	0.40921307	40.93	0.227639	7.59	3
4	1.518070	4.709731	0.21232635	0.658731	3.102446	0.32232635	32.24	0.289305	7.23	4
5	1.685058	6.227801	0.16057031	0.593451	3.695897	0.27057031	27.06	0.352852	7.06	5
6	1.870415	7.912860	0.12637656	0.534641	4.230538	0.23637656	23.64	0.418259	6.97	6
7	2.076160	9.783274	0.10221527	0.481658	4.712196	0.21221527	21.23	0.485507	6.94	7
8	2.304538	11.859434	0.08432105	0.433926	5.146123	0.19432105	19.44	0.554568	6.93	8
9	2.558037	14.163972	0.07060166	0.390925	5.537048	0.18060166	18.07	0.625415	6.95	9
10	2.839421	16.722009	0.05980143	0.352184	5.889232	0.16980143	16.99	0.698014	6.98	10
11	3.151757	19.561430	0.05112101	0.317283	6.206515	0.16112101	16.12	0.772331	7.02	11
12	3.498451	22.713187	0.04402729	0.285841	6.492356	0.15402729	15.41	0.848327	7.07	12
13	3.883280	26.211638	0.03815099	0.257514	6.749870	0.14815099	14.82	0.925963	7.12	13
14	4.310441	30.094918	0.03322820	0.231995	6.981865	0.14322820	14.33	1.005195	7.18	14
15	4.784589	34.405359	0.02906524	0.209004	7.190870	0.13906524	13.91	1.085979	7.24	15
16	5.310894	39.189948	0.02551675	0.188292	7.379162	0.13551675	13.56	1.168268	7.30	16
17	5.895093	44.500843	0.02247148	0.169633	7.548794	0.13247148	13.25	1.252015	7.36	17
18	6.543553	50.395936	0.01984287	0.152822	7.701617	0.12984287	12.99	1.337172	7.43	18
19	7.263344	56.939488	0.01756250	0.137678	7.839294	0.12756250	12.76	1.423688	7.49	19
20	8.062312	64.202832	0.01557564	0.124034	7.963328	0.12557564	12.56	1.511513	7.56	20
21	8.949166	72.265144	0.01383793	0.111742	8.075070	0.12383793	12.39	1.600597	7.62	21
22	9.933574	81.214309	0.01231310	0.100669	8.175739	0.12231310	12.24	1.690888	7.69	22
23	11.026267	91.147884	0.01097118	0.090693	8.266432	0.12097118	12.10	1.782337	7.75	23
24	12.239157	102.174151	0.00978721	0.081705	8.348137	0.11978721	11.98	1.874893	7.81	24
25	13.585464	114.413307	0.00874024	0.073608	8.421745	0.11874024	11.88	1.968506	7.87	25
26	15.079865	127.998771	0.00781258	0.066314	8.488058	0.11781258	11.79	2.063127	7.94	26
27	16.738650	143.078636	0.00698916	0.059742	8.547800	0.11698916	11.70	2.158707	8.00	27
28	18.579901	159.817286	0.00625715	0.053822	8.601622	0.11625715	11.63	2.255200	8.05	28
29	20.623691	178.397187	0.00560547	0.048488	8.650110	0.11560547	11.57	2.352559	8.11	29
30	22.892297	199.020878	0.00502460	0.043683	8.693793	0.11502460	11.51	2.450738	8.17	30
31	25.410449	221.913174	0.00450627	0.039354	8.733146	0.11450627	11.46	2.549694	8.22	31
32	28.205599	247.323624	0.00404329	0.035454	8.768600	0.11404329	11.41	2.649385	8.28	32
33	31.308214	275.529222	0.00362938	0.031940	8.800541	0.11362938	11.37	2.749770	8.33	33
34	34.752118	306.837437	0.00325905	0.028775	8.829316	0.11325905	11.33	2.850808	8.38	34
35	38.574851	341.589555	0.00292749	0.025924	8.855240	0.11292749	11.30	2.952462	8.44	35
36	42.818085	380.164406	0.00263044	0.023355	8.878594	0.11263044	11.27	3.054696	8.49	36
37	47.528074	422.982490	0.00236416	0.021040	8.899635	0.11236416	11.24	3.157474	8.53	37
38	52.756162	470.510564	0.00212535	0.018955	8.918590	0.11212535	11.22	3.260763	8.58	38
39	58.559340	523.266726	0.00191107	0.017077	8.935666	0.11191107	11.20	3.364532	8.63	39
40	65.000867	581.826066	0.00171873	0.015384	8.951051	0.11171873	11.18	3.468749	8.67	40
41	72.150963	646.826934	0.00154601	0.013860	8.964911	0.11154601	11.16	3.573386	8.72	41
42	80.087569	718.977896	0.00139086	0.012486	8.977397	0.11139086	11.14	3.678416	8.76	42
43	88.897201	799.065465	0.00125146	0.011249	8.988646	0.11125146	11.13	3.783813	8.80	43
44	98.675893	887.962666	0.00112617	0.010134	8.998780	0.11112617	11.12	3.889552	8.84	44
45	109.530242	986.638559	0.00101354	0.009130	9.007910	0.11101354	11.11	3.995609	8.88	45
46	121.578568	1096.168801	0.00091227	0.008225	9.016135	0.11091227	11.10	4.101964	8.92	46
47	134.952211	1217.747369	0.00082119	0.007410	9.023545	0.11082119	11.09	4.208596	8.95	47
48	149.796954	1352.699580	0.00073926	0.006676	9.030221	0.11073926	11.08	4.315485	8.99	48
49	166.274619	1502.496533	0.00066556	0.006014	9.036235	0.11066556	11.07	4.422612	9.03	49
50	184.564827	1668.771152	0.00059924	0.005418	9.041653	0.11059924	11.06	4.529962	9.06	50

COMPOUND INTEREST AND ANNUITY TABLE

12.00 % ANNUAL

	Amount Of 1	Amount Of 1 Per Period	Sinking Fund Payment	Present Worth Of 1	Present Worth Of 1 Per Period	Periodic Payment To Amortize 1	Constant Annual Percent	Total Interest	Annual Add-on Rate	
	What a single $1 deposit grows to in the future. The deposit is made at the beginning of the first period.	What a series of $1 deposits grow to in the future. A deposit is made at the end of each period	The amount to be deposited at the end of each period that grows to $1 in the future	What $1 to be paid in the future is worth today. Value today of a single payment tomorrow	What $1 to be paid at the end of each period is worth today. Value today of a series of payments tomorrow.	The mortgage payment to amortize a loan of $1. An annuity certain, payable at the end of each period, worth $1 today.	The annual payment, including interest and principal, to amortize completely a loan of $100.	The total interest paid over the term on a loan of $1. The loan is amortized by regular periodic payments.	The average annual interest rate on a loan that is completely amortized by regular periodic payments.	
	$S = (1+i)^n$	$S_n = \frac{(1+i)^n - 1}{i}$	$\frac{1}{S_n} = \frac{i}{(1+i)^n - 1}$	$V^n = \frac{1}{(1+i)^n}$	$A_n = \frac{1 - V^n}{i}$	$\frac{1}{A_n} = \frac{i}{1 - V^n}$				
YR										YR
1	1.120000	1.000000	1.00000000	0.892857	0.892857	1.12000000	112.00	0.120000	12.00	1
2	1.254400	2.120000	0.47169811	0.797194	1.690051	0.59169811	59.17	0.183396	9.17	2
3	1.404928	3.374400	0.29634898	0.711780	2.401831	0.41634898	41.64	0.249047	8.30	3
4	1.573519	4.779328	0.20923444	0.635518	3.037349	0.32923444	32.93	0.316938	7.92	4
5	1.762342	6.352847	0.15740973	0.567427	3.604776	0.27740973	27.75	0.387049	7.74	5
6	1.973823	8.115189	0.12322572	0.506631	4.111407	0.24322572	24.33	0.459354	7.66	6
7	2.210681	10.089012	0.09911774	0.452349	4.563757	0.21911774	21.92	0.533824	7.63	7
8	2.475963	12.299693	0.08130284	0.403883	4.967640	0.20130284	20.14	0.610423	7.63	8
9	2.773079	14.775656	0.06767889	0.360610	5.328250	0.18767889	18.77	0.689110	7.66	9
10	3.105848	17.548735	0.05698416	0.321973	5.650223	0.17698416	17.70	0.769842	7.70	10
11	3.478550	20.654583	0.04841540	0.287476	5.937699	0.16841540	16.85	0.852569	7.75	11
12	3.895976	24.133133	0.04143681	0.256675	6.194374	0.16143681	16.15	0.937242	7.81	12
13	4.363493	28.029109	0.03567720	0.229174	6.423548	0.15567720	15.57	1.023804	7.88	13
14	4.887112	32.392602	0.03087125	0.204620	6.628168	0.15087125	15.09	1.112197	7.94	14
15	5.473566	37.279715	0.02682424	0.182696	6.810864	0.14682424	14.69	1.202364	8.02	15
16	6.130394	42.753280	0.02339002	0.163122	6.973986	0.14339002	14.34	1.294240	8.09	16
17	6.866041	48.883674	0.02045673	0.145644	7.119630	0.14045673	14.05	1.387764	8.16	17
18	7.689966	55.749715	0.01793731	0.130040	7.249670	0.13793731	13.80	1.482872	8.24	18
19	8.612762	63.439681	0.01576300	0.116107	7.365777	0.13576300	13.58	1.579497	8.31	19
20	9.646293	72.052442	0.01387878	0.103667	7.469444	0.13387878	13.39	1.677576	8.39	20
21	10.803848	81.698736	0.01224009	0.092560	7.562003	0.13224009	13.23	1.777042	8.46	21
22	12.100310	92.502584	0.01081051	0.082643	7.644646	0.13081051	13.09	1.877831	8.54	22
23	13.552347	104.602894	0.00955996	0.073788	7.718434	0.12955996	12.96	1.979879	8.61	23
24	15.178629	118.155241	0.00846344	0.065882	7.784316	0.12846344	12.85	2.083123	8.68	24
25	17.000064	133.333870	0.00749997	0.058823	7.843139	0.12749997	12.75	2.187499	8.75	25
26	19.040072	150.333934	0.00665186	0.052521	7.895660	0.12665186	12.67	2.292948	8.82	26
27	21.324881	169.374007	0.00590409	0.046894	7.942554	0.12590409	12.60	2.399411	8.89	27
28	23.883866	190.698887	0.00524387	0.041869	7.984423	0.12524387	12.53	2.506828	8.95	28
29	26.749930	214.582754	0.00466021	0.037383	8.021806	0.12466021	12.47	2.615146	9.02	29
30	29.959922	241.332684	0.00414366	0.033378	8.055184	0.12414366	12.42	2.724310	9.08	30
31	33.555113	271.292606	0.00368606	0.029802	8.084986	0.12368606	12.37	2.834268	9.14	31
32	37.581726	304.847719	0.00328033	0.026609	8.111594	0.12328033	12.33	2.944970	9.20	32
33	42.091533	342.429446	0.00292031	0.023758	8.135352	0.12292031	12.30	3.056370	9.26	33
34	47.142517	384.520979	0.00260064	0.021212	8.156564	0.12260064	12.27	3.168422	9.32	34
35	52.799620	431.663496	0.00231662	0.018940	8.175504	0.12231662	12.24	3.281082	9.37	35
36	59.135574	484.463116	0.00206414	0.016910	8.192414	0.12206414	12.21	3.394309	9.43	36
37	66.231843	543.598690	0.00183959	0.015098	8.207513	0.12183959	12.19	3.508065	9.48	37
38	74.179664	609.830533	0.00163980	0.013481	8.220993	0.12163980	12.17	3.622312	9.53	38
39	83.081224	684.010197	0.00146197	0.012036	8.233030	0.12146197	12.15	3.737017	9.58	39
40	93.050970	767.091420	0.00130363	0.010747	8.243777	0.12130363	12.14	3.852145	9.63	40
41	104.217087	860.142391	0.00116260	0.009595	8.253372	0.12116260	12.12	3.967667	9.68	41
42	116.723137	964.359478	0.00103696	0.008567	8.261939	0.12103696	12.11	4.083552	9.72	42
43	130.729914	1081.082615	0.00092500	0.007649	8.269589	0.12092500	12.10	4.199775	9.77	43
44	146.417503	1211.812529	0.00082521	0.006830	8.276418	0.12082521	12.09	4.316309	9.81	44
45	163.987604	1358.230032	0.00073625	0.006098	8.282516	0.12073625	12.08	4.433131	9.85	45
46	183.666116	1522.217636	0.00065694	0.005445	8.287961	0.12065694	12.07	4.550219	9.89	46
47	205.706050	1705.883752	0.00058621	0.004861	8.292822	0.12058621	12.06	4.667552	9.93	47
48	230.390776	1911.589803	0.00052312	0.004340	8.297163	0.12052312	12.06	4.785110	9.97	48
49	258.037669	2141.980579	0.00046686	0.003875	8.301038	0.12046686	12.05	4.902876	10.01	49
50	289.002190	2400.018249	0.00041666	0.003460	8.304498	0.12041666	12.05	5.020833	10.04	50

COMPOUND INTEREST AND ANNUITY TABLE

13.00 % ANNUAL

	Amount Of 1	Amount Of 1 Per Period	Sinking Fund Payment	Present Worth Of 1	Present Worth Of 1 Per Period	Periodic Payment To Amortize 1	Constant Annual Percent	Total Interest	Annual Add-on Rate	
	What a single $1 deposit grows to in the future. The deposit is made at the beginning of the first period.	What a series of $1 deposits grow to in the future. A deposit is made at the end of each period.	The amount to be deposited at the end of each period that grows to $1 in the future.	What $1 to be paid in the future is worth today. Value today of a single payment tomorrow.	What $1 to be paid at the end of each period is worth today. Value today of a series of payments tomorrow.	The mortgage payment to amortize a loan of $1. An annuity certain, payable at the end of each period, worth $1 today.	The annual payment, including interest and principal, to amortize completely a loan of $100.	The total interest paid over the term on a loan of $1. The loan is amortized by regular periodic payments.	The average annual interest rate on a loan that is completely amortized by regular periodic payments.	
	$S=(1+i)^n$	$S_{\overline{n}|}=\frac{(1+i)^n-1}{i}$	$\frac{1}{S_{\overline{n}|}}=\frac{i}{(1+i)^n-1}$	$V^n=\frac{1}{(1+i)^n}$	$A_{\overline{n}|}=\frac{1-V^n}{i}$	$\frac{1}{A_{\overline{n}|}}=\frac{i}{1-V^n}$				
YR										YR
1	1.130000	1.000000	1.00000000	0.884956	0.884956	1.13000000	113.00	0.130000	13.00	1
2	1.276900	2.130000	0.46948357	0.783147	1.668102	0.59948357	59.95	0.198967	9.95	2
3	1.442897	3.406900	0.29352197	0.693050	2.361153	0.42352197	42.36	0.270566	9.02	3
4	1.630474	4.849797	0.20619420	0.613319	2.974471	0.33619420	33.62	0.344777	8.62	4
5	1.842435	6.480271	0.15431454	0.542760	3.517231	0.28431454	28.44	0.421573	8.43	5
6	2.081952	8.322706	0.12015323	0.480319	3.997550	0.25015323	25.02	0.500919	8.35	6
7	2.352605	10.404658	0.09611080	0.425061	4.422610	0.22611080	22.62	0.582776	8.33	7
8	2.658444	12.757263	0.07838672	0.376160	4.798770	0.20838672	20.84	0.667094	8.34	8
9	3.004042	15.415707	0.06486890	0.332885	5.131655	0.19486890	19.49	0.753820	8.38	9
10	3.394567	18.419749	0.05428956	0.294588	5.426243	0.18428956	18.43	0.842896	8.43	10
11	3.835861	21.814317	0.04584145	0.260698	5.686941	0.17584145	17.59	0.934256	8.49	11
12	4.334523	25.650178	0.03898608	0.230706	5.917647	0.16898608	16.90	1.027833	8.57	12
13	4.898011	29.984701	0.03335034	0.204165	6.121812	0.16335034	16.34	1.123554	8.64	13
14	5.534753	34.882712	0.02866750	0.180677	6.302488	0.15866750	15.87	1.221345	8.72	14
15	6.254270	40.417464	0.02474178	0.159891	6.462379	0.15474178	15.48	1.321127	8.81	15
16	7.067326	46.671735	0.02142624	0.141496	6.603875	0.15142624	15.15	1.422820	8.89	16
17	7.986078	53.739060	0.01860844	0.125218	6.729093	0.14860844	14.87	1.526343	8.98	17
18	9.024268	61.725138	0.01620085	0.110812	6.839905	0.14620085	14.63	1.631615	9.06	18
19	10.197423	70.749406	0.01413439	0.098064	6.937969	0.14413439	14.42	1.738553	9.15	19
20	11.523088	80.946829	0.01235379	0.086782	7.024752	0.14235379	14.24	1.847076	9.24	20
21	13.021089	92.469917	0.01081433	0.076798	7.101550	0.14081433	14.09	1.957101	9.32	21
22	14.713831	105.491006	0.00947948	0.067963	7.169513	0.13947948	13.95	2.068549	9.40	22
23	16.626629	120.204837	0.00831913	0.060144	7.229658	0.13831913	13.84	2.181340	9.48	23
24	18.788091	136.831465	0.00730826	0.053225	7.282883	0.13730826	13.74	2.295398	9.56	24
25	21.230542	155.619556	0.00642593	0.047102	7.329985	0.13642593	13.65	2.410648	9.64	25
26	23.990513	176.850098	0.00565451	0.041683	7.371668	0.13565451	13.57	2.527017	9.72	26
27	27.109279	200.840611	0.00497907	0.036888	7.408556	0.13497907	13.50	2.644435	9.79	27
28	30.633486	227.949890	0.00438693	0.032644	7.441200	0.13438693	13.44	2.762834	9.87	28
29	34.615839	258.583376	0.00386722	0.028889	7.470088	0.13386722	13.39	2.882150	9.94	29
30	39.115898	293.199215	0.00341065	0.025565	7.495653	0.13341065	13.35	3.002320	10.01	30
31	44.200965	332.315113	0.00300919	0.022624	7.518277	0.13300919	13.31	3.123285	10.08	31
32	49.947090	376.516078	0.00265593	0.020021	7.538299	0.13265593	13.27	3.244990	10.14	32
33	56.440212	426.463168	0.00234487	0.017718	7.556016	0.13234487	13.24	3.367381	10.20	33
34	63.777439	482.903380	0.00207081	0.015680	7.571696	0.13207081	13.21	3.490407	10.27	34
35	72.068506	546.680819	0.00182922	0.013876	7.585572	0.13182922	13.19	3.614023	10.33	35
36	81.437412	618.749325	0.00161616	0.012279	7.597851	0.13161616	13.17	3.738182	10.38	36
37	92.024276	700.186738	0.00142819	0.010867	7.608718	0.13142819	13.15	3.862843	10.44	37
38	103.987432	792.211014	0.00126229	0.009617	7.618334	0.13126229	13.13	3.987967	10.49	38
39	117.505798	896.198445	0.00111582	0.008510	7.626844	0.13111582	13.12	4.113517	10.55	39
40	132.781552	1013.704243	0.00098648	0.007531	7.634376	0.13098648	13.10	4.239459	10.60	40
41	150.043153	1146.485795	0.00087223	0.006665	7.641040	0.13087223	13.09	4.365761	10.65	41
42	169.548763	1296.528948	0.00077129	0.005898	7.646938	0.13077129	13.08	4.492394	10.70	42
43	191.590103	1466.077712	0.00068209	0.005219	7.652158	0.13068209	13.07	4.619330	10.74	43
44	216.496816	1657.667814	0.00060326	0.004619	7.656777	0.13060326	13.07	4.746543	10.79	44
45	244.641402	1874.164630	0.00053357	0.004088	7.660864	0.13053357	13.06	4.874011	10.83	45
46	276.444784	2118.806032	0.00047196	0.003617	7.664482	0.13047196	13.05	5.001710	10.87	46
47	312.382606	2395.250816	0.00041749	0.003201	7.667683	0.13041749	13.05	5.129622	10.91	47
48	352.992345	2707.633422	0.00036933	0.002833	7.670516	0.13036933	13.04	5.257728	10.95	48
49	398.881350	3060.625767	0.00032673	0.002507	7.673023	0.13032673	13.04	5.386010	10.99	49
50	450.735925	3459.507117	0.00028906	0.002219	7.675242	0.13028906	13.03	5.514453	11.03	50

COMPOUND INTEREST AND ANNUITY TABLE

14.00 % ANNUAL

	Amount Of 1	Amount Of 1 Per Period	Sinking Fund Payment	Present Worth Of 1	Present Worth Of 1 Per Period	Periodic Payment To Amortize 1	Constant Annual Percent	Total Interest	Annual Add-on Rate	
	What a single $1 deposit grows to in the future. The deposit is made at the beginning of the first period.	What a series of $1 deposits grow to in the future. A deposit is made at the end of each period.	The amount to be deposited at the end of each period that grows to $1 in the future.	What $1 to be paid in the future is worth today. Value today of a single payment tomorrow.	What $1 to be paid at the end of each period is worth today. Value today of a series of payments tomorrow.	The mortgage payment to amortize a loan of $1. An annuity certain, payable at the end of each period, worth $1 today.	The annual payment, including interest and principal, to amortize completely a loan of $100.	The total interest paid over the term on a loan of $1. The loan is amortized by regular periodic payments.	The average annual interest rate on a loan that is completely amortized by regular periodic payments.	
	$S = (1+i)^n$	$S_{\overline{n}} = \frac{(1+i)^n - 1}{i}$	$\frac{1}{S_{\overline{n}}} = \frac{i}{(1+i)^n - 1}$	$V^n = \frac{1}{(1+i)^n}$	$A_{\overline{n}} = \frac{1 - V^n}{i}$	$\frac{1}{A_{\overline{n}}} = \frac{i}{1 - V^n}$				

YR										YR
1	1.140000	1.000000	1.00000000	0.877193	0.877193	1.14000000	114.00	0.140000	14.00	1
2	1.299600	2.140000	0.46728972	0.769468	1.646661	0.60728972	60.73	0.214579	10.73	2
3	1.481544	3.439600	0.29073148	0.674972	2.321632	0.43073148	43.08	0.292194	9.74	3
4	1.688960	4.921144	0.20320478	0.592080	2.913712	0.34320478	34.33	0.372819	9.32	4
5	1.925415	6.610104	0.15128355	0.519369	3.433081	0.29128355	29.13	0.456418	9.13	5
6	2.194973	8.535519	0.11715750	0.455587	3.888668	0.25715750	25.72	0.542945	9.05	6
7	2.502269	10.730491	0.09319238	0.399637	4.288305	0.23319238	23.32	0.632347	9.03	7
8	2.852586	13.232760	0.07557002	0.350559	4.638864	0.21557002	21.56	0.724560	9.06	8
9	3.251949	16.085347	0.06216838	0.307508	4.946372	0.20216838	20.22	0.819515	9.11	9
10	3.707221	19.337295	0.05171354	0.269744	5.216116	0.19171354	19.18	0.917135	9.17	10
11	4.226232	23.044516	0.04339427	0.236617	5.452733	0.18339427	18.34	1.017337	9.25	11
12	4.817905	27.270749	0.03666933	0.207559	5.660292	0.17666933	17.67	1.120032	9.33	12
13	5.492411	32.088654	0.03116366	0.182069	5.842362	0.17116366	17.12	1.225128	9.42	13
14	6.261349	37.581065	0.02660914	0.159710	6.002072	0.16660914	16.67	1.332528	9.52	14
15	7.137938	43.842414	0.02280896	0.140096	6.142168	0.16280896	16.29	1.442134	9.61	15
16	8.137249	50.980352	0.01961540	0.122892	6.265060	0.15961540	15.97	1.553846	9.71	16
17	9.276464	59.117601	0.01691544	0.107800	6.372859	0.15691544	15.70	1.667562	9.81	17
18	10.575169	68.394066	0.01462115	0.094561	6.467420	0.15462115	15.47	1.783181	9.91	18
19	12.055693	78.969235	0.01266316	0.082948	6.550369	0.15266316	15.27	1.900600	10.00	19
20	13.743490	91.024928	0.01098600	0.072762	6.623131	0.15098600	15.10	2.019720	10.10	20
21	15.667578	104.768418	0.00954486	0.063826	6.686957	0.14954486	14.96	2.140442	10.19	21
22	17.861039	120.435996	0.00830317	0.055988	6.742944	0.14830317	14.84	2.262670	10.28	22
23	20.361585	138.297035	0.00723081	0.049112	6.792056	0.14723081	14.73	2.386309	10.38	23
24	23.212207	158.658620	0.00630284	0.043081	6.835137	0.14630284	14.64	2.511268	10.46	24
25	26.461916	181.870827	0.00549841	0.037790	6.872927	0.14549841	14.55	2.637460	10.55	25
26	30.166584	208.332743	0.00480001	0.033149	6.906077	0.14480001	14.49	2.764800	10.63	26
27	34.389906	238.499327	0.00419288	0.029078	6.935155	0.14419288	14.42	2.893208	10.72	27
28	39.204493	272.889233	0.00366449	0.025507	6.960662	0.14366449	14.37	3.022606	10.80	28
29	44.693122	312.093725	0.00320417	0.022375	6.983037	0.14320417	14.33	3.152921	10.87	29
30	50.950159	356.786847	0.00280279	0.019627	7.002664	0.14280279	14.29	3.284084	10.95	30
31	58.083181	407.737006	0.00245256	0.017217	7.019881	0.14245256	14.25	3.416029	11.02	31
32	66.214826	465.820186	0.00214675	0.015102	7.034983	0.14214675	14.22	3.548696	11.09	32
33	75.484902	532.035012	0.00187958	0.013248	7.048231	0.14187958	14.19	3.682026	11.16	33
34	86.052788	607.519914	0.00164604	0.011621	7.059852	0.14164604	14.17	3.815965	11.22	34
35	98.100178	693.572702	0.00144181	0.010194	7.070045	0.14144181	14.15	3.950463	11.29	35
36	111.834203	791.672881	0.00126315	0.008942	7.078987	0.14126315	14.13	4.085473	11.35	36
37	127.490992	903.507084	0.00110680	0.007844	7.086831	0.14110680	14.12	4.220952	11.41	37
38	145.339731	1030.998076	0.00096993	0.006880	7.093711	0.14096993	14.10	4.356857	11.47	38
39	165.687293	1176.337806	0.00085010	0.006035	7.099747	0.14085010	14.09	4.493154	11.52	39
40	188.883514	1342.025099	0.00074514	0.005294	7.105041	0.14074514	14.08	4.629806	11.57	40
41	215.327206	1530.908613	0.00065321	0.004644	7.109685	0.14065321	14.07	4.766781	11.63	41
42	245.473015	1746.235819	0.00057266	0.004074	7.113759	0.14057266	14.06	4.904052	11.68	42
43	279.839237	1991.708833	0.00050208	0.003573	7.117332	0.14050208	14.06	5.041590	11.72	43
44	319.016730	2271.548070	0.00044023	0.003135	7.120467	0.14044023	14.05	5.179370	11.77	44
45	363.679072	2590.564800	0.00038602	0.002750	7.123217	0.14038602	14.04	5.317371	11.82	45
46	414.594142	2954.243872	0.00033850	0.002412	7.125629	0.14033850	14.04	5.455571	11.86	46
47	472.637322	3368.838014	0.00029684	0.002116	7.127744	0.14029684	14.03	5.593951	11.90	47
48	538.806547	3841.475336	0.00026032	0.001856	7.129600	0.14026032	14.03	5.732495	11.94	48
49	614.239464	4380.281883	0.00022830	0.001628	7.131228	0.14022830	14.03	5.871186	11.98	49
50	700.232988	4994.521346	0.00020022	0.001428	7.132656	0.14020022	14.03	6.010011	12.02	50

COMPOUND INTEREST AND ANNUITY TABLE

15.00 % ANNUAL

	Amount Of 1	Amount Of 1 Per Period	Sinking Fund Payment	Present Worth Of 1	Present Worth Of 1 Per Period	Periodic Payment To Amortize 1	Constant Annual Percent	Total Interest	Annual Add-on Rate	
	What a single $1 deposit grows to in the future. The deposit is made at the beginning of the first period.	What a series of $1 deposits grow to in the future. A deposit is made at the end of each period.	The amount to be deposited at the end of each period that grows to $1 in the future.	What $1 to be paid in the future is worth today.	What $1 to be paid at the end of each period is worth today. Value today of a series of payments tomorrow.	The mortgage payment to amortize a loan of $1. An annuity certain, payable at the end of each period, worth $1 today.	The annual payment, including interest and principal, to amortize completely a loan of $100.	The total interest paid over the term of $1. The loan is amortized by regular periodic payments.	The average annual interest rate on a loan that is completely amortized by regular periodic payments.	
	$S=(1+i)^n$	$S_{\overline{n}}=\frac{(1+i)^n-1}{i}$	$\frac{1}{S_{\overline{n}}}=\frac{i}{(1+i)^n-1}$	$V^n=\frac{1}{(1+i)^n}$	$A_{\overline{n}}=\frac{1-V^n}{i}$	$\frac{1}{A_{\overline{n}}}=\frac{i}{1-V^n}$				
YR										YR
1	1.150000	1.000000	1.00000000	0.869565	0.869565	1.15000000	115.00	0.150000	15.00	1
2	1.322500	2.150000	0.46511628	0.756144	1.625709	0.61511628	61.52	0.230233	11.51	2
3	1.520875	3.472500	0.28797696	0.657516	2.283225	0.43797696	43.80	0.313931	10.46	3
4	1.749006	4.993375	0.20026535	0.571753	2.854978	0.35026535	35.03	0.401061	10.03	4
5	2.011357	6.742863	0.14831555	0.497177	3.352155	0.29831555	29.84	0.491578	9.83	5
6	2.313061	8.753738	0.11423691	0.432328	3.784483	0.26423691	26.43	0.585421	9.76	6
7	2.660020	11.066799	0.09036036	0.375937	4.160420	0.24036036	24.04	0.682523	9.75	7
8	3.059023	13.726819	0.07285009	0.326902	4.487322	0.22285009	22.29	0.782801	9.79	8
9	3.517876	16.785842	0.05957402	0.284262	4.771584	0.20957402	20.96	0.886166	9.85	9
10	4.045558	20.303718	0.04925206	0.247185	5.018769	0.19925206	19.93	0.992521	9.93	10
11	4.652391	24.349276	0.04106898	0.214943	5.233712	0.19106898	19.11	1.101759	10.02	11
12	5.350250	29.001667	0.03448078	0.186907	5.420619	0.18448078	18.45	1.213769	10.11	12
13	6.152788	34.351917	0.02911046	0.162528	5.583147	0.17911046	17.92	1.328436	10.22	13
14	7.075706	40.504705	0.02468849	0.141329	5.724476	0.17468849	17.47	1.445639	10.33	14
15	8.137062	47.580411	0.02101705	0.122894	5.847370	0.17101705	17.11	1.565256	10.44	15
16	9.357621	55.717472	0.01794769	0.106865	5.954235	0.16794769	16.80	1.687163	10.54	16
17	10.761264	65.075093	0.01536686	0.092926	6.047161	0.16536686	16.54	1.811237	10.65	17
18	12.375454	75.836357	0.01318629	0.080805	6.127966	0.16318629	16.32	1.937353	10.76	18
19	14.231772	88.211811	0.01133635	0.070265	6.198231	0.16133635	16.14	2.065391	10.87	19
20	16.366537	102.443583	0.00976147	0.061100	6.259331	0.15976147	15.98	2.195229	10.98	20
21	18.821518	118.810130	0.00841679	0.053131	6.312462	0.15841679	15.85	2.326753	11.08	21
22	21.644746	137.631638	0.00726577	0.046201	6.358663	0.15726577	15.73	2.459847	11.18	22
23	24.891458	159.276384	0.00627839	0.040174	6.398837	0.15627839	15.63	2.594403	11.28	23
24	28.625176	184.167841	0.00542983	0.034934	6.433771	0.15542983	15.55	2.730316	11.38	24
25	32.918953	212.793017	0.00469940	0.030378	6.464149	0.15469940	15.47	2.867485	11.47	25
26	37.856796	245.711970	0.00406981	0.026415	6.490564	0.15406981	15.41	3.005815	11.56	26
27	43.535315	283.568766	0.00352648	0.022970	6.513534	0.15352648	15.36	3.145215	11.65	27
28	50.065612	327.104080	0.00305713	0.019974	6.533508	0.15305713	15.31	3.285600	11.73	28
29	57.575454	377.169693	0.00265133	0.017369	6.550877	0.15265133	15.27	3.426888	11.82	29
30	66.211772	434.745146	0.00230020	0.015103	6.565980	0.15230020	15.24	3.569006	11.90	30
31	76.143538	500.956918	0.00199618	0.013133	6.579113	0.15199618	15.20	3.711882	11.97	31
32	87.565068	577.100456	0.00173280	0.011420	6.590533	0.15173280	15.18	3.855450	12.05	32
33	100.699829	664.665524	0.00150452	0.009931	6.600463	0.15150452	15.16	3.999649	12.12	33
34	115.804803	765.365353	0.00130657	0.008635	6.609099	0.15130657	15.14	4.144423	12.19	34
35	133.175523	881.170156	0.00113485	0.007509	6.616607	0.15113485	15.12	4.289720	12.26	35
36	153.151852	1014.345680	0.00098586	0.006529	6.623137	0.15098586	15.10	4.435491	12.32	36
37	176.124630	1167.497532	0.00085653	0.005678	6.628815	0.15085653	15.09	4.581692	12.38	37
38	202.543324	1343.622161	0.00074426	0.004937	6.633752	0.15074426	15.08	4.728282	12.44	38
39	232.924823	1546.165485	0.00064676	0.004293	6.638045	0.15064676	15.07	4.875224	12.50	39
40	267.863546	1779.090308	0.00056209	0.003733	6.641778	0.15056209	15.06	5.022483	12.56	40
41	308.043078	2046.953854	0.00048853	0.003246	6.645025	0.15048853	15.05	5.170030	12.61	41
42	354.249540	2354.996933	0.00042463	0.002823	6.647848	0.15042463	15.05	5.317834	12.66	42
43	407.386971	2709.246473	0.00036911	0.002455	6.650302	0.15036911	15.04	5.465872	12.71	43
44	468.495017	3116.633443	0.00032086	0.002134	6.652437	0.15032086	15.04	5.614118	12.76	44
45	538.769269	3585.128460	0.00027893	0.001856	6.654293	0.15027893	15.03	5.762552	12.81	45
46	619.584659	4123.897729	0.00024249	0.001614	6.655907	0.15024249	15.03	5.911154	12.85	46
47	712.522358	4743.482388	0.00021082	0.001403	6.657310	0.15021082	15.03	6.059908	12.89	47
48	819.400712	5456.004746	0.00018328	0.001220	6.658531	0.15018328	15.02	6.208798	12.93	48
49	942.310819	6275.405458	0.00015935	0.001061	6.659592	0.15015935	15.02	6.357808	12.98	49
50	1083.657442	7217.716277	0.00013855	0.000923	6.660515	0.15013855	15.02	6.506927	13.01	50

COMPOUND INTEREST AND ANNUITY TABLE

16.00 % ANNUAL

	Amount Of 1	Amount Of 1 Per Period	Sinking Fund Payment	Present Worth Of 1	Present Worth Of 1 Per Period	Periodic Payment To Amortize 1	Constant Annual Percent	Total Interest	Annual Add-on Rate	
	What a single $1 deposit grows to in the future. The deposit is made at the beginning of the first period.	What a series of $1 deposits grow to in the future. A deposit is made at the end of each period.	The amount to be deposited at the end of each period that grows to $1 in the future.	What $1 to be paid in the future is worth today. Value today of a single payment tomorrow.	What $1 to be paid at the end of each period is worth today. Value today of a series of payments tomorrow.	The mortgage payment to amortize a loan of $1. An annuity certain, payable at the end of each period, worth $1 today.	The annual payment, including interest and principal, to amortize completely by regular payments of $100.	The total interest paid over the term on a loan of $1. The loan is amortized by regular periodic payments.	The average annual interest rate on a loan that is completely amortized by regular periodic payments.	
	$S=(1+i)^n$	$S_{\overline{n}}=\frac{(1+i)^n-1}{i}$	$\frac{1}{S_{\overline{n}}}=\frac{i}{(1+i)^n-1}$	$V^n=\frac{1}{(1+i)^n}$	$A_{\overline{n}}=\frac{1-V^n}{i}$	$\frac{1}{A_{\overline{n}}}=\frac{i}{1-V^n}$				

YR										YR
1	1.160000	1.000000	1.00000000	0.862069	0.862069	1.16000000	116.00	0.160000	16.00	1
2	1.345600	2.160000	0.46296296	0.743163	1.605232	0.62296296	62.30	0.245926	12.30	2
3	1.560896	3.505600	0.28525787	0.640658	2.245890	0.44525787	44.53	0.335774	11.19	3
4	1.810639	5.066496	0.19737507	0.552291	2.798181	0.35737507	35.74	0.429500	10.74	4
5	2.100342	6.877135	0.14540938	0.476113	3.274294	0.30540938	30.55	0.527047	10.54	5
6	2.436396	8.977477	0.11138987	0.410442	3.684736	0.27138987	27.14	0.628339	10.47	6
7	2.826220	11.413873	0.08761268	0.353830	4.038565	0.24761268	24.77	0.733289	10.48	7
8	3.278415	14.240093	0.07022426	0.305025	4.343591	0.23022426	23.03	0.841794	10.52	8
9	3.802961	17.518508	0.05708249	0.262953	4.606544	0.21708249	21.71	0.953742	10.60	9
10	4.411435	21.321469	0.04690108	0.226684	4.833227	0.20690108	20.70	1.069011	10.69	10
11	5.117265	25.732904	0.03886075	0.195417	5.028644	0.19886075	19.89	1.187468	10.80	11
12	5.936027	30.850169	0.03241473	0.168463	5.197107	0.19241473	19.25	1.308977	10.91	12
13	6.885791	36.786196	0.02718411	0.145227	5.342334	0.18718411	18.72	1.433393	11.03	13
14	7.987518	43.671987	0.02289797	0.125195	5.467529	0.18289797	18.29	1.560572	11.15	14
15	9.265521	51.659505	0.01935752	0.107927	5.575456	0.17935752	17.94	1.690363	11.27	15

17.00 % ANNUAL

YR										YR
1	1.170000	1.000000	1.00000000	0.854701	0.854701	1.17000000	117.00	0.170000	17.00	1
2	1.368900	2.170000	0.46082949	0.730514	1.585214	0.63082949	63.09	0.261659	13.08	2
3	1.601613	3.538900	0.28257368	0.624371	2.209585	0.45257368	45.26	0.357721	11.92	3
4	1.873887	5.140513	0.19453311	0.533650	2.743235	0.36453311	36.46	0.458132	11.45	4
5	2.192448	7.014400	0.14256386	0.456111	3.199346	0.31256386	31.26	0.562819	11.26	5
6	2.565164	9.206848	0.10861480	0.389839	3.589185	0.27861480	27.87	0.671689	11.19	6
7	3.001242	11.772012	0.08494724	0.333195	3.922380	0.25494724	25.50	0.784631	11.21	7
8	3.511453	14.773255	0.06768989	0.284782	4.207163	0.23768989	23.77	0.901519	11.27	8
9	4.108400	18.284708	0.05469051	0.243404	4.450566	0.22469051	22.47	1.022215	11.36	9
10	4.806828	22.393108	0.04465660	0.208037	4.658604	0.21465660	21.47	1.146566	11.47	10
11	5.623989	27.199937	0.03676479	0.177810	4.836413	0.20676479	20.68	1.274413	11.59	11
12	6.580067	32.823926	0.03046558	0.151974	4.988387	0.20046558	20.05	1.405587	11.71	12
13	7.698679	39.403993	0.02537814	0.129892	5.118280	0.19537814	19.54	1.539916	11.85	13
14	9.007454	47.102672	0.02123022	0.111019	5.229299	0.19123022	19.13	1.677223	11.98	14
15	10.538721	56.110126	0.01782209	0.094888	5.324187	0.18782209	18.79	1.817331	12.12	15

COMPOUND INTEREST AND ANNUITY TABLE

18.00 % ANNUAL

	Amount Of 1	Amount Of 1 Per Period	Sinking Fund Payment	Present Worth Of 1	Present Worth Of 1 Per Period	Periodic Payment To Amortize 1	Constant Annual Percent	Total Interest	Annual Add-on Rate	
	What a single $1 deposit grows to in the future. The deposit is made at the beginning of the first period. $S=(1+i)^n$	What a series of $1 deposits grow to in the future. A deposit is made at the end of each period. $S_{\overline{n}\|}=\frac{(1+i)^n-1}{i}$	The amount to be deposited at the end of each period that grows to $1 in the future. $\frac{1}{S_{\overline{n}\|}}=\frac{i}{(1+i)^n-1}$	What $1 to be paid in the future is worth today. Value today of a single payment tomorrow. $V^n=\frac{1}{(1+i)^n}$	What $1 to be paid at the end of each period is worth today. Value today of a series of payments tomorrow.	The mortgage payment to amortize a loan of $1. An annuity certain, payable at the end of each period, worth $1 today. $\frac{1}{A_{\overline{n}\|}}=\frac{i}{1-V^n}$	The annual payment, including interest and principal, to amortize completely a loan of $100.	The total interest paid over the term on a loan of $1. The loan is amortized by regular periodic payments.	The average annual interest rate on a loan that is completely amortized by regular periodic payments.	
YR						$A_{\overline{n}\|}=\frac{1-V^n}{i}$				YR
1	1.180000	1.000000	1.00000000	0.847458	0.847458	1.18000000	118.00	0.180000	18.00	1
2	1.392400	2.180000	0.45871560	0.718184	1.565642	0.63871560	63.88	0.277431	13.87	2
3	1.643032	3.572400	0.27992386	0.608631	2.174273	0.45992386	46.00	0.379772	12.66	3
4	1.938778	5.215432	0.19173867	0.515789	2.690062	0.37173867	37.18	0.486955	12.17	4
5	2.287758	7.154210	0.13977784	0.437109	3.127171	0.31977784	31.98	0.598889	11.98	5
6	2.699554	9.441968	0.10591013	0.370432	3.497603	0.28591013	28.60	0.715461	11.92	6
7	3.185474	12.141522	0.08236200	0.313925	3.811528	0.26236200	26.24	0.836534	11.95	7
8	3.758859	15.326996	0.06524436	0.266038	4.077566	0.24524436	24.53	0.961955	12.02	8
9	4.435454	19.085855	0.05239482	0.225456	4.303022	0.23239482	23.24	1.091553	12.13	9
10	5.233836	23.521309	0.04251464	0.191064	4.494086	0.22251464	22.26	1.225146	12.25	10
11	6.175926	28.755144	0.03477639	0.161919	4.656005	0.21477639	21.48	1.362540	12.39	11
12	7.287593	34.931070	0.02862781	0.137220	4.793225	0.20862781	20.87	1.503534	12.53	12
13	8.599359	42.218663	0.02368621	0.116288	4.909513	0.20368621	20.37	1.647921	12.68	13
14	10.147244	50.818022	0.01967806	0.098549	5.008062	0.19967806	19.97	1.795493	12.82	14
15	11.973748	60.965266	0.01640278	0.083516	5.091578	0.19640278	19.65	1.946042	12.97	15

19.00 % ANNUAL

YR										YR
1	1.190000	1.000000	1.00000000	0.840336	0.840336	1.19000000	119.00	0.190000	19.00	1
2	1.416100	2.190000	0.45662100	0.706165	1.546501	0.64662100	64.67	0.293242	14.66	2
3	1.685159	3.606100	0.27730789	0.593416	2.139917	0.46730789	46.74	0.401924	13.40	3
4	2.005339	5.291259	0.18899094	0.498669	2.638586	0.37899094	37.90	0.515964	12.90	4
5	2.386354	7.296598	0.13705017	0.419049	3.057635	0.32705017	32.71	0.635251	12.71	5
6	2.839761	9.682952	0.10327429	0.352142	3.409777	0.29327429	29.33	0.759646	12.66	6
7	3.379315	12.522713	0.07985490	0.295918	3.705695	0.26985490	26.99	0.888984	12.70	7
8	4.021385	15.902028	0.06288506	0.248671	3.954366	0.25288506	25.29	1.023080	12.79	8
9	4.785449	19.923413	0.05019220	0.208967	4.163332	0.24019220	24.02	1.161730	12.91	9
10	5.694684	24.708862	0.04047131	0.175602	4.338935	0.23047131	23.05	1.304713	13.05	10
11	6.776674	30.403546	0.03289090	0.147565	4.486500	0.22289090	22.29	1.451800	13.20	11
12	8.064242	37.180220	0.02689602	0.124004	4.610504	0.21689602	21.69	1.602752	13.36	12
13	9.596448	45.244461	0.02210215	0.104205	4.714709	0.21210215	21.22	1.757328	13.52	13
14	11.419773	54.840909	0.01823456	0.087567	4.802277	0.20823456	20.83	1.915284	13.68	14
15	13.589530	66.260682	0.01509191	0.073586	4.875863	0.20509191	20.51	2.076379	13.84	15

COMPOUND INTEREST AND ANNUITY TABLE

20.00 % ANNUAL

	Amount Of 1	Amount Of 1 Per Period	Sinking Fund Payment	Present Worth Of 1	Present Worth Of 1 Per Period	Periodic Payment To Amortize 1	Constant Annual Percent	Total Interest	Annual Add-on Rate	
	What a single $1 deposit grows to in the future. The deposit is made at the beginning of the first period.	What a series of $1 deposits grow to in the future. A deposit is made at the end of each period.	The amount to be deposited at the end of each period that grows to $1 in the future.	What $1 to be paid in the future is worth today. Value today of a single payment tomorrow.	What $1 to be paid at the end of each period is worth today. Value today of a series of payments tomorrow.	The mortgage payment to amortize a loan of $1. An annuity certain, payable at the end of each period, worth $1 today.	The annual payment, including interest and principal, to amortize completely a loan of $100.	The total interest paid over the term of $1. The loan is amortized by regular periodic payments.	The average annual interest rate on a loan that is completely amortized by regular periodic payments.	
	$S=(1+i)^n$	$S_n = \frac{(1+i)^n - 1}{i}$	$\frac{1}{S_n} = \frac{i}{(1+i)^n - 1}$	$V^n = \frac{1}{(1+i)^n}$	$A_n = \frac{1 - V^n}{i}$	$\frac{1}{A_n} = \frac{i}{1 - V^n}$				
YR										YR
1	1.200000	1.000000	1.00000000	0.833333	0.833333	1.20000000	120.00	0.200000	20.00	1
2	1.440000	2.200000	0.45454545	0.694444	1.527778	0.65454545	65.46	0.309091	15.45	2
3	1.728000	3.640000	0.27472527	0.578704	2.106481	0.47472527	47.48	0.424176	14.14	3
4	2.073600	5.368000	0.18628912	0.482253	2.588735	0.38628912	38.63	0.545156	13.63	4
5	2.488320	7.441600	0.13437970	0.401878	2.990612	0.33437970	33.44	0.671899	13.44	5
6	2.985984	9.929920	0.10070575	0.334898	3.325510	0.30070575	30.08	0.804234	13.40	6
7	3.583181	12.915904	0.07742393	0.279082	3.604592	0.27742393	27.75	0.941967	13.46	7
8	4.299817	16.499085	0.06060942	0.232568	3.837160	0.26060942	26.07	1.084875	13.56	8
9	5.159780	20.798902	0.04807946	0.193807	4.030967	0.24807946	24.81	1.232715	13.70	9
10	6.191736	25.958682	0.03852276	0.161506	4.192472	0.23852276	23.86	1.385228	13.85	10
11	7.430084	32.150419	0.03110379	0.134588	4.327060	0.23110379	23.12	1.542142	14.02	11
12	8.916100	39.580502	0.02526496	0.112157	4.439217	0.22526496	22.53	1.703180	14.19	12
13	10.699321	48.496603	0.02062000	0.093464	4.532681	0.22062000	22.07	1.868060	14.37	13
14	12.839185	59.195923	0.01689306	0.077887	4.610567	0.21689306	21.69	2.036503	14.55	14
15	15.407022	72.035108	0.01388212	0.064905	4.675473	0.21388212	21.39	2.208232	14.72	15

21.00 % ANNUAL

YR										YR
1	1.210000	1.000000	1.00000000	0.826446	0.826446	1.21000000	121.00	0.210000	21.00	1
2	1.464100	2.210000	0.45248869	0.683013	1.509460	0.66248869	66.25	0.324977	16.25	2
3	1.771561	3.674100	0.27217550	0.564474	2.073934	0.48217550	48.22	0.446526	14.88	3
4	2.143589	5.445661	0.18363244	0.466507	2.540441	0.39363244	39.37	0.574530	14.36	4
5	2.593742	7.589520	0.13176533	0.385543	2.925984	0.34176533	34.18	0.708827	14.18	5
6	3.138428	10.182992	0.09820296	0.318631	3.244615	0.30820296	30.83	0.849218	14.15	6
7	3.797498	13.321421	0.07506707	0.263331	3.507946	0.28506707	28.51	0.995469	14.22	7
8	4.594973	17.118919	0.05841490	0.217629	3.725576	0.26841490	26.85	1.147319	14.34	8
9	5.559917	21.713892	0.04605347	0.179859	3.905434	0.25605347	25.61	1.304481	14.49	9
10	6.727500	27.273809	0.03666521	0.148644	4.054078	0.24666521	24.67	1.466652	14.67	10
11	8.140275	34.001309	0.02941063	0.122846	4.176924	0.23941063	23.95	1.633517	14.85	11
12	9.849733	42.141584	0.02372953	0.101526	4.278450	0.23372953	23.38	1.804754	15.04	12
13	11.918177	51.991317	0.01923398	0.083905	4.362355	0.22923398	22.93	1.980042	15.23	13
14	14.420994	63.909493	0.01564713	0.069343	4.431698	0.22564713	22.57	2.159060	15.42	14
15	17.449402	78.330487	0.01276642	0.057309	4.489007	0.22276642	22.28	2.341496	15.61	15

COMPOUND INTEREST AND ANNUITY TABLE

22.00 % ANNUAL

	Amount Of 1	Amount Of 1 Per Period	Sinking Fund Payment	Present Worth Of 1	Present Worth Of 1 Per Period	Periodic Payment To Amortize 1	Constant Annual Percent	Total Interest	Annual Add-on Rate	
	What a single $1 deposit grows to in the future. The deposit is made at the beginning of the first period.	What a series of $1 deposits grow to in the future. A deposit is made at the end of each period.	The amount to be deposited at the end of each period that grows to $1 in the future.	What $1 to be paid in the future is worth today. Value today of a single payment tomorrow.	What $1 to be paid at the end of each period is worth today. Value today of a series of payments tomorrow.	The mortgage payment to amortize a loan of $1. An annuity certain, payable at the end of each period, worth $1 today.	The annual payment, including interest and principal, to amortize completely a loan of $100.	The total interest paid over the term of $1. The loan is amortized by regular periodic payments.	The average annual interest rate on a loan that is completely amortized by regular periodic payments.	
	$S=(1+i)^n$	$S_{\overline{n}}=\frac{(1+i)^n-1}{i}$	$\frac{1}{S_{\overline{n}}}=\frac{i}{(1+i)^n-1}$	$V^n=\frac{1}{(1+i)^n}$	$A_{\overline{n}}=\frac{1-V^n}{i}$	$\frac{1}{A_{\overline{n}}}=\frac{i}{1-V^n}$				
YR										YR
1	1.220000	1.000000	1.00000000	0.819672	0.819672	1.22000000	122.00	0.220000	22.00	1
2	1.488400	2.220000	0.45045045	0.671862	1.491535	0.67045045	67.05	0.340901	17.05	2
3	1.815848	3.708400	0.26965807	0.550707	2.042241	0.48965807	48.97	0.468974	15.63	3
4	2.215335	5.524248	0.18102011	0.451399	2.493641	0.40102011	40.11	0.604080	15.10	4
5	2.702708	7.739583	0.12920593	0.369999	2.863640	0.34920593	34.93	0.746030	14.92	5
6	3.297304	10.442291	0.09576443	0.303278	3.166918	0.31576443	31.58	0.894587	14.91	6
7	4.022711	13.739595	0.07278235	0.248589	3.415506	0.29278235	29.28	1.049476	14.99	7
8	4.907707	17.762306	0.05629900	0.203761	3.619268	0.27629900	27.63	1.210392	15.13	8
9	5.987403	22.670013	0.04411114	0.167017	3.786285	0.26411114	26.42	1.377000	15.30	9
10	7.304631	28.657416	0.03489498	0.136899	3.923184	0.25489498	25.49	1.548950	15.49	10
11	8.911650	35.962047	0.02780709	0.112213	4.035397	0.24780709	24.79	1.725878	15.69	11
12	10.872213	44.873697	0.02228477	0.091978	4.127375	0.24228477	24.23	1.907417	15.90	12
13	13.264100	55.745911	0.01793854	0.075391	4.202766	0.23793854	23.80	2.093201	16.10	13
14	16.182202	69.010011	0.01449065	0.061796	4.264562	0.23449065	23.45	2.282869	16.31	14
15	19.742287	85.192213	0.01173816	0.050653	4.315215	0.23173816	23.18	2.476072	16.51	15

23.00 % ANNUAL

YR										YR
1	1.230000	1.000000	1.00000000	0.813008	0.813008	1.23000000	123.00	0.230000	23.00	1
2	1.512900	2.230000	0.44843049	0.660982	1.473990	0.67843049	67.85	0.356861	17.84	2
3	1.860867	3.742900	0.26717251	0.537384	2.011374	0.49717251	49.72	0.491518	16.38	3
4	2.288866	5.603767	0.17845139	0.436897	2.448272	0.40845139	40.85	0.633806	15.85	4
5	2.815306	7.892633	0.12670042	0.355201	2.803473	0.35670042	35.68	0.783502	15.67	5
6	3.462826	10.707939	0.09338865	0.288781	3.092254	0.32338865	32.34	0.940332	15.67	6
7	4.259276	14.170765	0.07056782	0.234782	3.327036	0.30056782	30.06	1.103975	15.77	7
8	5.238909	18.430041	0.05425924	0.190879	3.517916	0.28425924	28.43	1.274074	15.93	8
9	6.443859	23.668950	0.04224944	0.155187	3.673102	0.27224944	27.23	1.450245	16.11	9
10	7.925946	30.112809	0.03320846	0.126168	3.799270	0.26320846	26.33	1.632085	16.32	10
11	9.748914	38.038755	0.02628898	0.102576	3.901846	0.25628898	25.63	1.819179	16.54	11
12	11.991164	47.787669	0.02092590	0.083395	3.985240	0.25092590	25.10	2.011111	16.76	12
13	14.749132	59.778833	0.01672833	0.067801	4.053041	0.24672833	24.68	2.207468	16.98	13
14	18.141432	74.527964	0.01341778	0.055122	4.108163	0.24341778	24.35	2.407849	17.20	14
15	22.313961	92.669396	0.01079105	0.044815	4.152978	0.24079105	24.08	2.611866	17.41	15

THE LEASE / BUY DECISION

COMPOUND INTEREST AND ANNUITY TABLE

24.00 % ANNUAL

	Amount Of 1	Amount Of 1 Per Period	Sinking Fund Payment	Present Worth Of 1	Present Worth Of 1 Per Period	Periodic Payment To Amortize 1	Constant Annual Percent	Total Interest	Annual Add-on Rate	
	What a single $1 deposit grows to in the future. The deposit is made at the beginning of the first period.	What a series of $1 deposits grow to in the future. A deposit is made at the end of each period.	The amount to be deposited at the end of each period that grows to $1 in the future.	What $1 to be paid in the future is worth today. Value today of a single payment tomorrow.	What $1 to be paid at the end of each period is worth today. Value today of a series of payments tomorrow.	The mortgage payment to amortize a loan of $1. An annuity certain, payable at the end of each period, worth $1 today.	The annual payment, including interest and principal, to amortize completely a loan of $100.	The total interest paid over the term on a loan of $1. The loan is amortized by regular periodic payments.	The average annual interest rate on a loan that is completely amortized by regular periodic payments.	
	$S=(1+i)^n$	$S_n = \frac{(1+i)^n - 1}{i}$	$\frac{1}{S_n} = \frac{i}{(1+i)^n - 1}$	$V^n = \frac{1}{(1+i)^n}$	$A_n = \frac{1-V^n}{i}$	$\frac{1}{A_n} = \frac{i}{1-V^n}$				

YR										YR
1	1.240000	1.000000	1.00000000	0.806452	0.806452	1.24000000	124.00	0.240000	24.00	1
2	1.537600	2.240000	0.44642857	0.650364	1.456816	0.68642857	68.65	0.372857	18.64	2
3	1.906624	3.777600	0.26471834	0.524487	1.981303	0.50471834	50.48	0.514155	17.14	3
4	2.364214	5.684224	0.17592551	0.422974	2.404277	0.41592551	41.60	0.663702	16.59	4
5	2.931625	8.048438	0.12424771	0.341108	2.745384	0.36424771	36.43	0.821239	16.42	5
6	3.635215	10.980063	0.09107416	0.275087	3.020471	0.33107416	33.11	0.986445	16.44	6
7	4.507667	14.615278	0.06842155	0.221844	3.242316	0.30842155	30.85	1.158951	16.56	7
8	5.589507	19.122945	0.05229320	0.178907	3.421222	0.29229320	29.23	1.338346	16.73	8
9	6.930988	24.712451	0.04046543	0.144280	3.565502	0.28046543	28.05	1.524189	16.94	9
10	8.594426	31.643440	0.03160213	0.116354	3.681856	0.27160213	27.17	1.716021	17.16	10
11	10.657088	40.237865	0.02485221	0.093834	3.775691	0.26485221	26.49	1.913374	17.39	11
12	13.214789	50.894953	0.01964831	0.075673	3.851363	0.25964831	25.97	2.115780	17.63	12
13	16.386338	64.109741	0.01559825	0.061026	3.912390	0.25559825	25.56	2.322777	17.87	13
14	20.319059	80.496079	0.01242297	0.049215	3.961605	0.25242297	25.25	2.533922	18.10	14
15	25.195633	100.815138	0.00991915	0.039689	4.001294	0.24991915	25.00	2.748787	18.33	15

25.00 % ANNUAL

YR										YR
1	1.250000	1.000000	1.00000000	0.800000	0.800000	1.25000000	125.00	0.250000	25.00	1
2	1.562500	2.250000	0.44444444	0.640000	1.440000	0.69444444	69.45	0.388889	19.44	2
3	1.953125	3.812500	0.26229508	0.512000	1.952000	0.51229508	51.23	0.536885	17.90	3
4	2.441406	5.765625	0.17344173	0.409600	2.361600	0.42344173	42.35	0.693767	17.34	4
5	3.051758	8.207031	0.12184674	0.327680	2.689280	0.37184674	37.19	0.859234	17.18	5
6	3.814697	11.258789	0.08881950	0.262144	2.951424	0.33881950	33.89	1.032917	17.22	6
7	4.768372	15.073486	0.06634165	0.209715	3.161139	0.31634165	31.64	1.214392	17.35	7
8	5.960464	19.841858	0.05039851	0.167772	3.328911	0.30039851	30.04	1.403188	17.54	8
9	7.450581	25.802322	0.03875620	0.134218	3.463129	0.28875620	28.88	1.598806	17.76	9
10	9.313226	33.252903	0.03007256	0.107374	3.570503	0.28007256	28.01	1.800726	18.01	10
11	11.641532	42.566129	0.02349286	0.085899	3.656403	0.27349286	27.35	2.008421	18.26	11
12	14.551915	54.207661	0.01844758	0.068719	3.725122	0.26844758	26.85	2.221371	18.51	12
13	18.189894	68.759576	0.01454343	0.054976	3.780098	0.26454343	26.46	2.439065	18.76	13
14	22.737368	86.949470	0.01150093	0.043980	3.824078	0.26150093	26.16	2.661013	19.01	14
15	28.421709	109.686838	0.00911686	0.035184	3.859263	0.25911686	25.92	2.886753	19.25	15

COMPOUND INTEREST AND ANNUITY TABLE

30.00 % ANNUAL

	Amount Of 1	Amount Of 1 Per Period	Sinking Fund Payment	Present Worth Of 1	Present Worth Of 1 Per Period	Periodic Payment To Amortize 1	Constant Annual Percent	Total Interest	Annual Add-on Rate	
	What a single $1 deposit grows to in the future. The deposit is made at the beginning of the first period.	What a series of $1 deposits grow to in the future. A deposit is made at the end of each period.	The amount to be deposited at the end of each period that grows to $1 in the future.	What $1 to be paid in the future is worth today. Value today of a single payment tomorrow.	What $1 to be paid at the end of each period is worth today. Value today of a series of payments tomorrow.	The mortgage payment to amortize a loan of $1. An annuity certain, payable at the end of each period, worth $1 today.	The annual payment, including interest and principal, to amortize completely a loan of $100.	The total interest paid over the term on a loan of $1. The loan is amortized by regular periodic payments.	The average annual interest rate on a loan that is completely amortized by regular periodic payments.	
	$S=(1+i)^n$	$S_{\overline{n}}=\frac{(1+i)^n-1}{i}$	$\frac{1}{S_{\overline{n}}}=\frac{i}{(1+i)^n-1}$	$V^n=\frac{1}{(1+i)^n}$	$A_{\overline{n}}=\frac{1-V^n}{i}$	$\frac{1}{A_{\overline{n}}}=\frac{i}{1-V^n}$				
YR										YR
1	1.300000	1.000000	1.00000000	0.769231	0.769231	1.30000000	130.00	0.300000	30.00	1
2	1.690000	2.300000	0.43478261	0.591716	1.360947	0.73478261	73.48	0.469565	23.48	2
3	2.197000	3.990000	0.25062657	0.455166	1.816113	0.55062657	55.07	0.651880	21.73	3
4	2.856100	6.187000	0.16162922	0.350128	2.166241	0.46162922	46.17	0.846517	21.16	4
5	3.712930	9.043100	0.11058155	0.269329	2.435570	0.41058155	41.06	1.052908	21.06	5
6	4.826809	12.756030	0.07839430	0.207176	2.642746	0.37839430	37.84	1.270366	21.17	6
7	6.274852	17.582839	0.05687364	0.159366	2.802112	0.35687364	35.69	1.498115	21.40	7
8	8.157307	23.857691	0.04191521	0.122589	2.924702	0.34191521	34.20	1.735322	21.69	8
9	10.604499	32.014998	0.03123536	0.094300	3.019001	0.33123536	33.13	1.981118	22.01	9
10	13.785849	42.619497	0.02346344	0.072538	3.091539	0.32346344	32.35	2.234634	22.35	10
11	17.921604	56.405346	0.01772882	0.055799	3.147338	0.31772882	31.78	2.495017	22.68	11
12	23.298085	74.326950	0.01345407	0.042922	3.190260	0.31345407	31.35	2.761449	23.01	12
13	30.287511	97.625036	0.01024327	0.033017	3.223277	0.31024327	31.03	3.033163	23.33	13
14	39.373764	127.912546	0.00781784	0.025398	3.248675	0.30781784	30.79	3.309450	23.64	14
15	51.185893	167.286310	0.00597778	0.019537	3.268211	0.30597778	30.60	3.589667	23.93	15

35.00 % ANNUAL

YR										YR
1	1.350000	1.000000	1.00000000	0.740741	0.740741	1.35000000	135.00	0.350000	35.00	1
2	1.822500	2.350000	0.42553191	0.548697	1.289438	0.77553191	77.56	0.551064	27.55	2
3	2.460375	4.172500	0.23966447	0.406442	1.695880	0.58966447	58.97	0.768993	25.63	3
4	3.321506	6.632875	0.15076419	0.301068	1.996948	0.50076419	50.08	1.003057	25.08	4
5	4.484033	9.954381	0.10045828	0.223014	2.219961	0.45045828	45.05	1.252291	25.05	5
6	6.053445	14.438415	0.06925968	0.165195	2.385157	0.41925968	41.93	1.515558	25.26	6
7	8.172151	20.491860	0.04879987	0.122367	2.507523	0.39879987	39.88	1.791599	25.59	7
8	11.032404	28.664011	0.03488695	0.090642	2.598165	0.38488695	38.49	2.079096	25.99	8
9	14.893745	39.696415	0.02519119	0.067142	2.665308	0.37519119	37.52	2.376721	26.41	9
10	20.106556	54.590160	0.01831832	0.049735	2.715043	0.36831832	36.84	2.683183	26.83	10
11	27.143850	74.696715	0.01338747	0.036841	2.751884	0.36338747	36.34	2.997262	27.25	11
12	36.644198	101.840566	0.00981927	0.027289	2.779173	0.35981927	35.99	3.317831	27.65	12
13	49.469667	138.484764	0.00722101	0.020214	2.799387	0.35722101	35.73	3.643873	28.03	13
14	66.784051	187.954431	0.00532044	0.014974	2.814361	0.35532044	35.54	3.974486	28.39	14
15	90.158469	254.738482	0.00392559	0.011092	2.825453	0.35392559	35.40	4.308884	28.73	15

THE LEASE / BUY DECISION

COMPOUND INTEREST AND ANNUITY TABLE

40.00 % ANNUAL

	Amount Of 1	Amount Of 1 Per Period	Sinking Fund Payment	Present Worth Of 1	Present Worth Of 1 Per Period	Periodic Payment To Amortize 1	Constant Annual Percent	Total Interest	Annual Add-on Rate	
	What a single $1 deposit grows to in the future. The deposit is made at the beginning of the first period.	What a series of $1 deposits grow to in the future. A deposit is made at the end of each period.	The amount to be deposited at the end of each period that grows to $1 in the future.	What $1 to be paid in the future is worth today. Value today of a single payment tomorrow.	What $1 to be paid at the end of each period is worth today. Value today of a series of payments tomorrow.	The mortgage payment to amortize a loan of $1. An annuity certain, payable at the end of each period, worth $1 today.	The annual payment, including interest and principal, to amortize completely a loan of $100.	The total interest paid over the term of $1. The loan is amortized by regular periodic payments.	The average annual interest rate on a loan that is completely amortized by regular periodic payments.	
	$S=(1+i)^n$	$S_{\overline{n}}=\frac{(1+i)^n-1}{i}$	$\frac{1}{S_{\overline{n}}}=\frac{i}{(1+i)^n-1}$	$V^n=\frac{1}{(1+i)^n}$	$A_{\overline{n}}=\frac{1-V^n}{i}$	$\frac{1}{A_{\overline{n}}}=\frac{i}{1-V^n}$				
YR										YR
1	1.400000	1.000000	1.00000000	0.714286	0.714286	1.40000000	140.00	0.400000	40.00	1
2	1.960000	2.400000	0.41666667	0.510204	1.224490	0.81666667	81.67	0.633333	31.67	2
3	2.744000	4.360000	0.22935780	0.364431	1.588921	0.62935780	62.94	0.888073	29.60	3
4	3.841600	7.104000	0.14076577	0.260308	1.849229	0.54076577	54.08	1.163063	29.08	4
5	5.378240	10.945300	0.09136091	0.185934	2.035164	0.49136091	49.14	1.456805	29.14	5
6	7.529536	16.323840	0.06126010	0.132810	2.167974	0.46126010	46.13	1.767561	29.46	6
7	10.541350	23.853376	0.04192279	0.094865	2.262839	0.44192279	44.20	2.093460	29.91	7
8	14.757891	34.394726	0.02907422	0.067760	2.330599	0.42907422	42.91	2.432594	30.41	8
9	20.661047	49.152617	0.02034480	0.048400	2.378999	0.42034480	42.04	2.783103	30.92	9
10	28.925465	69.813664	0.01432384	0.034572	2.413571	0.41432384	41.44	3.143238	31.43	10
11	40.495652	98.739129	0.01012770	0.024694	2.438265	0.41012770	41.02	3.511405	31.92	11
12	56.693912	139.234781	0.00718211	0.017639	2.455904	0.40718211	40.72	3.886185	32.38	12
13	79.371477	195.928693	0.00510390	0.012599	2.468503	0.40510390	40.52	4.266351	32.82	13
14	111.120068	275.300171	0.00363240	0.008999	2.477502	0.40363240	40.37	4.650854	33.22	14
15	155.568096	386.420239	0.00258786	0.006428	2.483930	0.40258786	40.26	5.038818	33.59	15

APPENDIX E

Sources of Economic and Financial Information from The Conference Board

This annotated bibliography of well-known sources of economic data is limited to basic references. It should not be construed as a comprehensive listing of available material on economic information.

For the convenience of the user, the bibliography has been divided into several broad categories. All, except one devoted to international economic statistics, relate to the U.S. economy. Entries in the bibliography are listed by title, publisher, and frequency of issue.

Because economists generally depend to a great extent on official statistics, most of these entries are government publications. The bibliography includes, however, a selected sample of sources published by The Conference Board and other organizations.

Publications of the federal government, unless otherwise noted, can be obtained from The Superintendent of Documents, U.S. Government Printing Office, Washington, D.C. 20402. Entries published by The Conference Board are denoted by an asterisk (*). To order them, or to inquire about further details of their contents, please contact Information Service Division, The Conference Board, 845 Third Avenue, New York, N.Y. 10022.

The Conference Board, Inc., founded in 1916, is an independent, nonprofit institution for business and economic research. Its purpose is to promote broader understanding of business and the economy for the enlightenment both of those who manage business enterprises and of the society which shapes the business system. It pursues this by encouraging exchange of experience and opinion, by objective analyses of significant business and economic developments, and by widespread distribution of facts developed through these activities. The board is a fact-finding agency; it takes no positions on public policy issues nor does it act as a consulting organization. Its work is supported by more than 4,000 associates (members).

GENERAL REFERENCES

Survey of Current Business *Monthly*
U.S. Department of Commerce, Bureau of Economic Analysis
Each issue contains over 2,000 statistical series relating to Gross National Product (GNP), prices and employment, plus a wide variety of industrial data and other business indicators. July issue contains annual revisions of national income and product accounts.

Business Statistics *Biennial*
U.S. Department of Commerce, Office of Business Economics
A supplement to the *Survey of Current Business*. Presents historical data for the statistical series covered in that publication; also gives explanatory notes to their sources of data.

Business Conditions Digest *Monthly*
U.S. Department of Commerce, Bureau of Economic Analysis
A compilation of numerous economic statistical series, including charts, arranged for convenient analysis of business cycles.

Federal Reserve Bulletin *Monthly*
Board of Governors of the Federal Reserve System
Ordering address: Division of Administrative Services
Board of Governors of the Federal Reserve System
Washington, D.C. 20551
A compendium of financial, industrial and commercial statistics for the United States. Also includes data on the U.S. balance of payments and international exchange rates.

The Economic Report of the President and the Council of Economic Advisers
Annual
Executive Office of the President
The President's economic program and an elaboration of the goals of the U.S. economy by the Council of Economic Advisers. The analysis is supplemented by statistics on GNP, industrial production, personal income, employment, prices, profits and other aspects of the economy.

Statistical Abstract of the United States *Annual*
U.S. Department of Commerce
A basic reference source summarizing statistics on industrial, social, political and economic organizations of the United States; includes statistics obtained from both government and private sources.

Economic Indicators *Monthly*
U.S. Congress, Joint Economic Committee
Basic series on prices, wages, industrial production, consumer purchasing power, money supply, and receipts and expenditures of the Federal Government

The Conference Board Statistical Bulletin (*) *Monthly*
Gives GNP forecasts and information on various statistical series, including leading business indicators, help-wanted advertising indexes, diffusion indexes,

capital appropriations, profit margins, discretionary spending and automobile sales.

Current Economic Trends (*)   *Quarterly*
Presents current and historical statistics on major economic indicators in chart analysis form.

AGGREGATE MEASURES OF INCOME, DEMAND, AND PRODUCTION

GROSS NATIONAL PRODUCT AND INCOME

Survey of Current Business   *Monthly*
U.S. Department of Commerce, Bureau of Economic Analysis
See annotation under General References.

CONSUMER SPENDING

The Conference Board RECORD (*)   *Monthly*
Each issue includes a section on "Consumer Markets," which reports on various facets of consumer spending.

Consumer Attitudes and Buying Plans (*)   *Bimonthly*
Statistics measuring consumer attitudes toward current and future economic conditions; also interprets consumers' intentions to purchase durable goods.

Consumer Market Indicators (*)   *Monthly*
Statistics on consumption expenditures, consumer price index, consumer confidence index, and other market indicators.

Current Retail Trade Reports   *Weekly and Monthly*
U.S. Department of Commerce, Bureau of the Census
Data on estimated weekly and monthly retail sales, by lines of business, for the United States and for selected metropolitan statistical areas (SMSA's).

A Guide to Consumer Markets (*)   *Annual*
A statistical handbook. Contains data on employment, consumer income and expenditures, and the production and distribution of purchased goods and services.

Survey of Buying Power   *Annual*
Sales Management
630 Third Avenue
New York, New York 10017
Each edition includes data related to total retail sales and consumer buying indexes for the 50 states, their counties, and SMSA's.

Surveys of Consumers   *Annual*
Institute of Social Research
University of Michigan
Ann Arbor, Michigan 48106

National survey data on family incomes, household assets and liabilities, and consumer expenditures for durable goods. Also includes an outlook on consumer demand.

Survey of Consumer Expenditures *Irregular*
U.S. Department of Labor, Bureau of Labor Statistics
Data show expenditure patterns according to various family characteristics.

BUSINESS SPENDING

Survey of Current Business *Monthly*
U.S. Department of Commerce, Bureau of Economic Analysis
See annotation under General References.

Annual McGraw-Hill Survey of Business Plans for New Plants and Equipment *Annual*
McGraw-Hill Publications Co.
Economics Department,
1221 Avenue of the Americas
New York, New York 10020
Statistical data on planned capital investment, broken down by industry groups and regional areas.

Census of Manufacturers *Every five years, in years ending in 2 and 7*
U.S. Department of Commerce, Bureau of the Census
Statistical data on size of establishments, employment and expenditures by industry, and inventories by industry for regions of the United States.

Annual Survey of Manufacturers *Annual*
U.S. Department of Commerce, Bureau of the Census
Survey of manufacturing industries published in the years between the five-year Census of Manufactures.

Quarterly Survey of Capital Appropriations (*) *Quarterly*
Statistics on business investment in plant and equipment based on a survey of the nation's 1,000 largest manufacturers.

Capital Investment Conditions (*) *Semiannually*
Data on capacity utilization and factors affecting financing of capital spending based on a survey of the nation's 1,000 largest manufacturers.

CONSTRUCTION

Construction Reports *See entries below*
U.S. Department of Commerce, Bureau of the Census
Housing and construction statistics under the following categories:

C20. Housing Starts *Monthly*
Statistics on new housing starts by ownership, location and type of structure.

C22. Housing Completions   *Monthly*
Data on number of new units completed and currently under construction.

C25. New One-Family Sold and For Sale   *Monthly and Annually*
Corresponding data on sales and number of unsold new one-family dwellings.

C30. Value of New Construction Put in Place   *Monthly*
Current estimates of private and public construction, by aggregate value of these classifications.

C40. Housing Authorized by Building Permits and Public Contracts   *Monthly and Annually*
Statistics on the number of new housing units authorized in the United States under private building permits and public contracts.

C50. Residential Alterations and Repairs   *Quarterly and Annually*
Figures on quarterly and annual expenditures, according to type of work and size of property, for geographical regions of the United States.

Construction Review   *Monthly*
U.S. Department of Commerce, Bureau of Domestic Commerce
Contains timely, in-depth articles, as well as current data on expenditures, building starts, and employment levels in the construction industry.

Dodge Construction Potentials   *Monthly*
McGraw-Hill Information Systems Co.
F. W. Dodge Division
1221 Avenue of the Americas
New York, New York 10020
Statistical summary of construction contracts for new and major alteration projects; data are broken down by types of projects and by regions of the United States.

GOVERNMENT SPENDING

1. Federal Government

The Budget of the U.S. Government   *Annual*
U.S. Office of Management and Budget
Contains the official text of the President's budget message, a description of the budget system, data on budget receipts and expenditures, and line-item details of the budget as a whole.

The Budget of the U.S. Government: Appendix   *Annual*
U.S. Office of Management and Budget
Detailed information on the legislative authority for the budget; also data on programs in the budget, requests for supplemental appropriations and new program proposals.

The U.S. Budget in Brief   *Annual*
   U.S. Office of Management and Budget
The President's budget message and a condensed overview of the budget. Includes major summary tables.

The Federal Budget: Its Impact on the Economy (*)   *Annual*
Analysis of the federal budget as a whole, special analysis of some of its programs, and background information on major expenditure patterns in relation to the national economy.

Treasury Bulletin   *Monthly*
   U.S. Department of the Treasury, Office of the Secretary
A monthly summary of the Treasury's activities as related to federal fiscal operations. Includes international financial statistics and data on capital transfers between the United States and foreign countries.

Monthly Statement of Receipts and Outlays of the U.S. Government   *Monthly*
   U.S. Department of the Treasury, Bureau of Accounts
Details on receipts and expenditures for the U.S. budget and trust accounts.

Annual Report of the Secretary of the Treasury with Statistical Appendix
Annual
   U.S. Department of the Treasury, Bureau of Accounts
Statistical tables include summary of the Treasury's receipts and expenditures; also data on federal aid to states and other activities of the Treasury Department.

Facts and Figures on Government Finance   *Biennial*
   Tax Foundation, Inc.
   50 Rockefeller Plaza
   New York, New York 10020
Information about taxes, expenditures and debts for federal, state and local governments.

2. *State and Local Governments*

Governmental Finances   *Annual*
   U.S. Department of Commerce, Bureau of the Census
A series of reports that give fiscal data for the Federal Government, the 50 states, numerous cities, and selected SMSA's.

Census of Governments   *Every five years, in years ending in 2 and 7*
   U.S. Department of Commerce, Bureau of the Census
Various series of fiscal data for state and local governments of the United States.

EXPORTS

U.S. Commodity Exports and Imports as Related to Output   *Annual*
   U.S. Department of Commerce, Bureau of the Census
Statistical data on relationship between domestic output and foreign trade in commodities.

Commodity Yearbook   *Annual*
   Commodity Research Bureau
   140 Broadway
   New York, New York 10005
Latest trends in the supply and demand of numerous commodities. Price data are illustrated by charts.

LABOR AND PRODUCTIVITY

GENERAL SOURCES

Handbook of Labor Statistics   *Annual*
   U.S. Department of Labor, Bureau of Labor Statistics
   A statistical compendium of all phases of labor economics.

Manpower Report of the President   *Annual*
   Executive Office of the President
Documents current and historical trends in population, labor force, employment and unemployment, productivity and occupational data.

EMPLOYMENT

Employment and Earnings   *Monthly*
   U.S. Department of Labor, Bureau of Labor Statistics
   Statistics on employment, work hours, earnings, and labor turnover.

Labor Turnover   *Monthly*
   U.S. Department of Labor, Bureau of Labor Statistics
   Summarizes factory labor-turnover rates for major industry groups.

Monthly Labor Review   *Monthly*
   U.S. Department of Labor, Bureau of Labor Statistics
Articles on employment, wages, prices, productivity and labor developments abroad. Also includes current statistics for most of these areas.

PRODUCTIVITY

Indexes of Output per Man-Hour for Selected Industries   *Annual*
   U.S. Department of Labor, Bureau of Labor Statistics
Updates indexes of output per man-hour and output per employee for industries currently included in the Federal Government's productivity measurement program.

DEMOGRAPHIC DATA

GENERAL SOURCES

Manpower Report of the President   *Annual*
   Executive Office of the President
   See annotation under Labor and Productivity (General Sources).

A Guide to Consumer Markets (*)   *Annual*
See annotation under Aggregate Measures of Income, Demand and Production (Consumer Spending).

POPULATION

Census of Population   *Every 10 years, when the last digit is 0*
U.S. Department of Commerce, Bureau of the Census
A compendium of statistics related to the population of the United States and the social and economic living patterns of the American people. Gives statistics for U.S. territories, the 50 states and their counties, the District of Columbia, and the country's major SMSA's.

Current Population Reports   *Irregular*
U.S. Department of Commerce, Bureau of the Census
Up-to-date statistics on population, economic and social characteristics, and other demographic trends of the American people. Statistics are published in eight separate series of reports:

P-20 Population Characteristics   *Irregular*
Current national data on school enrollment, mobility and household characteristics.

P-23 Special Studies   *Irregular*
Infrequent reports containing specialized demographic data.

P-25 Population Estimates and Projections   *Irregular*
Monthly estimates of the total population of the United States, broken down by geographic area and other classifications. Includes projections on the future population of the entire United States—the 50 states, the District of Columbia, and the territories.

P-26 Federal-State Cooperative Program for Population Estimates   *Irregular*
Population estimates for counties in selected states where figures are prepared by state agencies as part of the Federal-State Cooperative Program for Local Population Estimates.

P-27 Farm Population   *Irregular*
Data on size and other selected characteristics of the U.S. farm population. Issued jointly with the Economic Research Service, U.S. Department of Agriculture.

P-28 Special Censuses   *Irregular*
Results of population censuses requested and funded by city or county governments. Reports show population changes in each locality since the last general census.

P-60 Consumer Income   *Irregular*
Information on the number of families and employed individuals at various income levels.

P-65 Consumer Buying Indicators *Annual*
Information on home ownership and purchases of automobiles and major household appliances. Statistics are broken down by income, age of family head, residence, and other characteristics.

Vital Statistics of the United States *Annual*
U.S. Department of Health, Education and Welfare, National Center for Health Statistics
A source of data on births, deaths, marriages and divorces. Regional information is classified by cities, counties and SMSA's.

EDUCATION

Digest of Educational Statistics *Annual*
U.S. Department of Health, Education and Welfare, Office of Education
An abstract of statistical information on American education. Contains data compiled from both government and private sources on number of schools, enrollments and graduates.

Fall Enrollment in Higher Education *Annual*
U.S. Department of Health, Education and Welfare, Office of Education
Enrollment data broken down by state, regional area, and individual institution.

Projections of Educational Statistics *Annual*
U.S. Department of Health, Education and Welfare, Office of Education
Ten-year projections for enrollments, number of graduates and teachers, institutional budgets, and related matters.

WAGES AND PRICES

GENERAL SOURCES

Business Conditions Digest *Monthly*
U.S. Department of Commerce, Bureau of Economic Analysis
See annotation under General References.

Economic Indicators *Monthly*
U.S. Congress, Joint Economic Committee
See annotation under General References.

WAGE RATES

Employment and Earnings *Monthly*
U.S. Department of Labor, Bureau of Labor Statistics
See annotation under Labor and Productivity (Employment).

Handbook of Labor Statistics *Annual*
U.S. Department of Labor, Bureau of Labor Statistics
See annotation under Labor and Productivity (General Sources).

Manpower Report of the President   *Annual*
   Executive Office of the President
See annotation under Labor and Productivity (General Sources).

CONSUMER PRICES

The Consumer Price Index   *Monthly*
   U.S. Department of Labor, Bureau of Labor Statistics
Statistical measures of the average changes in prices of goods and services (about 400 items) purchased by urban wage earners and clerical workers living in 56 urban areas across the country.

A Guide to Consumer Markets (*)   *Annual*
   See annotation under Aggregate Measures of Income, Demand and Production (Consumer Spending).

WHOLESALE PRICES

Wholesale Prices and Price Indexes   *Monthly*
   U.S. Department of Labor, Bureau of Labor Statistics
A basic reference on wholesale price movements; includes statistical tables and technical notes.

INDUSTRY STATISTICS

GENERAL SOURCES

Survey of Current Business   *Monthly*
   U.S. Department of Commerce, Bureau of Economic Analysis
See annotation under General References.

Federal Reserve Bulletin   *Monthly*
   Board of Governors of the Federal Reserve System
See annotation under General References.

Industrial Production   *Monthly*
   Board of Governors of the Federal Reserve System
   Ordering address: Division of Administrative Services
   Board of Governors of the Federal Reserve System
   Washington, D.C. 20551
Preliminary statistics for the total FRB Index; also carries revisions of the previous month's figures.

Moody's Industrial Manual   *Biweekly and Annual*
   Moody's Investors Service, Inc.
   99 Church Street
   New York, New York 10007
Various statistics on U.S. industrial corporations; includes separate section on classification of companies by industries and products.

Predicasts *Quarterly*
Predicasts, Inc.
11001 Cedar Avenue
Cleveland, Ohio 44106
Abstracts published forecasts for general economic indicators, industries, products and services.

Standard & Poor's Industry Survey *Quarterly and Annual*
Standard & Poor's Corporation
345 Hudson Street
New York, New York 10014
More than 40 basic surveys, each devoted to a major industry group; provides both financial statistics and detailed industry data.

Industry Profiles *Annual*
U.S. Department of Commerce, Bureau of the Census
Published as part of *Annual Survey of Manufacturers;* gives basic data series for past decade for selected major industry groups.

U.S. Industrial Outlook *Annual*
U.S. Department of Commerce, Domestic and International Business Administration
Detailed analysis and projections for more than 200 individual manufacturing and nonmanufacturing industries.

SECTORS

1. Manufacturing

Current Industrial Reports *Monthly, Quarterly and Annual*
U.S. Department of Commerce, Bureau of the Census
Information on production, shipments and inventories for 5,000 manufactured items.

Annual Survey of Manufacturers *Annual*
U.S. Department of Commerce, Bureau of the Census
See annotation under Aggregate Measures of Income, Demand and Production (Business Spending).

Census of Manufactures *Every five years in years ending in 2 and 7*
U.S. Department of Commerce, Bureau of the Census
See annotation under Aggregate Measures of Income, Demand and Production (Business Spending).

2. Mining and Energy

Mineral Industry Surveys *Weekly, Monthly and Quarterly*
U.S. Department of the Interior, Bureau of Mines
Periodic reports update information published in the *Mineral Yearbook* (see below).

Mineral Yearbook   *Annual*
U.S. Department of the Interior, Bureau of Mines
A statistical handbook on U.S. production of all metallic, nonmetallic and mineral fuel commodities; also gives similar statistics for more than 100 countries.

Census of Mineral Industries   *Every five years, in years ending in 2 and 7*
U.S. Department of Commerce, Bureau of the Census
Statistical data for each of 42 extractive industries on quantity and value of products shipped, quantity and cost of fuels, and electrical energy produced.

3. Utilities

Electric Power Statistics   *Monthly*
U.S. Federal Power Commission
Summaries of statistics on production of electric power, capacities of power plants, and sales of electricity.

Statistics of Communications Common Carriers   *Annual*
U.S. Federal Power Commission
Financial and operating data for 42 major telephone and telegraph companies operating in the United States.

Statistics of Publicly Owned Electric Utilities in the U.S.   *Annual*
U.S. Federal Power Commission
Financial and operating data for publicly owned utilities operating in the United States.

Statistics of Privately Owned Electric Utilities in the U.S.   *Annual*
U.S. Federal Power Commission
Financial and operating data for privately owned utilities operating in the United States.

4. Financial

See section below on Financial Markets.

5. Trade and Services

Current Retail Trade Reports   *Weekly and Monthly*
U.S. Department of Commerce, Bureau of the Census
See annotation under Aggregate Measures of Income, Demand and Production (Consumer Spending).

Monthly Selected Service Receipts   *Monthly*
U.S. Department of Commerce, Bureau of the Census
Estimated monthly revenues for a number of service fields—including the hotel and motel trades, various personnel and office services, automobile and appliance repairs, and leisure-time industries.

Monthly Wholesale Trade: Sales and Inventories   *Monthly*
U.S. Department of Commerce, Bureau of the Census
Data on sales and inventory trends of merchant wholesalers in over 70 lines of business.

Census of Business   *Every five years in years ending in 2 and 7*
U.S. Department of Commerce, Bureau of the Census
National and regional statistics on retail and wholesale industries, as well as on selected service trades.

6. Agriculture

Agricultural Prices   *Monthly*
U.S. Department of Agriculture, Crop Reporting Board
Prices received and paid by farmers compared to parity prices for all groups of agricultural products; data include state and regional analyses.

Agricultural Statistics   *Annual*
U.S. Department of Agriculture
Compendium of principal statistical series on agricultural production and consumption; includes historical data for the most recent ten years.

Commodity Yearbook   *Annual*
Commodity Research Bureau
140 Broadway
New York, New York 10005
See annotation under Aggregate Measures of Income, Demand and Production (Exports).

7. Transportation

Transport Economics   *Monthly*
U.S. Interstate Commerce Commission
Ordering address: Bureau of Economics, Interstate Commerce Commission
Washington, D.C. 20423
Current statistics on the operating income and working capital of Class I railroads and Class A freight forwarders.

Transport Statistics in the United States   *Annual*
U.S. Interstate Commerce Commission
Statistics on rail, motor and water carriers; also includes statistics on oil pipelines.

Handbook of Airline Statistics   *Annual*
Civil Aeronautics Board
Data on finances and traffic of major U.S. trunk carriers; also similar data on local service and helicopter carriers. Includes glossary of air-transport terms.

Census of Transportation   *Every five years, in years ending in 2 and 7*
U.S. Department of Commerce, Bureau of the Census
Data on uses and modes of transportation in the United States.

FINANCIAL MARKETS

GENERAL SOURCES

Federal Reserve Bulletin   *Monthly*
Board of Governors of the Federal Reserve System
See annotation under General References.

THE FEDERAL RESERVE SYSTEM AND MONETARY POLICY

Annual Report of the Board of Governors of the Federal Reserve System
Annual
Board of Governors of the Federal Reserve System
Information about the operations and conditions of the Federal Reserve Banks for the most recent calendar year.

Deposits, Reserves and Borrowings of Member Banks   *Weekly*
Board of Governors of the Federal Reserve System
Deposits, reserves and borrowings of reserve city banks and other member banks, by district.

Factors Affecting Bank Reserves and Conditions Statement of Federal Reserve Banks   *Weekly*
Board of Governors of the Federal Reserve System
Weekly averages of daily figures on factors affecting bank reserves, along with changes from week-ago and year-ago figures.

COMMERCIAL BANKS

Annual Report of the Federal Deposit Insurance Corporation   *Annual*
Federal Deposit Insurance Corporation
550 17th Street
Washington, D.C. 20429
Data on both insured and noninsured banks in the United States; also discusses the structure of the nation's banking system and gives aggregate statistics on its assets and liabilities.

Assets and Liabilities—Commercial and Mutual Savings Banks   *Semiannual*
Federal Deposit Insurance Corporation
Assets and liabilities of both insured banks and all operating banks by class of bank and by state.

Assets and Liabilities of all Commercial Banks in the United States   *Weekly*
Board of Governors of the Federal Reserve System
Weekly statistics on the principal assets and liabilities of all U.S. commercial banks.

Summary of Accounts and Deposits in All Commercial Banks   *Annual*
   Federal Deposit Insurance Corporation
Summarizes accounts and deposits for all commercial banks by FDIC region, state and SMSA's.

Weekly Condition Report of Large Commercial Banks and Domestic Subsidiaries   *Weekly*
   Board of Governors of the Federal Reserve System
Weekly breakdowns of assets and liabilities of reporting member banks in New York, Chicago and other leading cities, with separate figures by Federal Reserve district.

FINANCIAL INTERMEDIARIES

Annual Report of the Federal Deposit Insurance Corporation   *Annual*
   Federal Deposit Insurance Corporation
See annotation under Commercial Banks.

Assets and Liabilities—Commercial and Mutual Savings Banks   *Semiannual*
   Federal Deposit Insurance Corporation
See annotation under Commercial banks.

Federal Home Loan Bank Board Journal   *Monthly*
   Federal Home Loan Bank Board
Statistical series on housing industry; includes articles on thrift institutions.

Life Insurance Fact Book   *Annual*
   Institute of Life Insurance
   277 Park Avenue
   New York, New York 10017
Statistical tables and charts for all U.S. life insurance companies; also includes interpretive text.

National Fact Book of Mutual Savings Banking   *Annual*
   National Association of Mutual Savings Banks
   200 Park Avenue
   New York, New York 10017
Basic data on all aspects of savings banking.

Savings and Home Financing Source Book   *Annual*
   Federal Home Loan Bank Board
Statistics on Federal Home Loan Banks, including selected balance-sheet data, flow of savings, and mortgage-lending activity.

Savings and Loan Fact Book   *Annual*
   United States Savings and Loan League
   221 North La Salle Street
   Chicago, Illinois 60601
A comprehensive reference source on savings and loan associations, giving statistics on savings, home ownership, and financing of residential construction.

Statistical Bulletin *Monthly*
U.S. Securities and Exchange Commission
Data on new securities, securities sales, common stock prices and transactions; periodically shows the asset composition of all private noninsured pension funds.

Summary of Accounts and Deposits in All Mutual Savings Banks *Annual*
Federal Deposit Insurance Corporation
Summarizes accounts and deposits for all mutual savings banks by state, county and SMSA's.

MONEY MARKETS

Monthly Chart Book *Monthly*
Board of Governors of the Federal Reserve System
A variety of leading financial and economic statistical series in chart from; updated monthly.

Moody's Bank and Finance Manual *Biweekly and Annual*
Moody's Investors Service, Inc.
99 Church Street
New York, New York 10007
A source of comprehensive financial information on banks, insurance companies, investment companies, and miscellaneous financial enterprises.

Open Market Money Rates and Bond Prices *Monthly*
Board of Governors of the Federal Reserve System
Weekly data on yields of U.S. Treasury issues, Federal Funds, and commercial paper.

Reserve Positions of Major Reserve City Banks *Weekly*
Board of Governors of the Federal Reserve System
Weekly reports on the Federal Funds market and related transactions of major reserve city banks.

Weekly Condition Report of Large Commercial Banks and Domestic Subsidiaries *Weekly*
Board of Governors of the Federal Reserve System
See annotation under Commercial Banks.

CAPITAL MARKETS

Bond Outlook *Weekly*
Standard & Poor's Corporation
345 Hudson Street
New York, New York 10014
Analyzes all phases of current bond markets.

Census of Shareowners *Irregular*
The New York Stock Exchange
11 Wall Street
New York, New York 10005

Data on the number of shareowners of public corporations by state, region, and personal income.

Fact Book   *Annual*
The New York Stock Exchange
11 Wall Street
New York, New York 10005
Summarizes various statistical series issued by the Exchange.

FHA Homes: Data for States and Selected Areas   *Annual*
U.S. Department of Housing and Urban Development, Federal Housing Administration
Data on mortgages, represented property values, and other FHA classifications for states and selected housing areas.

FHA Trends of Home Mortgage Characteristics   *Quarterly*
U.S. Department of Housing and Urban Development, Federal Housing Administration
Data on insured FHA mortgages for existing and proposed family homes.

The Money Manager   *Weekly*
The Bond Buyer
77 Water Street
New York, New York 10005
Daily quotations for U.S. Treasury issues and federal agency securities; also includes a weekly index of municipal and corporate bond yields.

Moody's Bank and Finance Manual   *Biweekly & Annual*
Moody's Investors Service, Inc.
99 Church Street
New York, New York 10007
See annotation under Money Markets

Moody's Municipal and Government Manual   *Biweekly & Annual*
Moody's Investors Service, Inc.
99 Church Street
New York, New York 10007
Financial statistics on state governments and municipalities; also rates municipal and corporate bonds for quality.

Standard Corporation Records   *Daily & Bimonthly*
Standard & Poor's Corporation
345 Hudson Street
New York, New York 10014
Factual information on corporations and their securities—for example, description and history of the company, abstracts of financial statements, and related data. Updated by daily news bulletins.

Statistical Bulletin   *Monthly*
U.S. Securities and Exchange Commission
See annotation under Financial Intermediaries.

Value Line Investment Survey   *Weekly*
Arnold Bernhard & Co.
5 East 44th Street
New York, New York 10017
Continuous review and analysis of 1,000 leading corporate stocks.

INTERNATIONAL ECONOMIC STATISTICS

GENERAL SOURCES

Federal Reserve Bulletin   *Monthly*
See annotation under General References.

General Statistics   *Monthly*
Statistical Office of the European Communities
P.O. Box 1003
Luxembourg
Gives key economic statistics for the European Community.

International Economic Report of the President   *Annual*
Executive Office of the President
Discusses international economic goals of the United States and related issues. Statistical appendix on U.S. foreign trade, balance of payments, overseas investment, and economic aid.

International Financial Statistics   *Monthly*
International Monetary Fund
19th and H Streets, N.W.
Washington, D.C. 20431
Statistics, by country, on exports and imports, exchange rates, and monetary reserves.

Main Economic Indicators   *Monthly*
Organization for Economic Cooperation and Development, Paris, France
Ordering address: OECD Publications Center
1750 Pennsylvania Avenue, N.W.
Washington, D.C. 20006
A basic source of international statistics; particularly useful for data on foreign trade.

Monthly Bulletin of Statistics   *Monthly*
United Nations, Sales Section
United Nations Plaza
New York, New York 10017
Statistics on trade, national accounts, and financial markets of over 100 countries.

Statistical Yearbook   *Annual*
United Nations, Sales Section
United Nations Plaza
New York, New York 10017

A comprehensive compilation of data on balance of payments, wages and prices, and national accounts of member countries.

FOREIGN ECONOMICS

Foreign Economic Trends and Their Implications for the United States *Irregular*
U.S. Department of Commerce, Bureau of International Commerce
Each issue is devoted to a particular trading partner of the United States, and summarizes that country's key economic indicators and their trends.

OECD Financial Statistics *Semiannual with bi-monthly supplements*
Organization for Economic Cooperation and Development, Paris, France
Ordering address: OECD Publications Center
1750 Pennsylvania Avenue, N.W.
Washington, D.C. 20006
Detailed financial statistics and descriptions of OECD countries' exchange-control regulations. Reports also discuss the institutional aspects and functioning of each country's financial system.

Overseas Business Reports *Irregular*
U.S. Department of Commerce, Bureau of International Commerce
Individual reports give basic market and investment information on various foreign countries; include statistics related to trade, regulations governing trade, and foreign market indicators.

Yearbook of National Accounts Statistics *Annual*
United Nations, Sales Section
United Nations Plaza
New York, New York 10017
Data on national income, disposable income, and per capita gross domestic product for over 100 countries.

FOREIGN TRADE

Direction of Trade *Annual and monthly*
International Monetary Fund
19th and H Streets, N.W.
Washington, D.C. 20431
Data on foreign trade, by country, for over 100 countries.

Foreign Trade Reports *Monthly*
U.S. Department of Commerce, Bureau of the Census
U.S. foreign trade as listed below:

FT135. U.S. Imports for Consumption and General Imports, Commodity by Country.
U.S. imports by commodities.

FT410. U.S. Exports of Domestic and Foreign Merchandise, Commodity by Country of Destination.

Quantity and value of exports of individual commodities, plus various consolidations of these items according to destination.

FT800. U.S. Trade with Puerto Rico and with U.S. Possessions
Quantity, value and tonnage of individual commodities shipped between the United States and its territories and possessions.

FT990. Highlights of U.S. Export and Import Trade
Interrelated statistical tables summarizing significant trade movements by commodity, country, U.S. Customs District, and shipping method.

Yearbook of International Trade Statistics *Annual*
United Nations, Sales Section
United Nations Plaza
New York, New York 10017
Detailed data for individual countries, with summary tables on trade in principal commodities, and their value in foreign currencies and U.S. dollars.

BALANCE OF PAYMENTS

Balance of Payments Yearbook *Monthly*
International Monetary Fund
19th and H Streets, N.W.
Washington, D.C. 20431
Balance-of-payments data for about 100 countries, presented in various formats.

EXCHANGE RATES

Foreign Exchange Rates *Weekly*
Board of Governors of the Federal Reserve System
Ordering address: Division of Administrative Services
Board of Governors of the Federal Reserve System
Washington, D.C. 20551
Statistical release gives current exchange rates for various countries.

APPENDIX F

Table of Normal Distribution

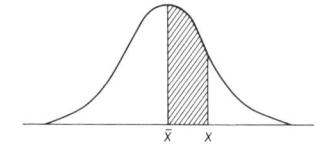

The table of areas of the normal curve between $\overline{X}$ and X for Z values is computed as follows:

$$Z = \frac{X - \overline{X}}{\sigma}$$

Normal Curve

Z	.00	.01	.02	.03	.04	.05	.06	.07	.08	.09
0.0	.0000	.0041	.0080	.0120	.0160	.0199	.0239	.0279	.0319	.0359
0.1	.0398	.0438	.0478	.0517	.0557	.0596	.0636	.0675	.0714	.0753
0.2	.0793	.0832	.0871	.0910	.0948	.0987	.1026	.1064	.1103	.1141
0.3	.1179	.1217	.1255	.1293	.1331	.1368	.1406	.1443	.1480	.1517
0.4	.1554	.1591	.1628	.1664	.1700	.1736	.1772	.1808	.1844	.1879
0.5	.1915	.1950	.1985	.2019	.2054	.2088	.2123	.2157	.2190	.2224
0.6	.2257	.2291	.2324	.2357	.2389	.2422	.2454	.2486	.2517	.2549
0.7	.2580	.2611	.2642	.2673	.2704	.2734	.2764	.2794	.2823	.2852
0.8	.2881	.2910	.2939	.2967	.2995	.3023	.3051	.3078	.3106	.3133
0.9	.3159	.3186	.3212	.3238	.3264	.3289	.3315	.3340	.3365	.3389
1.0	.3413	.3438	.3461	.3485	.3508	.3531	.3554	.3577	.3599	.3621
1.1	.3643	.3665	.3686	.3708	.3729	.3749	.3770	.3790	.3810	.3830
1.2	.3849	.3869	.3888	.3907	.3925	.3944	.3962	.3980	.3997	.4015
1.3	.4032	.4049	.4066	.4082	.4099	.4115	.4131	.4147	.4162	.4177
1.4	.4192	.4207	.4222	.4236	.4251	.4265	.4279	.4292	.4306	.4319
1.5	.4332	.4345	.4357	.4370	.4382	.4391	.4406	.4418	.4429	.4441
1.6	.4452	.4463	.4474	.4484	.4495	.4505	.4515	.4525	.4535	.4545
1.7	.4554	.4564	.4573	.4582	.4591	.4599	.4608	.4616	.4625	.4633
1.8	.4641	.4649	.4656	.4664	.4671	.4678	.4686	.4693	.4699	.4706
1.9	.4713	.4719	.4726	.4732	.4738	.4744	.4750	.4756	.4761	.4767
2.0	.4772	.4778	.4783	.4788	.4793	.4798	.4803	.4808	.4812	4817
2.1	.4821	.4826	.4830	.4834	.4838	.4842	.4846	.4850	.4854	.4857

Normal Curve (*continued*)

Z	.00	.01	.02	.03	.04	.05	.06	.07	.08	.09
2.2	.4861	.4864	.4868	.4871	.4875	.4878	.4881	.4884	.4887	.4890
2.3	.4893	.4896	.4898	.4901	.4904	.4906	.4909	.4911	.4913	.4916
2.4	.4918	.4920	.4922	.4925	.4927	.4929	.4931	.4932	.4934	.4936
2.5	.4938	.4940	.4941	.4943	.4945	.4946	.4948	.4949	.4951	.4952
2.6	.4953	.4955	.4956	.4957	.4959	.4960	.4961	.4962	.4963	.4964
2.7	.4965	.4966	.4967	.4968	.4969	.4970	.4971	.4972	.4973	.4974
2.8	.4974	.4975	.4976	.4977	.4977	.4978	.4979	.4979	.4980	.4981
2.9	.4981	.4982	.4982	.4983	.4984	.4984	.4985	.4985	.4986	.4986
3.0	.4987	.4987	.4987	.4988	.4988	.4989	.4989	.4989	.4990	.4990

BIBLIOGRAPHY

Books

American Institute of Certified Public Accountants, Accounting Principles Board. *Opinion 5,* "Reporting of Leases in Financial Statements of Lessee" (September 1964), and *Opinion 31,* "Disclosure of Lease Commitments by Lessees" (June 1973).

American Management Association, *Taking Stock of Leasing: A Practical Appraisal,* New York, 1965.

Anderson, Paul F. *Financial Aspects of Industrial Leasing Decisions: Implications for Marketing.* East Lansing, MI, Division of Research, Graduate School of Business Administration, Michigan State University, 1977.

Anthony, R. N., and S. Schwartz. *Office Equipment: Buy or Rent?* Boston: Management Analysis Center, Inc., 1957.

Bierman, Harold, Jr., and Seymour Smidt. *The Capital Budgeting Decision,* 4th edition. New York: Macmillan, 1975.

Clark, John J., Thomas J. Hindelang, and Robert E. Pritchard. *Capital Budgeting: Planning and Control of Capital Expenditures.* Englewood Cliffs, N.J.: Prentice-Hall, 1979.

Cohen, Albert B. *Long Term Leases: Problems of Taxation, Finance, and Accounting.* Ann Arbor: University of Michigan Press, 1954.

Cunnane, Thomas F. *Tax Aspects of Buying and Leasing Business Property and Equipment.* Englewood Cliffs, N.J.: Prentice-Hall, Inc., 1974.

Ferrara, William L. *The Lease–Purchase Decision: How Some Companies Make It.* New York: National Association of Accountants, 1978.

Financial Accounting Standards Board. *FASB No. 13: Accounting for Leases.* High Ridge Park, Stamford, Conn., November 1976.

———. *FASB No. 17: Accounting for Leases—Initial Direct Costs,* November 1977.

———. *Interpretations of 19, 21, and 26 of FASB No. 13,* October 1977, April 1978, and September 1978.

Hamel, Henry G. *Leasing in Industry.* New York: National Industrial Conference Board, 1968.

Hawkins, D. F., and M. M. Wehle. *Accounting for Leases.* New York: Financial Executives Research Foundation, 1973.

Jackson, James F., Jr. *An Evaluation of Finance Leasing.* Austin, Texas: Bureau of Business Research, University of Texas, 1967.

Kares, Peter. "Some Economic Implications of Equipment Lease Financing." Ph.D. dissertation, Purdue University, 1968.

Law, W. A., and M. C. Crum. *Equipment Leasing and Commercial Banks.* Chicago: Association of Reserve City Bankers, 1963.

Machinery and Allied Products Institute. *Leasing of Industrial Equipment.* Washington, D.C.: Machinery and Allied Products Institute, 1965.

Mao, James C. T. *Quantitative Analysis of Financial Decisions.* New York: Macmillan, 1969.

McGugan, Vincent John. *Competition and Adjustment in the Equipment Leasing Industry.* Boston: Federal Reserve Bank of Boston, 1972.

Metz, Donald H. *Leasing Standards and Procedures.* Kaudauna, Wisconsin: Thomas Publication, 1968.

National Association of Accountants. *Financial Analysis to Guide Capital Expenditure Decisions.* Research Report No. 43. New York: National Association of Accountants, 1967.

Nelson, Andrew T. "The Impact of Leases on Financial Analysis." Ph.D. dissertation, Michigan State University, 1962.

Opinions of the Accounting Principles Board (No. 7). *Accounting for Leases in Financial Statements of Lessors.* New York: American Institute of Certified Public Accountants, May 1966.

Opinions of the Accounting Principles Board (No. 27). *Accounting for Lease Transactions by Manufacturer or Dealer Lessors.* New York: American Institute of Certified Public Accountants, November 1972.

Opinions of the Accounting Principles Board (No. 31). *Disclosure of Lease Commitments by Lessees.* New York: American Institute of Certified Public Accountants, June 1973.

Opinions of the Accounting Principles Board (No. 5). *Reporting of Leases in Financial Statements of Lessee.* New York: American Institute of Certified Public Accountants, September 1974.

Porterfield, James T. S. *Investment Decisions and Capital Costs.* Englewood Cliffs, N.J.: Prentice–Hall, 1965.

Pritchard, Robert E. *Operational Financial Management.* Englewood Cliffs, N.J.: Prentice–Hall, 1977.

Quirin, G. David. *The Capital Expenditure Decision.* Homewood, Ill.: Richard D. Irwin, 1967.

Robichek, Alexander A., and Steward C. Myers. *Optimal Financing Decisions.* Englewood Cliffs, N.J.: Prentice–Hall, 1965.

Roulac, Stephen E. *Tax Shelter Sale–Leaseback Financing: The Economic Realities.* Cambridge, Mass.: Ballinger Publishing Co., 1976.

Solomon, Ezra. *The Theory of Financial Management.* New York: Columbia University Press, 1963.

Vancil, Richard F. *Leasing of Industrial Equipment.* New York: McGraw–Hill, 1963.

Van Horne, James C. *Financial Management and Policy,* 4th edition. Englewood Cliffs, N.J.: Prentice–Hall, 1977.

Wehle, Mary M. "Lessee Decision Criteria and Accounting Implications." Ph.D. dissertation, Harvard University, 1972.

Weston, J. Fred, and Eugene F. Brigham. *Managerial Finance,* 6th edition, Hinsdale, Ill.: The Dryden Press, 1978.

Articles

Alvin, Gerald. "Resolving the Inconsistency in Accounting for Leases." *The New York Certified Public Accountant,* March 1970, 223–230.

Aly, Hamdi F. "The Lease-or-Borrow Decision: An Opportunity Cost Approach." *Cost and Management,* January–February 1971, 37–41.

Archer, W. R. V. "Lease or Buy Decisions." *Accountant,* February 5, 1970, 193–196.

Axelson, Kenneth S. "Needed: A Generally Accepted Method for Measuring Lease Commitments." *Financial Executive,* July 1971, 40–52.

Babione, Francis A. "The Role of Rentals in Demand Stimulation." *Michigan Business Review,* May 1964, 17–22.

Basi, Bart A. "Tax Aspects of Leasing: Lessee's Viewpoint." *Tax Executive,* July 1975, 365–378.

Batkin, A. "Leasing vs. Buying: A Guide for the Perplexed." *Financial Executive,* June 1973, 63–68.

Beechy, T. H. "The Cost of Leasing: Comment and Correction." *Accounting Review,* October 1970, 769–773.

———. "Quasi-Debt Analysis of Financial Leases." *Accounting Review,* April 1969, 375–381.

Benjamin, James J., and Robert H. Strawser. "Developments in Lease Accounting." *CPA Journal,* November 1976, 33–36.

Bierman, Harold, Jr. "Accounting for Capitalized Leases: Tax Considerations." *Accounting Review,* April 1973, 421–424.

———. "Analysis of the Lease-or-Buy Decision: Comment." *Journal of Finance,* September 1973, 1019–1021.

Bower, Richard S. "Issues in Lease Financing." *Financial Management,* Winter 1973, 25–34.

Bower, Richard S., Frank C. Herringer, and Peter J. Williamson. "Lease Evaluation." *Accounting Review,* April 1966, 257–265.

Bower, Richard S., and Donald R. Lessard. "An Operational Approach to Risk-Screening." *Journal of Finance,* May 1973, 321–337.

Brigham, Eugene F. "Equipment Lease Financing: A Bank Management Imperative." *The Banker's Magazine,* Winter 1966, 65–75.

———. "The Impact of Bank Entry on Market Conditions in the Equipment Leasing Industry." *National Banking Review,* September 1964, 11–26.

———. "Hurdle Rates for Screening Capital Expenditure Proposals." *Financial Management,* Autumn 1975, 17–26.

Brown, E. Cary. "Tax Incentive for Investment." *American Economic Review,* May 1960, 335–345.

Brown, Norman M. "Return on Investment and Book Accounting for Leverage Lease Investments." *The Journal of Commercial Bank Lending,* August 1972, 24–33.

Burke, Arthur J. "Third-Party Leasing from a User's Viewpoint." *Datamation,* November 1969, 143–47.

Carlson, C. Robert, and Donald H. Wort. "A New Look at the Lease-*vs.*-Purchase Decision." *Journal of Economics and Business,* Spring 1974, 199–202.

Chamberlain, Douglas C. "Capitalization of Lease Obligations." *Management Accounting,* December 1975, 37–38, 42.

Chasteen, Lanny G. "Implicit Factors in the Evaluation of Lease vs. Buy Alternatives." *Accounting Review,* October 1973, 764–767.

Clark, David C. "Leases as Loan Security." *Journal of Commercial Bank Lending,* April 1972, 25–30.

Clark, Robert A., Joan M. Jantorni, and Robert R. Gann. "Analysis of the Lease-or-Buy Decision: Comment." *Journal of Finance,* September 1973, 1015–1016.

Cook, Donald C. "The Case Against Capitalizing Leases." *Harvard Business Review,* January–February 1963, 145–155.

Cooper, Kerry, and Robert H. Strawser. "Evaluation of Capital Investment Projects Involving Asset Leases." *Financial Management,* Spring 1976, 44–49.

Davidson, Sidney, and Roman L. Weil. "Lease Capitalization and Inflation Accounting." *Financial Analysts Journal,* November–December 1975, 22–29, 57.

Defliese, Philip L. "Accounting for Leases: A Broader Perspective." *Financial Executive,* July 1974, 14–23.

Doenges, E. C. "The Cost of Leasing." *Engineering Economist,* Winter 1971, 31–44.

Elam, Rick. "The Effect of Lease Data on the Predictive Ability of Financial Ratios." *The Accounting Review,* January 1975, 25–43.

Elliott, Grover S. "Leasing of Capital Equipment." *Management Accounting,* December 1975, 39–42.

Feet, Howard M., and Donald T. Barsky. "Purchase vs. Lease: Computer Obsolescence." *Management Accounting,* October 1969, 29–32.

Ferrara, William L. "Lease vs. Purchase: A Quasi-Financing Approach," *Management Accounting,* May 1974, 37–41.

———. "Capital Budgeting and Financing or Leasing Decision," *Management Accounting,* July 1968, 55–63.

———. "Should Investment and Financing Decisions Be Separated?" *Accounting Review,* January 1966, 106–114.

———. "Lease-Purchase Decisions: The Quasi-Financing Approach—Revised and Extended. *Management Accounting,* January 1974, 21–26.

Ferrara, William L., and Wojdak, Joseph F. "Valuation of Long-Term Leases." *Financial Analysts Journal,* November–December 1969, 29–32.

Findlay, III. M. Chapman, "Financial Lease Evaluation: Survey and Synthesis," *Financial Review,* 1974, pp. 1–15.

———. "A Sensitivity Analysis of IRR Leasing Models." *Engineering Economist,* Summer 1975, 231–241.

Finn, F. J. "Lease or Purchase: A Financing Decision." *Management Accounting* (British), April 1970, 145–150.

Fishback, J. Karl. "A Look at Lease Disclosure Requirements." *Financial Executive,* April, 1974, 24–37.

Gant, D. R. "A Critical Look at Lease Financing." *Controller*, June 1961, 274–277, 311–312.
——. "Illusion in Lease Financing." *Harvard Business Review*, March–April 1959, 121–142.
Golden, Raymond L., and Karl M. Parrish. "Leasing and Banks." *The Journal of Commercial Bank Lending*, March 1974, 2–16.
Gordon, M. J. "A General Solution to the Buy or Lease Decision: A Pedogogical Note." *Journal of Finance*, March 1974, 245–250.
Griesinger, F. K. "Pros and Cons of Leasing Equipment." *Harvard Business Review*, March–April 1955, 75–89.
Gustafson, George A. "Computers—Lease or Buy?" *Financial Executive*, July 1973, 64–66, 68–70.
Guy, Andrew D. "Caveat Emptor! Six Leasing Considerations." *Hospital Financial Management*, June 1976, 40–42, 44.
Hannon, John M. "Lease Accounting: A Current Controversy." *Management Accounting*, September 1976, 25–28.
Harris, Milton M. "Leveraged Leasing: Profits or Illusions?" *Bank Administration*, September 1975, 56–63.
——. "Lease Accounting: The FASB Exposure Draft." *Bank Administration*, June 1976, 25–27.
Harwood, Gordon B., and Roger H. Hermanson. "Lease-or-Buy Decision." *Journal of Accountancy*, September 1976, 83–87.
Hawkins, David F. "Objectives, Not Rules for Lease Accounting." *Financial Executive*, November 1970, 30–38.
Henry, James B. "Leasing: Cost Measurement and Disclosure." *Management Accounting*, May 1974, 42–47.
——. "Finding the True Cost of a True Lease." *Hospital Financial Management*, December 1976, 19–25.
Hershman, Arlene. "There's Leverage in Leasing." *Dun's Review*, May 1970, 43–44.
Hill, William H. "Should You Lease Company Cars?" *Financial Executive*, November 1973, 48–50, 52, 54.
Honig, Lawrence E., and Stephen C. Coley. "An After-Tax Equivalent Payment Approach to Conventional Lease Analysis." *Financial Management*, Winter 1975, 18–27.
Huefner, Ronald J. "A Debt Approach to Lease Accounting." *Financial Executive*, March 1970, 30–36.
Jenkins, David O. "Purchase or Cancellable Lease: Which Is Better?" *Financial Executive*, April 1970, 26–31.
Johnson, Robert W., and Wilbur G. Lewellen. "Analysis of the Lease or Buy Decision." *Journal of Finance*, September 1972, 815–823.
——. "Reply." *Journal of Finance*, September 1973, 1024–1028.
Keller, Thomas F., and Russell J. Peterson. "Optimal Financial Structure, Cost of Capital, and the Lease-or-Buy Decision." *Journal of Business, Finance and Accounting*, Autumn 1974, 405–14.

Kirchenbaum, Bruce J. "Lease-or-Buy Decisions Without Tears: The Present-Value Approach." *Financial Executive,* September 1974, 34–40.

Kirschbaum, Robert T. "Measuring Profitability in the Equipment Rental Business." *Management Accounting,* January 1972, 41–45.

Knutson, P. H. "Leased Equipment and Divisional Return on Capital." *N.A.A. Bulletin,* November 1962, 15–20.

Korn, Barry P. "Leveraged Leasing: A New Way to Manage Credit." *Credit and Financial Management,* September 1974, 34–40.

Leatham, John T. "No Letup in Leasing." *Conference Board Record,* March 1974, 61–64.

Lev, Baruch, and Yair E. Orgler. "Analysis of the Lease-or-Buy Decision: Comment." *Journal of Finance,* September 1973, 1022–1023.

Lewellen, Wilbur G., Michael S. Long, and John J. McConnell. "Asset Leasing in Competitive Capital Markets." *Journal of Finance,* June 1976, 787–798.

Lusztig, Peter. "Analysis of the Lease-or-Buy Decision: Comment." *Journal of Finance,* September 1973, 1017–1018.

Malernee, James K., Jr., and Andrew J. Senchack, Jr. "Secured Residual Values in Bank Leasing Arrangements." *The Journal of Commercial Bank Lending,* September 1975, 56–61.

Marcus, Robert P. "The Buy vs. Lease Decision Revisited." *Financial Executive,* December 1976, 34–38.

MacEachron, W. D. "Leasing: A Discounted Cash-Flow Approach." *Controller,* May 1961, 213–219.

McLean, J. H. "Economic and Accounting Aspects of Lease Financing." *Financial Executive,* December 1963, 18–23.

Miller, Merton H., and Charles W. Upton. "Leasing, Buying, and the Cost of Capital Services." *Journal of Finance,* June 1976, 761–786.

Mitchell, G. B. "After-Tax Cost of Leasing." *Accounting Review,* April 1979), 308–14.

Moyer, Charles R. "Lease Evaluation and the Investment Tax Credit: A Framework for Analysis." *Financial Management,* Summer 1975, 39–44.

Myers, Stewart C., David A. Dill, and Alberto J. Bautista. "Valuation of Financial Lease Contracts." *Journal of Finance,* June 1976, 799–819.

Nantell, Timothy J. "Equivalence of Lease versus Buy Analyses." *Financial Management,* Autumn 1973, 61–65.

Nelson, A. Thomas. "Capitalized Leases—The Effect on Financial Ratios." *Journal of Accountancy,* July 1963, 49–58.

Ofer, Aharon R. "The Evaluation of the Lease versus Purchase Alternatives." *Financial Management,* Summer 1976, 67–72.

O'Shea, J. E. "A Clarification of APB Opinions on Accounting for Leases." *The CPA Journal,* August 1972, 665–670.

Packham, E. Richard. "An Analysis of the Risks of Leveraged Leasing." *Journal of Commercial Bank Lending,* March 1975, 2–29.

Randolph, John M. "Computer Leasing Today." *Financial Executive,* May 1974, 50–56.

Reilly, F. "A Direct Cost Lease Evaluation Method." *Bank Administration*, July 1972, 22–26.

Roenfeldt, Rodney L., and James B. Henry. "Lease vs. Debt Purchase of Automobiles." *Management Accounting*, October 1976, 49–54.

Roenfeldt, Rodney L., and J. S. Osteryoung. "Analysis of Financial Leases." *Financial Management*, Spring 1973, 74–87.

Roesner, Paul I. "The Lease or Buy Decision in 'Truck Fleet' Expansion." *Management Accounting*, January 1972, 46–48.

Sartoris, William L., and Ronda, S. Paul. "Lease Evaluation—Another Capital Budgeting Decision." *Financial Management*, Summer 1973, 46–52.

Sax, F. S. "Lease or Purchase Decision—Present Value Method." *Management Accounting*, October 1965, 55–61.

Schall, Lawrence D. "The Lease-or-Buy and Asset Acquisition Decisions." *Journal of Finance*, September 1974, 1203–1214.

Schmidt, Henry W., and Richard G. Larsen. "Leveraged Lease Arrangements: Tax Factors That Contribute to Their Attractiveness." *The Journal of Taxation*, October 1974.

Singhvi, Surendra S. "The Lease or Buy Decision: A Practical Approach." *The Journal of Commercial Bank Lending*, October 1974, 60–65.

Smith, Pierce R. "A Straightforward Approach to Leveraged Leasing. *The Journal of Commercial Bank Lending*, July 1973.

Stiles, Ned B., and Mark A. Walker. "Leveraged Lease Financing of Capital Equipment." *The Journal of Commercial Bank Lending*, July 1973, 19–39.

Straus, Lee E. "Leveraged Lease Analysis: Some Additional Considerations." *The Journal of Commercial Bank Lending*, January 1974.

Sunblad, Harry A. "Automobile Leasing." *Management Accounting*, March 1975, 53–54.

Towles, Martin F. "Leases and the Relevant APB Opinions." *Management Accounting*, May 1974, 37–41.

Thulin, W. B. "Own or Lease: Underlying Financial Theory." *Financial Executive*, April 1964, 23–24, 28–31.

Vancil, Richard F. "Lease or Borrow: New Method of Analysis." *Harvard Business Review*, September–October 1961; reprinted in *Leasing Series*. Boston: Harvard Business Review, n.d., pp. 79–93.

———. "Lease or Borrow: Steps in Negotiation." *Harvard Business Review*, November–December 1961; reprinted in *Leasing Series*. Boston: Harvard Business Review, n.d., pp. 94–109.

Vancil, Richard F., and Robert N. Anthony. "The Financial Community Looks at Leasing." *Harvard Business Review*, November–December 1959; reprinted in *Leasing Series*. Boston: Harvard Business Review, n.d., pp. 31–48.

Vanderwicken, Peter. "The Powerful Logic of the Leasing Boom." *Fortune* 88 (November 1973), 132–136.

Vatter, William J. "Accounting for Leases." *Journal of Accounting Research*, Autumn 1966, 133–138, 147–148.

Watt, George C. "Setting Standards for Reporting Lease Transactions." *Price Waterhouse Review,* January 1975, 29–31.

Weiss, Steven J., and Vincent John McGugan. "The Equipment Leasing Industry and Emerging Role of Banking Organizations." *New England Economic Review of the Federal Reserve Bank of Boston,* November–December 1973, 3–30.

Westbrook, David N. "Accounting for Long-Term Leases." *Cost and Management,* May–June 1974, 54–58.

Weston, J. F., and R. Craig. "Understanding Lease Financing." *California Management Review,* Winter 1960, 67–75.

Wilson, C. J. "The Operating Lease and the Risk of Obsolescence." *Management Accounting,* December 1973, 41–44.

Wright, Ivor B. "Review of APB Opinion No. 27—Accounting for Lease Transactions by Manufacturer or Dealer Lessors." *The CPA Journal,* July 1973, 563–566.

Wyatt, Arthur R. "Accounting for Leveraged Leases." *The Arthur Anderson Chronicle,* April 1974, 38–49.

Wyman, H. E. "Financial Lease Evaluation under Conditions of Uncertainty." *Accounting Review,* July 1973, 489–493.

Zises, Alvin. "Lease Financing: A Reply." *Controller,* September 1961, 414–423.

———. "Disclosure of Long-Term Leases." *Journal of Accountancy,* February 1961, 37–47.

———. "Law and Order in Lease Accounting." *Financial Executive,* July 1970.

———. "The Pseudo-lease—Trap and Time Bomb." *Financial Executive,* August 1973, 20–25.

INDEX

accounting
  for depreciation, 40
  for financial reporting and taxes, 42–47
  inflation and, 66
  types of leases and, 15, 16
accounts receivable financing, 157, 160
Aetna Business Credit, Inc., 157–158
airplanes, 6, 61
American Association of Equipment Lessors, 167, 170
American Rental Association, 8
American Research and Development, 164–165
annuities
  compound sums (future values) of, 49–51
  present values of, 52–53
arithmetic means, 68
ASR 190, 66
assets
  corporate taxes and, 32–36
  depreciation of, 29–32
  economic life of, 61–63
  purchase options for, 144–145
AT&T, 173
audits, tax, 141
automobile leasing, 142–143, 184–191

Babylon, 2
Bacon, G. Pat, 156–161
balloon payments, 155
balloon-repayment automobile loans, 186
Baltimore, Lord, 2
BankAmerica, 175
BankAmeriLease, 179–183
bankruptcies, 15

banks
  joint lending involving commercial finance companies and, 161
  in lease transactions, 152
  in leasing industry, 170
  as lessors, 9–10, 174
  secured lending plans through, 154
  Small Business Administration guaranteed loans from, 162
Barnes, Charles F., 156
Beny, Marvin, 14
bookkeeping
  for leasing, 7
  see also accounting
Bossidy, Lawrence A., 156
Bower, R. S., 90
brokers, 179
  evaluating, 181–183
budgeting, leasing for flexibility in, 5
business risks, 57
  see also risks

Campbell, Dennis G., 44*n*., 47
capital
  freed by leasing, 189–190
  leasing as alternative source of, 5
capital gains and losses, 32–34
capital investments, impact of risks on, 60–62
capital leases, 16–18, 121
  financial accounting for, 43, 44
capital losses, 33–34
cash flows, 36–40
  accounting for, 43
  in automobile leasing, 188–189
  in certainty equivalent method, 83, 84
  depreciation and, 176–177

cash flows—*Cont.*
  in lease versus purchase analysis, 94–97, 103–109, 112–115
  leasing and timing of, 6
  in risk-adjusted discount rate technique, 74, 77–81
  in sensitivity analysis, 126, 131–135
Caves, Richard E., 18, 170
certainty conditions, 62
certainty equivalent factors, 83–84
certainty equivalent method, 83–87
certainty equivalent values, 84–87
Chrysler Leasing, 185
Cincinnati Milacron Inc., 156
CIT Financial Corp., 156
Clark, John J., 58
closed-end automobile leases, 185–188, 190–191
coefficients of variation, 70, 84
collateral
  inventory as, 162
  receivables as, 157, 160
Collins, William A., 121
Commerce, U.S. Department of, 167–169
commercial finance companies, 154–162
commercial lending sources, 154–156
communications equipment, 173
compound interest, 48–49
  on annuities, 50–51
compound sums of annuities, 49–51
computer industry
  leasing in, 171
  obsolescence in, 60–61
conditional sales agreements, 11–14
  tax considerations of, 140, 142, 143, 145–148
construction industry, 172
corporate leasing of automobiles, 190
corporate taxes, *see* taxes
costs
  of automobile leasing, 185–188, 190
  of commercial financing, 161
  depreciable, 30
  of evaluation, 58–59

costs—*Cont.*
  forecasting of, 63
  included in lease package, 6
  as reason for leasing, 4–5
  replacement, for equipment, 176–177
  unit, 178
Cowin, Lawrence R., Jr., 156
credit
  alternative sources of, 156
  automobile leasing and, 189
  costs of, from commercial finance companies, 161
  leasing to conserve, 6
  unsecured, 158–159
CSVLI, 165
current ratios, 45
customers, loans from, 165

data, changes in, for evaluation modules, 126–139
dealers, automobile, 184–185
Dean, Joel, 3
debt-to-equity ratios, 45
deductions
  timing of, 148–149
  see also depreciation; investment tax credits
Deliottle, Haskins, and Sells, 168
deposits, *see* security deposits
depreciation, 29–32, 175–177
  accounting and tax records of, 40
  in automobile leasing, 185
  on conditional sales agreements, 145–146
  financial accounting of, 43, 44
  in lease versus purchase analysis, 107, 108, 110
  leasing deductions compared with, 149
  recapture of, 33
  salvage value not equal to, 7
  on used equipment, 178
Digital Equipment Corporation, 165
direct leases, 21–22
discounted cash flow analysis, 48–59

INDEX

discount rates
  in lease versus purchase analysis, 95–97, 107, 108
  in risk-adjusted discount rate technique, 71, 81–82
  risk-adjusted evaluation of changes in, 135–139
Displaced Business Loans (SBA), 163
double-declining balance depreciation, 30–32
dry leases, 23

earnings per share (EPS), depreciation and, 40
"ecology" equipment, 172–173
Economic Development Assistance (SBA), 163–164
economic life of assets, estimating, 61–63
Economic Opportunity Loans (SBA), 163
"economic reality" test, 14
electronics equipment, 173
employees financing from, 165
Employee Stock Ownership Plan (or Trust) (ESOP/ESOT), 165
equipment
  financing of, 154–157
  history of leasing of, 2–3
equipment leasing industry, 167–183
equity financing, 159
estimated economic life, 17
estimated residual value, 17
estimation of risks, 61–62
evaluations
  certainty equivalent method for, 83–87
  discounted cash flow analysis for, 48–59
  in lease versus purchase analysis, 89–117
  of lessors, 179–181
  of packagers, 181–183
  risk-adjusted discount rate technique for, 71–83
  sensitivity analysis for, 120–139

Ex-Cell-O Corp., 156
expected returns, 68, 69
expected values, 68, 69

factoring, 157, 158
fair value of leased property, 17
Farmers Home Administration loans, 164
farming equipment, 172
FASB (Financial Accounting Standards Board)
  on direct leasing, 21
  on inflation accounting, 66
FASB 13, 7, 16, 143
  amendments to, 121
  financial accounting for, 42–47
  leases defined under, 18
FASB 17, 121
FASB 22, 121
Federal Reserve Board, 154
finance companies, 154–162
Financial Accounting Standards Board, see FASB
financial cash flows, 133–134
financial leases, 20–21
  net leases as, 23–24
financial ratios, FASB 13's effects on, 44–47
financial reporting, 42–47, 121
  of depreciation, 40
financial risks, 57
financial statements, 42–47
financing
  alternative sources of, 153–166
  in lease versus purchase analysis, 91–93, 108, 121–124
  leasing for flexibility in, 6–7
financing evaluation module, 91–93, 97, 102, 107–112
First National Bank of Boston, 9
food processing industry, 172
Ford Leasing, 185
Ford Maintenance Coupon program, 186
forecasting, 63–64
front-end costs, 6

272 INDEX

Frost & Sullivan, Inc., 9, 167, 171–173
full payout leases, 20–21, 143
future values of annuities, 49–51

General Electric Credit Corp., 156
GMAC, 185
goals
 discounted cash flow analysis for evaluations of, 58
 in forecasting, 63, 64
Golden, C. L., 24
government, financing through, 162–164

hearses, 8
"hell or high water" clauses, 13, 14
Hindelang, Thomas J., 58

IBM, 171
identification on leased equipment, 178
implicit interest rate, 17
improved version obsolescence, 19
inception of lease, 18
income taxes, *see* taxes
incremental borrowing rate, 18
indenture trustees (in leveraged leases), 25
indenture trusts, 25
industrial equipment, 172
inflation, 64–67
 higher interest rates during, 154
 leasing as hedge against, 6
inflows, cash, 37–38
 forecasting of, 63
 see also cash flows
instruments (measurement, analysis, and control), 173
insurance, in automobile leasing, 188
insurance companies
 financial affiliates of, 164
 as lessors, 10
"intent to purchase" test, 14
interest
 in automobile leasing, 186–187
 charged by commercial finance companies, 161

interest—*Cont.*
 in conditional sales agreements, 146–148
 financial accounting of, 44
 floating rates of, 154
 mathematics for, 48–53
 volatility of rates of, 61
intermediate term commercial loans, 157
internal rates of return, 55–56
Internal Revenue Service, U.S. (IRS)
 automobile leasing and, 189, 191
 guidelines on leases by, 141–143
 guidelines on useful life by, 30
 leveraged leases and, 27
 on operating leases, 19
 rulings requested from, 152
 sale-and-leaseback rulings of, 15
 true leases and, 11–13, 144
 see also taxes
international leasing industry, 168–169
inventory, as collateral, 162
inventory to net working capital ratios, 47
investment and financing evaluation module, 93, 97, 102–103, 112–117
investment firms, 164
investment tax credits, 34–36, 149–152
 in automobile leasing, 187
 in lease versus purchase analysis, 94, 97, 102, 103, 108, 109

Johnson, R. W., 90
joint lending arrangements, 161

Kalata, John J., 44*n.*, 47
Kasper, L. J., 90

laboratory equipment, 173
land
 history of leasing of, 2
 not depreciable, 30
 tax advantages of leasing, 7
lease agreements (in leveraged leases), 25–27
leased assets to total assets ratios, 47

INDEX

lease terms, 17
  in automobile leasing, 186
  on operating leases, 19
Leaseurope Trade Association, 159
lease versus purchase analysis, 89–117
  for automobiles, 188–190
    qualitative factors in, 120–125
    sensitivity analysis in, 120–139
lease-with-option-to-purchase agreements, *see* purchase options, leases with
leasing
  alternative sources of financing and, 153–166
  of automobiles, 184–191
  of equipment, 167–183
  financial statements for, 42–47
  history of, 1–4
  impact of risk on, 60–62
  as inflation hedge, 67
  reasons for, 4–7
  renting versus, 8
  tax aspects of, 140–152
  types of, 11–27
leasing industry, 167–183
  structure of, 8–10
  tax audits of, 141
Lerner, Eugene M., 58
lessors, selection of, 179–181
leveraged leases, 4, 21, 24–27
  evaluating packagers or brokers for, 181–183
  middle-market leases and, 22
  not used internationally, 169
Lewellen, W. G., 90
loan participants, 25
loans
  alternative sources of, 165
  automobile, balloon-repayment, 186
  from commercial finance companies, 161–162
  commercial sources of, 154–156
  in lease versus purchase analysis, 110–112, 124
  receivables as collateral for, 157, 160
  SBA, 162–164

loans—*Cont.*
  volatility of interest rates on, 61
losses
  capital, 33–34
  tax laws on, 32

McGugan, Vincent J., 18, 170
machine tool industry, 155–156, 172, 174–175
Main Line Fleets Inc., 184
maintenance
  in automobile leasing, 186, 190
  provided by lessor, 20
  requirements for, 178
maintenance leases, 18
management
  assumptions on, in forecasting, 64
  lease evaluation by, 58–59
  operating leases for flexibility of, 20
manufacturers
  financing from, 155–156
  as lessors, 174, 175
  in leveraged leases, 26
Manufacturers Hanover Leasing Company, 24–26
marketability of leased equipment, 178
market values of assets, forecasting of, 63
Maryland, leasing of, 2
master leases, 22
materials-handling equipment, 172–173
mathematics
  of interest and discounted cash flow, 48–53
  in lease versus purchase analysis, 96–97, 108–109, 115, 126
  for risk analysis, 68–87
means (arithmetic), 68
medical and dental instruments and equipment, 173
middle-market leases, 22
mileage, in automobile leasing, 185, 186, 191
military aircraft obsolescence, 19
mineral property leases, 2, 23
minimum lease payments, 17

minority enterprise small business investment companies (MESBICs), 164

National Commercial Finance Conference, 158
net leases, 23–24
net-net leases, 23–24
net operating cash inflows, 131–135
net present values (NPV), 54–55
   in lease versus purchase analysis, 90, 93, 103–107, 114–117
   in risk-adjusted discount rate technique, 71, 74–76, 79–83
   in sensitivity analysis, 127–139
net profit to net working capital ratios, 47
net sales to net working capital ratios, 47
non-full payout leases, 21

obsolescence
   leasing for reducing risks of, 7, 19
   risks of, 60–61, 178
office equipment, 171–172
Oloffo, Joseph R., 156
one and one-half declining balance depreciation, 30
one and one-quarter declining balance depreciation, 30
open-end automobile leases, 186, 188, 190–191
operating leases, 18–20, 121
   financial accounting for, 43
owner participants (in leveraged leases), 25
ownership, risks of, 19–20
owner trustees (in leveraged leases), 25

packagers
   evaluating, 181–183
   in leveraged leases, 26
Parrish, K. M., 24
participation agreements, 24–25
pass-through elections, 150, 151
Patton, J. R., Jr., 13

payments, in automobile leasing, 185–188
percentage leases, 23
   history of, 2
Peterson, Howell, and Heather, Inc., 184
Phoenicians, 1–2
portability of leased equipment, 178
prepayments on leases, 94
   tax aspects of, 144
present values, 52–55
   in lease versus purchase analysis, 94, 95, 97–114
   in sensitivity analysis, 127–139
Pritchard, Robert E., 59
project lease financing, 168
pseudo-leases, 13
purchase agreement assignments (in leveraged leases), 26
purchase agreements (in leveraged leases), 26
purchase options, leases with
   banks and, 152
   in machine tool industry, 174–175
   tax rulings on, 14, 144
purchase prices, in automobile leasing, 188
purchasing
   with financial leases, 20
   leasing versus, 4–7
   versus leasing analysis, 89–117

qualitative factors, in lease versus purchase analysis, 120–125
quantitative methods, *see* mathematics

Rappaport, Alfred, 58
rates of return
   in evaluation of changes in risk-adjusted discount rates, 139
   internal, 55–56
rates of utilization, 8
receivable financing, 157, 160
Regular Business Loans (SBA), 163
renewal periods, tax considerations on, 144

renting, leasing versus, 8
replacement costs, 176–177
residual values, obsolescence and, 61
retail store fixtures, 171–172
return on assets ratios, 47
returns, risks and, 68–71
returns on investment, in financial leases, 20–21
Revenue Act of 1978 (U.S.), 149
Revenue Proceeding 75-21, 27
Revenue Proceeding 75-28, 27
Revenue Ruling 55-540, 11–12, 143
risk-adjusted discount rate technique (RADR), 71–83
  evaluation of changes in rates in, 135–139
risks
  in automobile leasing, 186, 190–191
  evaluations of, 57–58
  forecasting of, 60–67
  of obsolescence, 7, 19
  quantitative methods for analysis of, 68–87
Rollins Leasing Inc., 184
rule of 78's, 146, 147

Safeway, 2
sale-and-leaseback arrangements, 22–23
  for office equipment, 172
  tax rulings on, 15
sales taxes, 186, 190
salvage values, 7, 30
  discount rates for, 108n.
  estimation of, 61
  in sensitivity analysis, 127–131
Section 38, 149–151
Section 1231 assets, 33–34, 145
secured lending plans, 154
Securities and Exchange Commission, U.S. (SEC), on inflation, 66
security deposits, 6, 94
  in automobile leasing, 187, 190
  in lease versus purchase analysis, 112, 115–116
  for machine tools, 175

security deposits—*Cont.*
  salvage values in, 108n.
  sensitivity analysis, 91, 120–139
service leases, 18
services, provided by lessor, 20
shareholders' equity to property, plant, and equipment ratios, 47
Shumaker, Ian K., 44n., 47
simple interest, 48–49
sinking funds, 51–52
Small Business Administration, U.S. (SBA), 162–164
small business investment companies (SBICs), 164
Small Business Loans (SBA), 163
specialization in leasing industry, 170
standard deviations, 68, 69
  for risk-adjusted discount rate technique distributions, 75–80
statements, financial, 42–47
states, Economic Development Assistance from, 163–164
Stiles, N. B., 27
stocks, risk evaluation for, 57
straight-line depreciation, 30–31
  cash flows and, 40
sum-of-the-years'-digits depreciation, 30, 31, 110
suppliers, loans from, 165

tax credits, *see* investment tax credits
taxes, 32–36, 140–152
  automobile leasing and, 189
  on equipment leases, 3
  financial reporting for, 42–43
  leased land and, 7
  in lease versus purchase analysis, 107–110, 121
  lease-with-option-to-purchase agreements and, 14
  nonprofit organizations and, 2
  sale-and-leaseback agreements and, 15
  sales, 186, 190
  state, Economic Development Assistance and, 163

taxes—*Cont.*
   true leases and, 11–13
   see also depreciation; Internal Revenue Service; investment tax credits
Technical Advise Memorandum (TAM; IRS), on leasing, 142
technological change, obsolescence from, 60–61
textile industry, 172, 174
third-party leasing companies, 9, 170
time sales financing, 157
times interest charges earned ratios, 47
tool-making industry, 155–156, 172, 174–175
trade-ins, investment tax credits and, 35
true leases, 11–15
   leveraged leases as, 27
   tax considerations of, 143–145
trust agreements, 25
trustees-in-bankruptcy, 15
trust estates (in leveraged leases), 25

uncertainty conditions, 62
   risk-adjusted discount rate technique in, 80
unguaranteed residual value, 17
Uniform Commercial Code (UCC), 155
unit costs, 178
unsecured credit, 158–159
used property
   investment tax credits on, 150
   not preferred for leasing, 178

used property—*Cont.*
   purchase options on, 144–145
useful life of assets, 30
   conditional sales agreements and, 146

values (economic)
   depreciable, 30–31
   future, of annuities, 49–51
   see also net present values; present values; salvage values
variability
   in certainty equivalent distribution, 86–87
   in risk-adjusted discount rate technique distribution, 74–80
vehicle leasing, 142–143, 184–191
vendor lessors, 9
venture capital, 164–165
Vitale, Frank A., 155, 156
volatility of interest rates, 61

Wajnert, T. J., 22
Walker, M. A., 27
Warner & Swasey Co., 155–156, 174
wet leases, 23
wholesale values, in automobile leasing, 185–188, 191
Wilson, C. J., 19

yields, in financial leases, 21

Zises, Alvin, 13